Law and Economics in India

This is one of the first volumes that uses economic tools to analyse and evaluate law and policy in India. Applying economic theories such as incentive analysis, cost–benefit studies and game theory, the essays in the volume negotiate contentious issues in law, including property, contracts, torts, nuclear liability regime, bankruptcy law, criminal law and procedure, constitutional law, administrative law, environmental law and family law.

A radical take on commercial and socio-legal issues in India, this book will greatly interest scholars and researchers of law, political economy and public policy.

Bimal N. Patel is Director and Distinguished Professor of Public International Law, Gujarat National Law University, Gandhinagar, India.

Ranita Nagar is Professor of Economics, Dean of the Department of Research and the Head of the Department of Social Sciences at Gujarat National Law University, Gandhinagar, India.

Hiteshkumar Thakkar is Assistant Professor of Economics at Gujarat National Law University, Gandhinagar, India.

Law and Economics in India

Understanding and practice

Edited by
Bimal N. Patel, Ranita Nagar
and Hiteshkumar Thakkar

Routledge
Taylor & Francis Group
LONDON AND NEW YORK

First published 2017 by Routledge

2 Park Square, Milton Park, Abingdon, Oxfordshire OX14 4RN
52 Vanderbilt Avenue, New York, NY 10017

Routledge is an imprint of the Taylor & Francis Group, an informa business

First issued in paperback 2019

British Library Cataloguing in Publication Data
A catalogue record for this book is available from the British Library

Library of Congress Cataloging-in-Publication Data
A catalog record has been requested for this book

ISBN: 978-1-138-68556-7 (hbk)
ISBN: 978-0-367-17729-4 (pbk)

Typeset in Sabon
by Apex CoVantage, LLC

Contents

Figures and tables

Figures

Tables

Notes on contributors

Shivansh Agarwal is a student at the Gujarat National Law University, Gandhinagar, India.

Madhuja Barman is a student at the Gujarat National Law University, Gandhinagar, India.

Jashaswi Ghosh is a student at the Gujarat National Law University, Gandhinagar, India.

Aonkan Ghosh is Associate at Shardul Amarchand Mangaldas & Co., New Delhi. He is a B.COM, LLB (Honours), Graduate from Gujarat National Law University, Gandhinagar, India.

Esha Goel is a student of Masters in Corporate Law at the University of Cambridge, UK. She is a graduate in BCom, LLB (Honours) from Gujarat National Law University, Gandhinagar, India.

Supratim Guha is a student at the Gujarat National Law University, Gandhinagar, India.

Amudavalli Kannan is a student at the Gujarat National Law University, Gandhinagar, India.

Aanchal Kapoor is a Master's student at the National University of Singapore. She is a graduate in BCom, LLB (Honours) from Gujarat National Law University, Gandhinagar, India.

Prateek Kumar is Advocate at the High Court of Delhi, India. He is a graduate in BA, LLB (Honours) from Gujarat National Law University, Gandhinagar, India.

Amrita Mohan is a student at the Gujarat National Law University, Gandhinagar, India.

Aishwarya Mohapatra is Advocate at the High Court of Delhi, India. She is a graduate in BA, LLB (Honours) from Gujarat National Law University, Gandhinagar, India.

Lalit Panda is a student at the Gujarat National Law University, Gandhinagar, India.

Aakanksha Parashar is a student at the Gujarat National Law University, Gandhinagar, India.

Chandni Patel is a student at the Gujarat National Law University, Gandhinagar, India.

Shreya Ramakrishanan is Associate at Lakshmikumaran and Sridharan, Advocates and Attorneys, New Delhi, India. She is a graduate in BA, LLB (Honours) from Gujarat National Law University, Gandhinagar, India.

Kaustubh Rastogi is a student at the Gujarat National Law University, Gandhinagar, India.

Anamika Ray is a student at the Gujarat National Law University, Gandhinagar, India.

Shubhangi Roy is a student at the Gujarat National Law University, Gandhinagar, India.

Ifrah Shaikh is a student at the Gujarat National Law University, Gandhinagar, India.

Rumani Sheth is an LLM student at the National University of Singapore. She is a BA, LLB (Honours) graduate from Gujarat National Law University, Gandhinagar, India.

Kundhavi Suresh is Associate at Cyril Amarchand Mangaldas, Bangalore, India. He is a BA, LLB (Honours) graduate from Gujarat National Law University, Gandhinagar, India.

Suriti is Advocate at the High Court of Delhi, India. She is a BA, LLB (Honours) graduate from Gujarat National Law University, Gandhinagar, India.

Gayathree Devi Kalliyat Thazhathuveetil is a student at the Gujarat National Law University, Gandhinagar, India.

Preface

The *corpus juris* that governs every aspect of communal life is a manifestation of our collective experience. It is this body of the law that harmonises the disjoint, and often conflicted, interest baskets while creating and moulding the cluster of interpersonal relations, which is human society. Being a tool of behavioural manipulation, the lawmakers must necessarily devise an appropriate set of laws that pushes social behaviour towards the socially desirable end. It therefore follows that the designing of laws requires a studied and cautious approach, backed by accurate empirical research, which is sensitive to positive realities and is accordingly structured to address the same. Law and economics provides the theoretical foundations for a systematic analysis of socio-legal circumstances, with the objective of allowing lawmakers to fine-tune legal rules to fit the societal model in which they must function. Most important, this increasingly influential technique of analysis has revolutionised the way one views the functioning of the legal system. The 'efficiency' argument it stands for sheds an all-new perspective to how legal rules must be fashioned in order to obtain the socially desirable end, often challenging the sanctity of traditional legal frameworks while attempting to design more 'efficient' laws.

At this point, it would not be imprudent to point out that available literature in this interdisciplinary field remains confined to exclusive socio-cultural settings. Under these circumstances, there is an immediate need to develop a body of literature that would sufficiently address the social variables endemic to a particular domestic setting. Keeping this in mind, the Centre for Law and Economics of Gujarat National Law University has consolidated its efforts into producing a compendium of chapters tracing the contours of several specific laws and policies, and analysing these using the magnifying glass of law and economics. The book is an advanced version of its predecessor, *Economic Analysis of Law: An Indian Perspective*. Each chapter not only sheds light on various fundamental theories of law and economics but also employs economic tools to gauge the effectiveness of specialised areas of law. Each touches upon various facets of the law, such as contract law, company law, competition law, sports law, labour law, bankruptcy law, nuclear liability regime, law of crimes and other socially relevant bills.

This publication is not meant to be an authoritative commentary upon the present legal regime. Rather, it is an attempt to persuade greater debate in our understanding of the way in which laws influence social behaviour. The views are expressed in the personal capacity of individual authors. The editors accept responsibility for any editorial errors or oversights. The editors shall not however be held liable for any omission or commission in terms of facts, figures and legal propositions. The Centre for Law and Economics of Gujarat National Law University hopes that this book would fulfil its purpose of encouraging greater debate and discussion in law and economics among students and academicians in India, and promoting the application of these principles by lawmakers.

Acknowledgements

Our deep sense of appreciation is extended to the following student editors from the Gujarat National Law University (GNLU) for their continuous assistance and efforts towards the publication of this volume: Kundhavi Suresh (batch 2010–2015), Supratim Guha (batch 2011–2016), Amudavalli Kannan (batch 2011–2016), Dhruv Malhotra (batch 2012–2017), Aditi Gupta (batch 2013–2018), Gayathree Devi Kalliyat Thazhathuveetil (batch 2013–2018) and Shivansh Agarwal (batch 2013–2018).

We also extend due appreciation to all the previous members of the GNLU Law and Economics Committee and to the present members of the Centre for Law and Economics for their involvement, contribution and commitment to this field.

Introduction

Law and economics provides the theoretical foundations for a systematic analysis of socio-legal circumstances, with the objective of allowing lawmakers to fine-tune legal rules so that they may fit the societal model in which they must function. An inquiry into economic analysis of law leads to the realization of two pertinent questions: first, what the effect of legal rules on the relevant sectors and individuals is; and second, whether the effects of such legal rules are socially desirable. This book is an endeavour towards the analysis of the effects of such legal rules on select contemporary issues which are not adequately addressed in the Indian academic debate. In order to undertake a systematic analysis, this book has been divided into six parts on the basis of the type of economic parameter used in the analysis and the kind of the law being analysed; the parts are property rights, contract theory and efficiency, economics of corporate law, game theory and law, regulatory economics and markets and economic analysis of media laws.

Property law and economics is perhaps one of the most often explored areas in the discipline of law and economics. In this part, the authors have attempted to provide insights to further the dialogue that Coase started decades before. The chapters within juxtapose the existing tools of economic analyses into the many contemporaneous issues – environment law, carbon footprint and information exchange – through the efficient allocation of property rights.

In the first chapter, 'Economic analysis of environmental law and policy', the author focuses on the economic rationale for tortious liability in environmental law regime. It explains the method of determining which stakeholders should bear the environmental costs and why using an economic analysis of externalities of cost of production, welfare system and Coase Theorem would be beneficial. The various systems of the tort regime like strict liability and polluter pays principle are analysed. The last part of the chapter juxtaposes the theory developed above to the Indian environmental law system. The second chapter, 'Economic analysis of carbon credit laws', deals with the controversial and upcoming market for carbon credits as an innovative method of managing greenhouse gas emissions in the atmosphere. It compares the discrepancies in allotment of credits to developed–developing countries. As the market matures, the potential fraudulent practices that may be indulged in and need to be regulated are discussed.

Chapter 3, 'The economic analysis of blackmail: the case for an alternate legal regime', uses property rights to postulate an alternate legal regime where 'informational blackmail' can be bargained upon as in an ordinary transaction with the sale of silence by someone who is otherwise free to disclose what he or she knows. The chapter relies on works of Posner, McAdams, Coase and others to create a demarcation between blackmails, which should be considered as prohibited bargain.

Moving forward from property rights, the book delves into the intricacies of negotiations between two individuals in the form of contracts, and the legal regime that can produce the most efficient outcome in its enforcement. The analysis of efficiency in contract theory is largely based on the underlying purpose that the contract seeks to achieve. Part II identifies the contemporary loopholes in certain contracts (domestic or international) and uses the traditional concepts of contract theory to search for an optimum solution.

Intention of the parties involved is the cornerstone of any arbitration. It is accepted jurisprudence that all contractual transactions impose an underlying good faith obligation on the parties involved. The best efforts clauses in contracts may be perceived as express good faith obligations. The question then arises as to what standard the courts must apply to enforce these express best efforts clauses. Chapter 4, '"Best efforts": search for the optimal performance standard – an economic analysis', seeks to find an optimum solution with a focus on the intention of parties. The analysis further proceeds to address the 'rules versus standards' debate to address the efficiency of an ex post determination of liabilities that such a clause imposes. The chapter identifies two models that the courts may follow, namely implied good faith standard and absolute obligation. The efficiency analysis of the two models leads to a discovery of trade-offs between investments and transaction costs. In their search for the most efficient model, the authors of this chapter seek to maximize aggregate social benefits with an incentive for the parties to internalize costs.

Efficiency is an important parameter to be considered while entertaining thoughts of expropriation. Expropriation or 'wealth deprivation' could take different forms: it could be direct where an investment is nationalized or otherwise directly expropriated through formal transfer of title or outright physical seizure. A high degree of complexity arises in cases where the host states interfere with the rights of the foreign owner without formal removal of title. It thus becomes pertinent to identify whether a 'taking' is an expropriation that can be compensated or whether it is an uncompensated government regulation. Chapter 5, 'The economically efficient expropriation: an economic analysis of expropriation under international investment law', proceeds to evaluate the economic efficiency of the two most widely used doctrines in wealth deprivation, that is the police power doctrine and the substantial deprivation doctrine. A litmus test for the two is prepared by applying each to the same hypothetical situation. In the process, the common problems of underinvestment and overinvestment are encountered, respectively, along with added complications of moral hazards, increased social cost and so on. However, the greater symmetry of information and expert knowledge unique to foreign investments has been used to find a solution to the paradox of compensation in the field of international investment. This attempt is based on a modified proportionality doctrine, which is dealt with in the conclusive notes of the chapter.

Part III deals with the economic analysis of corporate law. This field dates back to the collaboration between a law professor and an economist: Berle and Means. They identified the separation of ownership and control, with public corporations owned by a dispersed group of shareholders, none of whom owned enough shares to have the incentive to rigorously monitor managerial behaviour. From these 'agency problems', Ronald Coase developed the theory of a firm, which explains the transactions within firms and between firms. Subsequently, Oliver Williamson filled in the gaps left by Coase, by focusing on asset specificity. Jensen and Meckling's contribution must be acknowledged, as they coined the idea of firm as a nexus of contracts. The enquiry into the reasons for the existence of the concept of the company is interesting. Courts propounded the meanings of traditional concepts of limited liability, corporate veil, shareholder primacy and so on through sound logical reasoning. As Easterbrook and Fischel rightly stated, corporate law is a set of terms available off the rack so that participants in corporate ventures can save the cost of contracting. The tool of economic analysis has been used in this part to refine the existing state of corporate law in India, and delve into the corporate debt restructuring in India, a tool for corporates to deal with financial difficulties and the economics of dispute resolution mechanism under the Companies Act, 2013, in terms of the National Company Law Tribunal and the introduction of class action.

Chapter 6, 'Economic analysis of corporate laws', seeks to economically analyse the traditional concepts of corporate law to evaluate the underlying rationale for the same. An efficiency analysis of company law in India is required to compare and contrast the same with other jurisdictions. Newer corporate actions such as squeeze-outs, hostile takeovers, staggered voting, strategic assets and investment management are a result of the internalization of the demonstrated need to perform better in markets. Their behavioural analysis and trans-deal effects have not been documented till date in a comprehensive manner. This chapter is an attempt at such an analysis. While this theory does explain some plenary concepts, it suffers from certain flaws, which have been highlighted in the chapter. One of the principal objections to this theory would be that it would be difficult to agree that there exists one straightjacket approach, which explains all aspects of corporate governance. This chapter attempts to dissect various aspects of company law and apply distinct analytical principles to different aspects such as game theory for strategic voting and takeover bids and defences, modified contractarian theory to explain the IPO process and the efficiency argument for distribution of powers. As an additional aspect to the economic analysis of corporate law, note must be taken of the dispute settlement mechanism applicable to companies. The validity of arbitration or alternate dispute resolution arguments is also an important issue, fit for analysis.

In 2001, the Reserve Bank of India introduced the Corporate Debt Restructuring (CDR) Scheme to act as a solution to a company in organizing its outstanding debts. The Indian mechanism is based on the London approach. Comprehensive guidelines for both institutional and non-institutional CDR were issued in 2008. Later on, in 2012, master guidelines were issued. CDR guidelines were further issued in May 2013. The Reserve Bank of India's efficient guidelines on restructuring of advances have developed slowly from simple instructions directing the rescheduling of the loans to disaster-affected people in the 1970s to comprehensive guidelines on restructuring of loans to large corporate houses under multiple banking arrangement. India's stance clearly reveals that it believes in an interventionist approach. In Chapter 7, 'Economic analysis of the corporate debt restructuring mechanism in India', the authors are of the view that this approach needs to be looked into, as it includes problems like excessive leveraging and deficient project appraisals for cash-flow analyses. The mechanism was meant to act as a tool for corporates to deal with financial difficulties 'because of factors out of their control and due to internal reasons'. The chapter seeks to analyse the CDR mechanism and verify if it is timely or transparent and deigns to restructure debts of entities facing problems.

India's corporate law regime has undertaken a complete overhaul with the introduction of the Companies Act, 2013. Two major highlights in this regard include the establishment of the National Company Law Tribunal and the introduction of class action suits as a tool for creditors and shareholders to pin the companies' liability. Chapter 8, 'An economic analysis of the dispute resolution mechanism under the Companies Act, 2013', seeks to evaluate the efficiency of the dispute resolution mechanism under the act solely on established economics tools without delving too much into the constitutional controversies of the subject matter. The first part of the chapter deals with the economic analysis of the tribunal by employing microeconomic tools to evaluate its projected efficiency. The aim of this research is to rationalize the efficiency of the newly introduced provisions to evaluate if they lubricate the system or cause further hurdles. Presently, company law disputes are adjudicated through several forums like the Company Law Board, high courts and the Supreme Court. The establishment of a single tribunal to adjudicate all company law disputes holds the key to shaping the corporate sector growth in India. The latter part of the chapter deals with the idea of class action suits evaluated through the lens of property rights in economics.

Part IV takes the readers to a different aspect of law and economics, namely game theory and its application to the law. There can be little doubt that the legal system is primarily concerned with predicting the response of human beings to various institutional arrangements so that their behaviour can be influenced through suitable sanctions and incentives. Growing recognition of this functional aspect of the legal system permitted the employment of tools of economics to improve the field of law. Game theory is one such invaluable methodological tool popularized by the field of 'law and economics'. It owes much of its success to the fact that it can effectively address the problems of asymmetric information and bargaining. The theory allows regulators to identify the key actors in a situation and to appreciate strategic actions of a group of such actors. The most common form of the theory functions on the postulate that while all individuals in the game take into account the incentives and sanctions that accompany their decisions, they are equally conscious of the effect their decisions would have on what other players do. The theory studies different types of games, formed on the basis of the number of players involved, symmetry of the game and co-operation among the players. This part focuses on two types of games: WHAT and the Dictator Game.

Chapter 9, 'An economic analysis of cybercrimes', uses game theory to analyse cybercrimes, a rising phenomenon that poses a global threat to security owing to their untraceable nature. Recent years have witnessed an unprecedented growth in cybercrimes, particularly hacking and cyberterrorism. While from the perspective of fame-hackers and crackers, hacking is a cost-efficient choice, from the societal perspective, it amounts to an undesirable invasion of privacy. Thus, the authors point out the need to formulate effective laws to address the problem of asymmetry of information. The authors then delve into an efficiency analysis of the existing regulatory framework in India embodied in the Information Technology Act. The chapter also provides an economic perspective of cyberterrorism, by characterizing the terrorist as a rational actor who chooses between legal and terrorist activities, after appreciating the costs and benefits of pursuing his political goals. Most important, the authors envision a standard game with two players (the government and the terrorist) and two potential targets, with the constraint that the government can defend only one of the targets. The model appreciates the pay-offs involved, before arriving at the best strategic decision. The chapter concludes on a recommendatory note, encouraging regulators to apply the game theory to cybercrimes in a more extensive manner.

In Chapter 10, 'Economics of child labour', an attempt has been made to appreciate the economics of child labour, another global phenomenon having socio-economic implications. The author uses a Dictator Game model, which is a peculiar variant of the game theory inasmuch as it allows only one party to dictate terms to the other. This model explains the phenomenon by using the parents and the child as the key players and by requiring the child to choose between the options of going to school and working. The author introduces the notion of 'altruism' and uses the Rotten Kid Theorem to explain how dictators in the game are incentivized to act in the interest of the recipient as well. It is postulated further that child labour is economically inefficient, and this is explained in terms of the short-run and long-run impacts of child labour on household and individual incomes and the adult labour market. The author next uses the Basu and Van model to discuss the effectiveness of the Child Labour (Prohibition and Regulation) Act, 1986, in curbing child labour. The chapter concludes with a recommendation to implement a broader policy mix that aims at reducing poverty, child labour and the costs of education for poor households.

The process of formulating and designing institutions to regulate aspects of the law is made simpler by the use of economic analysis, as the latter is grounded in the principles of welfare maximization through the use of the market. Hence Part V of the book delves into regulatory economics and markets. Regulatory economics has, in the recent past, become an important tool in the drafting and assessment of institutions, legislations and policies, making it an integral part of any collection of works that aim to analyse the law. This part focuses on the question of efficiency of the countermajoritarian institution of judicial review, an economic analysis of competition law in India and an analysis of the pricing policy in the pharmaceutical market in India, specifically with reference to the Drugs (Prices Control) Order, 2013.

The 'countermajoritarian difficulty' is best understood as an aspersion cast on the legitimacy of the institutions of governance, which run parallel to the democratically elected government. Popularly, it examines judicial review as a countermajoritarian institution. Chapter 11, 'The limits of democracy: an economic analysis of countermajoritarian institutions', deals with whether judicial review meets the criterion of efficiency in the provision of good governance. To assess this, the author has looked into whether the democratic process, as understood today, tends to bring about equilibrium at the point of maximum utility. A review of seminal works on public choice theory and its applications in the analyses of democracy and political activity has been undertaken, based on which an economic framework of analysis has been devised to examine the relationships between the votes of conflicting interest groups and the rights that actually are protected. From the point of view of the government, the analysis argues that there is a production and consumption of rights at the same time for each interest group, in a manner as to maximize utility in the form of obtaining an optimum amount of votes. However, the point of maximum utility to the government is not always the point where economic efficiency would be at maximum utility. Judicial review, as a countermajoritarian institution, steps in here to address the deficiencies in the operation of a democratic government. The author further analyses the position in India and proposes certain methods to create a better model of governance to obtain maximum utility in economic efficiency.

Chapter 12, 'Economic analysis of competition law', undertakes an exhaustive review of various facets of the regulation of competition in the market. It takes into account the influence of the Chicago School of Economic Thought in the framing of legislations governing competition, and the development of the law since the Chicago influence. It analyses the definitions of market, market power and relevant market in India. The author further adopts an economic approach when looking into abuse of dominance and predatory pricing from an Indian perspective. In detailing the functioning of cartels, the author has used game theory to demonstrate how individual players in cartels have incentives to deviate from the cartelized prices, in situations of conflict. Further, the author argues that the best option that an individual in a collusion can make is by following Nash equilibrium. The author has also scrutinized the effect of competition laws on mergers.

Chapter 13, 'An economic analysis of Indian pharmaceutical pricing policy (Drugs (Prices Control) Order, 2013)', looks into the current pricing policy of medicines in the pharmaceutical sector in India from the lens of an economist. The market for pharmaceuticals in India is an imperfectly competitive one, and players, that is manufacturers of medicines, will consistently increase their prices, necessitating government intervention as an alternative to market forces. The Drugs (Prices Control) Order, 2013, has introduced the market-based pricing mechanism for determining the price ceiling for drugs, in a bid to address concerns regarding availability and accessibility of drugs. The authors have critically analysed the provisions of the order and attempted to evaluate its economic efficiency in achieving its objective. They have concluded that while the order will lead to a better allocation of the gains between the consumer and the manufacturer in the long run, the true potential of the order in improving accessibility to medicines will be visible only when competition in the pharmaceutical sector for both the low-cost and the high-cost drugs reaches a saturation point.

Part VI, 'Economic analysis of media laws', probes into the laws and policies relating to the media in India. Popularly regarded as the fourth pillar of India's governmental structure, the media has emerged as a powerful tool that influences the making of policy decisions and legislations in our country. The media is generally believed to contribute to some of the ideals of democracy, such as transparency and accountability. Consequently, it is no doubt that the efficiency of the ownership structures of our media needs to be looked into, which is what the authors have attempted in Chapter 14. Another important aspect of the media is the role of advertisements as an efficient tool for marketing products and services, albeit within the cost–benefit constraint towards which the scope of alternative dispute resolution mechanisms with reference to comparative advertising has been looked at in Chapter 15.

Media ownership is an interesting subject that has caught the limelight of several debates and discussions in both democratic and non-democratic countries. Given the significance of ownership of multiple media houses by a single person, there is little data on the measurements of media concentration and diversity in countries across the globe. India has taken a positive initiative in requiring a survey of cross-media ownership, which found that even if businessmen and influential persons are disallowed from owning media houses, they always find other indirect ways to control them. However, the foray of cross-media ownership in the Indian media sector is comparably less, due to governmental interference. In Chapter 14, 'Economic analysis of cross-media ownership', the authors delve into an analysis of whether allowing cross-media ownership itself is efficient, and whether the laws in India governing it are effective or not.

Advertisements are an integral part of any mass media campaign, be it for a product, a service, an information and so on. In Chapter 15, 'Comparative advertising: case analysis of *Colgate Palmolive v. Hindustan Unilever Ltd*', the authors have focused on comparative advertising as an efficient tool of marketing and have made special reference to the highly publicized case of *Colgate Palmolive v. Hindustan Unilever*. The case has been analysed using economic tools like efficiency of the judiciary, game theory and cost–benefit analysis. The authors observe that an effective way to reduce costs borne by parties in comparative advertising cases is through the use of alternative dispute resolution mechanisms. The authors conclude that in order to increase overall social welfare, it is inadvisable to impose a complete ban on comparative advertising, as long as firms provide truthful information about their products. The judiciary will play a role in deciding the efficacy of the claims. The judgement of *Colgate Palmolive* was found to be sound from a law and economics standpoint, as the court chose to encourage comparative advertising as long as it adheres to certain standards.

In this manner, this book has attempted to provide a comprehensive analysis of various different facts of law in India. The type of economic parameter used in the analysis and the kind of the law being analysed are the key factors taken into consideration in the division of the book into 6 parts, comprising 15 chapters. Each chapter provides an in-depth analysis of the relevant law or policy, through the lens of law and economics. The analyses have been made keeping the Indian position in mind. This book is the first major attempt to apply law and economic theory to the Indian legal regime.

Part I

Property rights

Chapter 1

Economic analysis of environmental law and policy

Esha Goel

Background note

Environmental law has become the news, which features on the front page of newspapers and hits headlines on prime time. The spread of industrialization and urbanization has caused significant and direct impact on the environment. Environmental problems are soaring and are increasing at an alarming rate.[1] The degradation of the environment has raised concerns and has alarmed the society. These constant changes and direct impact on the environment prompted the legislatures to enact rules, regulations and by-laws for the protection of the environment. The international arena has dedicated institutions and organizations, which have laid down model code of conduct for protecting the environment. The Rio conferences, inclusion of environment in corporate social responsibility norms and other endeavours have shown the importance of including this social endeavour as a prime consideration. Property law, contract law and tort law have become the basis on which environmental liability is modelled. All production activities affect the environment, which in turn has severe consequences on the health and well-being of people affected. This social cost has now become an imperative part of all environmental economics. In this chapter the author seeks to analyse the economic rationale behind environmental torts. The first part of the chapter addresses the existence of environmental social costs. It then focuses on the manner in which such costs can be successfully internalized with the help of the welfare theory. The next part of the chapter addresses the interpretation of environmental torts and its effect on property rights with the help of the Coase Theorem. The chapter then proceeds to address concepts of environmental nuisance and the conflict between injunctive remedies and damages remedies. Finally, the chapter deals with economic analysis of environmental torts in India.

Internalizing environment externalities

Every market works on the basis of simple supply and demand. It is assumed that when the prices are low the demand is high and when the prices are high the demand is low. In the case of supply, the very opposite is true. It is important that we consider an example for better understanding. Assume an automobile industry. We know that people purchase cars when the price is low and the supply corresponds to it. There is a point where an equilibrium is reached. Nowhere in this have we considered indirect effect such vehicles have on the environment. This makes environment cost and externality. There is a need to include these costs while determining the cost of production.[2] There is however one significant concern as there is no known method of putting a monetary value to environmental damage. It can be assumed that in the case of air pollution, the amount that is spent on replenishing whatever is damaged, medical expenses would form the basis of calculation. But the smoggy air, which lasts for many years, is still not valued.[3] There are a few methods by which the social cost of environment can be internalized. The most common and effective way is through pollution tax. With the imposition of pollution tax, the price of the automobiles will increase, thereby reducing the number of cars sold. This in turn will reduce pollution. There are other ways in which costs can be internalized. The government or policy makers can impose environment safety standards, requirement of emission standards and so on.

The theory of welfare analysis

The difference between the points of equilibrium can be evidenced from Figure 1.1. If we do not consider environment externalities, then equilibrium is achieved at Rs 2.5. However, in case environmental externalities are considered, then equilibrium is reached at Rs 3. Hence, if we rely only on the former case, then incorrect numbers of cars are produced and sold at the wrong price because important externalities have not been internalized to reach the most efficient equilibrium.[4]

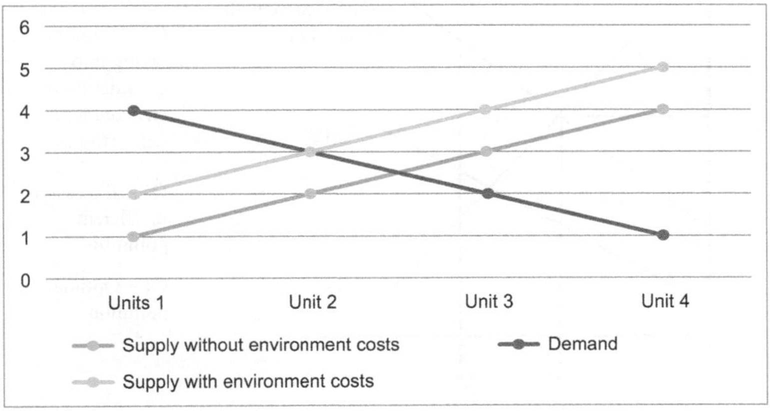

Figure 1.1 Welfare analysis – environmental costs with rise in demand

Source: Author's own compilation.

From Figure 1.1 we notice that production can continue only till it does not cross Rs 3, as any production over that will amount to extreme pollution and will lead to inefficiency. This gives rise to another consideration of optimal pollution, which will be discussed in the next section.

Optimal pollution

The doctrine of optimal pollution can be aptly explained with the help of Figure 1.2. Q1 represents the most optimal efficient point. At this point also we can see that there are some pollution costs (C1). This is the optimal amount of pollution that can be permitted given the current production costs and technologies.[5] It is believed that optimal pollution should be zero. However, there is an explanation for this belief, which has been given by economists. According to them, zero pollution can be achieved when there is zero production. It must be borne in mind that with any kind of manufacturing endeavour, there will be some resultant pollution. We as a society must decide what level of pollution we are willing to accept. The level of pollution can be reduced over the period of time with the help of better technologies and pollution-efficient inventions.[6]

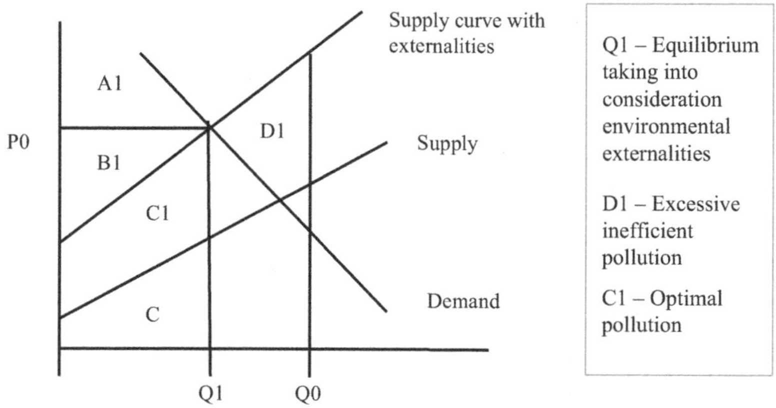

Figure 1.2 Supply curve with externalities (optimal pollution)

Source: Author's own compilation.

Environmental costs: Coase Theorem

Society's concern with regard to defining, allocating and enforcing environmental property rights has led to the development of environmental law. It seems like an uphill task because of the dependence of environmental resources and its non-exclusivity and also because environmental elements are difficult to define and allocate. The legislatures and courts have tried to derive the most efficient model to protect the environment by applying several economic theorems. One of the most effective and popular is the interpretation of nuisance law with the help of the Coase Theorem. Nuisance law and the attempts of resolving conflicts between the police power of the state and the citizen's right are difficult to internalize. The most desirable policy is lacking, and the courts and legislatures have been slow in making use of the cost–benefit analysis. The Coase Theorem was developed by Ronald Coase with regard to determining property rights. For the purposes of understanding the applicability of this theorem to environmental jurisprudence, the authors have proposed an example.

Example: Consider a cement factory whose residue causes damage to about three residents whose houses are situated near the factory. If no corrective measures are taken, then each resident would suffer damages worth Rs 100 each, which would total Rs 300. However, the damage can be eliminated in two ways: (1) a filter can be installed in the chimney, which would cost Rs 150; (2) each resident can be provided with a filter, which would cost Rs 70 each totalling Rs 210.

From the example we can see that it would be more viable to install the filter in the factory as it would eliminate the damages of Rs 300 in Rs 150 and it is a more efficient solution in comparison to the cost that would have been incurred providing a filter to each resident. Coase explained the applicability of the theorem in the following two situations.

Zero transaction costs

Transaction cost is the cost of exchange.[7] It involves three basic steps. The first step is determining an exchange partner, the second step involves the process of bargaining and finally, it must result in a bargain. However on the other hand, if no costs are incurred for the above, it is called 'zero transaction costs'. Now assuming there are no transaction costs, the theorem assumes two viable situations:

1 If the factory has the right to pollute: The citizens would consider purchasing the filter for the factory as it would be the most cost efficient in comparison to purchasing individual filters.
2 If the citizens have the right to clean air: The factory would consider installing the filter in the factory as it is most cost efficient in comparison to the damages of Rs 300 and the installation of individual filters for each resident which amounts to Rs 210.

Therefore, if there is zero transaction cost, the most efficient solution would occur irrespective of the legal rule. Even though it does not affect the efficiency of the legal rule, it most definitely affects the allocation of income. In the case that there is a right to pollute, then the residents would incur the costs; however, in the case there is a right to clean air, then the factory would incur the costs Thus, the choice of the legal rule redistributes income by the amount of the least-cost solution to the conflict. Since it is assumed for now that income can be costlessly redistributed, this distributional effect is of no consequence – if it is not desired, it can be easily corrected.[8]

Positive transaction costs

It is unrealistic to assume zero transaction costs. It is obvious that parties have to spend time, money and effort in organizing the resources for putting together a transaction.[9] In order to understand the applicability of the positive transaction costs, assume the following changes to the example.

> Example: Consider a cement factory whose residue causes damage to about three residents whose houses are situated near the factory. If no corrective measures are taken, then each resident would suffer damages worth Rs 100 each, which would total Rs 300. However, the damage can be eliminated in two ways: (1) a filter can be installed in the chimney, which would cost Rs 150; (2) each resident can be provided with a filter, which would cost Rs 70 each totalling Rs 210. It costs the residents Rs 100 in meeting up and negotiating, therefore now costing the residents Rs 250 in installing the filter in the factory.

On considering the example again, two situations arise:

1. If the citizens have the right to clean air: The factory would still consider installing the filter in the factory as it would cost Rs 150, which is cheaper in comparison to purchasing three individual filters which would cost Rs 210.
2. If the factory had the right to pollute: The citizens from among the choices they have would consider installing the filters in their respective homes as it would cost Rs 210, which is lesser than Rs 250.

Therefore, from the preceding two situations, we can see that the most efficient solution is the right to clean air. Here the cost is just Rs 150, therefore becoming the most efficient bargain. The factory here did not have any transaction costs, and whether the residents are bearing any transaction cost is also a point of irrelevance for the factory. However under the right to pollute, the residents had to make an efficient choice.[10] A more complicated version of the Coase Theorem urges the parties to identify the relevant transaction costs and negate the unnecessary and futile costs.[11] It provides a useful way to begin thinking about the legal problems because it suggests the kinds of transactions that would have to occur under each legal rule in order for that rule to become efficient.[12]

Environmental nuisance

Nuisance disputes arise from activities that injure the neighbour's activity.[13] A few typical examples can be emissions from factories that harm the neighbour's property and blaring noise and light, which disturb the neighbour. Most cases of pollution fall under the ambit of nuisance.[14] In this section, environmental nuisance is analysed keeping in mind the Coase Theorem, and a comparison of two private remedies of injunction and damages is done. The economic analysis of nuisance law got a new definition and dimension with the Coase Theorem. Coase believed that both parties to a nuisance cause the nuisance. He states that nuisance arises when there are two conflicting property uses. His analysis was based primarily on property law but indirectly gave an interpretation to nuisance law as the examples used by him to explain the conflict were based on principles of nuisance. He stated that transaction costs are positive in nature. He used examples of nuisance and noted that in the presence of positive transaction costs the initial distribution of property rights does *affect allocative efficiently and courts are inclined towards* ruling in favour of the most efficient outcome. Calabresi and Melamed[15] moved this theory to a whole new level and established the modern approach to nuisance law. They constructed a unified framework for the analysis of entitlement of property laws and torts. Here they established the following points.

Recipient of the entitlement

Entitlements are synonymous to rights. They are absolute in nature and provide that either the resident is entitled to be free of all pollution or the factory has the right to pollute without any restriction. If there are absolute entitlements, then there is no conflict between the most efficient forms of remedy. If entitlement rests with the victim, then the question arises whether the polluter must purchase the entitlement from the victim, and the opposite is applicable when the entitlement rests with the polluter. However, this does not mean the most efficient solution. There is a need to reach middle ground where both parties can benefit. Injunctions and damages can be combined to reach the most desired result. A positive damage remedy combined with a negative injunctive remedy would protect the resident's entitlement by requiring the factory to pay the resident court-determined damages for increases in its output, and the resident would benefit as the output of the factory will decrease.[16]

Methods of protecting the entitlement

For any tort claim, two types of remedies are available: (1) injunctive remedies and (2) damages remedies. This part of the chapter will discuss these remedies in brief, and the later part of the chapter will clearly highlight the difference between the two with the help of an example. Before progressing with the kinds of remedies available, it is essential to understand the three factors that determine the liability system.

Efficiency

Efficiency means the creation of the greatest aggregate profit from an activity while taking into account costs and benefits incurred by all affected parties.[17] Efficient behaviour can take two forms. The first form is when parties choose to coexist but adjust their behaviour to maximize benefits. The second is when one party shuts down and moves away.[18]

Distributional income

The next potentially important concern in any nuisance dispute is distribution of income.[19] Upon attaining the efficient solution, it is important to determine who is going to bear the gains from trade created by reaching the efficient solution.

Social welfare

Social welfare is the weighted average of the two aforementioned goals. Therefore, this provides a single measure for comparing the two remedies, injunctive and damages. Injunctive remedies are the remedies in which the aggrieved gets an injunction against the wrongdoer and the production or business is then stalled. Damages remedies relate to court-determined damages, which the wrongdoer pays to the aggrieved. In this case, the business of the wrongdoer continues and the victim stands compensated.

The most efficient remedy

Calabresi and Melamed also listed the means and ways through which the courts have determined the most efficient solutions for resolving nuisance disputes.

Plaintiff has the right of entitlement

Plaintiff has a right to get an order of injunction against the defendant. The defendant is duty-bound to halt the nuisance-generating activity unless the defendant pays a price for the transfer of entitlement to itself. This is popularly known as the *property rule*. The court awards the plaintiff the entitlement under the *liability rule*. However, the defendant on payment of court-determined damages continues to use his or her property in a nuisance-causing manner.

Defendant is awarded the entitlement

In such cases, the property rule will apply and the defendant can continue using the land in a nuisance-causing manner, and no injunction will be imposed against such use. However, the plaintiff can purchase the entitlement from the defendant upon payment of a specified agreed price.

Reverse liability rule

There is an interesting fourth rule. Here the defendant is awarded the entitlement, but the plaintiff may obtain an injunction against the acts of the defendants upon paying damages to the defendant which is decided by the judiciary. There exists a conflict between the property rule (injunction) and the liability rule (damages) as to which is the most efficient rule. Most authors on nuisance law have suggested that the damages rule is the most efficient.[20]

Assume a factory polluting the air, which is causing harmful detriment to the crops of the residents. It must be assumed that the case relates between one polluter and a few pollutees. It must also be assumed that all factories cause the same kind of pollution. Table 1.1 shows the various permutations and combinations:

Table 1.1 Cost–benefit analysis of pollution

Factory output	*Total profits of the factory (in Rs)*	*Total damages to residents (in Rs)*	*Total profits less total damages (in Rs)*
0	–	–	–
1	10,000	1,000	9,000
2	8,000	10,000	–2,000
3	6,000	16,000	–10,000

Now we look at the most efficient solution in two situations:

Injunctive remedy (where the resident has the right to clean air): The resident through an injunction can force the factory to have zero output. But taking into consideration business and the need for manufacturing, the most efficient would be the production of one unit. The reason is that for one unit produced the factory would earn a profit of Rs 10,000 and the resident would suffer damages of just Rs 1,000. Therefore, the parties can agree to allow the factory to purchase the entitlement by paying a price from anywhere between Rs 1,000 and Rs 10,000. It is not advisable to produce the second unit as the factory gains an additional profit of just Rs 8,000 and the resident suffers additional damages of Rs 9,000. Therefore, the third option would also be inefficient.

Damage remedy: Again the most efficient solution will be the production of one unit, as the factory is suffering damages lesser than the profit earned. However, in the case of units two and three, the damages supersede the profits earned. Hence, the factory will go ahead and produce one unit and pay damages.

Other determinants for efficient remedy

According to Polinsky, efficiency of each remedy also depends on the following three character traits:

1 *Extortion*: Injunctive remedy gives rise to extortion on behalf of the plaintiff. Taking into consideration the preceding example, if at one output, the plaintiff (residents) claims for injunction, then the factory will suffer the loss of the factory shutting down, which is much more than the actual damage caused to the plaintiff which is just Rs 1,000. Injunctive remedy may attract the element of extortion. Therefore, the damages remedy or court remedy is desirable as the court will dictate the plaintiff's compensation which will not be more than 1,000.
2 *Strategic behaviour*: Behaviour patterns of the party also play a significant role in determining the kind of remedy that can be availed. In the example discussed earlier, suppose the resident demands damages worth Rs 7,000 during the course of negotiations, but the factory is unwilling to budge from Rs 5,000.

The resident might just rely on an injunction and cause irreparable losses to the factory. Therefore, the factory will choose to pay a court-determined damage award between Rs 1,000 and Rs 9,000 and keep its plant in operation.

3 *Bonus payment argument*: This argument does not feature too often; however, it states that once the damages have been decided, the next step is the distribution of the same. It is possible that there might be certain concerns on the point. Therefore, the defendants and the plaintiffs would rely on the distributional pattern set by the court to avoid inefficiency.
4 *Asymmetrical information*: This is a situation under which the court does not have absolute information about certain aspects of the case. It is possible that the court is unaware of the schedule of profits of the factory. In such cases, injunctive remedies are not a viable solution and are inefficient. To reach an effective outcome under this remedy, strategic behaviour must be avoided, which requires that the entitlement point coincide with the efficient output.[21] On the other hand, damages remedies are the most effective and efficient only when the court ensures that an absolute entitlement is awarded to the resident and sets liability equal to actual damage suffered.

Economic analysis of environmental torts in India

Every owner in possession of property, subjected to encumbrances, is entitled to absolute and uninterrupted enjoyment of the same. If there is improper use of someone else's property, it results in unlawful interference in the enjoyment of that property, which is popularly termed as negligence. There are three important topics that require discussion:

1 The tort of nuisance in India
2 The trend in environment jurisprudence in India
3 The nexus between environmental damage and nuisance

The first point discusses how nuisance law is treated in India. The Indian judiciary has from time to time deferred to economically analyse the problems to reach an efficient outcome. This is a good case, and the analysis will be easy to gauge. The second, more broader object is to see the judicial activism of the Indian courts in environment matters and thus the concern that although private nuisance as a tort may not be as burning an issue in India as in other countries like the United States right now, in the coming days a well-thought-out mechanism needs to be in place to tackle such issues between two parties that affect environment in a manner that calls for efficient solutions.

We can use an example to better understand the concept. If a factory releases toxic substances into the river, which is used to irrigate the crops of the plaintiff, then most likely under the tort of private nuisance an injunction will be granted. It is however important to note that as environment consciousness increases, such pollution is not just a matter relating to one private individual but becomes a social concern. Hence, it is in these situations that there arises a need to have economically efficient and socially efficient solutions to a problem. In due course of this chapter, the economic tools will be used to draw efficient conclusions for environmental concerns. The law of torts in India is un-codified and rests primarily on the common law regime. Because of it being un-codified, it has not received due credit in the Indian judicial system. Moreover, law of nuisance too is un-codified and receives precedential value from the English Law. However, over time it has expanded through a plethora of judgements. Particularly, nuisance-causing environmental damage has seen a lot of reaction from the apex court from time to time. In this chapter, a brief overview of the use of environmental doctrines, such as the polluter pays principle and the precautionary principle, is provided. A brief economic analysis of the same has also been provided for.

Indian judiciary: environmental torts

The tortious liability for environmental wrongs emerges from public nuisance. The Environment Protection legislation in India is derived from the understanding of liability of nuisance under the law of torts. The *M.C. Mehta* cases have helped in the development of this law in India. His cases are credited for the evolution of the concept of absolute liability. The Constitution of India guarantees the right to life under Article 21, which includes the right to live in an unpolluted environment. Article 48A of the Constitution of India further imposes a duty on state to protect and improve the environment. According to Ramaswamy Iyer, nuisance means anything, which annoys or hurts. Pollution of water is nuisance if it changes the natural qualities of water.

In cases of corporate governance, the Supreme Court of India granted a remedy of injunction to the plaintiff and asked for the removal of advertisements painted on the historic rocks enroute Kulu Manali area near Himachal Pradesh and imposed a heavy fine of Rs 5 crore for polluting the naturally formed environmentally valuable geographic rocks. In another case, the court resorted to the concept of negligence. The Andhra Pradesh High Court found that the permit granted by the municipality for connecting the sewerage pipeline of the builder to the underground municipal pipeline was illegal as no one can be permitted to pollute the atmosphere of an area by letting out offensive material from his or her premises. The court held that it was incumbent upon the builders and those who are engaged in the construction work to comply with the approved plans of the drainage system.[22]

In an issue involving a complaint by local residents against the use of loud speakers by a nearby church, the Supreme Court of India found the excessive noise caused to be contrary to the Environment (Protection) Act 1986.[23] The High Court directed the church to turn down the volume. On appeal to the Supreme Court of India, it was contended that it infringed their right to practice religion of their choice. The Supreme Court of India stated that the right to religion is not an absolute right and is subject to public order, morality and health. In a civilized society, religious activities disturbing the peace of others cannot be justified (noting that no religion prescribes or preaches that prayers must be performed through voice amplifiers or by beating drums) and that there is no religious right to breach the permissible limits of the 1986 Act; and even if the noise pollution in certain cities may already exceed those limits, this is not a sufficient ground for permitting others to increase the noise.

Polluter pays principle

The polluter pays principle rests on the premise that the polluter must pay for the damage caused by him or her. Principle 16 of the Rio Declaration on Environmental Law provides that national authorities should endeavour to promote the internalization of environmental costs and the use of economic instruments, taking into account the approach that the polluter should, in principle, bear the cost of pollution, with due regard to the public interest and without distorting international trade and investment.[24]

India has implemented this principle in its entirety. The following paragraphs will highlight the growth of the law with the application of this principle. The Supreme Court of India has been really proactive in matters concerning the environment in the past many decades. The most famous case on the point is that of *M.C. Mehta v. Union of India* & Ors. (1987) 1 SCC 395.[25] The case was concerning the escape of oleum gas from one of the units of Sriram Foods and Fertilizer Industries. The court held that the rule of *Rylands v. Fletcher* that evolved in the 19th century did not fully meet the needs of modern industrial society with highly developed scientific knowledge and technology where hazardous or inherently dangerous industries were necessary to lay down a new rule not yet recognized by English Law to adequately deal with the problems arising in a highly industrialized economy.

The court pointed out that the duty to protect the escape of hazardous substances is absolute and non-derogable and the enterprise cannot escape liability by showing that all due reasonable care had been taken and that there was negligence on its part. The bases of this new rule are based on two basic principles: (1) if an enterprise is permitted to carry on an hazardous or inherently dangerous activity for its profit, the law must presume that such permission is conditional on the enterprise absorbing the cost of any accident arising on account of such hazardous or inherently dangerous activity as an appropriate item of its overheads; and (2) the enterprise alone has the resource to discover and guard against hazards or dangers and to provide warning against potential hazards.

There are many points of distinction between the *Rylands v. Fletcher* rule and the rule established in the *M.C. Mehta* case. On the point of damages, the norm under the *Rylands v. Fletcher* case was that damages will be normal, ordinary and compensatory. However, in the *M.C. Mehta* case it was pointed out that the damages that will be awarded will be exemplary in nature, and the more larger the enterprise, greater will be the amount that will be liable for payment. In yet another *M.C. Mehta* decision, the Supreme Court of India held that environment pollution is not merely civil torts but also a violation of fundamental rights as enshrined under the Constitution of India, hence are redressable directly by the Supreme Court through the Public Interest Litigation route under Article 32 of the Constitution of India.[26] Since then the Supreme Court has addressed several cases concerning the use of hazardous substances, which has an irreparable damage on the environment. This can be noticed in the tanneries case[27] and the Taj Mahal Pollution case.[28] The Ganga Water pollution case,[29] Yamuna Water pollution case,[30] the ban on toxic waste case[31] and noise pollution by crackers case[32] are other important examples.[33] The Public Insurance Liability Act, 1991, is an important legislation for promptly compensating members of the public from accidents arising from hazardous accidents. This is an act to provide for public liability insurance for the purpose of providing immediate relief to persons affected by accident occurring while handling any hazardous substance. Section 3 of the act provides for liability on no fault basis to the extent mentioned in the schedule of the act. Provisions for reimbursement of medical expenses and so on have also been provided for.

In the case of *Kendra v. State of U.P.*, the case concerned limestone mining activities in Mussorie – Dehradun region, which caused ecological disturbances, and it thus violated the right to life under Article 21 of the Constitution of India. The court held that the activities polluted the environment and thus violated the right to life. Carrying out the haphazard and dangerous limestone quarrying practices in Mussorie hills was banned by the SC, and it observed that this would undoubtedly cause hardship to the residents, but it is a price that has to be paid for protecting and safeguarding the right of the people to live in a healthy environment with minimal disturbances in ecological balance.[34] In a case involving the production of hydrochloric acid at levels that were toxic to the environment, the court extended the polluter pays principle to the industries that flouted the environmental standards and licenses persistently. The Supreme Court of India held that the principle of strict liability as it is known in England cannot form the law of the land and must go a step higher.[35] The Supreme Court of India held that the question of damages must be determined by the now-universally accepted polluter pays principle. 'The Polluters Pays Principle demands that the financial costs of remedying damage caused by pollution should lie with the undertakings which cause the pollution, or produce the goods which cause the pollution.'[36]

The implementation of the polluter pays principle has overall consequences economically. There is a necessity to implement this via market-based instruments. The principle must be developed keeping in mind safeguards against the potentially harmful effects while at the same time there must be a reduction in its economic impact.

In urban areas, where there is stiff competition between the industrial sector and small and medium enterprises and higher costs are incurred from emission or other effluent clean-up, the application of the principle might put the larger enterprises on a better footing as they will be able to afford the liability of the damage caused. This will severely affect the competition in the market, as there is a possibility of harm. It is evident that the corporations will try and offset this cost by charging their consumers more. This again is not the most viable option in a developing country. Representing a larger objection to the inclusion of polluter pays principle in Indian law is the consequence it will have in the realm of the common property resource. The application of the principle will lead to the appropriation of rights by wealthy landlords to the disadvantage of the small land owners, if curbs are imposed on the manner in which a resource can be used, in this instance land.[37]

Therefore, it is quite clear that the polluter pays principle functions on the strict liability rule. It seeks to hold the polluter responsible for all the damages caused by him or her. However, it is important that the government apply this principle to create the adequate incentive such that the polluter is able to internalize the costs.

Precautionary principle

In an interesting case before the Allahabad High Court, a doctor complained against the brick powdering mill that was generating a lot of dust, which entered the plaintiff's chambers causing inconvenience to him and his patients. The High Court held that everyone has the right to use his or her property in the manner he or she likes. The court went on to state that no person has the right to make such use of his property as materially interferes with the similar right of the neighbour.[38] Precautionary principle as a tool for environmental protection got international recognition in the Rio Conference on Environment and Development in 1992. Principle 15 of the Declaration states that

> in order to protect the environment, the precautionary approach shall be widely applied by states according to their capabilities. Where there are threats of serious or irreversible damage, lack of full scientific certainty shall not be used as a reason for postponing cost effective measures to prevent environmental degradation.

In the *Vellore Citizen*'s case, the Supreme Court of India appraised the pollution caused by the enormous discharge of untreated effluent by tanneries and other industries in the state of Tamil Nadu. The petitioner stated that as per a survey conducted by the petitioner's group, this discharge affected the underground water causing severe agricultural losses. The Supreme Court observed that the precautionary principle and the polluter pays principle have been accepted as the law of the land, by quoting various provisions of the Constitution of India and environment specific legislations such as the Air Act, Water Act and the Environment Protection Act. It has become a part of customary international law.[39] This was further emphasized by the Supreme Court in the case of *Andhra Pradesh Pollution Control Board v. MV Naydu*.[40] The court held that the principle involves the anticipation of environmental harm and taking measures to avoid it or to choose the least environment-harmful activity. It is based on scientific uncertainty. In *M.C. Mehta v. Union of India*[41] the Supreme Court of India stated that the precautionary principle is enshrined within the contours of sustainable development. This principle imposes upon the government and health authorities to take appropriate action and prevent pollution.

The concept of precautionary principle seeks to tap on the economic requirement to take precaution before the damage is done and it also pins liability in case such precaution is not taken. It is applicable in cases where there is a threat of irreversible damage. The precautionary principle urges the pollutant to take cost-effective measures as a precaution to avoid the escape of the pollutant. Therefore, it seeks to create an incentive on the polluter to take adequate precaution, else the polluter shall be held liable.

Environmental legislations in India

Indian environment legislations started with the Stockholm Declaration in 1972 in which India agreed with other 113 nations that steps will be taken to protect the environment. This eventually resulted in a Constitutional Amendment where Articles 48A and 51A(g) were added and the Environment Protection Act, 1989, Water Act, 1974, and the Air Act, 1981, were enacted. The Water Act, 1974, was the first legislation that was passed, which dealt with environment protection in India. It primarily dealt with ensuring that domestic and industrial pollutants are not discharged into rivers and lakes without the necessary treatment of the same. It set up national- and state-level boards to monitor the same. Soon the Air Act was enacted, which was also modelled along similar lines.

The Bhopal gas tragedy rocked the nation, which then led to the enactment of a series of legislations. The most important one is the Environment Protection Act, 1989. This legislation gave the government extensive power to monitor and regulate industries.[42] The act further empowered the government to make rules, regulations and by-laws for the protection of the environment and imposed standards of safeguards. The legislation and the rules established the polluter pays principle and imposed a civil liability for improper compliance.[43] The Bhopal gas tragedy also led to the enactment of yet another set of regulations for the management and proper disposal of solid wastes under the Environment Protection Act, 1986. Through this act the government was specifically empowered to protect the environment from hazardous substances. The polluter pays principle and the no-fault liability regime were incorporated as the liability principles under the regulations.[44]

The Public Liability Insurance Act is conclusive evidence of the polluter pays principle in India. It is for the first time the government acknowledged the payment of absolute liability for accidents caused due to hazardous substances. The Public Liability Insurance Act, 1991, is an important legislation for promptly compensating members of the public from accidents arising from hazardous accidents. This is an act to provide for public liability insurance for the purpose of providing immediate relief to persons affected by accident occurring while handling any hazardous substance. Section 3 of the act provides for liability on no-fault basis to the extent mentioned in the schedule of the act. Provisions for reimbursement of medical expenses and so on have also been provided for.

Far cry from reality

It is assumed that due to such well-established legislations on environment protection, Indians are protected from accidents and can be assured of due compensation as they follow the no-fault liability principle. It is unfortunate, but India is nowhere close to being a perfect example. The Environment Policy of India is nothing but the best example of over-legislation and under-enforcement. The legislations in India were a result of some incident and were a result of obligations under the United Nations. One of the main reasons for the failure is the governance structure in India. The pollution control boards are overburdened and have too much on their plate, much more than what they can handle.

Remedies resorted

It is noticeable that a lot has been done to award damages for tortious claims in India. However, the concept of damages is shied away from awarding exemplary damages. Mostly temporary injunctions are granted, which are in no way useful as they do not serve a long-lasting purpose. This can be seen in the case of *Radhey Shyam v. Gar Prasad and Anr*, where a suit was filed against Radhey Shyam for the remedy of permanent injunction against the running of a flour mill in the premises as it was causing the tort of nuisance to the plaintiffs who lived on the first-floor portion of the same premises. They were losing their peace due to the noise. Injunction was thus granted. Here the remedy resorted to was just injunction, and no damages were given. It does not seem to be the most efficient trend.

India is not far from the day when activities leading to nuisance-causing environmental damage will be viewed as a major socio-legal problem. When that happens, remedies that are more sustainable than injunctions will need to replace the status quo. The problem may be seen economically, and the benefits of each remedy, whether injunction, compensation or precautionary measures, must be calculated. Social costs of each solution must be accounted for. What may be an efficient solution for one party in a dispute may not be the most economically efficient solution as a whole. To come to a conclusion, the court can resort to various solutions that may be best suited for the situation, but these solutions must be first analysed to be economically most efficient in a given set of factors.

Conclusion

India faces an economic and political necessity to address the environmental concerns that have plagued the country for many years. India has seen growth in budget deficits, sluggish productivity and international foreign competition in the market. The public is also aggrieved with the minimal expenditure that the government is undertaking in addressing these issues. India is a developing nation, and it never had the ability to consider environmental protection in isolation from costs. A lot of money is spent by companies and industries to comply with the environment protection rules and regulations. There is a growing concern with regard to the impact of these legislations on the strength of the economy and its ability to compete in the international markets. It is argued that environmental problems are economic problems. Market failures cause these economic problems such as profit maximization decisions and social costs divergence. All are socially inefficient. It is also believed that this can be corrected by requiring private decision makers to internalize these externalities in such a manner that the profit motive is achieved keeping in mind the social costs that are involved. When this is done, it is believed that pollution can be controlled.

It is my conclusion that environmental legislations have failed to make the economic common sense. They have failed to maximize satisfaction of consumer demand over the long run. It is quite shocking to note that the government has devised methods of stopping or curbing pollution through many of its legislations but has not provided for a solution of the economic problems that arise. Most of the laws have moral convictions rather than economic considerations. The main problems that are faced by the Indian environment protection liability regime are highlighted through the following points:

1 The harms resulting from the derogation of the environment are externalized, and the benefits of environmental litigation are also externalized. Hence, what is observed is that the damage borne by an individual is very small and the compensation he or she receives is also very small but the cost of environmental litigation is extremely high. Hence, there exists a problem of rational disinterest as the compensation that is received is not enough for the victim to sue injurer. The concept of rational disinterest is further elaborated in the cases of health problems for which the victims are insured. India has seen the prevalence of this situation the most as the common man is disillusioned with the Indian judiciary and the justice delivery system in general. This problem is to be mitigated with the help of Public Interest Litigation or class action tort claims. It is quite interesting to note that in practice most legal systems have very little exposure to such litigations.
2 The whole aspect of civil liability will become inefficient when the injurer has the opportunity of settling with a few victims in return for continuing his business which causes pollution. This form of out-of-court settlement is a huge threat, as a large part of the victims are left to their own fate. This leaves the economy in a suboptimal equilibrium where the socially damaging activity is oversupplied.

3 In the strict liability even if one does not have to prove fault, the causal link needs to be established. It is common knowledge that there are many sources or causes for a particular pollutant, and it may not always be possible to impute liability or draw the relevant link. It also becomes difficult when the time period between the damage and the harm is heightened, which becomes more difficult to impute liability. It is also difficult or impossible to determine harm in cases where the environment increases the probability of a certain disease, but may not be the only manifest cause.
4 There is another problem that is often faced by the courts. It relates to the fact that the injury suffered by an individual due to the pollution must be protected by a legal right. When the dispute involves many victims and many injurers and the amount of damages is very large, it becomes problematic when the injurer is insolvent or may not have the required solvency to pay for the claims or damages. This problem however may be mitigated with the use of insurance for environment liability.
5 There is another concern which is daunting, the assessment of damages. This is often faced by the courts. It is difficult to determine the exact amount of damage that is caused. In most cases, the effects of certain environmental harms are still unknown, and therefore, it becomes more difficult to estimate damages.
6 Even if the causation is determined, the poverty in India and subsistence farmers cannot afford any additional costs for waste disposal. They are therefore fully dependent on the polluter pays principle.

The main conclusion through this chapter is that the basic principles of strict liability and negligence in pollution control are not affected if the victims can reduce their damages by taking precautions. The main problem under the negligence rule is that it does not reflect the true damages incurred; rather, it focuses on the residual damages only. This is remedied by the strict liability regime. Under strict liability all residual damages are accounted for. It is also necessary to add the defence of contributory negligence to the strict liability rule when the victims can affect the level of damages. This creates incentives for them to take proper precautions. However, while awarding remedies, courts will have to make an informed choice after carefully evaluating the sustainability of each remedy available. The social costs of both injunctions and damages must be accounted for, since what may be an efficient solution for one party in a dispute may not be the most economically efficient solution as a whole. To come to a conclusion, the court can resort to various solutions that may be best suited for the situation, but these solutions must be first analysed to be economically most efficient in a given set of factors.

The author would like to make the following suggestions for improving the environmental legislations in India. These suggestions are academic in nature, and the author hopes they can be added to the pool of research.

- *Harness market forces*: While drafting the legislations, the legislators must take into consideration the true picture of the existing market. The adoption of such an approach suggests that some political leaders recognize that market forces form a potential part of the problem. By constantly monitoring behaviour and removing the opportunity to make profits, the past regulations and laws in India have placed a lot of burden on the economy and have slowed down the process of development of new and better technologies. As a result of this poor balance, a lot of money has been spent in litigation costs and other forms of conflict among parties. There is a need to mobilize and harness the power of market forces and make an incentive for the market to enter the industry where there is a potential of environmental harm. There is a necessity to make economic and environmental interests compatible with each other.
- *Policies for environment protection*: The formation of an environment policy has two basic steps. The first one is choosing an overall goal, and the second one is the establishment of means to achieve this goal. Uniform standards must be set, which can force some businesses to use unduly expensive means of controlling pollution because the costs of controlling emissions can vary greatly between and within businesses and the right technology in one situation might not be so in another situation. This kind of a command and control policy tends to freeze the development of new technologies that could provide a greater degree of control.

- *Need for market-based policies*: Market-based policies are policies which train their sights on the overall pollution in a given area. What is important to the propounders of this policy is not how many particulates are being released into the air but the quality of air that one is breathing while walking or sitting in a yard. The market-based policy creates incentives that are financial in nature, which drives that entire industry to reduce the aggregate level of pollution and ensure that the same is in tandem with the required environmental standards that are set by experts. This kind of a policy creates the same kind of effect as the type created through the command and control policy, but it in fact gives an opportunity to share the burden and pollution control more effectively and efficiently among businesses. In economic terms, market-based policies equalize the level of marginal costs of control among businesses rather than the level of control. As a result, the market-based policies provide a monetary incentive for the greatest reduction in pollution by businesses that can do so most cheaply. Therefore, the government will be able to achieve this by setting different standards for each business and equating the marginal costs of control.
- *Pollution charges*: the levying of pollution charges means the charging of a few on the amount of pollution generated by the industry. One example of pollution charges is the deposit refund system under which all or part of some initial charge is rebated if the individual performs certain actions. The pollution charge that is levied should be on the basis of the level of pollution caused and not on how it was caused. The Organisation for Economic Co-operation and Development has identified five types of pollution charges, which are as follows:

    1 Effluent charges, which are based on the quantity that is discharged.
    2 User charges, which are payments for public treatment facilities.
    3 Production charges, which are levied by estimating the amount of pollution that is caused by a product.
    4 Government charges, which are levied by the government for certain government facilities such as registration.
    5 Tax differentiation is a special tax that is levied on green products. It is a special incentive that is extended to companies.

There are several advantages for pollution charges, which are as follows:

1 It provides an incentive to businesses and individuals to reduce emissions as it is less expensive.
2 It helps the business externalize costs such as health costs, property damage and aesthetic impacts. It forces the businesses to pay for these external costs and therefore incorporate it in their daily business decisions.
3 Charges are fixed not on the basis of a standard but for each increase in pollution. This therefore always puts an element of caution on the companies while expanding or upping their productions.
4 Thus, companies are always eager to invest in green technologies, which will help them in their business and in turn protect the environment.
5 By charging polluters a fee or tax on the amount of pollution they generate and not on their pollution-generating activities, the government gives businesses an incentive to reduce pollution up to the point at which their marginal control costs are equal to their pollution tax rates. As a result of this, businesses will control pollution as it will land up being a cheaper option.
6 *Tradable permit system*: Under this system the authorities demarcate certain level of air that can be polluted. They then allocate permits to businesses in the relevant geographic area so that each is allowed to emit some fraction of the overall total. The companies that keep their emission levels below the allocated level may sell or lease their surplus permits to other firms or use them to offset excess emissions in other parts of their own facilities.
7 *Removal of market barriers*: Sometimes a lot of difference can be made to environmental protection with the removal of government-made market barriers.
8 *Imposition of waste disposal charges*: Citizens should be charged with a fee for the amount of waste that they generate. This is necessary as there is a direct nexus between households and the expenses incurred in disposal and management of the same. Charging such rates will motivate the citizens to reuse and recycle and generate environment-friendly waste. This will promote simple practices like reusing plastic and using environment-friendly reusable bags while shopping.

9 *Polluter pays principle*: The implementation of the polluter pays principle has overall consequences economically. There is a necessity to implement this via market-based instruments. The principle must be developed keeping in mind safeguards against the potentially harmful effects while there must be a reduction in its economic impact. The application of the principle in urban areas might prove to be more advantageous to large enterprises as compared to small and medium enterprises, since the former are in a better position, financially, to pay damages. This will severely affect the competition in the market, as there is a possibility of harm. It is evident that the corporations will try and offset this cost by charging their consumers more. This again is not the most viable option in a developing country. Representing a larger objection to the inclusion of polluter pays principle in Indian law is the consequence it will have in the realm of the common property resource. The application of the principle will lead to the appropriation of rights by wealthy landlords to the disadvantage of the small land owners, if curbs are imposed on the manner in which a resource can be used, in this instance land.[45]

10 *Sustainable development*: The author urges that all nations must adopt the principles of sustainable development, which requires that the resources of today must be used in such a manner that there is enough left for the future generations. It is clear that this principle is urging states to have efficient laws that permit exploitation of resources (which includes pollution) but curbing unnecessary exploitation. Therefore, legislators need to put in a lot of checks and balances in order to curb incessant exploitation. Enough incentives need to be created to stop polluters from exploiting.

These initiatives will create the right incentive for both parties to take steps towards the protection of the environment and yet be an economically viable option.

Notes

1 John E. Vellentezas, Kyriahi K. Sauuidor and George K. Broni, 'Economic Analysis of Environmental Law: Pollution Control and Nuisance Law', *International Conference on Applied Economics* (2009): 753, http://kastoria.teikoz.gr/icoae2/wordpress/wp-content/uploads/articles/2011/10/066-2009.pdf.

2 Donald A. Wittman, 'First Come, First Served: An Economic Analysis of "Coming to the Nuisance"', *Journal of Legal Studies* 9 (1980): 557; Christopher M. Snyder and Rohan Pitchford, 'Coming to the Nuisance: An Economic Analysis from an Incomplete Contracts Perspective', *Journal of Law, Economics and Organisation* 19 (2003): 491.
3 Office of Mobile Sources. *Opportunities to Improve Air Quality through Transportation Pricing Programs: A Report Prepared for the Office of Mobile Sources, U.S. Environmental Protection Agency*, accessed 13 December 2015, http://www3.epa.gov/otaq/market/pricing.pdf.
4 Clifford W. Cobb, 'The Roads Aren't Free: Estimating the Full Social Costs of Driving and the Effects of Accurate Pricing', *Resource Incentives Program Working Paper No. 3. San Francisco: Redefining Progress* (1998), http://rprogress.org/publications/1998/wpts3_execsum.htm.
5 Daniel W. Bromley, *Handbook of Environmental Economics* (Cambridge, MA, and Oxford, UK: Basil Blackwell, 1995).
6 William J. Baumol and Wallace E. Oates, 'The Use of Standards and Prices for Protection of the Environment', In *Environmental Economics: A Reader*, edited by Anil Markandya and Julie Richardson (New York: St. Martin's Press, 1993): 229.
7 Robert Cooter and Thomas Ulen, *Law & Economics* (Delhi: Pearson, 2006).
8 Ronald Coase, 'The Problem of Social Cost', *Journal of Law and Economics* 3 (1960): 40.
9 M.T. Maloney and G.L. Brady, 'Capital Turnover and Marketable Pollution Right', *Journal of Law and Economics* 31 (1988): 203.
10 A. Allan Schmid, *The Environment and Property Rights Issues, Handbook of Environmental Economics* (Oxford–Cambridge: Basil Blackwell Ltd, 1995): 45–60.
11 R.W. Crandall, *Controlling Industrial Pollution: The Economics and Politics of Clean Air* (Washington, DC: Brookings Institution, 1983).
12 John E. Vellentezas, Kyriahi K. Sauuidor and George K. Broni, 'Economic Analysis of Environmental Law: Pollution Control and Nuisance Law', *Journal of International Trade Law and Policy* 8 (3) (2009): 252–271.
13 Thomas W. Merrill, 'Trespass, Nuisance, and the Costs of Determining Property Rights', *Journal of Legal Studies* 14 (1) (1985): Article 3, pp. 15–16.
14 A. Mitchell Polinsky, 'Resolving Nuisance Disputes: The Simple Economics of Injunctive and Damage Remedies', *Stanford Law Review* 32 (6) (1980): 1075–1112.
15 Guido Calabresi and A. Douglas Melamed, 'Property Rules, Liability Rules, and Inalienability: One View of the Cathedral', *Harvard Law Review* 85 (6) (1972): 1089–1128.
16 Polinsky, 'Resolving Nuisance Disputes'.
17 Ibid.
18 Michelle J. White and Donald Wittman, 'Optimal Spatial Location under Pollution: Liability Rules and Zoning', *The Journal of Legal Studies* 1 (1969): 249.
19 A. Mitchell Polinsky, 'Economic Analysis as a Potentially Defective Product: A Buyer's Guide to Posner's "Economic Analysis of Law"', *Harvard Law Review* 87 (1974): 1655.

20 Robert C. Ellickson, 'Alternatives to Zoning: Covenants, Nuisance Rules, and Fines as Land Use Controls', *The University of Chicago Law Review* 40 (4) (1973): 681–781.
21 Polinsky, 'Resolving Nuisance Disputes'.
22 *Ajay Construction v. Kakateeya Nagar Cooperative Housing Society Ltd & Ors.*, AIR 1991 AP 291.
23 *India v. KRR Majestic Colony Welfare Association* (2000) 7 SCC 282.
24 Regulation 16, Rio Declaration on Environment and Development (1992), accessed 5 November 2014, http://www.jus.uio.no/lm/environmental.development.rio.declaration.1992/portrait.a4.pdf.
25 *M.C. Mehta v. Union of India* (1987) 1 SCC 395.
26 *M.C. Mehta v. Union of India*, AIR 1987 SC 1086.
27 *Vellore Citizens Welfare Forum v. Union of India & Ors.*, (1996) 5 SCC 647.
28 *M.C. Mehta v. UOI & Others*, Writ Petition (Civil) No. 4677/1985.
29 *M.C. Mehta v. UOI & Others*, Writ Petition (Civil) No. 3727/1985.
30 *AQFM Yamuna v. Central Pollution Control Board* (2000) 9 SCC 499.
31 *Research Foundation for Science Technology National Resource Policy v. Union of India and Anr.* (1999) 1 SCC 223.
32 *In Re Noise Pollution* (2005) 5 SCC 733.
33 *Indian Council for Enviro-Legal Action v. Union of India*, AIR 1996 SC 1446; *Imtiaz Ahmad v. UOI & Ors.*, Writ Petition (Civil) No. 418/1998; *The United Communist Party of India v. The Union of India & Ors.*, CWP No. 1640/2001; *Hemraj & Ors. v. Commissioner of Police & Ors.*, CWP No. 3419/1999 in the High Court of Delhi; *Buffalo Traders Welfare Association v. Union of India & Ors.* (2004) 11 SCC 333; *B.L. Wadhera v. Union of India and Ors.* (1996) 2 SCC 594; *Acti-Recti & Others v. UOI & Others*, CWP No. 3105/1999.
34 Decision of Apex Court on Ecology and Air Pollution, 2012, Legal Services India, http://legalservicesindia.com/article/article/decision-of-apex-court-on-ecology-&-air-pollution-978-1.html.
35 *Indian Council for Enviro-Legal Action v. Union of India*, AIR 1996 SC 1446.
36 Ibid.
37 Kirit Parikh, 'The Polluter Pays Principle for Developing Countries: Merits, Drawbacks and Feasibility c. Villod Rege, GATT Law and Environment Related Issues Affecting the Trade of Developing Countries', *Journal of World Trade* 26 (95) (1994): 150.
38 *Ram Baj Singh v. Babulal*, AIR 1982 All 285.
39 *Vellore Citizens Welfare Forum v. Union of India*, AIR 1996 SC 2175.
40 AIR 1999 SC 812.
41 AIR 2002 SC 1696.
42 Section 3, Environment Protection Act, 1989.
43 Section 15, Environment Protection Act, 1989.
44 Rule 16, Hazardous Wastes Management and Handling Rules, 1989.
45 Parikh, 'The Polluter Pays Principle for Developing Countries'.

Chapter 2

Economic analysis of carbon credit laws

Jashaswi Ghosh

Background note

Since the 1900s, there has been a great deal of deliberation and research regarding the state of the environmental degradation, which has been a steady and ever-increasing phenomenon enhanced by the industrial revolution which has spread across the length and breadth of this planet. Scientific evidence has always pointed out irresponsible human activities and industrial pollution and waste as a primary reason of this degradation. The field of modern international environmental law has its origins in a dispute between the United States and Canada over air pollution damages in Washington State from an ore smelter in Trail, British Columbia.[1] The resolution of this dispute established the norm of customary international law that it is the state's duty to avoid letting its activities produce harm in other states. Failing that duty, a state is liable to compensate for environmental damages.[2] International environmental law in the 1950s and 1960s proceeded almost exclusively in the form of such customary laws. In the 1970s, treaties began to codify the customary norms of international environmental law. The 1980s and 1990s witnessed a proliferation in the magnitude, complexity and scope of international environmental law treaties.[3] No longer content to merely codify existing norms, these new treaties imposed new duties and standards on states and other actors. In response to this scientific evidence, the global community agreed in 1992 to an international treaty, the United Nations Framework Convention on Climate Change. The treaty requires countries to cooperatively consider what they could do to limit average global temperature increases and the resulting climate change and to cope with whatever impacts were, by then, inevitable. As of June 2013, the treaty has been ratified by 195 parties.[4]

While the Kyoto Protocol requires signatory countries to meet their targets primarily through domestic measures,[5] it also provides for a number of flexible mechanisms that allow them to offset their emissions by purchasing reductions made in other countries.[6] This is done by purchasing 'units', each unit being equivalent to one tonne of CO_2 (emissions of other greenhouse gases being converted to the equivalent number of tonnes of CO_2). Through the trading of these units to offset emissions of greenhouse gases, a new commodity has been created in the form of emission reductions or removals. Since carbon dioxide (CO_2) is the principal greenhouse gas, this market is widely referred to as the 'carbon market', with each of the units traded commonly referred to as 'carbon credits'. A very clear record of this carbon credit trade transaction is maintained by the United Nations Climate Change Secretariat, in Bonn, Germany, for not only keeping records but also for checking whether these transactions are following the procedures prescribed by the Kyoto Protocol. In spite of the regulatory procedures that are followed in the carbon market to maintain the legality of the trade, several counterfeiting methods are being used by potential traders in this market to increase their profits exponentially and thus enhancing the environmental degradation procedure. INTERPOL, through its Environmental Crime Programme and the Economic and Financial Crimes Sub-Directorate, recognizes that emerging carbon markets, like any market, are at risk of exploitation through criminal means and therefore require proper monitoring and enforcement to ensure environmental and financial integrity.[7] Thus, we see that linkages between the international trading regime and efforts to address climate change require governments and policy makers in each area to take account of the other. Trade rules may both constrain and facilitate action to address climate change, while actions taken to address climate change will in some cases have important implications for trading relationships. Thus, to address several problems that are arising in the carbon market, we have to begin by knowing the kinds of problems that are existing and then try to find out methods of solving these problems.

Income effect and demand for environmental quality

The answer to the question as to why developing countries tend to have more lax environmental regulations than rich countries comes from the very basic effect that income seems to have on the demand for environmental regulations and quality. As people become wealthier, they seem to demand more and more environmental protection. Conversely, at any point in time, the poor seem to demand less protection than the rich.[8]

We know that environmental quality is not a homogeneous good, for example we have different requirements of these goods like quality of water, ambient air quality and global climate. However, the major issue that is to be scrutinized and answered is how the demand for these goods increases with an increase in the income. As the world becomes wealthier, the extent to which environmental protection is to be provided becomes more or less dependent on the income elasticity of demand for the environmental quality. Thus, we can clearly explain the differences in pollution levels in the various countries of the world by means of the differences that are existing in their income.

This is because of the simple reason that individual demand for the environmental quality will depend on his or her own income. If a person does not have a high income, he or she will demand for goods that are cheaper in order to afford them. Now, an aggregate of these individual demands will represent the demand from the particular society. Now, the government will act upon such demands, and if the government is democratically elected, such demand will be the basis of the government's regulations. Thus, we can see how income is implicitly interlinked with the regulations that a particular government applies on its industries. Thus, it follows that the countries which are developing or are poor are not interested in their environmental quality and pollution; this disinterest is because their economic condition is not such that they can sustain a society that has stringent economic regulations which will not be favourable for the industries that are providing the economic opportunities to their society. Thus, their primary aim is to sustain and improve their economic condition rather than improve the quality of the surrounding environment.

The Kyoto Protocol also recognizes the plight of these developing countries. Simon Kuznets developed curves showing how income inequality changed as per capita income of the country increases. He found that income inequality initially increased and then decreased. Because of the similarity, curves showing how environmental quality or pollution changes with changes in income in a country are known as environmental Kuznets curves.[9]This helps to determine policy questions that deal with improvement of environmental quality in poor countries.[10]

The competitive aspect in a market economy is of vital importance. Just as firms compete against each other by providing better goods, cheaper prices and so on, the governments also compete against each other by providing incentives to the industries in order to attract these industries to establish their factories in the jurisdiction of the government. They do this in a number of ways, such as providing tax reductions and cheap land for building the factories. The governments have their own incentives in providing such amenities, like job opportunities for its citizens and economic boost. However, one of the most important problems arising out of this is that of environmental degradation. Though this process is economically efficient at first glance, in the long run, it has severe detrimental effects on the environment. Thus, at the international level, regulations vary substantially from one country to another. A simple reason for this variation is that environmental quality is a normal good; the wealthier people are, the more environmental quality they demand Thus, we would expect the citizens of a rich country to demand more environmental quality than citizens of a poor country. However, one negative impact of such process is the creation of 'pollution havens', which are countries that are full of polluting factories and industries because such countries have extremely relaxed environmental regulations and so on.

According to Coase Theorem[11] it makes no difference whether the polluter must compensate the victim of the pollution or the victim must pay the polluter not to pollute. There is an analogous issue in the context of Pigovian fees, which can be defined as a fee paid by the polluter per unit of pollution exactly equal to the aggregate marginal damage caused by the pollution when evaluated at the efficient level of pollution. The fee is generally paid to the government.[12] Thus, a major question that arises out of this context is whether the outcome of subsidizing firms is the same as the outcome obtained by imposing fees or taxes. This is an important question since subsidies are usually much more politically popular than taxes or fees.[13]

Thus, the determination of the market price of the good under these three regimes, that is taxes, subsidies and unregulated, is of utmost importance. The demand function for the good is typical, downward sloping, and the quantity demanded is inversely proportional to the price. Further, the market analysis is to be carried out using short-run supply functions for the industry in all three cases.

Recall that firms will operate on the portion of their marginal cost curve that lies above the variable cost.

The determination of the market price in the cases of unregulated circumstances and subsidies would operate to yield product prices Pu and Ps, respectively. In the case of Pigovian tax, only the newer firms operate, yielding product price Pt. Thus, it can be concluded that taxes and subsidies have different effects in the short run. A subsidy may allow firms to continue operating, which would not have happened in the case of tax. The subsidy requires a lump-sum transfer, which has to be obtained from somewhere. More important, the subsidy involves the operation of firms that are really losing money. This is not efficient.[14] Thus, from the earlier analysis, it can easily be concluded that though the theoretical concept of Coase Theorem tells us that subsidies and taxes have the same impact upon efficiency, we see that in case of practical application, as illustrated earlier, it has a detrimental effect, not only on the economy but also, more important, on the environment by allowing the loss-making and polluting firms to continue.[15]

The aspect of subsidy is undesirable because it does not allow the market to communicate the true costs of the product being consumed to the consumer. Thus, suppose there are two factories, one of which makes goods from recycled materials while the other is the polluting industry. Now subsidies would basically require giving money to the polluting industry to enable it to clean up. This would however create an interest or incentive in investing in those polluting industries rather than industries that are using the recycled materials. Moreover, as stated earlier, we would want the consumers to see the full costs associated with producing the product so that the consumers know what to buy and how much of it to buy.

To summarize, we could clearly suggest that, if jurisdictions/countries offer foreign firms tax-free status, it would not be in the best interest of these jurisdictions to loosen environmental regulations to attract capital. If, on the other hand, conditions are such that the jurisdiction must tax capital, we might see the complementary use of weak environmental regulations to make up for the capital taxation. In reality, we might expect positive capital taxation to exist in countries that are not excessively worried about attracting capital. It seems logical that such countries would not feel strongly enough about attracting capital that they would resort to substantial weakening of environmental regulations. This is just speculation; what happens in reality is an empirical question.

International trade

Environmental regulations cost polluters money. Firms subject to tighter environmental regulations will incur higher costs than firms subject to weaker or nonexistent environmental regulations. Thus, we can infer that economic theory would indicate that in the countries where there are relaxed environmental regulations there would be a concentration of polluting industries. Every industry would naturally (due to reasons of apparent economic efficiency) like to shift to a country where there are less environmental regulations because this condition would enable industries to produce goods without investing a substantial amount of capital on either using cleaner technology or paying penalty for the pollution generated by them. Thus, this leads to the development of areas/countries that have only pollution-intensive industries due to their weak environmental regulations and areas/countries that specialize in clean industries due to their strong environmental regulations. Moreover, if we have significant amount of such specialization, the establishment of free trade areas would be of major concern to the environmental groups. In fact, the environment was a major issue in the debate in the United States over the North American Free Trade Agreement.[16] The issue was whether a free trade zone involving Canada, the United States and Mexico would result in a significant number of Canadian and US industries moving to Mexico, seeking out weaker environmental regulations. Similarly, should Eastern Europe join the European Union, and will firms migrate to the East where environmental regulations may be more relaxed? Furthermore, tight environmental regulations tend to drive the industries elsewhere to places where they can find more relaxed regulations and weak government monitoring of the industries present.

Thus, we can see that certain countries/specific areas specialize in certain industries, depending on the assimilative capacity of the area. One of the primary models of explaining international specialization is the Heckscher–Ohlin model of international trade.[17] The Heckscher–Ohlin Theorem states that countries export those commodities which require, for their production, relatively intensive use of those productive factors found locally in relative abundance. The twin concepts of relative factor intensity and relative factor abundance are most easily defined in the small-dimensional context in which the basic theory is usually developed. Thus, there are two basic things that determine the environmental regulations of a particular country, the first being the assimilative capacity of the area. For example, a country with stringent environmental regulations will have clean industries, a country having weak environmental regulations is likely to have pollution-intensive industries, a country with plentiful labour will specialize in labour-intensive markets and so on. The second aspect on which the environmental regulations of a region depend on is the income of individuals[18] residing in the region. The more the income of the residents, the more stringent are the laws. This has been illustrated before.

One problem with finding evidence that differential environmental regulations influence international trade is that the effect is probably small. Because of this, some authors have focused on the margin most likely to be sensitive to the effect: international flows of capital.[19] The logic is that the nature of the capital stock in any country, and thus that country's specialization in a particular industry, is the result of investments made over many decades. Movement of capital from one country to another for investing in the industry of the other country is called foreign direct investment (FDI).[20] If lax environmental regulations tend to attract dirty industries, then we should expect to see FDI for dirty industries concentrated in countries with lax environmental regulations, all else being equal.

Now we shall discuss one of the most pertinent problems that arise as a result of the creation of pollution havens: that is the problem of transfer mispricing.[21] It is possible that companies that need to purchase carbon credits to offset their emissions may also have investments in derivatives trading and in businesses responsible for generating carbon credits. This raises the potential for those related companies to engage in transfer mispricing. Transfer mispricing, also known as transfer pricing manipulation, refers to trades between two related parties at artificial prices for the purposes of tax avoidance.[22]

If two unrelated companies trade with each other, it is generally accepted that they will deal with each at the market price for the transaction because it is the product of genuine negotiation in a market. But when two related companies – that is a parent company and a subsidiary, or two subsidiaries controlled by a common parent – trade with each other, they may artificially distort the price at which the trade is recorded, to minimize the overall tax bill. This might, for example, help the company record as much of its profit as possible in a tax haven with low or zero taxes.[23]

In the case of the carbon market, for example, a company (the 'parent company') may need to purchase carbon credits to offset its own emissions. It may invest in an offset project in Africa to generate those carbon credits. But first it establishes a trading company in a tax haven (with zero taxes). The subsidiary company in Africa sells its carbon credits (at a very low price) to the trading company, which then sells those carbon credits (at a very high price) to the parent company. In this case the subsidiary company in Africa receives an artificially low price for the carbon credits, resulting in low profits – and consequently an artificially low tax bill in Africa. The company in the tax haven sells the credits at a high price – artificially transferring all of the profits there – but being a tax haven, no tax is paid.[24]

Thus, as a result of the aforementioned phenomenon, we see that there has been complete avoidance of payment of taxes in the country in which the offset project was set up; the polluting industry in the main country can produce unlimited pollution, but it can save itself from any adverse effect, because it has an unlimited source of production of carbon credits which will meet its requirement. Thus, we see that such tax havens or pollution havens that are developed in specific countries due to their lax environmental regulations have an extremely negative effect on the environment. We have to remember that the basic reason why the environmental regulations were enacted in the first place was to protect the environment from degradation and provide overall welfare of the society as a whole. Thus, when one industry can generate immense amount of pollution, not caring about the carbon cap because it has an unlimited supply of carbon credits, it is extremely detrimental to the overall environment. Thus, this leads to the loss of the very reason for which such carbon caps were incorporated in the system in the very first place. If the environmental pollution is not reduced and the polluting industries continue to carry out their detrimental procedures, then the institution of carbon credits and the carbon-related regulations are of no use. Moreover, from the economic prospective, such transfer mispricing also leads to tax fraud in the country (say Africa, in the example stated earlier) in which the set-off industry is set up to produce carbon credit, because the set-off industry sold off the carbon credits at an extremely low price and as a result the regulatory authorities could not charge the normal taxes or charged zero taxes for such transaction because of the extremely low financial amount involved in the transaction.

Thus, we see that the economic benefit that the country (Africa in the example) should be receiving from the taxes is lost because of the fraud. This situation is not Pareto efficient because Pareto efficiency requires that one person should be better off (in his or her own estimation) and no other person may be made worse off (again in his or her own estimation). Thus, clearly from the aforementioned situation we can see that the polluting industry is made better off as a result of the entire set-up of the tax haven/or pollution haven (this is apparent at first glance); however, the country in which the set-off industry is situated is made worse off due to the tax fraud, and the overall society is made worse off as a result of the environmental degradation. Thus, we see that the set-up as a whole is inefficient on the whole from both the economic and the environmental prospective.

Tax fraud in international trade

Carbon trading in the European Union has already been hit by a particular form of tax fraud involving the theft of value-added tax (VAT) (also known as carousel fraud or missing trader intra-community fraud).[25] This type of fraud exploits how VAT is treated in multi-jurisdictional trading in Europe. In this type of fraud, the criminal utilizes the fact that VAT is not charged when a good is traded across the boundary between member states of the European Union; thus, a good, say, from Country A is traded to a Country B, and since the countries are member states of the European Union, such a transfer of that good is VAT-free. Now person 1 who obtained this good by means of the trans-boundary trade will sell it to another person within his or her country, and such a sale will include both sale price and VAT. Now person 2 who obtains this good is supposed to pass on the VAT to the relevant government to which this is owed; however, in the situation where there is a tax fraud, such a person usually disappears without paying the relevant tax, and subsequently the goods and the VAT may then be sold on through a number of companies, passing across a number of borders, with each additional layer of transactions making it more difficult to trace the link between the final VAT that is owed to the relevant government authority and the original importer, who by this time has disappeared without paying the tax.

In 2009 authorities began to observe high volumes of trade on France's BlueNext carbon exchange. Subsequent investigations revealed the sudden spike in trading was the result of highly organized criminals trading large volumes of carbon credits as part of a carousel fraud scheme. The European police agency, Europol, subsequently estimated that up to 90% of all carbon trading in some countries was a result of these fraudulent activities.[26] This fraud was estimated to have resulted in losses to several governments of around 5 billion euro in just over 18 months. Moreover, in the case of *R v. Dosanjh, Chahal and Gill* (2012), in June 2012, at Southwark Crown Court in the United Kingdom, three defendants were found guilty of carbon trading carousel fraud and jailed for a combined total of 35 years.

The three VAT fraudsters had established a number of bogus companies to import the carbon credits into the United Kingdom, and when those credits were sold on the original, companies were dissolved. The credits were sold on again between three further 'buffer' companies – also run by the gang – to make the trading chain appear legitimate, before the credits were finally sold to legitimate companies, charging VAT which was never paid back to the government. During the 69 days of trading, the total turnover was 276 million euro, of which 41 million euro was due in VAT. The trades were made in a matter of minutes via a computer system, and the stolen VAT was transferred to offshore bank accounts in the United Arab Emirates to 'clean' the stolen cash which the gang then spent.[27]

Thus, we see as a result of such tax fraud by not paying the VAT to the required authorities, there has been an immense amount of economic loss to the respective countries, and as a result we see that such processes are basically inefficient and cause widespread economic loss. Now, if we look into the background as to why frauds in general take place, we will see that while committing such offences, the major thought process of such violators is that even if they get caught, the penalty which they will have to pay or the loss they suffer is less than the total profit that is generated as a result of this violation. Now, this is efficient according to Potential Pareto Improvements or Kaldor–Hicks efficiency.[28] Now this theory of efficiency was developed by economists who wanted to overcome the restriction that was laid down by the Pareto criterion, which is to achieve Pareto efficiency, one person must be made better off while no other person can be made worse off. However, economists wanted to develop a more practical approach, and as a result, they developed the Potential Pareto Improvements or Kaldor–Hicks efficiency, which said that in a situation there can be both persons, one who has obtained a profit and another who has suffered a loss; however, the person who has obtained a gain must be better off than the person who has suffered a loss, that is the gainer's gain must be more than the loser's loss, and as a result even after compensating the loser the gainer must have surplus left as a result of which such a situation is efficient.

However, the situation which is being dealt with in the present scenario is not efficient according to Kaldor–Hicks efficiency. Here, the loss of the loser is greater than the gainer's gain, which is very evident from the reports that specify that around 90% of trade in carbon credit is the result of fraudulent activities (in certain countries), and moreover, there is no instance of payment of compensation by the violator to the person who has suffered the loss as these people do not pay compensation for the VAT fraud as it is extremely difficult to locate such violators due to the presence of a number of transactions and foreign exchanges and the relaxation in regulation and cross-checking in these foreign exchanges. As a result, such a situation is not efficient and is highly detrimental to the global economy.

Recycling of carbon credits

As a result of the intangible nature of carbon credits, a number of problems arise, with the major one being the problem of double-counting. Double-counting is the process by means of which the same carbon credits are sold to multiple parties, and it is the lax legal regulation that enables the owner of the carbon credits to indulge in such a process. Moreover, because of the intangible nature of the carbon credits, it is difficult to prevent an owner of carbon credits to sell his carbon credits through a number of foreign exchanges with different regulations and lax standards of monitoring or cross-checking between exchanges.

In one recent example of double-counting, carbon credits were traded on the European Union Emission Trading System (EU-ETS)[29] and then after being used to offset emissions found their way back onto the EU-ETS via a number of international transfers. In effect, this allowed those same carbon credits to offset emissions twice. In March 2010, the Hungarian government resold 2 million carbon credits, which had been surrendered by businesses to the government.[30] The rules of the EU-ETS allowed the Hungarian government to legally sell these carbon credits because Hungary anticipated being below its Kyoto Protocol target. However, the rules prevented these used or recycled credits from being reused within the EU.[31] On this occasion, Hungary sold the carbon credits to a recently created company, Hungarian Energy Power, with restrictions that they were ineligible for use in Europe and notified the European Commission of the sale. This company then sold the credits to a British trading company, which resold them to a firm in Hong Kong. The Hong Kong firm, however, then put those same recycled carbon credits on BlueNext, a Paris carbon exchange, where a number of European brokers and banks purchased them not knowing the carbon credits had already been used in Europe.[32] A major reason why this entire debacle regarding the double-counting occurred is that there was lax in the regulations which dealt with cross-checking between different foreign exchanges which in turn dealt with the exchange in carbon credits. Now before we further elucidate this point, we have to understand that every regime has its own set of specific regulations regarding emission of greenhouse gases and thus this creates a lack of co-ordination and cross-checking between these regimes, which leads to tax fraud, double-counting, transfer mispricing and so on. The Hungarian situation is a prime and clear-cut example of such a situation. The reselling of carbon credits within the boundaries of Hungary was allowed and justified due to the prevailing situation in that country and owing to the fact that it was below the target set by the Kyoto Protocol. However, the very fact that this carbon credit found its way to the Paris-based carbon exchange BlueNext and it was bought by European industries and bankers to offset their limit is proof of lax regulations and lack of countercheck between the foreign exchanges, and as a result, a lot of fraudulent processes take place. Now in the present situation, we see that since the carbon credit that was meant to be resold in Hungary only is sold elsewhere, there is a two-pronged loss: (1) there will be an increase in the opportunity cost and (2) there will be aggravated environmental degradation. Coming to the first situation, we see that since the carbon credit that was meant to be sold within Hungary was sold outside, there has been a reduction in the number of carbon credits available in Hungary, as a result of which another carbon credit is required to be produced to return to the situation as it was at the beginning. This is because carbon credit is a rival good. Once one such good (which is available in limited numbers) is consumed, then the opportunity for others to get the same good is reduced. As a result of this, the opportunity cost rises, and thus, there has been inefficient use of resources. Moreover, we have to keep in mind that the very reason why such environmental law and regulations were brought into place was to protect the environment, and if they are failing to do the very basic purpose for which they were instituted, then they are inefficient and must be replaced. We see in the present scenario that the recycling of carbon credits in Europe (where such recycling had been prohibited) is causing environmental degradation. This is because once a carbon credit is used to offset limit, its work is done. Now, again if the same one is used to offset another limit, then only one carbon credit is being used though double the amount of pollution is being cancelled out by its usage. Thus, pollution in the global environment increases. Thus, it is detrimental for the global environment.

Conclusion

Thus, we see that when we go on to analyse international trade or the provisions on the basis of which regulations (legislations) are made in countries, there are severe defaults in the practical application of theoretically successfully provisions. As illustrated earlier, we have already seen that income and assimilative capacities are two major aspects that influence the making of laws. Economic benefits have been the only drive that has influenced the countries and industries. It is true the developing or underdeveloped countries cannot afford to implement stringent environmental regulations because they need the development of industries for their economic development, but this factor has been mis-utilized by several factories and thus has resulted in areas specializing in polluting industries giving rise to pollution havens. Thus, we see that there is an overall detrimental effect on the environment, because on the one hand there are countries that have implemented strong environmental laws to improve the quality of the environment, and on the other hand, there are these countries with weak environmental regulations that are polluting the environment. Since environment is a public good and can be used in equal amounts by all countries, individuals or groups can take the position of a free rider not contributing to the cost of environmental quality. Constitutional mechanisms have to be developed, which ensure that free-rider behaviour in evaluating environmental quality is reduced.

Now coming to the concept of whether subsidies or penalties should be made applicable for such environmental pollution – we have seen that though the Coase Theorem says that penalties and subsidies have the same effect on efficiency – practical application has shown that providing subsidies is inefficient. Thus, we can say that practical application of certain laws should be reconsidered in terms of its environmental implication, and if such laws are not consistent with the environment/or have a detrimental impact on the environment, such laws should be removed because environmental laws should not only be economically efficient but should also promote the betterment of the environment (in its practical application) because that is the basic reason of the institution of such laws.

We have already seen the problems associated with international trade. Thus, let us see provisions which may help to improve the situation. One of such provisions is the implementation of sanctions against such polluted countries. Trade is one of the several aspects that control international relations; however, there are several other aspects that govern international relations, like the fact that countries deal with each other on a multitude of issues, not only economic but political and cultural as well. It may be that the victim country has little ability to coerce the polluter to reduce emissions; however, the victim country may have a great deal of power on a totally unrelated issue, such as involvement in a joint defence treaty. By withholding agreement on the joint defence treaty, the victim country may be able to force the polluter to reduce pollution levels. In essence, the victim country can threaten sanction of one sort or another against the polluter country that does not adopt pollution regulations to achieve the efficient amount of pollution. Another means of controlling the pollution situation is by having a stringent multinational international agreement, which involves as many countries as possible so that the deviance from the agreement is not in the scope of events, because it is only when majority of the countries are not subject to a uniform law that such problems like pollution haven and tax haven arise. The basic problem in designing an effective international environmental agreement is that there is no super-national organization to enforce such an agreement. In effect, the agreement must not only be self-enforcing but also be sufficiently appealing to all parties involved for them to agree to it in the first place.

Thus, there are three desirable characteristics of an international environmental agreement: (1) the agreement should be self-enforcing, (2) each country should be better off as part of the agreement than not and (3) pollution levels obtained by the agreement should be Pareto improvement over the status quo and, ideally, a Pareto optimum. It is easy to contemplate an international agreement that meets the first two of these three criteria; it is quite another thing to design an agreement that meets all three conditions.[33]

Notes

1 Trail Smelter Arbitration (*United States v. Can.*), Arbitral Trib., 3 U.N. Rep. Int'l Arb Awards 1905 (1941).
2 Peter H. Huang, 'International Environmental Law and Emotional Rational Choice', *The Journal of Legal Studies* 31 (2002): 237–258.
3 Ibid.
4 United Nations Framework Convention on Climate Change, 'Status of Ratification of the Convention', accessed 10 September 2014, http://unfccc.int/essential_background/convention/status_of_ratification/items/2631.php.
5 International Criminal Police Organisation (INTERPOL), 'Interpol Guide to Carbon Trading Crime (2013)', accessed 10 September 2014, www.interpol.int/. . ./Crime. . .crime/Guide-to-Carbon-Trading-Crime-2013.
6 Ibid.
7 United Nations Framework Convention on Climate Change, 'Status of Ratification of the Convention'.
8 Charles D. Kolstad, *Environmental Economics* (New York: Oxford University Press, 2000), 246.
9 Ibid., 248.
10 Ibid., 249.
11 Ibid., 124.
12 Ibid.
13 Ibid.
14 Ibid., 127.
15 Ibid.
16 Ibid.
17 Eli F. Heckscher and Bertil Ohlin, *Heckscher–Ohlin Trade Theory*, edited by Harry Flam and M. June Flanders (Cambridge, MA: MIT Press, 1991), accessed 11 October 2014, http://www.econ.rochester.edu/people/jones/Palgrave_Jones_on_Heckscher_Ohlin.pdf.
18 *See* Kolstad, *Environmental Economics*.
19 United Nations Framework Convention on Climate Change, 'Status of Ratification of the Convention'.
20 Ibid.
21 Tax Justice Network, 'Transfer Pricing – Tax Justice Network', accessed 11 October 2014, http://www.taxjustice.net/topics/corporate-tax/transfer-pricing/.
22 United Nations Framework Convention on Climate Change, 'Status of Ratification of the Convention'.

23 Ibid.
24 Ibid.
25 Ibid.
26 Rowena Mason, 'Copenhagen Climate Summit: Carbon Trading Fraudsters in Europe Pocket €5bn', *The Telegraph* (2009), accessed 8 November 2014, http://www.telegraph.co.uk/earth/copenhagen-climate-change-confe/6778003/Copenhagen-climate-summit-Carbon-trading-fraudsters-in-Europe-pocket-5bn.html.
27 Emily Allen, 'Fraud Mastermind Cheated Taxpayer Out of £39 Million in Just 69 Days and Spent the Money on £1 million Home and a Rolls Royce Is Jailed for 15 Years', *Mail Online* (2012), accessed 11 October 2014, http://www.dailymail.co.uk/news/article-2161520/Fraud-mastermind-cheated-taxpayer-39million-just-69-DAYS-spent-money-1million-home-Rolls-Royce-jailed-15-years.html#ixzz29O6SfXtp.
28 Robert Cooter and Thomas Ulen, *Law and Economics* (Delhi: Pearson, 2004), 48.
29 United Nations Framework Convention on Climate Change, 'Status of Ratification of the Convention'.
30 Ibid.
31 Catherine Airlie, 'BlueNext Arranges "Swap Back" of Recycled CO_2 Credits after Trading Halt', *Bloomberg* (2010), accessed 11 October 2014, http://www.bloomberg.com/news/2010-04-14/bluenext-arranges-swap-backs-of-recycled-co2-credits-after-trading-halt.html.
32 Danny Fortson and Jonathan Leake, 'Hunt for "Rogue Trader" over Recycled Carbon Credits', *The Times* (2010), accessed 11 October 2014, http://www.timesonline.co.uk/tol/news/environment/article7069741.ece.
33 International Criminal Police Organisation (INTERPOL), 'Interpol Guide to Carbon Trading Crime (2013)'.

Chapter 3

The economic analysis of blackmail

The case for an alternate legal regime

Anamika Ray

Background note

The term 'blackmail' has been attached to a number of relations where one person extracts something of value from another with pressure. This chapter is limited to 'pure' or 'informational' blackmail: the sale of silence by someone who is otherwise free to disclose what he or she knows.[1] The case of character in a blackmail must number at least three: 'A', 'B' and 'C'. B (for 'blackmailer') is the holder of information that he or she threatens to disclose unless compensated. A is the person to whom B offers to sell his or her silence and is usually the subject of the information to be kept silent. C is the person or group of persons to whom B threatens to disclose the information, unless he or she and A reach an understanding or an agreement. C may be an individual, a group or the general public.[2] In this triangle, B is an intermediary who, depending on the legal regime, may advance or impede the flow of information concerning A to C.

A key element of pure blackmail, which has led some to question whether it should be treated as a crime, is that B is initially free to make the disclosure over which he or she bargains with A.[3] It is pertinent to note here that blackmail, as addressed here, does not include threats of disclosure barred by statute or contract, such as a doctor's threat to reveal a patient's disease, which belongs to the broader class of 'extortion'. Extortion, that is obtaining something with the threat of inflicting *unlawful* harm, is a form of threat by force. Most violent crimes have an element of extortion. 'Give me your wallet or I will kill you' is a threat to do something that is no more permitted absent the threat, than with it. In contrast, B's bargaining lever in a blackmail is something that normally is within B's right. The criminal prohibition of blackmail – essentially a prohibition on bargaining between B and A over control of information – denies B the right to seek compensation from A for not doing something B is otherwise free to do.

On first encounter there is no obvious reason for this restraint of B's (and A's) freedom: why impede the allocation of rights in information that unconstrained bargaining would otherwise produce? This question is one way of framing what is called the 'paradox of blackmail'.[4] In most contexts other than the disclosure of information, people are free to bargain over permissible courses of action. It is through bargaining that rights in property (note that information is a kind of property) migrate to the hands of owners who value them the most.[5] For example, when A and B own contiguous parcels of land on which construction is allowed, it is no crime for B to threaten to build on his or her lot and impair A's view unless A pays him not to do so. The case of contiguous lots serves in the literature as a standard counterpoint to informational blackmail.[6] Numerous other transactions recognized as legitimate, or even statutory, involve some form of 'threats' to do something lawful unless paid otherwise or otherwise rewarded to abstain. 'Pay me higher wages or I will go on strike or quit' and 'pay me the price I am asking for this good or I will sell it to someone else' are permissible threats almost everywhere, while 'pay me or I will reveal compromising photographs' and 'if you fire me I'll tell the Revenue Department about your secret Swiss bank account' are blackmail.[7]

Threats of the latter type often elicit a strong aesthetic reaction. Indeed, blackmail has drawn unusually intense condemnations from otherwise sober sources. 'The blackmailer is both contemptible and dangerous; from the standpoint of his victim, he is more to be feared than a burglar or a thief.'[8] This response resists fully satisfactory explanation, however, even upon prolonged introspection. Scholarly accounts of the prohibition of blackmail are widely contradictory; none seems to be entirely convincing. Despite the obvious difficulty of explaining the crime of bargaining over permissible conduct, commentators have generally defended the prohibition of blackmail.

Two broad ideas run through the writing on blackmail. One condemns the threat to privacy. In this view, A is B's victim, forced to pay to protect a personal sphere that should remain private. The other finds in blackmail the opposite vice of concealing wrongs that should be revealed. In this latter view of blackmail, B and A are cooperating, conspiring even, to keep valuable information from C. In fact – and this is where the paradox of blackmail ultimately lies – the prohibition of blackmail serves both ends to a degree. The concern in this chapter is whether prohibition of blackmail serves these ends well enough, or whether some other legal regime for bargaining over private information might be preferable.

The prohibition of blackmail affects the allocation of rights in information.[9] It is argued in this chapter that the prohibition of blackmail leads to relatively greater disclosure of a smaller body of information, because on the one hand, B is more likely to disclose information about A to C when prevented from bargaining with A, but on the other hand, not being able to extract the full return from bargaining with A, B has less incentive to seek out information about A in the first place.[10] In a frictionless world (one in which it was costless to bargain over the value of information), prohibition of blackmail would surely not be correct. For most rights in property *other* than information, even in our world of significant transaction costs, both analysis and experience suggest that prohibition of bargaining is likely to impede the appropriate allocation of those rights.[11]

The justification for the prohibition of blackmail, if there is one, must therefore lie in the particular nature of information. The transactional difficulty and cost of bargaining over the disclosure of information are greater than for other forms of property. Unrestricted blackmail might lead to vexatious and ultimately sterile bargaining.[12] This is specially so if the cost of bargaining over information is understood broadly to include even the inducement of efforts by would-be blackmailers to unearth information destined simply to be reburied. Even with such an extended notion of cost, however, the prohibition of blackmail is not self-evidently justified. The costs saved under prohibition must be weighed against the possibility of better allocation of rights in information under a regime of freer bargaining.[13]

Blackmail as prohibited bargaining

What is prohibited under the law of blackmail is a certain type of bargaining over the disclosure of information, rather than the bare result, which is some sort of compensation given for silence. It is B's threat of disclosure that is barred, not any reward from A for

B's discretion.[14] Thus, if A spontaneously offers to reward B's discretion regarding private information, or simply does so without bargaining, there is no prohibited blackmail, even if it is likely that B's discretion would end with the withdrawal of the reward.[15] Once B has acquired private information about A, blackmail is, much like gambling or trade in narcotics, a victimless crime. A (who is often identified as B's victim) would almost invariably prefer the possibility of bargaining with B over the alternatives. If there is a victim of a blackmail in the conventional sense (someone who bears the uncompensated external cost of a transaction benefitting others), it is C.[16]

The extent of blackmail

Blackmail is not a major day-to-day concern of the criminal justice system. On first encounter, in fact, blackmail seems a matter of mainly academic concern. Scholars have written about it with some regularity, but on any given day, there are probably a thousand times more prisoners serving time in our jails for crimes related to cocaine than for blackmail.[17] It is very possible that there may be no one in an Indian jail convicted of what might be called 'classical' or pure 'informational' blackmail. The actual extent of blackmail in daily life is not readily knowable to an academic observer, but it is very likely greater than what the scarcity of appellate decisions on the subject might indicate.[18] Certainly many proscribed acts are carried out beyond the immediate attention of the criminal courts. A successful blackmail (one in which B and A come to an agreement) by its nature tends to remain hidden.

A further difficulty is determining the point at which ubiquitous minor threats moult into prohibited blackmail. A parent's threat to tell a child's playmates that he or she sleeps with a nightlight unless he or she cleans his or her room falls literally within the Model Penal Code's definition of criminal coercion,[19] so does an employee's threat to inform the revenue department of his or her employer's concealed income unless promoted.[20] The largest single class of blackmail, both subtle and overt, involves tax obligations that A has slighted in some way and that B knows about. The Model Penal Code clearly makes it a crime for an employee to seek advantage by threatening to reveal an employer's tax evasion and would also make it a crime for a spouse to seek a larger divorce settlement with a similar threat.[21]

Blackmail and property rights

Property rights are largely shaped by the law of crimes. The assignment of property rights to those who value them most reduces the necessity of exchanges or other transactions to bring them to higher-valued uses.[22] An important function of a legal regime is, therefore, to maintain property rights in the hands of owners who value them most.[23]

The definition of most crimes is easily understood in the light of these principles. The prohibition of murder accords an individual the property right in his or her own life; the prohibition of battery frames an individual's rights in his or her body; the prohibition of theft sets the contours of other property rights. That life is worth more a priori to its owner than to any other person is revealed by the rarity of exchanges in which someone consents to being killed for a payment from another who would enjoy doing it. That people value their bodies more than batterers can similarly be inferred from the infrequency of their consenting to being beaten for a fee. If homicide and accidental killing were legal, people would have to take far greater pains to protect their lives through individual force, bargaining and other transactions aimed at regaining control over survival.[24] Relations between people in such a world would have the character of blackmail. People would abstain from killing each other in consideration of some advantage implicitly or explicitly bargained for.

At issue in blackmail is the right to control the disclosure of information.[25] The starting point of any blackmail is B's possession of information, usually about A, that A does not want it to be communicated to C. Almost always, C will gain something from learning the information. One way for B to derive a benefit from the information, absent the prohibition of blackmail, is to offer not to disclose the information to C in exchange for payment from A.[26] The most B can get from A with the threat of disclosure is what the disclosure would cost A. This cost may involve money (e.g. an income tax deficiency and fraud penalties), jail time, embarrassment and so on.[27] The full cost to A of disclosure may be called the 'value' of the information to A. B will bargain for something like the monetary equivalent of this value, but in practice, given the uncertainties of measurement and A's likely limited means, B is bound to settle for less. The value of the information to C is what C stands to gain from learning the information.[28] Depending on who C is, this value may be the collection of a tax deficiency and penalties, a tort recovery or simply the requital of animosity against A. The value of the information to C may even be negative.[29] That is, it may concern something that would compel some sort of change in C's actions or attitude towards A and that C would accordingly rather not know.

A predicate of blackmail is that B's disclosure would be costly to A, whether or not the underlying information is of value to C.[30] Also necessary is that B values the information less than A. Often the element of greatest uncertainty is the value of the information to C. If we could determine the flow of information costlessly from some sort of a vantage point, we would want the information held by B to be disclosed to C when its value to C was greater than its value to A, but to be kept private when it was worth more to A.[31] Since it is usually impossible to determine the value of the information to each party, it is generally left to private bargaining to steer property rights to owners who value them most. In the case of private information, however, the prohibition of blackmail prevents bargaining between B and someone with a large stake in controlling the information, namely A. Immediate questions are (a) whether the prohibition thereby prevents the flow of information to those who value it most and (b) if it does, what is gained.[32]

Bargaining over information

When the right at issue between A and B (and ultimately C) is control over information, the same outcome is desirable in the abstract. B's information should be controlled by A or disclosed to C according to whether A or C values the information more. However, the regime of free bargaining between B and A does not clearly tend towards that result.[33] What shapes the particular course of bargaining in blackmail is that the underlying rights consist entirely of information, a form of property different from others in significant respects. Information is less susceptible to exclusive ownership than other property; it is hence more costly to appropriate and to transmit, and the return from information is generally independent of the amount invested in it. Bargaining over information raises unique problems.[34]

If allowed to bargain without constraint, B would be more likely to sell silence to A than to disclose the information to C, regardless of the value of the information to C. With information concerning A, the course of bargaining between B and A is by far the easier.

B and A already know the information; C does not. Indeed, in the normal setting of blackmail, A knows more of the value of the information than C knows of its very existence.[35] Regardless of who ultimately values the information the most, at the time of a potential blackmail bargain, B stands to gain more from the effort of bargaining with A, who already knows the value of the information. B cannot bargain with C over the value of the information without revealing some part of it, thereby reducing the amount still undisclosed.[36] If C is the public, B must bargain with some proxy, such as a newspaper or a magazine that will pay for a circulation-boosting story. If blackmail were legal, in short, B would tend consistently to try to sell silence to A rather than disclose it to C. The outcome of the bargaining that leaves no change in the surface distribution of rights is more likely when information is at issue, regardless of the values assigned to the information by A and C.[37]

We can safely posit, therefore, that unfettered bargaining between B and A would not lead to the same allocation of rights as in a world of perfect information. That does not mean, of course, that *prohibition* of bargaining induces the best possible allocation of rights in information. In practice, the prohibition of blackmail prevents bargaining from following its natural course between B and A, and, indirectly, strengthens C's hand in acquiring information held by B.[38]

When B is denied the (legal) benefit of bargaining with A, disclosure to C is more likely. B also has less to gain from acquiring information about A in the first place. The prohibition of blackmail, therefore, leads to *more* disclosure from a *smaller* body of information held by B. Perhaps that is why defenders of privacy and proponents of disclosure both find merit in the prohibition of blackmail. Whether the absolute amount of information disclosed to C is greater or lesser in a situation of prohibition rather than under the regime of free bargaining is hard to say. While the prohibition of blackmail is likely to have little effect on the type of information adventitiously discovered by B about A, it may bear on what sort of information B deliberately seeks out.[39] Under prohibition, B has more reason to seek out information of interest to C than information merely costly to A. This effect is likely to be small, however, because it is difficult in any event for B to get full value for information in dealings with C.

The prohibition of blackmail creates for C leverage that C would not otherwise have with respect to information concerning A. The prohibition of blackmail, in broad terms, shifts the rights in private information discovered by B to C. While it is not a tax, it is similar to one in that it reduces the value to B of a certain kind of economic activity, to the advantage of A's piracy. The 'tax' also reaches information obtained by B as a windfall and shifts part of the windfall advantage to C. Some part of the potential windfall – possibly larger than C's average – goes back to A in the cases where B simply remains silent without seeking compensation from anyone.[40] Across the full range of situations, both C and A get part of the value that is denied to B, which is why the prohibition of blackmail can plausibly be viewed as serving the ends of disclosure *and* privacy.

An alternative regime for bargaining over private information

While the particular nature of rights in information lends plausibility to the prohibition of blackmail, it by no means disposes of the question whether prohibition leads to the best practical allocation of those rights. In weighing a change in the legal regime for blackmail, three considerations come into play.[41] The most important concern in framing a regime for bargaining over private information is to enhance the likelihood that it will be controlled by the one who values it most. Two other concerns, both related to the main concern, involve the effect of a given regime on underlying conduct: first, the incentives to invest resources in discovering information and bargaining over it (in our triangular scenario, these are the incentives for B); and second, the incentives for those whom the information concerns (A) to leave it exposed to discovery by B in the first place.[42] These elements are specially correlated under different regimes for bargaining over information.

Prohibition of blackmail limits cooperation between B and A to keep C uninformed, thereby apparently increasing disclosure to C; the prohibition, however, also likely cuts down effort by B to acquire information concerning A, thereby reducing the body of disclosable information, and thus may, in the end, make it somewhat easier for A to engage costlessly in the course of action that gives rise to the information.[43] These three effects are increasingly accentuated in the order just given. If blackmail were permitted, C would on balance find out less of the information concerning A held by B, B would invest more effort in uncovering information held by A and

A would accordingly want to be somewhat more guarded in leaving a trail of information, either by changing conduct or by engaging in the same conduct more discreetly.[44]

In this light the following tentative rule for bargaining over private information may be offered: B cannot legally bargain with A to suppress information about a prosecutable crime for tortuous act committed by A. Although perhaps not obvious, it is unnecessary to treat as crimes bargains that are invalid under this rule. It is sufficient, indeed preferable, simply to make them unenforceable. A gains no real control over disclosure from an unenforceable bargain with B. And if B cannot assure A of any increased control over disclosure, B cannot extract much from A and therefore has little reason to invest much effort in bargaining. In contrast, if blackmail is made a crime, A gains considerable control over disclosure from entering into a bargain with B, because B, by incurring the criminal exposure of a blackmailer, can now sell A a much higher likelihood of silence. To be sure, after a blackmail bargain between B and A, B's disclosure is not literally proscribed. But B's disclosure also exposes the blackmail and so may be costly to B. If the penalty for blackmail is severe, B's disclosure after having bargained to agreement with A is in fact prohibitive. The criminal prohibition of blackmail, therefore, makes the blackmail bargains entered into across the threshold of prohibition highly enforceable. If A and B both want to bargain, they will often do so despite the prohibition of blackmail. When they do, the prohibition, on balance, strengthens A's hand. To make a blackmail agreement enforceable is likely, in sum, to cut down bargaining and increase disclosure compared to the alternative of making them crimes.

In summary, the new legal regime for bargaining over private information[45] would be the following:

1 Contracts not to disclose knowledge of prosecutable crimes and torts would be invalid and unenforceable. To enter into such a contract would, in addition, imply a measure of complicity in the underlying crime or tort.
2 Contracts not to disclose private information entered into between persons with no prior course of dealing would also be invalid and unenforceable.
3 Other contracts not to disclose private information would be valid.

This regime would give rise, between persons who have had some prior dealing, to a new class of enforceable contracts of silence. The existence of a binding obligation between A and B would largely eliminate the routine that arouses the indignation of commentators. Once B has been compensated for remaining silent, B's subsequent try for a second helping with the threat of disclosure can be countered by A's own threat of a damage action or even prosecution, depending on the strength of the sanctions backing the enforceability of contracts of silence. A is no worse off than if there had been no initial agreement.

Conclusion

The problem of blackmail belongs to the broader problem of framing a legal regime for rights in information. The analysis of social cost in blackmail transaction is, for this reason, more difficult than that for other crimes. The paradox of blackmail, restated in these terms, is that the prohibition of blackmail leads to a distribution of rights in information which, though not optimal in a world of zero transaction costs, may nonetheless be the best attainable.

Several commentators concerned with social cost have concluded that the prohibition of blackmail is desirable because agreements to suppress information are non-productive. But when the information is worth more to A (i.e. concealed) than to C (i.e. revealed), the blackmail bargain, viewed in isolation, is productive. A's control of the information is more secure, and the alternative – disclosure – leaves A, B and C in the aggregate worse off. Possible gains from blackmail bargains viewed in isolation, however, do not in themselves justify the regime of free bargaining over private information, which is worthwhile only if the larger cost of bargaining (which includes the creation of incentives for would-be blackmailers to seek out private information) is offset by a more valuable allocation of information resulting from the bargaining. The balance of advantage between these two regimes is not self-evident.

Across-the-board prohibition of blackmail has the advantage of simplicity. Its cost lies in the potential denial of control of private information to the one who values it most. To permit bargaining without restraint might also, however, given the asymmetry of bargaining opportunities between B and A, and B and C, lead to the suppression of some information that would be profitable if disclosed. Furthermore, unrestricted blackmail might induce excessive investment in the discovery of, and bargaining over, information of lesser value to C than to A. Nonetheless, a plausible case can be made for freer bargaining between B and A over the disclosure of private information, not concerning A's crimes or torts, when A and B have had a prior course of dealing.

This conclusion is reached even though it may well be that the gains from improved allocation of rights in information would be roughly balanced by a possible increase in costly transactions. What tips the scales towards freer bargaining is, first, the suspicion that the prohibition of blackmail is widely ineffective. Much bargaining over private information, explicit and implicit, doubtless goes on in the teeth of prohibition, which itself adds a measure of anxiety and risk to the process. Second in the balance favouring freer bargaining are possible gains, little noticed in the literature on blackmail, in A's incentives to guard his or her own privacy.

Notes

1 Steven Shavell, 'An Economic Analysis of Threats and Their Illegality: Blackmail, Extortion, and Robbery', *University of Pennsylvania Law Review* 141 (1993): 1877.
2 Ibid.
3 Ibid.
4 F.E. Guerra-Pujol, 'The Problem of Blackmail: A Critique of Coase, and the Case for Blackmail Markets', *The Critical Studies Journal* 5 (2012): 1.
5 Richard H. McAdams, 'Group Norms, Gossip, and Blackmail', *University of Pennsylvania Law Review* 144 (1996): 2237.
6 Ronald H. Coase, 'The 1987 McCorkle Lecture: Blackmail', *Virginia Law Review* 74 (1988): 655, 670–71.
7 Walter Block, 'Blackmail and Economic Analysis', *Thomas Jefferson Law Review* 21 (1996): 165.
8 Arthur L. Goodhart, *Essays in Jurisprudence and the Common Law* (London: Cambridge University Press, 1931): 175.
9 Ibid.
10 Richard A. Posner, 'Blackmail, Privacy, and Freedom of Contract', *University of Pennsylvania Law Review* 141 (1993): 1817.
11 Guerra Pujol, 'The Problem of Blackmail': 3.
12 Posner, 'Blackmail, Privacy, and Freedom of Contract': 1818.
13 Fernando Gomez, 'Civil and Criminal Sanctions against Blackmail: An Economic Analysis', *International Review of Law and Economics* 21 (2002): 475.
14 Model Penal Code § 212.5 (Official Draft and Explanatory Notes, 1985).
15 Ibid.
16 James Lindgren, 'Blackmail: On Waste, Morals, and Ronald Coase', *UCLA Law Review* 36 (1989): 597.

17 Joseph Isenbergh, 'Blackmail from A to C', *University of Pennsylvania Law Review* 141 (1993): 1905.
18 Ibid.
19 Model Penal Code § 212.5(1)(c) (Official Draft and Explanatory Notes, 1985).
20 Ibid., § 212.5(1)(b).
21 George P. Fletcher, 'Blackmail: The Paradigmatic Crime', *University of Pennsylvania Law Review* 141 (1993): 1617.
22 David B. Sentelle, 'Law and Economics Should Be Used for Economic Questions', *Harvard Journal of Law and Public Policy* 21 (1997): 112.
23 Isenbergh, 'Blackmail from A to C': 1905.
24 Sentelle, 'Law and Economics Should Be Used for Economic Questions': 121.
25 Fletcher, 'Blackmail': 1619.
26 Ibid.
27 Ibid.
28 Isenbergh, 'Blackmail from A to C': 1908.
29 Ibid.
30 Lindgren, 'Blackmail': 599.
31 Ibid.
32 Lindgren, 'Blackmail': 597.
33 Gomez, 'Civil and Criminal Sanctions against Blackmail': 479.
34 Kenneth Arrow, *Information and Economic Behaviour*, reprinted in '4 Collected Papers of Kenneth J. Arrow' 136 (1984): 142–143.
35 Ibid.
36 Posner, 'Blackmail, Privacy, and Freedom of Contract': 1819.
37 Goodhart, *Essays in Jurisprudence*: 655, 673.
38 Block, 'Blackmail and Economic Analysis': 168.
39 Goodhart, *Essays in Jurisprudence*: 175, 180.
40 Ibid.
41 McAdams, 'Group Norms, Gossip, and Blackmail': 2237.
42 Ibid.
43 Shavell, 'An Economic Analysis of Threats and Their Illegality :152.
44 McAdams, 'Group Norms, Gossip, and Blackmail': 149.
45 Coase, 'The 1987 McCorkle Lecture': 692.

Part II

Contract theory and efficiency

Chapter 4

'Best efforts'

Search for the optimal performance standard – an economic analysis

Supratim Guha and Amudavalli Kannan

Background note

The law of contracts is founded upon mutual good faith of the parties. Every transaction is inherently risky, and contracts function as tools in aid of better planning by the contracting parties. In other words, contract law supplies the contracting parties with much-needed clarity of information, enabling them to undertake risky ventures for mutual gain; transactions are efficiently carried out on the basis of the relatively secure knowledge that all rights and obligations are enforceable under the law. It therefore follows that the law demarcates standards of care that must be observed by the parties in the course of any transaction. In this regard, the obligation of 'good faith' is taken as a thumb rule, a common minimum, in the process of allocation of risks and costs between the parties. A constant rule of contractual interpretation in the form of good faith obligations acts as a 'safety net' for parties of varying levels of sophistry and enables them to deal with one another without undue suspicion. In other words, this legal standard imposed seeks to level the playing field for parties with unequal bargaining strengths. In a recent judgement, the Delhi High Court affirmed

> the fiduciary principle of every contract containing an implied covenant of good faith and fair dealing because in every contract each party reposes trust and confidence in the other, that each would refrain from doing anything which will have the effect of destroying or injuring the right of the other party to receive the fruits of the contract.[1]

In this regard, the use of 'best efforts' clauses, or any of its variants, poses as a special problem. For instance, where a distributor agrees to use his or her best efforts to sell some goods, the standard of care that must be observed by the dealer remains unclear; the use of the verb in the superlative degree does not convey any definite meaning, leaving much to the ex post determination of the courts. The only definite yardstick available is the 'implied covenant of good faith'.[2] Indeed, courts across the world have taken a wide variety of approaches to interpreting best efforts. Some jurisdictions in the United States, such as those in Illinois, do not give any effect at all to the provision, holding that the obligation of best efforts is lacking in mutuality and merely emphasises the underlying duty of good faith in contracts.[3] On the other hand, the Second Circuit Court in New York State, in *Bloor v. Falstaff Brewing Corp.*,[4] a landmark judgement on the topic, imposed a duty that was greater than good faith but lesser than a fiduciary duty, similar to that required of an agent.[5] Similarly, in the United Kingdom, the recent ruling in *Jet2.com Limited v. Blackpool Airport Limited*[6] held that the courts would strive to enforce an agreement between parties to use their best efforts, so long as there was clarity in the obligations sought to be imposed; a vague or too uncertain obligation will not be enforceable in law.

In India too, parties often make use of best efforts clauses in their contracts, presumably relying on the plain meaning of the phrase, that is a more onerous obligation to perform. However, in the absence of any authoritative pronouncement on the subject, the performance standards that parties set for themselves remain uncertain. The lack of scholarship or judicial interpretation on best efforts clauses may be attributable to conservative business practices in India. However, recent years have witnessed the re-invigoration of the commercial enterprise in India, bringing with it demands for greater efficiency and the need for a higher degree of commitment to purpose. This assumes great importance in trade and commerce where, especially in India's expanding business sector, the investors look to the stability and certainty of their obligations while undertaking risky ventures. Today, the law of best efforts obligations is urgently in need of clarity. This chapter seeks to provide a framework to guide parties in setting performance standards while negotiating agreements.

The position in India

Quite interestingly, there is a dearth of authoritative literature on the use of best efforts clauses in India. P. Ramanatha Aiyar's *Advanced Law Lexicon* indicates that as a standard, a best-efforts obligation should be stronger than a good faith obligation.[7] This interpretation implies that an obligation to exert best efforts cannot be absolute and the nature of the duty will depend on several factors, which may even be extraneous of the express terms of the contract.[8] Material factors such as the price or the degree of risk involved in achieving the result, or the prevailing legal position, are relevant to the determination of the nature of the obligation to be imposed.[9] Where the contract is contingent upon the fulfilment of a condition precedent, there is no undertaking by either party that such condition shall be fulfilled, but a contractual clause may also specify that one of the parties will use all reasonable efforts to secure the fulfilment of such condition or event. Thus, there cannot be any absolute obligation to do that which the law forbids.[10] However, there is nothing improper or illegal for a party to bind himself or herself to an absolute obligation.[11] That being said, these interpretations shed no light on the legal standard actually applicable to parties in best efforts agreements in India. Two standards may be identified from the aforementioned musings of the courts:

- First, a conditional standard where the party must make reasonable efforts to perform the thing promised. This re-emphasises the implied covenant of good faith in contracts, that is the parties must engage in the transaction in a manner that will maximise mutual benefits and refrain from anything that would impair the ability of the other party to partake in the joint benefits arising out of the contract. In other words, the obligation imposed on the promisor is no more onerous than under an ordinary contract.
- Second, on the other end of the spectrum is an absolute standard. Parties are bound absolutely and to an unlimited extent. Here, the obligation imposed is highly onerous and must be performed even to the detriment of the promisor himself. Thus, where the person has promised to do something which he or she knew, or, with reasonable diligence, might have known, and which the promisee did not know to be impossible or unlawful, such promisor must make compensation to such promise for any loss which such promise sustains through the non-performance of the promise.[12] In *Gwalior Rayon Silk Mfg Co Ltd v. Shri Andavar & Co*,[13] it was held that a party agreeing to supply firewood of a specified type and girth from the plantation cannot plead impossibility of

performance on the ground that later the party found that it was not available in the plantation.

These approaches adopted by the Indian courts cannot be effective standards for guiding parties in the allocation of risks and costs. Using the first standard, a best efforts obligation is a conditional standard and, in effect, the same as an ordinary contract with the inherent good faith obligation at its core. On the other hand, imputing an absolute obligation on the promisor to perform is far too burdensome and cannot be an acceptable general standard. Such refusal to give effect to the plain meaning of best efforts clauses thwarts the parties' intentions because it is unlikely that they included a best effort clause without intending to create a binding obligation.[14] Similarly, the proposition that best effort clauses embody the intention of parties to bind themselves absolutely to the performance of an obligation is naive and unrealistic. Parties are free to contract around good faith obligations and bind themselves to more onerous standards of performance. Agreements frequently require parties to exert their 'best endeavours' towards the performance of the task agreed upon. Uncertainty in default rules can be especially pernicious in contract law; contracting parties must have adequate information in order to allocate risks and assign the appropriate price to the performance of the contracts. This emphasises the need for a set legal standard to provide incentives to parties to contract efficiently. This comment puts forth an efficient legal standard which bestows a reasonable degree of certainty to the parties, allowing them to structure their contractual relationships efficiently.

Party autonomy and contract design

Party autonomy, that is the principle of contractual freedom, is at the core of contractual jurisprudence. In other words, upholding the contractual intent of the parties is the central objective of contract law.[15] The law of contracts aims at facilitating easy and efficient transactions. The enforceability of promises is the basis of contracts, and it encourages exchange and cooperation among people. For instance, in the case of deferred exchanges, where the passage of time is required for completion, a cautious buyer may refuse to pay now for future delivery of goods in a situation where promises are unenforceable. The passage of time between the exchange of promises and their performance creates uncertainties and risks, which present barriers to efficient contracting.[16] The buyer will want something more than the moral obligation of the seller to deliver the goods. Deferred exchanges can thus be made possible only by legal rules set down by contract law. It is therefore efficient to enforce a promise because both the promisor and promisee wanted the assurance of enforceability when it was made. In other words, the law is instrumental in safeguarding contractual autonomy.

Contracting parties design contracts using terms that will best serve the purpose or the 'ends' of their collaboration. Accordingly, the parties will include particular provisions that will function as the means towards the achievement of the shared intention. In this regard, the interpretation doctrines of contract law are meant to work as devices for discovering and effectuating contractual intent.[17] Conventionally, contract analysis depends on an objective understanding of the parties' intentions: a party is taken to have meant what his or her contract partner could plausibly believe he or she meant when the parties contracted.[18] Parties put forth their intention by choosing between vague terms or precise terms. Where the parties have identified the standard of performance by which they wish to bind themselves, their contract would employ specific terms; in such a situation, the law must necessarily abide by that standard decided upon.[19] It follows that where parties contracted to employ their best efforts towards the attainment of something, they obviously set themselves to a peculiar standard of performance which may be gauged after reading the contract as a whole. In other words, by including precise terms, the parties withdraw authority from courts to determine their particular performance obligations, and instead direct the courts to enforce the obligations already decided between the two parties at the time of formation of the contract.

It cannot therefore be concluded that there is but one criterion to which the best efforts agreement is subject. It would be inefficient to subject parties to standards which they have not contracted for, such as a standard which is not enforceable, as in the case of good faith obligations of ordinary contracts, or a standard which is far too onerous, as in the case of 'absolute obligations'. Setting a standard different from that which is understood between the parties lays down incorrect incentives and would fail to guide parties while contracting with each other. If these standards are what the court imposes on the parties, it makes little sense as to why parties would opt for the use of the relatively uncertain wording of a best effort clause or its variants, if the 'end' was indeed the achievement of well-defined and mutually accepted performance standards, which do not flow directly from the text of the contractual provision, as in the case of an intended standard of good faith or absolute obligations.

In reality, neither a good faith standard nor that of an absolute obligation can be made out from the plain meaning of the text of best efforts clauses. The same end of good faith or absolute obligation, if indeed the true end is sought, could instead have been reached using an unambiguous text for the contractual provision as would precisely indicate the obligations of the parties. In other words, in such a case, parties would have rationally opted to specify in lucid and certain terms each other's absolute obligation that has been mutually decided upon. This is rational: if parties are certain of the performance standards to which they are subjecting themselves, it would be less costly to specify the precise performance obligations at the time of formation.

However, by using vague terms (e.g. an obligation to use best efforts), parties delegate the identification of a concrete and specific performance requirement to a court at the time of adjudication, as part of the process of interpretation.[20] This strategy additionally imposes on the parties the expected costs of litigation. This is thus an absurd strategy, where parties are aware of their respective performance obligations and are therefore able to specify the same in their contracts. It is pertinent to note here that the mix of specific and vague terms in any contract constitutes the contractual means that the parties have chosen to trade off investments in transaction costs at the time of formation of the contract, against the enforcement costs at the time of litigation due to a contractual dispute, so as to best achieve their particular contractual ends at least cost.

Despite the indefinite and inconsistent standards according to judicial interpretation of the best efforts clause, it still appears frequently in contracts.[21] The reasons for this may be manifold. Employing a strategy for specific terms in the contract would require the parties to specify their performance obligations based solely on estimates of the likelihood of various future events.[22] This means that the parties will set standards only on the basis of foreseeable future events. Any unforeseeable event that could potentially have changed their performance standard is not accounted for in the standard pre-decided at the time of contracting. By using vague terms, however, the parties are able to save costs of specifying precise performance obligations at the time of formation. This allows the parties to benefit from more efficient performance standards than they could have specified at the time of formation. The courts, having the benefit of information that was not available to the parties at the time of formation of contract, are able to determine the optimal standard of performance at a relatively lower cost. Thus, there are good reasons for the parties, under certain conditions, to let courts determine the content of vague terms ex post.

Further strategies of the contracting parties in inserting such a clause, for the purpose of this analysis, may be approximated to three:

1. The parties are both ignorant of the rules prescribed by the law with respect to good faith and absolute obligations, and therefore use the phrase 'best efforts' to define what they want.
2. There is information asymmetry between the two parties – one party is ignorant of the two rules of the law, and the other party, being more informed and sophisticated, is aware of the lack of judicial interpretation of best efforts and chooses to use it to his or her advantage.
3. The parties want a performance standard that is greater than a good faith obligation but lesser than an absolute obligation, and resort to the phrase 'best efforts' to define such an obligation. In this manner, it is quite possible for sophisticated parties to manoeuvre unsophisticated parties into non-effective or unintended obligations.

Keeping in mind the aforementioned diversity of intention of parties from one contract to another, it would be erroneous on the part of the courts to apply a uniform rule in the interpretation of all contracts. As in the case of best efforts contracts, such a rigid rule is undesirable, due to the conflict between the intentions of the parties in different cases and the understanding of the courts. In other words, such an approach thwarts the well-informed intentions of the parties to design an efficient contract and thereby defeats the very purpose of contracting. Further, where rights are indeterminate, rent-seeking becomes inevitable.[23] To clarify, the determination of the optimal judicial interpretation of best efforts that the authors seek to propose draws from the 'rules-versus-standards' debate that is ubiquitous in law.[24] Rules are sharp communicating devices, which clearly define the judicial interpretation of a particular phrase. Standards, however, are open-ended and heuristic directives which set parameters based on which an interpretation is to be formulated by judicial authorities. The form of a directive as a rule or a standard depends on various factors – for instance, a legal system might penalise drivers for driving beyond 100 kilometres per hour, because it finds that speeds in excess of 100 kilometres per hour are more likely to result in accidents. Such a directive is a rule. A standard, on the other hand, is more likely to be used when the lawmakers do not know the specific speed that is likely to result in an accident. The cost of gathering information is a major factor that determines the form of a legal directive. Another difference between the two is the amount of work required to be done in order to generate the content of the law before or after actors act.[25] If the directive is a rule, it will involve less work after the act; if the directive is a standard, it will involve more work after the act.

Developing jurisprudence indicates that there is a slow, but steady movement in legal scholarship towards a more 'purposive' approach to the construction of contracts. Courts are willing to look beyond dogmatic considerations for a more responsive theory of contractual interpretation. The parties are taken to have contracted on the basis that they both accept the obligations in the same sense, fully understanding the true import of the language they employ, applying the standard of the reasonable man.

Identifying the appropriate model

While interpreting best efforts clauses, courts often apply certain default rules based on their understanding of the intention of the parties. Two default rules that the courts in India have applied in different cases are the Rule of 'Good Faith' and the Rule of 'Absolute Obligation'. A legal system that adopts such a rule-based approach will define the standard of performance to be followed by the parties, thereby allocating the obligations and liabilities with certainty. This will allow the contracting parties to negotiate the terms of the contract keeping in mind the applicable rule, thereby defining the performance standards between them. In this manner, the parties are incentivised to reveal more information and internalise their estimable costs. The default rules thus provide efficient incentives to both parties. To the party having more knowledge, it acts as a penalty for default of providing that knowledge to the other party; it thus imposes costs upon the cheapest cost avoider. In the long run, it would enable contracts to spell out with precision the accuracy of the expectations of both parties.[26]

However, defining such a rigid rule structure is undesirable as it restricts the freedom of the parties to define a performance standard between them. Imputing a good faith obligation or an absolute obligation to parties when this was not their intention at the time of formation of the contract results in a violation of the sanctity of the contract; this is because the interpretation of the contract becomes a representation of the court's interpretation rather than the parties' intention. Further, allocation of liabilities and costs would give one party greater bargaining power, as he or she would be reasonably certain of the outcome of litigation. This leaves room for exploitation. As a result, in the ex post determination of the best efforts clause, it is more efficient for the courts to base their interpretation on certain parameters or 'standards'. Doing so would allow the contracting parties to freely negotiate the terms of the contract. In the determination of the standards to be applied for the interpretation of the best efforts clause, the authors have come across three different models.

Fiduciary duty/good faith standards

It is an established principle that fiduciary duty implies the duty owed by the promisor to the promisee, which can be described as 'loyalty, of constant, unqualified fidelity . . . The fiduciary must subordinate his individual and private interests to his duty, whenever the two conflict'.[27] In other words, the fiduciary (or the promisor, in our analysis) is bound to take the promisee's situation into consideration, and not his own, while performing his duty. If he does not keep the promisee's interests in mind, liability would accrue against him.

Fiduciary duties exist so that parties can deal with problems stemming from 'unequal costs of information'. An agent, who is an example of a fiduciary, is hired to deal with others on parity of information. The legal rules in case of a standard of fiduciary duty are meant to incentivise the agent to internalise all costs of negligence. The duty of care requires that the promisor make reasonable decisions on behalf of the promisee. It is similar to a good faith obligation promised by the promisor or the fiduciary, but a little more than mere good faith. This is to be understood with the duty of loyalty, which imposes a higher legal standard than mere good faith and yet is not burdensome. The obligation imposes a combination of care, loyalty and obedience.

In order to understand this standard of care, one must take note of *Bloor v. Falstaff Brewing Corp.*, where Falstaff acquired Bloor's assets as Bloor was facing losses in the beer industry, on the promise that he will use his 'best efforts to promote and maintain a high volume of sales'. Having done this, Falstaff allowed Bloor's sales to drop and maximised his own profit in the market. The court in this case held that Falstaff, by undertaking to use best efforts, was under a duty to uphold a standard of performance that was greater than mere good faith. Falstaff was supposed to have managed Bloor's beer manufacture and distribution better than his own. This was the closest that the Second Circuit Court came to identifying characteristics of fiduciary duty as the standard of performance attached to the best efforts clause.

Diligence insurance

Diligence insurance is an economic concept to be understood as describing that standard of performance which requires that 'only the promisor maximises his own profit'. The only consideration that the promisor is required to take in this situation is his or her own situation. Liability accrues when the promisor does not act in his or her own benefit.[28] This standard is often rejected by the courts as being 'profit uber alles', or that situation where profit is the only motive to carry out any act. In *Zilg v. Prentice-Hall*, Prentice-Hall had the exclusive right to determine the printing volume, sales price, publishing style and all promotional details of Gerald Colby Zilg's book. Prentice-Hall slashed its printing volume and advertising budget, causing Zilg to sue Prentice-Hall on the ground that the latter had 'privished' the book in order to 'fulfil the technical requirements of the contract to publish, but to avoid adding to [their] losses, by throwing "good money after bad"'.[29] The same court, in this case, held that privishing was permissible so long as it proceeded from its profit motive. The absence of an explicit best efforts promise required Prentice-Hall to merely supply 'a first printing and advertising budget adequate to give the book a reasonable chance of achieving market success', even though there was an implied duty of good faith. This can be described as a 'good faith business judgement' and faintly incorporates the standards of diligence insurance.

In both cases, unknown future contingencies might result in one party regretting having entered into contract with the other, since he or she can no longer derive any profit. This risk of regret contingency creates a sharp conflict of interest between the two parties to a contract. The risk is borne by one or the other of the parties, depending on the standard of performance that is used to interpret the best efforts requirement. For example, in a manufacturer–distributor relationship, under a fiduciary standard, the distributor bears the risk since he or she is required to maximise the manufacturer's royalty-based profits notwithstanding his or her own losses. With diligence insurance being the standard, conversely, the manufacturer bears the risk since a profit-maximising distributor will immediately choose to cease distribution in case the distribution of an additional unit will incur losses.

In case the standard of fiduciary duty was attached to the performance in a best efforts clause, it would disincentivise the promisee from taking all necessary precaution, as he or she would be compensated for any losses by the promisor, who will bear the cost. This would also allocate the risk of regret to the promisor, who is required to maximise the profits of the promisee. As a result, it would induce the promisor to internalise all costs and ensure that the promisee receives profits, even at his or her expense, as long as the liability exceeds the costs faced by him or her. In the contrasting standard of diligent insurance, the promisee will have to bear all costs because the promisor is required to maximise his or her own profits and work on the principle of profit uber alles. As a result, the promisor will make no real effort to perform and the promisee will have to internalise all costs.

Both the aforementioned standards result in disjoint costs and benefits, due to which the total social welfare is never increased to a maximum. These methods of allocation of liability do not achieve efficiency, due to the internalisation of the costs by a single person, who may or may not be the cheapest cost avoider. In other words, joint maximisation under a polar standard like fiduciary duty or diligence insurance is not a viable option as these standards virtually assure one party of litigation victory. As a result, this party gains tremendous bargaining power in the contractual negotiations. This party will have every incentive to convert all the additional benefits gained from joint maximisations since he or she can legally impose the loss on the other party if no agreement is reached.[30] This increases the probability that the other party will walk away and take a loss, and prevent the achievement of joint maximisation.

Intermediate standard: joint maximisation

The standard applied in most cases is the one that is intermediate to the two approaches mentioned earlier. It is more lenient than the standard of fiduciary duty but stricter than that of diligence insurance. In other words, the level of effort required for performance is to be determined by both the promisor's and promisee's situations. This intermediate standard is indeterminate, that is not well defined, in sharp contrast to the well-defined extremes of fiduciary duty and diligence insurance.

The economics behind the application of this intermediate standard is that in an exclusive deal between two parties, specifying performance in advance would be impracticable due to the uncertainty of surrounding conditions (e.g. the demand in the market, for manufacturer–distributor agreements) and the complexity of the arrangement. The uniqueness of the intermediate standard is that the very uncertain nature of the standard will induce both the parties to jointly share the regret contingency risk. This is because, under the intermediate standard, the risk of regret is not allocated in advance to either party due to the indeterminacy of the current position in courts of law. As a result, the promisor will perform as long as his or her benefits exceed his costs, and the promisee agrees to forego performance when there is a surplus of costs. In order to understand this, consider a simple manufacturer–distributor relationship. If a single actor is both manufacturer and distributor, he or she would maximise his or her profits by continuing to produce and distribute so long as the sales price exceeds the sum of marginal manufacturing costs and marginal distribution costs. When there are two actors, the situation can be viewed as the distributor (promisor) who obtains exclusive right over the assets of the manufacturer (promisee), and promises to use best efforts to maintain distribution, thereby giving the manufacturer a high royalty.

'Best efforts' in this case may be defined as the point of joint maximisation of the benefits accruing to both the manufacturer (promisee) and the distributor (promisor), and would require the distributor to set that volume of products which maximises the sum of his or her and the manufacturer's profits. Both the risk of regret and the profit is shared between the parties, by virtue of the contractual promise of best efforts. This is the perfect example of the intermediate standard which puts the standard of performance between fiduciary duty and diligence insurance. The distributor must distribute unprofitable units up to the joint maximisation volume, but the manufacturer must forego royalties on any units above that volume. Although this method is suboptimal for each party, joint maximisation optimises the total value of the arrangement.

Conclusion: testing the proposition in the Indian context

In India, the use of best efforts clauses is fairly common. Best efforts clauses figure in contracts and agreements in several areas of the Indian economy, such as in real estate agreements, distributor agreements, patent licences, sports players' contracts, technical assistance agreements, agency agreements and research agreements. The commercial jurisprudence in India is still expanding and has not yet reached the level of maturity that can be seen in developed countries, such as the United States. With greater inflow of investments in Indian businesses, it is not surprising that the investors rely on higher performance standards of their contracting partners. Conservative business practices in India dictate that all contractual obligations be defined ex ante by parties. This allows courts to enforce accurately the crystallised intention of the parties at the time of formation of the contract. As was seen in the case of *H. T. Somashekar Reddy v. Government of Karnataka & Anr.*,[31] the High Court of Karnataka enforced the terms of the contract, which stipulated that best efforts would mean that the Government of Karnataka (Respondent 1) would *use all legal avenues possible* to get the necessary laws enacted or carry out necessary amendments to achieve the purposes of the project. However, pursuing such a practice of ex ante decision-making is not always cost-effective as has been discussed and demonstrated earlier in this chapter, as it does not allow parties to exploit the efficient performance-setting functions of the courts, where an agreement could not be reached or where parties deliberately leave it to the ex post determination of the courts.

The situation in India, however, is not conducive for parties to leave to the determination of courts the appropriate level of performance. In cases that have been discussed earlier, it can be seen that courts have adopted divergent viewpoints for the interpretation of the best efforts clauses. The legal position on the interpretation of this clause is unclear and ambiguous as the relevant precedents appear to lean towards interpreting the standard as nothing more than a simple good faith obligation, while keeping it open to the parties to set a standard of their choice, including an absolute obligation. This is done without the courts guiding parties in any manner on how their contractual intentions must be expressed so as to be interpreted appropriately. There is, therefore, no set standard on the basis of which parties can contract on the best efforts to be utilised.

The authors have already highlighted the advantages of an intermediate standard as the most efficient tool to determine the appropriate level of performance. This would enable parties to design their contracts in a cost-effective manner distributing transaction costs of determining performance levels, between the parties mutually and the courts. Further, taking into account the conservative business strategies in vogue in India, the adoption of an intermediate standard would communicate to the parties the appropriate methodology of devising their contracts. This would have twin effects:

1 That it would promote contractual freedom, allowing parties to leave to the ex post determination of courts the appropriate performance level.
2 Flowing from the first effect, it would also enable parties to choose the correct performance standard as required of their transaction.

Moreover, the presence of unsophisticated parties in large numbers in India also adds strength to this argument. The use of an intermediate standard is the same as a contextual approach to the interpretation of contracts. This is a more responsive approach, which takes into account the true intention of the parties and does not disregard their levels of sophistry.

However, the authors concede that this model is not without certain drawbacks:

1 Indeterminacy of joint maximisation: The distributor, in the earlier example, will not be able to discern the joint maximisation volume since he or she will not know the manufacturer's cost function. This might induce the manufacturer to underestimate his or her costs so as to deceive the distributor into performing beyond joint maximisation.

2 Costs of uncertainty: The manufacturer may think he or she is being promised something like a fiduciary obligation, whereas the distributor thinks he or she is promising little more than diligence insurance. In fact, neither knows what he or she is entitled to give or receive until a post hoc judicial determination that will likely disappoint one if not both parties. The expectations of both parties are thus not secure by this standard. Further, the standard will increase the probability of litigation in the event of a regret contingency, as each party may rationally anticipate victory, giving each an incentive to litigate without out-of-court settlements.

This approach may not attain efficiency in its true sense, but it is the best alternative that can be had at the moment.

Notes

1 *Association of Unified Telecom Service Providers of India & Ors v. Union of India & Ors* WP(C) No. 3673 and 2679/2010.
2 George M. Cohen, 'Interpretation and Implied Terms in Contract Law', *University of Virginia School of Law, John M. Olin Law and Economics Research Paper Series No. 2009–2012* (2009).
3 *Kraftco Corp. v. Kolbus*, 1 Ill App. 3d 635 (1971).
4 *Bloor v. Falstaff Brewing Corp.*, 601 F.2d 609.
5 Ibid.
6 *Jet2.com Limited v. Blackpool Airport Limited* [2012] EWCA Civ. 417.
7 P. Ramanatha Aiyar, *Advanced Law Lexicon* (New Delhi: LexisNexis, 2012).
8 Fredirick Pollock and Sir Dinshaw Fardunji Mulla – *Indian Contract and Specific Relief Act* (New Delhi: Lexis Nexis, Butterworths, 2006): 324.
9 Ibid.
10 *In Re, Anglo-Russian Traders Ltd v. John Bait & Co. (London) Ltd* (1917) 2 KB 679.
11 *Pattahmull Rajeshwar v. KC Sethia* [1951] 2 All ER 352.
12 Section 56, Indian Contract Act 1872.
13 *Gwalior Rayon Silk Mfg Co. Ltd v. Shri Andavar & Co.*, AIR 1991 Ker 134.
14 Marcel Fontaine and Filip De Ly, *Drafting International Contracts: An Analysis of Contract Clauses* (the Netherlands: Martinus Nijhoff, 2009).
15 Mo Zhang, 'Contractual Choice of Law in Contracts of Adhesion and Party Autonomy', *Akron Law Review* 41 (2008): 123.
16 Daniel A. Farber, 'Contract Law and Modern Economic Theory', *Northwestern University Law Review* 78 (1983): 303.
17 Fontaine and Ly, *Drafting International Contracts.*

18 Cohen, 'Interpretation and Implied Terms in Contract Law'.
19 Jody S. Kraus and Robert Scott, 'Contract Design and the Structure of Contractual Intent', *New York University Law Review* 84 (2009): 1023.
20 Ibid.
21 Deborah Fosbrook and Adrian C. Laing, *The A-Z of Contract Clauses* (London: Sweet & Maxwell, 2010).
22 Kraus and Scott, 'Contract Design and the Structure of Contractual Intent': 1023.
23 Rob Park, 'Putting the Best in Best Efforts', *Chicago Law Review* 73 (2006): 705.
24 Pierre Schlag, 'Rules and Standards', *University of California Los Angeles Law Review* 33 (1985): 379.
25 Louis Kaplow, 'Rules versus Standards: An Economic Analysis', *Duke Law Journal* 43 (1992): 557–559.
26 Lawrence S. Long, 'Best Efforts as Diligence Insurance: In Defense of "Profit Uber Alles"', *Columbia Law Review* 86 (1986): 1728–1740.
27 Ibid.
28 Ibid.
29 Ibid.
30 Ibid.
31 *H.T. Somashekar Reddy v. Government of Karnataka & Anr.*, 2000 (1) Kar. L.J. 224.

Chapter 5

The economically efficient expropriation

An economic analysis of expropriation under international investment law

Kaustubh Rastogi and Shubhangi Roy

Background note

In the international investment regime (as is the case in most municipal legal systems as well), any encroachment of an investor's right to enjoyment of his or her property or investment by the government of the host state should necessarily be followed by compensating the same.[1] As in most legal propositions, there is a dispute with this as well. The dispute in this particular case is regarding what factors need to be considered in order to classify an act/policy of the host state as an expropriation, thereby entitling the investor to compensation while the remaining can be put in the category of 'regulation' to prevent giving rise to any liability for the host state.

Through an exhaustive perusal of the available literature on the same, the three tests evolved by the various international tribunals and courts are the substantial deprivation doctrine, the police power doctrine and a less frequently employed proportionality doctrine.[2] There is some literature available comparing the three. However, none of them delve into the economic efficiency argument to augment the comparison. This research endeavour is to employ existing concepts of law and economics to arrive at an economically efficient test for classification of an act of a government as expropriation or taking. The most evident concept that fits the situation is that of the economics of land acquisition. Since international investment employs more sophisticated knowledge on part of the investor and a greater symmetry of information, the assumptions need to be considerably altered to make it applicable to the present dilemma

Post a summary description of the present law on the subject, the chapter proceeds to evaluate the economic efficiency of the two most widely used doctrines, that is the police power doctrine and the substantial deprivation doctrine. A litmus test for the two is prepared by applying each to the same hypothetical situation. In the process, the common problems of underinvestment and overinvestment are encountered, respectively, along with added complications of moral hazards, increased social cost and so on. However, the greater symmetry of information and expert knowledge unique to foreign investments allows us to offer a solution to the paradox of compensation in the field of international investment through a modified proportionality doctrine, which has been dealt with in the last section of the chapter.

Expropriation: analysing the relevant concepts

It is a well-recognised rule in international law that the property of aliens cannot be taken, whether for public purposes or not, without adequate compensation.[3] The classical rules of international law have accepted the host state's right to expropriate alien property in principle.[4] This is the accepted position, unless the Bilateral Investment Treaty explicitly excludes the right to lawful expropriation. Expropriation or 'wealth deprivation' could take different forms: it could be direct where an investment is nationalised or otherwise directly expropriated through formal transfer of title or outright physical seizure. In addition to the term 'expropriation', terms such as 'dispossession', 'taking', 'deprivation' or 'privation' are used. It is important to establish the requirements for a lawful expropriation.[5] The right to expropriation raises no questions in case of a formal expropriation (e.g. nationalisation); however, a high degree of complexity arises in cases where the host states interfere with the rights of the foreign owner without the formal removal of title. Looking at state practice in the past few years, it is important to notice that a pertinent question that has come up is whether a particular situation is a 'taking' that requires compensation (expropriation) or it is an uncompensated 'regulation' that falls within the sovereign rights of the state.

Types of expropriation

There are two distinct types of expropriation, direct and indirect. The concept of direct expropriation is a simple understanding where the legal title of the property transfers from the investor to the host state. However, most states are reluctant to jeopardise their investment climate by taking such a drastic step.[6] Therefore, indirect expropriation has gained importance. An indirect expropriation leaves the investor's title untouched but deprives him or her of the possibility to utilise his or her investment in a meaningful way. This is the situation where the host state will deny the existence of an expropriation, that is one where adequate compensation needs to be provided.[7]

Creeping expropriation is a form of indirect expropriation with a distinctive temporal quality in the sense that it encapsulates the situation whereby a series of acts attributable to the state over a period of time culminate in the expropriatory taking of such property.[8] It has long been accepted that expropriation may take effect 'outright or in stages'.[9]

Standard of indirect expropriation

As a consequence to the earlier discussion, it becomes essential to draw a line between non-compensable regulatory and other governmental activities and measures amounting to indirect compensable expropriation.[10] There are a number of international texts and instruments, including standard Bilateral Investment Treaty (BITs),[11] that define indirect expropriation as something being tantamount to nationalisation. Nouvel has pointed out that in the case of nationalisation or direct expropriation, the dispossession to the detriment of a private person coincides with the appropriation to the profit of a public person;[12] the measures tantamount to expropriation do not have this linkage.[13] To determine whether or not an action or a series of actions by a party, in a specific situation, constitute an expropriation requires a case-by-case, fact-based inquiry that considers[14]

1. the impact of the government action, although the fact that an action or a series of actions by a party have an adverse effect on the economic value of an investment, standing alone, does not establish that an indirect expropriation has occurred.
2. the extent to which the government action interferes with distinct, reasonable investment-backed expectations; and
3. the character of the government action.

Criteria to determine indirect expropriation/taking

In *Metalclad v. Mexico*,[15] the arbitral tribunal held that the term 'expropriation' includes covert or incidental interference with the use of the property which has the effect of depriving the owner, in whole or in significant part, of the use or reasonably-to-be expected economic benefit of property even if not necessarily to the obvious benefit of the host state. Professor Shruer has laid down a few tests to determine what could contribute to an indirect expropriation. The phrases 'unreasonable interference' and 'measures having the effect of an expropriation' or 'measures which substantially deprive the owner of the use of the property' are vague.[16]

It is also pertinent to note that the effect of the measure upon economic benefit and value as well as upon the control over the investment will be the key question when it comes to deciding whether an indirect expropriation has taken place. Whenever this effect is substantial and lasts for a significant period of time, it will be assumed prima facie that a taking of the property has occurred.[17]

Need for regulatory measure

It has been held by various investment tribunals and by the European Court of Human Rights that in addition to a legitimate claim in the public interest there has to be a 'reasonable relationship of proportionality between the means employed and the aim sought to be realized'.[18] This is termed as the fair balance test where the tribunal must balance two competing interests: the degree of the measure's interference with the right of ownership and the power of the state to adopt its policies.[19] This may also be termed as the 'proportionality doctrine'. Originating in German administrative law, it is now employed by many international and supranational courts and tribunals in a variety of contexts, is evolving as the dominant judicial technique for mediating between the competing values of rights protection (or protection of the legal regime's primary interest, such as free movement of goods) and the public interest pursued by government policy, and may be emerging as a general principle of international law.[20] A finding of proportionality requires that where a range of alternative measures exist, the option that intrudes least upon the right or interest should be preferred, and that the greater the limitation on a right or interest, the more compelling the social need or public objective should be.[21]

Duration of the measure

The duration of a governmental measure affecting the interests of a foreign investor is important for the assessment of whether an expropriation has occurred.[22] In *SD Myers v. Canada*,[23] the tribunal held that an expropriation usually amounts to a lasting removal of the ability of an owner to make use of his or her economic rights although it may be that, in some circumstances, it would be appropriate to view a deprivation as amounting to an expropriation, even if partial or temporary. However, this consideration is very subjective, and different tribunals have held different time periods to be considerable enough to constitute a compensable taking.

Consideration of legitimate expectation of the investor

There are various formulations of what constitutes a legitimate expectation. In *Thunderbird v. Mexico*,[24] the arbitral tribunal defines legitimate expectation as a situation where a contracting party's conduct creates reasonable and justifiable expectations on the part of an investor to act in reliance of said conduct, such that a failure by the party to honour those expectations could cause the investor to suffer damages. Therefore, not every change in the host state's legal system affecting foreign property will violate legitimate expectations. No such violation will occur if the change remains within the boundaries of normal adjustment customary in the host state and accepted in other states.

In *RFCC v. Morocco*,[25] the tribunal stated that an indirect expropriation exists in case the measures have 'substantial effects of an intensity that reduces and/or removes the legitimate benefits related with the use of the rights targeted by the measure to an extent that they render their further possession useless'.[26] This has also been used in *Metalclad v. Mexico*, where an International Centre for Settlement of Investment Disputes (ICSID) tribunal held that there has been indirect expropriation because *Metalclad*'s investment was completely lost because of Mexico's action.

Total and substantial deprivation

In terms of indirect expropriation, Schreuer emphasises 'judicial practice indicates that the severity of the economic impact is the decisive criterion'[27] in determining the occurrence of indirect expropriation. In other words, an indirect expropriation cannot be established if the investor did not study 'substantial deprivation',[28] where the degree of substantiality is often conveyed as meaning that interference from the state must approach total impairment.[29]

The substantial deprivation test triggered by governmental regulatory measures was first identified in *Pope & Talbot v. Canada*[30] to draw a distinction between non-compensable regulatory measures and measures that amount to expropriation. The test lays down that an indirect expropriation cannot be established when the interference from the host state has affected only a portion of the investment, where the investor was able to continue to export despite a reduction in profit.[31] This test has led the tribunal in numerous awards, to deny the existence of an expropriation where the investor had retained control over the overall investment even though it had been deprived of specific rights.[32] In such cases, the tribunal may come to a decision of the violation of a standard of fair and equitable treatment; however, it will not be considered as expropriation. This criterion is not satisfied even if there has been a reduction in the profits from the investment. This illustrates the significance of a test that includes criteria other than control, such as economic use and benefit. Any attempt to define an indirect expropriation on the basis of one factor alone will not lead to a satisfactory result in all cases.[33]

What constitutes 'regulation'?

Protection against indirect expropriation has been included in various forms of international instruments. Literally all relevant treaties and draft treaties provide for indirect expropriation or measures tantamount to expropriation. However, most of them stay mute on the treatment of the non-compensable regulatory measures, with the exception of the European Convention on Human Rights and Fundamental Freedoms (hereafter the European Convention on Human Rights), the recently concluded US-Free Trade Agreements and the new model US and Canada BITs.[34] We shall first discuss scenarios that have been held by arbitral tribunals to constitute a non-compensable regulation, through a series of awards. Emphasis on the host state's sovereignty supports the argument that the investor should not expect compensation for a measure of general application.[35] One way to identify whether a measure is a non-compensable regulation is to clarify whether the measure in question was taken in the exercise of functions that are generally considered part of the government's powers to regulate the general welfare.[36]

Since all lawful expropriations must be for a public purpose, the general public utility of a measure does not justify taking property from a property owner without compensation. In order to maintain a conceptual distinction between expropriations and regulation, reference cannot be made solely to public utility or benefit to justify non-compensation. In US takings jurisprudence, police power regulation of the use of property is justified by the prevention of harm or protection of the public. This approach believes that measures imposed because of economic nationalism require compensation. According to the doctrine of police powers, certain acts of states are not subject to compensation under the international law of expropriation. Although there is no universally accepted definition, in a narrow sense, this doctrine covers state acts such as (a) forfeiture or a fine to punish or suppress crime; (b) seizure of property by way of taxation; (c) legislation restricting the use of property, including planning, environment, safety, health and the concomitant restrictions to property rights; and (d) defence against external threats, destruction of property of neutrals as a consequence of military operations and the taking of enemy property as part payment of reparation for the consequences of an illegal war.[37]

In the Iran–US claims case and *Feldman v. Mexico*, the tribunal has opined that a state is not responsible for a loss of property or for other economic disadvantages resulting from bona fide general measures. Further, it has been held that governments must be free to act in the broader public interest through protection of the environment, new or modified tax regimes, the granting or withdrawal of government subsidies, reductions or increases in tariff levels, imposition of zoning restrictions and the like.[38] An exercise of police powers by a state may manifest itself in adopting new regulations or enforcing existing regulations in relation to a particular investor.[39] This would in turn imply that these measures shall be considered within the limits of the regulatory powers of the state and not in violation of the treaty. It also leads to the conclusion that such a regulation will not require adequate compensation as it would not amount to expropriation.

Economic analysis of the popular doctrines of expropriation in international investment law

The purpose of an economic analysis is to arrive at an economically efficient solution where the total benefit from performing an activity or not performing the same is higher than the total cost incurred by the society. However, a point of great relevancy that is often missed out due to its subtlety is that profit-maximising activities need not be the most economically efficient solution and vice versa.[40] As is clear from the preceding sections, the standards for determining whether an act of the host nation's government falls within the category of expropriation are myriad and ambiguous, with each tribunal focusing on a separate element of the government action.[41] The following section deals with each of the diverging jurisprudential tests that have been espoused through various judgements and tribunal awards in the light of their competence in arriving at an economically efficient solution.

To better understand expropriation through the prism of economic analyses, the best approach would be to employ the help of a common illustration of expropriation and arrive at a situation, which maximises the economic efficiency of the society. For the chapter, we shall take the example where the host country is a developing country with an agrarian economy (say Eastland). It would not be a stretch of imagination but a fact grounded in reality if we were to propose that the investor is an established company (say Kaash Industries) from a developed country investing in the developing country.[42] The investment was considered highly lucrative due to the abundant availability of inexpensive indigo (for example), which was the fundamental raw material employed by Kaash Industries in manufacturing its goods. At the time the investment was made, the prices of indigo were Rs 100 per kilogram. The per unit cost of production in the particular case would be Rs 200 and the per unit selling price was Rs 500.

At the time of making the investment, Eastland had lax regulations on indigo cultivation, and the same was considered an important incentive for Kaash Industries while deciding to invest there. However, continuous and intensive cultivation of indigo depletes the fertility of soil drastically.[43] As time progressed and Kaash Industries flourished, more and more of lands in Eastland were getting barren. In order to prevent this situation, the government came up with a regulation that altered the land use pattern and put an upper limit on the total land that could be employed in indigo cultivation. The scarcity in production results in the price of indigo rising from a mere Rs 100 to Rs 350 per kilogram, and the additional cost of transporting large quantities from different locations adds an additional transportation cost of Rs 100. Therefore, the cost of production rises to Rs 550, thereby making the venture unprofitable for Kaash Industries. Aggrieved, it sends in a notice of arbitration to the government of Eastland, claiming its interest has been expropriated. Along with the altered land use, the indigo policy also includes measures for rehabilitation of the indigo farmers and providing them with an alternative source of livelihood. With these common factual circumstances as the background to the discussion, we shall now proceed to delve into the possible outcomes to the arbitration on the basis of the existing doctrines in the subject and analyse which enables us to achieve the illusive economic efficiency that we seek.

Substantial deprivation doctrine

The substantial deprivation doctrine (as has been explained in the previous section) shall be applied to the given set of facts, and an analysis will reveal that giving undue importance to this doctrine will lead to inefficient outcomes. The incentives for the government and the investor will be misplaced, leading to economic inefficiency. The situation of law will be such that a measure leading to substantial deprivation of investor's right over the property will be considered a compensable taking. All other measures will be considered non-compensable regulations.

Potential behaviour of the investor in a regime of substantial deprivation principle

An investor who enters a foreign country does so in order to earn profits. There is a risk attached to every investment, that is the risk of governmental measures making the investment unviable. All investors consider this risk and on that basis invest in any country. Only if the profits accruing to them are more than what is the potential loss will they invest. In the present situation where the international investment tribunal follows the principle of substantial deprivation, the potential risk of loss due to change in governmental policies is relatively very low. This is so as at the very moment the loss becomes substantial, the same will be claimed in an investment tribunal and awarded as compensation to the investor. A situation where any substantial loss of the investor is compensated by the government, there is no disincentive for the investor. All the investor's risks shall be compensated. This raises the risk of moral hazard. 'Moral hazard' describes 'any situation in which one person makes the decisions about how much risk to take, while someone else bears the cost if things go badly'.[44] Investors might undertake projects without adequately assessing the externalities created by their projects, and the associated risk that future governments might redress such externalities when they begin to crystallise.[45] There is a possibility that such guarantee of return can lead to a situation of moral hazard. Moral hazard refers to a situation where economic actors make profit-maximising but inefficient decisions because they are able to avoid costs associated with their conduct. The problem of moral hazard is often associated with insurance – when someone takes out insurance against a given type of harm, they no longer have an incentive to take prudent (efficient) steps to reduce the risk of that harm occurring. The guarantee of compensation, in case of substantial harm, acts as insurance for the investor.

Applying this logic to Kaash Industries, there has been a substantial increase in the price of indigo due to government measures leading to substantial loss. The investor is aware of this risk; however, the investor enters into Eastland because he or she is aware that this substantial loss will be compensated by the government. Therefore, it does not internalise its risks, which leads to overinvestment. The benefit to the public by the indigo policy may be more than the harm that is caused to Kaash. However, Kaash is aware that irrespective of the purpose of the policy, any substantial deprivation will be compensated. Therefore, there shall be inefficient investment decisions that do not internalise the negative externalities as the investor need not compensate for it or bear any loss in case the government of the host state does attempt to correct the imbalance in sharing of harm.

Potential behaviour of the host government

In the instant case, the government of Eastland is aware that in all cases where its measures affect the investor, it will be made to compensate. The effect of its measures upon the public welfare is not considered. Therefore, it will not be incentivised to develop efficient policies that are beneficial to the public, but may be harmful to the investor. The government of Eastland has come out with the limit on the use of land for indigo. This has caused substantial deprivation to the investor, Kaash. The measures adopted by the government are for the benefit of the public, as overuse of the land would lead to barrenness of the land and loss in income. However, this will not be taken into account while determining whether the measure can be termed as expropriation. The moment it is established that there has been substantial deprivation to Kaash, it shall be termed as a compensable taking. Therefore, the government of Eastland will not be adequately incentivised to adopt measures that are beneficial to the public, in the fear of paying compensation.

Police power doctrine

The police power doctrine discussed earlier shall be applied to the given set of facts, and an analysis will reveal that giving undue importance to this doctrine will lead to inefficient outcomes. The result will be similar to applying the substantial deprivation doctrine, in so much that it shall misplace the incentives for the investor. The situation of law will be such that any action by the government that is in favour of the public but not for economic nationalism will be considered a non-compensable regulation.

It has been made clear that the investor must weigh the risk that a change in the laws of the host state entails, before investing in that state. The authors will use the example stated earlier to establish that if tribunals tend towards passing awards stating government measures to be non-compensable regulations, it will lead to underinvestment from foreign players. This will further lead to undersupply of the product and inflated prices. The government of Eastland has passed a law that places a cap on the land used for indigo cultivation. This leads to a substantial increase in price and pushes Kaash to withdraw its investment. The government has passed this law for the benefit of the indigo farmers as such a cap would open greater tracts for other gainful cultivation and also ensure that the land use is not harmful or leaves the tracts uncultivable in future. Stating this reason would lead the tribunal to employ the earlier-stated doctrine and decide in favour of the government. The measure shall be termed as a regulation, and the investor will not receive the fair and prompt compensation.

While investing, Kaash was aware of the risk that a change in the laws of the host state entails because if the investor knows the precedent of tribunal is to follow this doctrine, then it will be more careful when making investments. However, if the trend of the tribunal had been to rule in favour of the host state, this risk would increase substantially. The investor will be aware that even a substantial loss to it shall not be compensated by the host state. Therefore, investment by Kaash and all other investors would substantially decrease. A decrease in this investment would lead to undersupply of the product in the market, leading to a leftward shift of the supply curve and a subsequent increase in price. Therefore, employing this doctrine will act as a disincentive for the investor to enter foreign states and therefore hinder economic growth.

Conclusion: a potential solution to the paradox of compensation through a modified proportionality doctrine

A perusal of the aforementioned two doctrines clearly indicates a paradox, one which is often referred to in the discipline of law and economics as the 'paradox of compensation'.[46] The dilemma that the tribunal faces in such disputes is a choice between two separate constitutional rights – that of the sovereignty of a state to take measures for social welfare and the property rights of the investor.[47] The problem is heightened when taken in the context that most host states are developing countries and the need for intervention in their market to equalise the socio-economic differences is greater than the 'necessity' of intervention when viewed from a developed country perspective.[48]

Some scholars express that the application of the principle of proportionality allows judges to see the entire contextual field, which enables to provide equitable judgement, as it embraces balancing.[49] However, the assertion is one made more in generality than with any reasoning embedded in an analytical cost–benefit study of the decisions. Following the test of proportionality established in *Tecmed v. The United Mexican State*,[50] if the four criteria of 'legitimacy', 'necessity', 'suitability' and 'balancing in the strict sense' are followed, then the government regulation will not qualify as an expropriation and the host state will not be liable to pay compensation.[51] For understanding the economic implications of following the Doctrine of Proportionality, let us implement these tests and see the potential conclusion that the arbitral tribunal would arrive at in case of our hypothetical dispute between Eastland and Kaash Industries. The regulation, in the illustration, is one that allows for social welfare. Altering the land use pattern is within the legitimate power of the legislatures of Eastland and the same is not disputed. The need to protect the fertility of their land and the future of indigo farmers from the possible ruin is sufficiently necessary for a developing country like Eastland. Therefore, the first three criteria, namely legitimacy, necessity and suitability, are fulfilled. The balancing in the strict sense is the last criterion and one with greatest latent economic implications.

In the present case, the indigo legislation alters the land use pattern. This implies the following (in the short run):

1 The investor's cost of production (Rs 550) has exceeded the sale price (Rs 500), thereby making its investment unprofitable.
2 Part of the farmers involved in the cultivation of indigo would be out of their regular commission that they were receiving from the sale of their produce to Kaash Industries.
3 Considering the legislation is enforced, Kaash Industries would in most likelihood relocate, thereby resulting in layoffs, and this will create a situation of unemployment for those previously working as Kaash employees or workers.
4 Successful avoiding of a situation where most lands under indigo production would have gone barren, the owners of such tracts of land would have been permanently disabled from continuing cultivation and due to fall in production of indigo, Kaash Industries would have faced increasing raw material prices nonetheless.

The most important element is that each of these implications ensued no matter which doctrine was relied on by the tribunal, but it is only through the application of the proportionality test that each of them will be given due consideration by the tribunal before arriving at the award. Up until 2000, for determining a dispute under international investment law, the only point of consideration was the loss of the investor as compared to the social gain.

Principle of proportionality requires that the actions taken by the government do not exceed the necessary in achieving the objective of the government. However, its definition is disputed and one which varies with scholars. Most agree that it is a balancing tool between two conflicting interests.[52] Many have dismissed it as being merely a means by which the judges can manipulate and impose their own substantive rules.[53] However, if the proportionality doctrine were to be applied to a given dispute from an economic perspective, it would imply that if

> **the total loss of expected returns by the investor > social welfare created by the indigo legislation**

the same will be considered an expropriation, and the government will be liable to compensate Kaash Industries. On the other hand, if

> **the total loss of expected returns by the investor < social welfare created by the indigo legislation**

the government measure will not be an act of expropriation and Kaash Industries will not be entitled to any compensation.

The flexibility that such a host country enjoys in implementing social welfare increasing measures at the cost of the investor's investment will be determined on the basis of whether the advantages of the regulation outweigh the loss incurred by the investor. The resultant incentive from application of the aforementioned doctrine would be two fold:

1 The government would no longer shirk its responsibility towards its citizenry since it can balance off its responsibility as a welfare state sufficiently well with its obligations under international investment law. The compensation for expropriation will no longer have the penalising effect it did during the arbitral regime where the substantial deprivation doctrine was the sole criterion for determining expropriation. On the other hand, the government will not exploit its sovereign powers unnecessarily and indiscriminately due to the fear that its policies fail to meet the threshold where the benefit derived from them is not higher than the cost incurred by the investor. This would prompt them to channelise the money that would have otherwise gone into compensating the investor towards the more needy stakeholders. For example, in the present case the indigo policies did include a farmer rehabilitation programme. In the absence of possible threshold test of the proportionality doctrine, the government would have perhaps halted with

merely altering the land use pattern. This would imply that the investor would be out of business and so would the farmers. There would still be the benefit of preventing infertility of land. But there was a scope of a more holistic welfare maximising measure and the apprehension that merely protecting future fertility of soil might be rejected by a tribunal as not equivalent benefit for the loss incurred by the investor would prompt the government to take all measures possible. Through such threshold cost–benefit juxtaposing, the doctrine ensures that the most economically efficient behaviour is pursued by the government.

2 The investor would no longer suffer from the complacency and misguided ideas of entitlement that many foreign investors fall victim to in case of tribunals indiscriminately ruling any regulations which causes substantial deprivation to the investment of the foreign investor as expropriation, thereby handling the problem of moral hazard. The investors will be incentivised to enter into more extensive recce of potential countries to invest in prior to making the investment. Moreover, the investor would decide the country on the basis of its true potential and not merely on the basis of its technological or economical backwardness which enables it to bypass basic human rights, corporate social responsibility or environmental laws. This trend was one that dictated the colonial era and one we hope to not create again. On the other hand, the guarantee that if they were to follow the basic rules of foreseeability and market trend predictability their investment would not be arbitrarily expropriated is going to ensure that they continue investing in the various host countries.

Therefore, a means end test (proportionality) if augmented with a case-by-case cost–benefit analysis such as the one explained earlier would greatly further the cause of arriving at economically efficient arbitral decisions that encourage international investment.

Notes

1 Frank I. Michelman, 'Property, Utility, and Fairness: Comments on the Ethical Foundations of Just Compensation Law', *Harvard Law Review* 80 (6) (1967): 1165–1258.

2 Surya P. Subedi, *International Investment Law* (Oxford; Portland, OR: Hart Publishing, 2008).

3 OECD Working Paper on International Investment, *Indirect Expropriation and the Right to Regulate in International Investment Law*, accessed 7 November 2014, http://www.oecd.org/daf/inv/investment-policy/WP-2004_4.pdf.
4 Rudolf Dolzer and Christoph Schreuer, *Principles of International Investment Law* (Oxford: Oxford University Press, 2008): 89.
5 OECD Working Paper on International Investment, *Indirect Expropriation and the Right to Regulate in International Investment Law.*
6 Ibid.
7 Ibid.
8 Ibid., 114.
9 Louis Henkin, ed., *Restatement of the Law, the Foreign Relations Law of the United States*, Rev. and Enl. ed. Vol. 1. (St. Paul, MN: American Law Institute Publishers, 1987): 712.
10 OECD Working Paper on International Investment, *Indirect Expropriation and the Right to Regulate in International Investment Law*: 93.
11 W. Michael Reisman and Robert D. Sloane, 'Indirect Expropriation and Its Valuation in the BIT Generation', *British Year Book of International Law* 74 (2004): 115.
12 L. Yves Fortier and Stephen L. Drymer, 'Indirect Expropriation in the Law of International Investment: I Know It When I See It, or Caveat Investor', *Asia Pacific Law Review* 13 (2005): 79.
13 OECD Working Paper on International Investment, *Indirect Expropriation and the Right to Regulate in International Investment Law.*
14 Ibid., 94.
15 *Metalclad Corp. v. Mexico*, Award, 30 August 2000, 5 ICSID Reports (2002) 209.
16 OECD Working Paper on International Investment, *Indirect Expropriation and the Right to Regulate in International Investment Law*, 93.
17 *Norwegian Shipowners' Claims*, Norway v. USA, Award, I RIAA (1922) 307 (13 October 1922).
18 Benedict Kingsbury and Stephan Schill, *Investor-State Arbitration as Governance: Fair and Equitable Treatment, Proportionality and the Emerging Global Administrative Law* (2009), *New York University Public Law and Legal Theory Working Papers*. Paper 146. http://lsr.nellco.org/nyu_plltwp/146.
19 *LG&E v. Argentine Republic*, Award, 14 July 2006.
20 Caroline Henckels, 'Indirect Expropriation and the Right to Regulate: Revisiting Proportionality Analysis and the Standard of Review in Investor-State Arbitration', *Journal of International Economic Law* 15 (1) (2012): 223–255.
21 Robert Alexy, *A Theory of Constitutional Rights* (Oxford: Oxford University Press, 2002): 102.
22 G.C. Christie, 'What Constitutes a Taking of Property under International Law?' *The British Year Book of International Law* 38 (1962): 307.
23 *S.D. Myers v. Canada*, Award, 30 October 1998.
24 *Thunderbird v. Mexico*, Award, 26 January 2006.
25 *RFCC v. Morocco*, Award, 22 December 2003, 20 ICSID Review – FIJL (2005) 391.

26 Ibid., at para. 69.
27 Christoph Schreuer, 'The Concept of Expropriation under the ECT and Other Investment Protection Treaties', *Transnational Dispute Management* 2 (2005): 28.
28 *Pope & Talbot v. Canada*, Award, 26 June 2000, 7 ICSID Reports 69.
29 Christoph Schreuer, 'The Concept of Expropriation under the ECT and Other Investment Protection Treaties', *Transnational Dispute Management* 5 (2005): 28, available at www.transnational-dispute-management.com/article.asp?key=596.
30 *Pope & Talbot v. Canada*, Award, 26 June 2000, 7 ICSID Reports 69.
31 Ibid.
32 *Azurix v. Argnetina*, Decision on Liability, 3 October 2006, 46 ILM (2007) 36.
33 OECD Working Paper on International Investment, *Indirect Expropriation and the Right to Regulate in International Investment Law*,108.
34 Ibid.
35 Ibid., 109.
36 *Telenor v. Hungary*, Award, 13 September 2006.
37 'UNCTAD, Expropriation, UNCTAD Series on Issues in International Investment Agreements II', accessed 7 November 2014, http://unctad.org/en/Docs/unctaddiaeia2011d7_en.pdf.
38 *Feldman v. Mexico*, Award, 16 December 2002, 18 ICSID Review – FILJ (2003) 488.
39 Ibid.
40 Jonathan Bonitcha, 'The Problem of Moral Hazard and Its Implications for the Protection of "legitimate Expectations" under the Fair and Equitable Treatment Standard', *Investment Treaty News* (7 April 2011), accessed 31 August 2014, http://www.iisd.org/itn/2011/04/07/the-problem-of-moral-hazard/.
41 *RFCC v. Morocco*, Award, 22 December 2003, 20 ICSID Review – FIJL (2005) 391.
42 Muthucumaraswamy Sornarajah, *The International Law on Foreign Investment* (Cambridge: Cambridge University Press, 2010).
43 *Pope & Talbot v. Canada*, Award, 26 June 2000, 7 ICSID Reports 69.
44 P. Krugman, *The Return of Depression Economics and the Crisis of 2008* (New York: W. W. Norton, 2009), 63.
45 *Pope & Talbot v. Canada*, Award, 26 June 2000, 7 ICSID Reports 69.
46 Robert Cooter, 'Unity in Tort, Contract, and Property: The Model of Precaution', *California Law Review* 73 (1985): 1–51.
47 Alec Stone Sweet and Jud Mathews, 'Proportionality Balancing and Global Constitutionalism', 3 November 2008, accessed 31 August 2014, http://digitalcommons.law.yale.edu/cgi/viewcontent.cgi?article=1013&context=fss_papers.
48 *Pope & Talbot v. Canada*, Award, 26 June 2000, 7 ICSID Reports 69, 357.
49 *Telenor v. Hungary*, Award, 13 September 2006.
50 *Tecnicas Medioam Bientales Tecmed v. The United Mexican States* (Case no. ARB(AF)/00/2) Award, 29 May 2003, http://icsid.worldbank.org/ICSID/FrontServlet?requestType=CasesRH&actionVal=showDoc&docId=DC602_En&caseId=C186.

51 J. Ueda and M. Andenas, 'Proportionality in EU Environmental Law', 1998, http://www.soc.nii.ac.jp/eusa-japan/download/eusa_ap/paper_MadsAndenas_JunkoUeda.pdf.
52 Tor-Inge Harbo, 'The Function of the Proportionality Principle in EU Law', *European Law Journal* 16 (2) (2010): 158–185.
53 *Telenor v. Hungary*, Award, 13 September 2006.

Part III

Economics of corporate law

Chapter 6

Economic analysis of corporate laws

Aonkan Ghosh

Background note

The Companies Act, 1956, has been replaced with the new Companies Act, 2013, which purports to be a largely self-containing code with the integration of provisions for the reconstruction of sick industrial companies into the main company legislation. The mergers and acquisition provisions have also been revamped along with the introduction and recent notifications of the corporate social responsibility norms. These changes may or may not be the most optimal when seen from a behavioural perspective. Such enquiry is imperative.

The enquiry into the reasons for the existence of the concept of the company is interesting. The economic rationale for traditional concepts of limited liability, corporate veil, shareholder primacy and so on were all concepts the courts have propounded on the basis of sound logical reasoning. A core economic analysis of the traditional concepts is done to evaluate and, if such is the case, challenge the underlying rationale for the same. The contractarian theory of corporate law has been for quite some time the most reasonable classification of the types of interrelationship among the stakeholders in a company.[1] It assumes that a corporate action is part of a web of interlinked contract-like obligations. Under this premise, the theory predicts and evaluates behaviour on strength of the promises. For instance, in the case of an initial public offering (IPO), the theory would state that the prospective investors engage in a two-sided bargain with the existing shareholders of the company. The existing shareholder works under an expectation that the price of the share will be high owing to demand in the public. In exchange the company offers a 'promise' of effective corporate structure to the prospective investors.

Further, an efficiency analysis of company law in India is required to compare and contrast the same with other jurisdictions. Newer corporate actions such as squeeze outs, hostile takeovers, staggered voting, strategic assets and investment management are a result of the internalisation of the demonstrated need to perform better in markets. Their behavioural analysis and trans-deal effects have not been documented till date on a comprehensive basis. This chapter is an attempt at such an analysis. While this theory does explain some plenary concepts, it suffers from certain flaws, which have been highlighted in the chapter. One of the principal objections to this theory would be that it would be difficult to agree that there exists one straightjacket approach, which explains all aspects of corporate governance. This chapter attempts to dissect various aspects of company law and apply distinct analytical principles to different aspects such as game theory for strategic voting and takeover bids and defences, modified contractarian theory to explain the IPO process and the efficiency argument for distribution of powers. As an additional aspect to the economic analysis of corporate law, note must be taken of the dispute settlement mechanism applicable to companies. The validity of arbitration or alternate dispute resolution arguments is also an important issue, fit for analysis.

Economic analysis of company law: an overview

Philosophical underpinning for the existence of the company

There exists an important philosophical debate between the characterization of the company as a pure profit-chasing entity and the contrasting opinion that it also be aligned with societal interest and promote the same. These questions come to the fore where public corporate entities are in analysis. Expectedly, in shareholder derivative actions, these interests may stand in conflict with each other, such as the *Coal India* case where there seems to be a clear conflict between the role of the company as a pure profit-chasing vehicle, in the pursuit of profit motive, and the alleged role of that company as an avenue for dispersal of societal benefit by effecting equitable distribution of a material resource like coal. There is sizeable opinion that business is permitted and encouraged by the law primarily because it is of service to the community rather than because it is a source of profit to its owners.[2] Another author opines that one must remember that the corporation is legal fiction, a creature of law, and the benefits of participation in enterprise with limited liability are provided for the benefit of society, not of the shareholders themselves.[3] Distinguishing this opinion, another cogent argument relating to the efficiency of the company in society is introduced. It relies on the reasoning that the maximizing of profits for the equity investors assists the other 'constituencies' automatically. The participants in venture play complementary rather than agnostic roles. In market economy, each party to a transaction is better off. A successful firm provides job for workers and goods and services for consumers. The more appealing the goods to the community, the more profits (and perhaps employment). Under this line of thought, prosperity for shareholders, workers and communities goes hand in glove with better products for consumers. Quite often, the harmony between profit maximization and its service of other objectives goes unnoticed.[4] This work presumes that shareholder primacy is valid until a countervailing interest of the company or the society is established. It is within these contours that the author proceeds to the rudimentary examination of all legal issues of the concept of a company in the specific context of shareholder derivative litigation.

Legal characterization

Entity maximization is a well-accepted theory relating to the economic allegiance of the company and its role in the societal framework. Professor Andrew Keay, a notable economist, has, in the most succinct manner, laid down the role of a company and the implied role of the directors when he states:

> This focus on the company as a separate legal entity and maintains that the objective of the company is to maximize the wealth of the entity as an entity and, at the same time, to ensure that the company is sustained financially. The theory involves directors endeavoring to increase the overall long-run market value of the company as a whole, taking into account the investment made by various people and groups. But it maintains that maximization must be combined with aiming to ensure entity survival and feasible development.[5]

A pragmatic characterization of law itself, it may be looked as a tool to place adequately incentives and disincentives in a manner that would allow for persons, natural or artificial, to align their best interest with that of the community. In the essential distinction between ownership share vis-à-vis that of ordinary movable or immovable property, the share in a company is necessarily dynamic in nature. One who owns the share may sell or otherwise transfer the share as a property and realize its economic value. Apart from this, the share entitles him or her to be a member of a company, an artificial entity whose control is an incident of ownership of the shares.[6] While the terms 'members' and 'shareholders' are interchangeably used, they bring along with them separate theoretical undertones. In the light of the concept of the corporate veil, it is important to understand the shareholder may have right to enforce his or her direct rights as shareholder and his or her indirect right as a member-shareholder of the company on behalf of the company.

A seldom-discussed case, which illustrates this distinction, is *Northern Counties Securities Ltd v. Jackson and Steeple Ltd*,[7] which involved a company that had failed to fulfil its obligations under a contract and had been ordered by the court to perform those obligations. However, the company was required to take the consent of the shareholders in order to perform the contract as per the requirement of the stock exchange. The claimant in this regard argued that if the members fail to give assent then they would be liable for contempt of court's order. This argument was rejected on the basis that since the company is a separate person it was the only one subject to the court order and not the members. As a corollary of the fact that the members of a company do not bear any liability for the acts of the company in relation to court orders, the directors have a clear obligation that the company complies with orders of the court and the provision of any law that is applicable to the company.[8] This aspect is elaborated upon in the latter part of this work. The first aspect of the ownership of shares is that a share under all circumstances remains the property of the holder and can be treated as such, subject to specific restrictions imposed by law in the form of statutory lock-in periods and so on. Since it is property it is difficult to argue that there is any obligation at all on the shareholders to vote in a specific manner. It is therefore evident that at the time a shareholder is under no obligation to care for the interests of the company, it is not acting in a fiduciary character for the company.

This is the most relevant conclusion and is the basis of much of the corporate strategy that goes into operating groups of companies. In the spirit of judicial clarity, in *Peters' American Delicacy Co. Ltd v. Heath*[9] the court held that

> the shareholders are not trustees for one another and, unlike directors, they occupy not fiduciary position and are under not fiduciary duties. They vote in respect of their shares, which are property, and the right to vote is attached to the share itself as an incident of property to be enjoyed and exercised for the owner's personal advantage.

In *North West Transportation Co. Ltd v. Beatty*,[10] the court held that every shareholder has a perfect right to vote upon any question, although he or she may have a personal interest in the subject matter opposed to, or different from, the general or particular interests of the company. Therefore, the shareholder's right to property and prima facie may be exercised by a shareholder as he or she thinks fit in his or her own interest.[11] However, courts have come close and perhaps gone on to place fetters on the choices of a shareholder to vote in a certain manner over certain matters. In *Allen v. Gold Reefs of West Africa*,[12] the court insisted that members were under an obligation to vote in a bona fide manner for what they consider to be interests of the company. It would therefore seem that there is restriction on shareholders from voting for improper purposes.[13] Other instances where such duty has been implied have also been noticed such as that in *Re HR Harmer Ltd*[14] wherein the court held that during voting to appoint, a director must be made for the benefit of the company as a whole and not for any ulterior purpose. The second aspect concerns the rights that flow to a shareholder as an incidence of being a member of a company. These rights are discussed in the subsequent sections. The jurisprudence reproduced earlier must not be interpreted to mean that shareholders have an unfettered right to control and effect their will upon the company's dealing even in cases where they act collectively. No statutory power of dismissal was held to be available to the members in *Teck Corporation Ltd v. Millar*,[15] where the majority of the members of the company authorized legal proceedings against the directors seeking to halt an allotment of shares by the directors on the ground that it would be misuse of the powers. The court denied such request, stating that allotment would not be an abuse of the power of the directors. It also referred to the decision in *Ashburton Oil v. Alpha Minerals NL*,[16] which laid down that directors who are minded to do something which in their honest view is for the benefit of the company are not to be restrained because a majority shareholder or shareholders do not want the directors to so act.

Further, the primacy of the directors in the age of apparent shareholder primacy is rather interesting. In *Lonrho Ltd v. Shell Petroleum Co. Ltd* it was held that under English Law if a company's directors decide that a particular course of action is not in the interest of the company, then they may refuse to pursue that course of action even if it flies counter to the will of the entire membership of the company.[17] Though the earlier-stated precedent is unquestionable on the question of statutory interpretation, it cannot be considered as a final authority on the exact limitations of shareholder primacy. In the next section, the relation between the shareholders and directors is examined through the lens of shareholder primacy. The author prescribes the exercise of caution in the conjoint reading of the concept of shareholder primacy and shareholder derivative litigation. It is important to keep in mind that a shareholder derivative litigation is not an action in assertion of the rights of the shareholders but an action where the shareholder derives the right to sue on behalf of the company, in order to assert the rights of the company as an artificial entity against persons or bodies which have caused detriment to the company. These persons may be fellow shareholders, directors, executive officers or non-member officials.

With reference to the basic mode of running of company, it would be fair to say that a shareholder when one among a thousand is virtually powerless as against the management. The management on the other hand is completely aware of the running of the company's business and has the ability to conceal knowledge about its activities from the shareholders. Theoretically, this would allow the managers to divert income to themselves, stealing or otherwise mismanaging the assets beneficially owned by the company and indirectly held by the shareholders. Even when such acts do not occur, there remains the possibility of the same. This paradox had in the mid- to late 1990s given rise to academic discussion on the premise that managers have control over the company and they seek to exploit their investors and customers. This is the simplest logic to call for regulation of corporate behaviour.

Regulation of companies and the Coase Theorem

The famous and perhaps the most lucid expression of the Coase Theorem is that where transaction costs are zero or near it, the determination by-law or authority of rights and liabilities makes no difference to the efficiency of the outcomes. The simple logic is that the rights and liabilities in question will be reallocated through exchange until they reach their most efficient use. Where voluntary exchanges are costless, the process of bargaining between the parties will bring about a most Pareto optimal outcome.[18] This may provide a reasonable explanation as to why despite such an obvious difference in the rights and liabilities of the managers and shareholders in a company work effectively. If the Coase Theorem is assumed to be true, then the behaviour of the parties in the framework will reach the most efficient outcome, and therefore, there would not be any occasion for corporate law to exist. This brings us to another question: *does Corporate law even matter?*

Does corporate law even matter?

The answer to this question lies in the modifications, which need to be made to counter the fairly specific assumptions of the Coase Theorem. The most problematic is the limitation of *zero transaction cost*. In fact, Ronald Coase himself recognized it and defined the role of law in general in the following manner:

> Of course, if market transaction were costless, all that matters (questions of equity apart) is that the rights of the various parties should be well defined and the results of legal actions easy to forecast. But . . . the situation is quite different when market transactions are so costly as to make it difficult to change the arrangements of rights established by law. In such cases the courts directly influence economic activity. It would therefore seem desirable that the courts should understand the economic consequence of their decisions and should, wherever possible without creating too much uncertainty about the legal position itself, take these consequences into account when making their decisions.[19]

It would flow from logic that where transactions costs are high, regulators and the law must reduce such transactions by simply reducing barriers to exchange and guaranteeing the freedom of contract. Unregulated markets are necessarily characterized by high transaction costs, which arise from information asymmetry and other transaction costs. The only common conclusion of the two views on corporate law is that the law should only concern itself with causing the effective coordination of economic resources. There is however a general understanding that legislative and administrative interference would in its own right be a source of distortions and inefficiencies as well.[20]

The problem of agency costs

The structure of the company can be looked at as one of the principal–agent relationships between the shareholders and the management. In the context of Coase Theorem, we must first enquire the costs of transaction. Agency costs arise in this regard. They are subsets of transaction costs, which would include the cost of laying down a contractual mechanism from negotiating to enforcement.

Informational asymmetry

In the purported agency relationship, the agent – the management – has access to information about the dealings of the company. The owners however cannot at all times ask for such information and details. Even if they can, the transaction would be costless. It is essentially this information asymmetry that raises the transaction costs and thereby allocative efficiency is not reached in this framework.

Asset specificity and strategic behaviour

Asset specificity is of great relevance in the commercial world where interaction of parties leads one of the parties to invest capital and time in the maintenance of assets acquired or used for the specific purpose of fulfilment of a contractual obligation. For instance, where the laundry owner near a university seeks to provide for the laundry of all students, he may be prompted to invest in laundry machines and so on. He must insist on a contract to protect against the risk of either the university or students acting collectively to exploit the risk of failure of investment, unless there is a reduction in price of the service. Asset specificity therefore gives rise to rent-seeking behaviour where bargains are tilted without any real value being exchanged; this is a purely strategic action and can be viewed as such. Strategic actions, therefore, may refer to opportunistic behaviour by one or other of the parties, aimed at seeking an advantage for themselves at the cost of parties, which invariably increases the net social cost.

The market demand and supply idea does not squarely apply here since informational asymmetry and threat of strategic behaviour persist. Scholars have therefore endorsed the idea of a specialized structure of governance, which could address the continuing exchange.[21]

Corporate law as a solution for the non-Coasen world

In the earlier sections, we have discussed the fact that transactions in the real world are hardly ever costless. More so for the company, there are rigid and undeniable costs that are associated with the process of running the company. If corporate law is to serve the aim of the greatest welfare, it must bring the situation to a point where allocative efficiency is reached. Given that parties have an in-built incentive to transact towards the point of allocative efficiency, all that corporate law must really be called upon to do would be reduction of transactions costs.

Costs related to contracting itself are themselves very significant. Contracting must begin with information gathering, negotiating, drafting and expending resources on formation of contract as well as that of performance and enforcement of the contract. Logic law must effect the reduction of such costs. The Companies Act, 2013, contains as an annexure a document referred to as table A for the articles of association of the company in 'Table A', which applies automatically as the clauses for the AoA of any company unless excluded. These are more significant than they may first appear. Easterbrook and Fischel state that

> corporate law is a set of terms available of-the rack so that participants in corporate ventures can save the cost of contracting. There are a lot of terms, such as rules for voting, establishing quorums and so on, that almost everyone will want to adopt.

> Corporate Codes and existing judicial decisions supply these terms 'For free' to every corporation, enabling these ventures to concentrate on matters specific to their undertaking. Even when they work through all the issues they expect to arise, they are apt to miss something. Corporate Law – and in particular the fiduciary principle enforced by courts – fills in the blanks and oversights with the terms that people would have bargained for had they anticipated the problems and been able to transact costlessly in advance. On this view corporate law supplements but never replaces actual bargains, save in situations of third party effects or latecomer terms.[22]

It is pertinent to note that 'latecomer' terms deal with the position of parties joining after the 'nexus of contracts' after it was first formed.

The contractarian theory of corporate law

There is a need to understand the value of an automatic control system within a company. Lucidly, if the regulators were to govern the workings of the company or second guess every move of the mangers, then precious resources will be lost in this process given that there are a large number of companies. Hence, there would be a need to align the interest of the managers with the beneficiaries of the income streams and the corporate assets, the investors. The characterization of the company as a complex set of contracts is therefore helpful. The theoretical understanding of corporate law with its internal contracts is now called for. The managers in these firms have come about their position after competing against others to reach a position where they can control corporate assets. The corporate assets, bought from the capital provided by the shareholders, will arrive only if the managers *promise and deliver* value to the investor in terms of returns or the prospect of the same.

Let us return now to the classical concept of a market. The managers cannot limitlessly exploit the investors since at some point investors will just start paying less if the managers do not promise a feasible return. There is therefore an inherent limit on the ability of the manager to work for his or her own good using the investor's capital. In order to attract capital, managers will need to promise high returns. Only promising is likely to be less than enough; they need to act in order to supplement the purpose of the promise – the inducement of the investors to part with their money. The managers will need to make their promises believable in most cases, by reducing them into a binding form. Here again, carrying on from a simplistic analysis, two decisions need to be made. What must be the content of the promises? How does one make the promise believable? The second question may depend on a simple behavioural assumption: the more automatic the enforcement of the promise, the more likely an investor is to believe the promise. The first question and the answer to it is almost completely subjective. The method of enforcement and packaging of the promise may follow a simple rule, but the nature of the promise made must be enough for an investor to put money into a company. It would therefore be influenced by a variety of intrinsic and extrinsic factors. A promise suited to be made by a car dealer may not be of any value to a company like Chevrolet. Size, nature and strategy of the firm's growth are important in deciding what promises should be made. It would be beneficial to take a managerial view of the corporate law to understand the incentives at play. To illustrate, lets analyse two instances of the scope and reason for decision-making power of managers.

Managers select the place of incorporation

One must note here that there is a certain complexity involved in selecting a place of incorporation. Since managers intend to attract investment, they will have an incentive to look for the most commercially feasible location of incorporation. In addition, for entities such as private limited companies, the dynamics are different; the managers are initially the promoters of a company who will then have their own set of incentives to work towards the betterment of the company. Therefore, at the time of incorporation there is an undoubted incentive to select the most commercially feasible location of incorporation.

Managers decide when to issue public securities

Private companies and venture capital endeavours involve a great deal of private money, which allows the third-party regulator to assume low levels of information asymmetry. Venture capitalists (VCs) decide when the structure and management has become mature enough to handle public money or to expand.

The promises of the manager

Managers make a variety of implied and express promises, when they go public. They are mainly concerned with the risk involved in the operation of the company's business. Debt instruments like debentures generally drawn up in the form of an indenture deed have more detailed promises than, for instance, equity instruments like shares. In the next segment, the contractarian perspective is applied to questions of corporate governance.

An overview: contracts and corporate governance

There is evidence to suggest that firms, which fail to adapt their governance structures, are grounded under by sheer competition.[23] One of the central assumptions is that the choice of governance mechanisms does not create third-party effects. Investors have a plethora of opportunities to make investment in other places. Any clause, which has the effect of diluting the expected return, will normally cause a reduction in price offered. All terms in corporate governance are contractual in nature. The pricing and testing mechanisms of the promises made may be negotiated under a fairly Coasean framework and will have no effect on third parties.[24] The optimal nature of contracting exits only when the contracting parties bear the full costs of their decisions. The presumption of efficiency addition is applicable at enforcement of the contract. There must also be a full set of contracts.

The contractarian model assumes that the perfect contracts can be made in a purely private order. There are serious challenges to the presumption of this kind.[25] The contracts, not being market-based exchanges, are necessary due to the informational asymmetry given the separation of ownership and control. Contracts are looked at as responses to such asymmetry. It is highly realistic to assume that parties through contracting cannot design an arrangement to address all future contingencies. Even if they did, it would be too expensive to contract. So does corporate law seek to complete such contracts? Soon it will come to the future that even corporate law cannot take into account all circumstances or be an effective 'contract-perfecter'; rather the role of corporate governance is perceived as a different problem altogether. Governance defined in this context by a noted author is as follows: 'as the complex set of constraints that shape the ex post bargaining over the quasi rents generated in the course of a relationship'.

A system of corporate governance would refer to the set of constraints which deal with bargaining within specialized investments that cannot be replicated by the market.[26] The role of law is to put in a framework that ex post bargaining over rent-seeking behaviour takes place. The completion of hypothetical contracts covering all situations is an oxymoron, in so much as the hypothetical contracts must contain clauses, which by definition the parties remain unaware of. In the specific context of corporate governance, the additional transaction costs add as transactional costs, thereby leaving scope for beneficial intervention. Assume that a contract to hold an auction for a target is optimal, both ex ante and ex post, for investors. They might seek the highest possible price. However, strategy-wise any auctioneering strategy carries with it the risk of the bid falling through. If today's bids are not high enough, an auctioneer may take a painting off the market for a short time, until a higher-valuing bidder appears. It would be inefficient to do the same in the context of the actions of directors of companies. For publicly traded stock, the SEBI takeover code in Regulation 26 prevents from such an occurrence. As for the managers, there is a risk of them setting an unrealistic reservation price. The difficulty of assuring compliance with the terms of the corporate contract may make particular kinds of contracts less useful. The lack of certainty concerning the contractual strategy decided upon has an effect of the process of governance of other firms. This gives rise to another problem. Profit maximization strategy for each single entity for an investor with a diversified portfolio would be a rather unfounded assumption; he or she might seek only to maximize the average performance. Investors sometimes want to maximize the value of their holdings, not the value of a given stock. The value of holdings is highest if the value of each stock is highest.

Corporate veil

The fact that companies have perpetual existence has the effect of extinguishing the need for any agreement for limitation. However, there exists the inherent limitation in the quintessential rule of corporate veil, wherein the shareholders' liability is limited to their fractional or otherwise ownership of shares. The obvious advantage that is offered is that it allows investors to invest small sums in order to be able to diversify and reduce risk. In the opinion of the author, the structures of the corporate organs are all a result of the assessment of the magnitude attached to each role. For instance, if limited liability did not exist, then a shareholder like the partner of a firm would not be able to sell the shares in the company without the consent of the other shareholders. If he or she sold the shares to someone poorer than him or her, the risk of liability for the remaining shareholders would increase and thereby a right to seek consent is sought. Would it then be fair to say that the corporate structure is intended to eliminate the risk of management default? Decidedly, no. The corporate structure merely shifts the risk of such default at least marginally to the voluntary creditors of the corporation. It is often seen with much scepticism that practically, the principal risk of the affairs of the company is taken by persons outside of the company. The creditors therefore fear the risk of default. Richard Posner in his seminal work *Economic Analysis of Law* explains the situation in a more econometric sense in the following form to demonstrate why creditors must be paid for their risk. Consider a new venture with a stated 50% chance of success. The equity of the shareholders covers half of the required capital and the bank provides the other half. In the estimation of the bank, there is a 50% chance the debt will be repaid. In the event of failure, the bank would be able to recover 80% of the loan as assets of the company.

$$\text{The expected payback} = .5(K(1 + r)) + .5(.8K)$$

where K is the principal amount and r is the rate of interest.

Compared to this, let us assume the bank's ultimate aim is to achieve a standard 6% interest over its principal. So the desired return would be 1.06K as K(1 + 0.6). For the expected payback to be equal to the desired payback, we must consider that the following equality must be true:

$$\text{Expected payback } [.5(K(1 + r)) + .5(.8K)] = \text{desired payback } [1.06K]$$

$$.5K + .5Kr + .4K = 1.06K, \text{ which would imply } r = 32.$$

Now let us consider a situation where instead of the bank going in for the finance of the company, only equity holders financed the entire capital. In such cases, if the equity holders borrowed money on themselves, then the bank would have charged them just 6%.

It would then be fair to state that the difference between 62% and 32% represents the amount of compensation paid to the bank to assume the risk, which in another circumstance would lay with the investors. This shift of risk in lieu of compensation offers efficiency advantages. Quite logically, a bank that mainly operates with companies is likely to have a far greater grasp of the risks involved and will be able to operate with low information costs. An individual is also likely to be more risk averse from the bank. A secondary, yet immediate impact is on the actions and incentives placed before the shareholders change radically in a situation where limited liability does not exist. In such cases, the shareholders already are more risk averse than the bank; the investor will have to amend his or her strategy. Currently, an efficient method to reduce risk of investment in a venture lies in the diversification of portfolio. That method is completely incapable of application since the diversification of risk concept relies on the existence of the concept of limited liability and the same would not be possible since the fear of the default on one of the investments would add to the risk aversion and thereby cause the person to not invest at all. Diversification of risk would not matter. To consider the viability of the concept of the corporate veil, let us consider a situation where a car rental service is run wherein each car is incorporated individually, in order to limit their tortious liability. The separate incorporation therefore serves to externalize the cost of the car service.

To answer the question of why the corporate veil, we quite simply see that bringing the personal assets of the shareholders into the scope of possible liability will add to the risk, which we clearly know to be a cost against investment. The next solution sometimes offered is that the company could take insurance to limit its liability, yet the efficacy of such a method is questionable. There are far too many things that can go wrong and cause liability to attach to the property of the shareholder. The insurance companies may deny a certain claim; they may become insolvent, even when available payments from third party carry the risk of litigation and thereby delay, which would again contribute to the cost.

Directors and shareholders: an overview

An insight into the true nature of relationship between directors and shareholders is enquired into to understand the effects of the separation of ownership from control.

Quintessential question of corporate governance: relation between the directors of a company and its shareholders

One of the most interesting and unique features of a company is that decisions about its activities are taken by its directors.[27] Yet company law is often described as 'shareholder-centred' or based on a principle of shareholder primacy.[28] In this section, an inquiry is undertaken to answer the illusory question as to who has the ultimate right to control the affairs of the company in the theoretical sense, while the practical realities of contemporary company law are for all to see. It is therefore, at least tangentially, affected by the philosophical, yet important debate as to whether it is a pure profit-chasing entity or whether it must also be aligned with societal interest and promote the same. This question is relevant even in the shareholder derivative actions wherein these interests may stand in conflict with each other, such as the *Coal India* case where there seems to be a clear conflict between the role of the company as a pure profit-chasing vehicle, in the pursuit of profit motive, and the alleged role of that company as an avenue for dispersal of societal benefit by effecting equitable distribution of a material resource like coal. There is an opinion that business is permitted and encouraged by the law primarily because it serves the community rather than because it is a source of profit to its owners.[29] Another author opines that one must remember that the corporation is legal fiction – a creature of law – and the benefits of participation in enterprise with limited liability are provided for the benefit of society, not of the shareholders themselves.[30] Distinguishing this opinion, another cogent argument relating to the efficiency of the company in society is introduced. It relies on the reasoning that the maximizing of profits for the equity investors assists the other 'constituencies' automatically. The participants in venture play complementary rather than agnostic roles. In market economy, each party to a transaction is better off. A successful firm provides job for workers and goods and services for consumers. The more appealing the goods to the community, the more profits (and perhaps employment). Under this line of thought, prosperity for shareholders, workers and communities goes hand in glove with better products for consumers. Quite often, the harmony between profit maximization and its service of other objectives goes unnoticed.[31]

Relationship between the members and directors

The exact nature of relationship between the members of a company and directors has consistently been debated. It is important in understanding the obligation whether express or implied on the directors of the company vis-à-vis the shareholders and the company as a whole. It is also important to answer the question as to who among the directors and shareholders are or should be bestowed with the authority to control the affairs of the company, in a theoretical sense.

The question of agency

The question of the possibility of an agency relationship between the shareholders and directors is often contemplated. English Law answers this point in the negative in quite emphatic terms. In *Gramaphone and Typewriter Ltd v. Stanley*,[32] it was held that directors of a company, when acting as such, act as agents of the members of the company. Even a director who is an employee of a shareholder and has been nominated to his directorship by that shareholder does not act as agent for the shareholder when acting as a director of the company.[33] Such a director does not owe a duty to that shareholder under company law.[34] There are however cases where directors have acted as agents of the members. Two well-known English cases relate to such a situation. One such situation was witnessed in *Allen v. Hyatt*,[35] where certain directors made an undisclosed profit by selling shares of members. Under the concept of agency, they were held liable to the members. Further, in *Briess v. Woolley*,[36] the members were held liable for the acts of the managing director of a company; he made a fraudulent misrepresentation when arranging for the sale of shares of the members. However, these situations are very specific and cannot be taken as propounding a general rule of company law.

Shareholders and directors: independent entities?

As shown earlier, there is no relationship of agency between shareholders and directors. We now turn to see whether there is any relation fit to be categorized in general between shareholders and directors. A similar comment on the dilemma in strict legal categorization was made in *Imperial Hydropathic Hotel Co., Blackpool v.*

Hampson,[37] where it was held that when one seeks to categorize the directors into known roles such as agents, trustees or managing partners of the company, it is essential to recollect that such expressions are not exhaustive of the powers and responsibility of directors. Such categorization is dynamic and is useful when made applicable to a specific set of circumstances in order to ascertain the rights and duties of directors at such times and for such purpose. The court used the expression that the directors' role may seem in the moment and for the purpose 'be falling within the circle' or 'cutting the circle' of the roles referred to earlier. Such categorization must therefore be categorized only for the circumstance where the role of the director falls pro tanto within the principles, which govern the particular class. The starting point of this analysis must be to take into account the impact of the duty of director to exercise independent judgement to the relationship between a shareholder and the directors. Some benefit may also be gained from making an enquiry as to whose interest it is that the director should promote, the company's or the shareholder's.

Duty to exercise independent judgement

The duty on the director to exercise independent judgement is well established in law. It has backing within statutes of various jurisdictions as well as a general principle in the realm of corporate law. The case *Boulting v. Association of Cinematograph, Television and Allied Technicians*[38] is of particular relevance here. This case concerned an agreement entered between a shareholder and a director, which required that the director carry out his duties in a certain manner without regard to the interest of the company. Lord Denning, in describing such contracts as illegal on account of fettering the discretion of the company, ruled that no stipulation by which a director, a person having a fiduciary duty, agrees to act on the instruction of another instead of exercising his own independent judgement can be conferred legality. It would be unlawful to agree to subordinate the interest of the company, which the director is under an obligation to protect in order to protect the interest of someone else. There are, however, more moderate decisions on this point. In *Motherwell v. Schoof*,[39] the court declined from ordering the specific performance of the contract, which imposed fetters of such kind when such performance would go against the interest of the company. There is a significant difference between the two rulings. The ratio in *Boulting* case suggests that regardless of any conflict, or lack thereof, between the stipulations in an agreement and the interest of the company, such agreements are unlawful. However, the ratio in *Motherwell* implies that such agreements are unlawful and unenforceable to the extent they are against the interests of the company. Some concession is allowed insofar as the director is entitled to take into account the appointing members' interests. However, the duty to the company under the statute is paramount and of inescapable importance.[40]

Whom does the director serve?

Quite often the phrases 'success of the company' and 'beneficial to the company' become subjects of scrutiny in cases involving allegations of the breach of duties on the part of the directors. This problem is one, which is encountered due to the sheer structure of governance and is inherent in the concept of a company as an artificial entity with perpetual succession different from the ones who own, run or control it. In *Gaiman v. National Association for Mental Health*,[41] the court encountered a similar dilemma, which involved the question of expulsion of a member from the corporation. It stated that as a company is an artificial legal entity, it has an arduous task determining what is in its best interest without paying due regard to its present and prospective membership. In what may appear as a departure from other cases where it has been held that directors have no duties qua members, the court held that

> where there is a corporate personality, the directors are bound not merely by their duties towards the members but also towards the corporation. These duties [unlike in case of partnerships] may be inconsistent with the observance of natural justice. Since the duty towards the corporation impels the board to take action with great speed and the duty towards the members would prompt natural justice which would require delay, I think that indicates that the board is intended to be able to exercise its powers unfettered by natural justice.

Fiduciary duties of directors

It is true that directors of a company are under a fiduciary duty. Yet the question that often arises is, to whom do they owe this duty? What happens in case of conflict between the creditors' interest and the members? What happens when the company's interest differs from that of its members or a class of them? This section contains the analysis of the same in greater detail.

Origins and current state of fiduciary obligation towards the company

In the 19th century directors of companies, under English Law, were often referred to as trustees[42] of the company's property. Proceedings could therefore be brought under the head of 'breach of trust'. In *Re National Funds Assurance Co*,[43] the directors who had paid dividends out of capital were held guilty of a breach of trust for the purposes of misfeasance proceedings. There is, however, one essential difference between a trustee and a director – a trustee holds legal title to the property of the beneficiary which he or she holds in trust; a director, on the other hand, cannot under any circumstance assert legal title or associated right over company property. From the categorization of directors as trustees, the judicial pronouncements moved away from the strict categorization and in a case similar to *National Funds Assurance Co* held that managers were to be referred to as 'quasi trustee', presumably taking into account the essential difference highlighted earlier.[44] Into the 20th century the courts in England further departed from the strict categorization and enunciated the concept of fiduciary duty of the directors towards the company. In *Regal (Hastings) Ltd v. Gulliver*,[45] the court held that directors are, without a doubt, not trustees, yet they occupy a fiduciary duty towards the company whose boards they form. This case seems to imply the fiduciary of the board of directors and not specifically on each individual director. In the latter half of the 20th century the concept of the fiduciary duty of the directors seems to have become more clear in its definition and ambit, owing to increasing jurisprudence on the role of the director in the contemporary legal structure of companies.

Fiduciary duties towards members of the company

Courts in cases[46] such as *Multinational Gas and Petrochemical Co. v. Multinational Gas and Petrochemical Services Ltd*[47] have held that a director does not by virtue of being a director owe to the members of the company any fiduciary duties even though the director stands in a fiduciary position qua the company. In *Hawkes v.*

Cuddy Ltd[48] it was held that the fact that the director of a company has been nominated by a shareholder does not imply any obligation on such director towards the member whether of fiduciary character or otherwise.

Fiduciary duty towards creditors

Insofar as the creditors are concerned, the courts have expectedly held in cases[49] such as *Re: Wincham Shipbuilding Boiler and Salt Co., Poole, Jackson and Whyte's case*[50] that the directors of the company owe no fiduciary duty towards its creditors.

Fiduciary duty towards other directors

In *Brant Investments Ltd v. KeepRite Inc.*,[51] it was also held that a director cannot be said to be under a fiduciary duty towards fellow directors. However, in few cases such *as Elliott v. Wheeldon*,[52] the courts have left open the possibility in special circumstances that fiduciary duty be placed on directors towards other directors when two directors acted to pursue a joint venture as partners through the medium of a company of which they were directors. However, the court in *Peskin v. Anderson*[53] held that findings of such duties are owing to special circumstances and are quite separate from the duties considered to be owed to all directors in a company by a company director. It may also be important to mention that the company as a whole does not owe a fiduciary duty to its members.[54] As a result of the analysis of the aforementioned precedents and the concepts discussed, it is clear that there are no enforceable fiduciary obligations of directors towards the creditors, members, employees or any other entity apart from the artificial legal entity of the company itself.

Implication of the directors' duty to exercise reasonable care and diligence in the affairs of the company

A director is under an obligation to exercise reasonable skill and judgement in relation to the affairs of a company to the extent that is reasonably expected of a person of his or her knowledge and experience.[55] Such was the standard in most common law jurisdictions until recently when it was understood as being too low.[56] One must delve deep into the concept and origin of the duty to exercise skill and diligence in order to appreciate what is a squarely equitable duty, which may in some cases be codified.[57] The House of Lords in *Henderson v. Merrett Syndicates Ltd*[58] held that the duty of care owed by a director of a company towards the company is a product of the circumstances that the director assumes responsibility for the affairs of the company. Such duty might have two sources – a duty based on an equitable principle and another under the common law of tort.[59] It is however not a fiduciary duty of the director.[60] The duty of care encompasses within it the obligation to know the company's business. Directors are collectively and individually under a continuous obligation to keep themselves sufficiently informed and acquire understanding of the company's business to enable them to properly discharge their duties as directors.

The judicial pronouncements on this point take into account the age-old standard that the director must act in accordance with the skill which can be expected of him or her, taking into account his or her knowledge and expertise.[61] Clearly, this standard is subjective and prescribes different levels of skill for different directors. This formed the subject matter of *Re Brazilian Rubber Plantation and Estates Ltd*[62] where it was held that a man could lawfully discharge as a director of a rubber plantation company, without any semblance of knowledge about the business of the company and in complete ignorance of all things connected to rubber. The obligation to exercise reasonable care, skill and diligence must be balanced with the right of the board to take decisions by itself and its good sense. To preserve this and prevent a host of frivolous litigations, courts have imposed self-restraint on their powers. Courts have in this context resorted to the doctrine more commonly known as the *business judgement rule* in the United States and its variants. For instance, in *Howard Smith Ltd v. Ampol Petroleum*,[63] it was held that there is 'no appeal from the management decisions in a court of law; nor will courts of law assume to act as a kind of supervisory board over decisions within the powers of management honestly arrived at'. This opinion was relied upon and qualified in *Regentcrest Plc v. Cohen*,[64] where the court held that it would be wrong to assume that relevant question for determination for the court was whether the act in question was in fact in the interests of the company, or whether a better decision was possible. The true and justiciable question can only be related to the directors' state of mind. The point to be determined is whether or not in the opinion of the directors at the relevant point the course of action was in the best interest of the company. In order for such a vague parameter to be brought into the field of scrutiny by the courts, a test has been laid down in *Charterbridge Corporation Ltd v. Lloyds Bank*[65] in the following words, 'The proper test in the absence of actual separate consideration, must be whether an intelligent and honest man in the position of a director of the company concerned, *could*, in the whole of the existing circumstances, have reasonably believed that the transactions were for the benefit of the company.'

One of the examples comparable to a shareholder derivative litigation in this context is the case of *Fusion Interactive Communication Solutions Ltd v. Venture Investment Placement Ltd*,[66] where the minority shareholder of a company brought a legal proceeding in the name of the company when the directors of the company in breach of their duty towards the company refused to initiate legal proceedings that were in the company's best interest. The court held valid the action on behalf of the company by its minority shareholders. In the case of *Mafatlal v. Miheer H Mafatlal*,[67] the Supreme Court of India in the specific context of business decision by the board of directors and shareholders in relation to a merger has stated that the role of the court resembles that of an umpire in a game of cricket, where it only ensures that the parties interact within the four corners of the rules of the game but the court does not take upon itself the power or duty to tell the parties how to play the game.

Critique of parallel provision in the Companies Act, 2013

The preceding discussion is also relevant in the examination of Section 166 of the newly enacted Companies Act, 2013, which lays down the following duties on the directors. Under this provision, a director of a company must perform the following duties.

Positive duties

- 'Act according to the articles of association of the company.' This is a reflection of a fairly settled principle of law.
- 'Shall observe good faith in order to promote the objects of the company for the benefit of its members as a whole, and in the best interests of the company its employees, the shareholders, the community and for the protection of environment.'

The expansive inclusion of beneficiaries of the obligation of directors becomes normative without being pragmatic when almost all stakeholders excluding only the creditors are statutorily defined. Most disputes relate to which among the mentioned stakeholders are superior to another. Hence, this provision does not provide the tools to analyse situations where the directors face conflicting duties inter se the stakeholders. The strict literal interpretation taking into account the normal rule of emphasis of the punctuation in the English language might lead to an uncomfortable conclusion that the directors are to serve the best interest of the members of the company, before the interest of the company itself. The likelihood of such confusion to manifest is low given the outstanding common law jurisprudence in this regard.

- 'Act with duties with due and reasonable care, skill and diligence and shall exercise independent judgment'. Quite rightly this is an assertion of the relevant principle of common law, yet this provision is widely inadequate. It fails to provide any standard to judge the reasonable skill, which is to be demonstrated by a director. It does not completely rule out the possibility that a director, in manner of speaking, goes about his directorial duties without any knowledge of the nature of the business of the companies. This situation is rather oxymoronic since no supervision of activities is possible without the knowledge of the companies' business and operations. In failing to define whether an objective or subjective standard should be applied, the Parliament has left large scope for misinterpretation. It would not be too risky to predict significant amount of litigation on the basis of this provision in which case common law principles may be read into the provision.

Negative duties

- 'shall not involve himself in a situation which contain a conflict, whether direct or otherwise of his interests that of the corporate.
- shall not achieve or attempt to achieve any undue gain or advantage either to himself or to his relatives, partners, or associates. This requirement also carries an equal compensation provision, it being liable to paid to the company.
- shall not assign his office.'

These seem to adequately reflect the pre-existing obligations. Given the potential for divergent opinion of the law in its newest form, the preceding discussion on the existing Indian and common law jurisprudence on this point is likely to be relevant for litigators and adjudicators alike.

Economic analysis of law relating to directors and self-dealing

On a pure incentive-based view, only the law can prevent insiders from taking courses of action that maximize their own utility even at the expense of stockholders.[68] As the most noted authorities put it, 'Duty-of-loyalty problems often involve spectacular, one-shot appropriations, of the "take the money and run" sort, in which subsequent penalties through markets are inadequate.'[69] Before embarking on the assessment of various municipal laws on the issue, it would serve one well to get an understanding of what truly is the trade-off in terms of regulation of self-dealing. It is appropriate to introduce the subject of the basic regulatory options on self-dealing transactions by stating the obvious: self-dealing transactions do not necessarily result in damage to the company.[70] By definition, however, they cause harm to the company when they are *unfair*.

Self-dealing transactions are unfair when 'the[ir] outcome . . . is *less advantageous* [to the company] than the outcome would have been if the transaction had been agreed to, on [the company's] behalf, by a rational, well-informed decision maker who was independent and loyal, that is, not affected by a conflict of interest' (emphasis added).[71] Legal systems therefore balance the need for deterrence and avoid the risk of overkill, which would lead to efficiency losses. In the balance between the two lies a point where restrictions of the law find the most operation optimal level of deterrence. Therefore, the import of statistics that compare jurisdictions on the basis of number of self-dealing transactions must be tempered with the knowledge that the essence really lies in the *kind of violations* that occur.

Deterrence

Where an issue of incentive mismatch occurs, the law often takes the 'compensation route'. One such rule would be to mandate no ex ante regulation but the post facto right of the company to claim damages from the directors.[72] Another option would be to refrain from directly regulating self-dealing but prescribe for effective responses when self-dealing does occur. The voidability of self-dealing transactions has an adverse effect for the director similar to the disgorgement of any profits that the director had or sought to make. In this approach, the costs of recovery are avoided, and a more direct disincentive is created. The directors' viewpoint must be considered. A rational self-dealing director will decide on whether to go ahead with his or her assessment of the expected benefits which are offset by what he or she receives from the transaction, with the expected costs imposed on him or her by the legal system. Theoretically, the cost of judicial intervention coupled with information asymmetry in favour of the directors renders them in a superior position while entering into the transaction.[73]

Risk of overkill

The risk of overkill in terms of regulation is simply that regulation might in itself cause efficiency problems. If regulations are prohibitive and strict, it is possible that at a significant number of value increasing transactions will not be allowed. This is what is commonly known as a false-positive problem.[74] The probability of such an outcome is of course much higher when the decision to challenge a transaction is in the hands of each shareholder.[75] The analysis of various jurisdictions and their rules on self-dealing will stress on the same. In fact, 'that decision will be controlled by the settlement value of the challenge and the attendant opportunity for plaintiff's attorney's fees, rather than [by] an even-handed consideration of whether the transaction, on balance, is in the corporation's interest'.[76] These are then best described as intangible second-order effects to overkill regulation such as resignations and a general perception of increased cost to become director of a company as a direct extension of the false-positive problem.[77]

The role of disclosure

The value of disclosure is found in the rationale used for its employment. For any self-dealing transaction, at least three components exist. The disclosures are the first aspect. They contribute to the efficiency of the markets.[78] Prices will in most cases reflect the fairness of a transaction.[79] Second, the disclosures give all other recipients of information a reasonable and objective basis to judge the integrity of managers in so much as it affects the reputation of the manager.[80] Therefore, disclosure makes it ex ante less advantageous for managers. Third aspect is the classical problem of too much information. Quite simply, information or a document in isolation is better than relevant documents and information in a room full of similar documents owing to the cost of access and process of the information. Further, excessive information has a detrimental effect on the value of the information[81] in addition to causing increase in costs due to the high likelihood of a false positive.[82] In the next segment, an analysis of the law relating to self-dealing in a common law nation, the United Kingdom, and a civil law nation, such as France, is carried out.

United Kingdom

Disclosure per se

The law prevalent in the United Kingdom requires directors to disclose any credit transactions covered under a listing provision and transactions where a transaction either of the company or its subsidiary has a material interest.[83] The nature of the 'interest' also has to be disclosed[84] after which the board may decide on the same. It would only be in cases where the board fails to consider the matter that the courts would be empowered to review.[85] This legal position goes a step ahead and imposes blanket fine for any directors failing to disclose any such material interest to the board, regardless of its consequence without regard to subsequent ratification.[86] Quite obviously, this seeks to create a disincentive to evasion of disclosure duties. Questions are however raised in relation to the efficacy of this provision since the effect of however large a fine is severely diluted given the low likelihood of prosecution of the director.[87]

Disclosure as a procedural requirement

The standard clauses in Table A (*standard AoA*) enunciate what may be presumed the British legislators' most favoured clause on the subject. Article 85 states that directors may deal with the company, as long as disclosure is made. It also shields the directors from any liability that arises by 'reason of his office, be accountable to the company for any benefit which he derives from any [self-dealing] transaction'. It has been held that failure to disclose renders the transactions voidable at the option of the company.[88] Here the ratification of an act done without disclosure cannot be done without shareholder approval.[89] On a more basic theoretical note, this provision may be referenced as loosely defining the contours at which the shareholders are assessed to lose trust on the managers.

Ratification by (disinterested) stockholders

The concept of diversification of risk is looked at favourably on an efficiency basis. This would however entail that the shareholder of the company could possibly invest in two competing companies. In such a case, he or she would have the right to readjust the capital he or she owns. Therefore, as a general principle, stockholders may vote despite having a personal interest in the subject matter opposed to or different from the general or particular interests of the company.[90] Such course of action is not entirely without fetters. A provision in the UK company law provides for a safeguard wherein the court may interfere to prohibit the interested shareholders from causing unfair prejudice to the interest of the stockholders.[91] For publicly traded company stocks the London Stock Exchange lays down strict rules on self-dealing transactions in what is referred to as the *Yellow Book*.[92] It lays down similar rules as to ratification by shareholders without the participation of the interested party director. The related party should not be permitted to vote at the meeting. The Companies Act, 2013, newly enacted in India, takes a leaf out of such provisions.

France

In France, company law requires that internal auditors report to the general meeting on all self-dealing transactions authorized by the board of directors. For the most part, such a report is related to the general meeting vote on the transactions. However, one must note that information to be given to stockholders by the auditors is independent of approval by the former.[93] Theoretically, this is an effective safeguard if alternate disincentives are created to ensure to preserve the independent role of the auditor. In that vein to prevent risk of collusion, auditors are at risk of criminal liability if they fail to report such transaction to the shareholders in spite of knowing such information to be true.

Disclosure per se

French law requires internal auditors to report to the shareholders in a general meeting all self-dealing transactions either authorized by the board or the ones that should have but did not go to the board for authorization.[94] Once again the provision (Section 457) has limited deterrent effect since a causal link between the fault and the damage to the company is very difficult to establish.[95]

Disclosure as a procedural requirement

In France, the scope of disclosure to the board is rather limited. The director has to inform only the board of the existence of a proposed transaction in which he or she has an interest without the relevant details as to what is the interest in question. The intent can therefore only be that the director inform the board that an authorization is required.[96] Even if this seems rather lacking on the first look, it makes no difference as to what the exact nature of interest a director has as long as the requirement of board approval evinces itself. The extra details are void of much use, and its omission does not seem to affect the core efficacy of the provision. The director is required to raise alarm and necessitate the need for board approval in a broad range of cases where there exists even an indirect interest.

Approval or ratification by disinterested directors

In any case the interested director has a duty to abstain from voting. However, 'current transactions entered into at normal conditions', that is transactions which, by definition, do not expose the company to any danger of expropriation on the part of managers, are exempted. Even where they involve damage to the company, the general meeting can ratify them. Void transactions may be challenged either by the company or by its stockholders. Corresponding deterrence is provided in so much as the directors will be criminally liable and may face imprisonment for up to five years and a fine in cases where the directors have used bad faith for the personal use, contrary to the interest of the company. This provision is frequently used.

Approval or ratification by (disinterested) stockholders

Any self-dealing transaction, subject to some exceptions, has to be submitted to the general meeting for evaluation by stockholders.[97]

The auditors play a central role in the information dispensation regarding the conflict. The general shareholder meet may ratify the transactions not authorized by the directors.[98] Interested directors do not vote in such a meeting. Fraud aside, ratification of other transaction immunizes the directors from liability.

In India as well, Section 188 of the Companies Act, 2013, read with the rules contains three essential characteristics. Requirement of disclosure for transactions over prescribed thresholds, interested directors mandated to refrain from voting from those transactions and interested shareholders to refrain when such transactions are subject to ratification in a general meeting of the shareholders.

Conclusion

Policy making for ages has been mostly about the borrowing of the experience of yesteryears. By the end of the 20th century, the developed world policy makers began understanding the economic perspective in policy making. There is a cogent argument towards the use of economic analysis for the formulation of law and policy. The company is the most efficient form of risk distribution, and its merit as legal entity is undoubted. It allows for capital to be invested in a fair manner without too much of risk concentration. It also allows owners to be among those who do not really understand the workings of a certain business. In employing specifically trained and educated managers, the efficiency advantage is conferred and the net social cost is reduced.

Problems have however arisen due to the separation of ownership and control. *Coase Theorem*–based incentive schemes do fairly well to regulate the behaviour, yet the high transaction costs associated with such a structure call for corporate regulation in order to improve informational symmetry. Problems do arise even with regulation; there remains a possibility of an overkill whereby the legislation itself creates transaction costs. An analysis of the working of the common and civil law system reveals that the self-dealing with directors is a highly regulated issue, being the overlap of the incentive towards self and duties towards company for the directors; this area is logically regulated in most nations. The disclosure rules and ratification rules reflect each legal system's understanding of the economic incentive at play. The tool economic analysis may be used to refine the existing state of corporate law in India as well as the world. The behavioural analysis involved in the chapter must also be backed up by empirical evidence, which remains outside the scope of this endeavour. It is easy to conclude that most policy making does in fact bring in the behavioural rationale, but only considers direct effects of policy making. Since the different market factors and regulations apply simultaneously, there are a variety of second-order effects that need to be made reference to on a more detailed incentive-disincentive-based paradigm.

Notes

1 Thomas Donaldson and Lee E. Preston, 'The Stakeholder Theory of the Corporation: Concepts, Evidence, and Implications', *Academy of Management Review* 20 (1) (1995): 65–91.
2 E.M. Dodd Jr., 'For Whom Are Corporate Managers Trustees?', *Harvard Law Review* 45 (1932): 1149.
3 T.S. Norwitz, 'The Metaphysics of *Time:* A Radical Corporate Vision', *Business Lawyer* 46 (1991): 387.
4 Andrew Keay, 'Ascertaining the Corporate Objective: An Entity Maximisation and Shareholder Value', *Modern Law Review* 71 (2008): 663.
5 Ibid.
6 *Vodafone International Holdings B.V. v. Union of India & Anr.*, Civil Appeal No. 733 of 2012.
7 [1974] 1 WLR 1133.
8 *Attorney General for Tuvalu v. Philatelic Distribution Corporation* [1990] 1 WLR 926.
9 (1939) 61 CLR 457.
10 (1887) 12 App. Cas 589.
11 *Carruth v. Imperial Chemical Industries Ltd* [1937] AC 707, 765.
12 [1900] 1 Ch 656.
13 *Re Western Mines Ltd* (1975) 65 DLR (3d) 307, 313.
14 [1959] 1 WLR 62, 82.
15 (1972) 33 DLR (3d) 288.
16 (1971) 123 CLR 614, 620.
17 *Lonrho Ltd v. Shell Petroleum Co. Ltd* [1980] 1 WLR 627.
18 Robert Cooter, 'The Coase Theorem', In *Information, Allocation and Exchange*, edited by J. Eatwell, M. Milgate and P. Newman (London: Macmillan, 1990): 64–70.
19 Ronald H. Coase, 'The Problem of Social Cost', *Journal of Law and Economics* 3 (1960): 1–44.
20 Anthoy Ogus, *Regulation: Legal Form and Economic Theory* (Oxford: Clarendon Press, 1994): 78.
21 L. Zingalies, 'Corporate Governance', In *The New Palgrave Dictionary of Economics and Law*, edited by P. Newman (London and Basingstoke: Macmillan, 1998): 495.
22 F. Easterbrook and D. Fischel, *The Economic Structure of Corporate Law* (Cambridge: Harvard University Press, 1991): 35.
23 O. Williamson, *The Economic Institutions of Capitalism* (New York: The Free Press, 1985).

24 Coase, 'The Problem of Social Cost': 1.
25 S. Deakin and J. Michie, 'The Theory and Practice of Contracting', In *Contracts, Cooperation and Competition: Studies in Economics, Management and Law*, edited by S. Deakin and J. Michie (Oxford: OUP, 1997): 1–42.
26 Zingalies, 'Corporate Governance': 498.
27 Derek French, Stephen Mayson and Christopher Ryan, *Mayson, French and Ryan on Company Law* (Oxford: OUP, 2012): 31.
28 Ibid.
29 Dodd Jr., 'For Whom Are Corporate Managers Trustees?': 1149.
30 Norwitz, 'The Metaphysics of *Time*': 387.
31 Keay, 'Ascertaining the Corporate Objective': 663.
32 [1908] 2 KB 89.
33 *Kuwait Asia Bank EC v. National Mutual Life Nominees Ltd* [1991] 1 AC 187.
34 *Hawkes v. Cuddy* [2009] EWCA Civ 291, LTL 2/4/2009, 32.
35 (1914) 30 TLR 444.
36 [1954] AC 333.
37 (1882) 23 Ch. D. 1, 12.
38 [1963] 2 QB 606.
39 (1949) 4 DLR 812.
40 *Hawkes v. Cuddy* [2009] EWCA Civ 291, ITL 2/4/2009, 33.
41 [1971] Ch. 317.
42 French, Mayson and Ryan, *Mayson, French and Ryan on Company Law*: 231.
43 L.R. 10 Ch. D. 118.
44 *Re Exchange Banking Co., Flitcroft's Case* (1882) 21 Chd 519.
45 [1967] 2 AC 134.
46 *Brant Investments Ltd v. KeepRite Inc.* (1991) 80 DLR 161.
47 [1983] Ch. 258.
48 [2009] EWCA Civ 291, LTL 2/4/2009.
49 *Western Finance Co. Ltd v. Tasker Enterprises Ltd* (1979) 106 DLR (3d) 81.
50 (1878) 9 Ch. D. 322.
51 (1991) 80 DLR 161.
52 [1993] BCLC 53.
53 [2001] 1 BCLC 372.
54 *Esplanade Developments Ltd v. Divine Holdings Pty Ltd* [1980] WAR 151.
55 *In Re City Equitable Fire Insurance Co. Ltd* [1925] Ch. 407.
56 Paul Davies and Sarah Worthington, *Gower and Davies Principles of Modern Company Law* (London: Sweet and Maxwell, 2012): 488.
57 Ibid.
58 [1995] 2 AC 145.
59 *Bristol and West Building Society v. Mothew* [1998] Ch. 1, 16–17; *Base Metal Trading Ltd v. Shamurin* [2004] EWCA Civ 1316.
60 *Henderson v. Merrett Syndicates Ltd* [1995] 2 AC 145.
61 *Re City Equitable Fire Insurance Co. Ltd* [1925] Ch. 407.
62 [1911] 1 Ch. 425.

63 [1974] AC 821, 832.
64 [2001] 2 BCLC 80, 105.
65 [1970] Ch. 62, 74.
66 [2005] EWHC 736 (Ch.).
67 AIR 1997 SC 506.
68 Adolf A. Berle and Gardiner C. Means, *The Modern Corporation and Private Property* (New Brunswick, NJ: Transaction Publishers, 1982): 221; Tullio Ascarelli, 'Postilla in tema dinominatività', *Rivista delle Società* (1957): 370.
69 Easterbrook and Fischel, *The Economic Structure of Corporate Law*: 103.
70 Robert C. Clark, 'Agency Costs versus Fiduciary Duties', In *Principals and Agents: The Structure of Business*, edited by John W. Pratt and Richard J. Zeckhauser (Boston: Harvard Business School Press, 1985): 148–149.
71 Ibid.
72 Yvan Balensi, *Collection Étudesjuridiques SérieDroit des affaires, Volume 1 of Étudesjuridiques (Economica): Droit des affaires, Les Conventions Entre les Sociétés Commerciales et Leurs Dirigeants* (1975): 4.
73 Robert Cooter and Bradley J. Freedman, 'The Fiduciary Relationship: Its Economic Character and Legal Consequences', *New York University Law Review* 66 (1991): 1045, 1052.
74 Ibid.
75 Harry G. Henn and John R. Alexander, *Laws of Corporations* (Eagan, MN: West Publishing Co., 1983): 1035–1044.
76 Jonathan P. Charkham, *Keeping Good Company: A Study of Corporate Governance in Five Countries* (Oxford: OUP, 1995): 152.
77 Law Commission and the Scottish Law Commission, *Company Directors: Regulating Conflicts of Interests and Formulating a Statement of Duties* (Consultation Paper No. 153, 1998), 39, accessed 5 November 2014, http://www.gtnet.gov.uk/lawcomm.
78 John C. Coffee Jr., 'Market Failure and the Economic Case for a Mandatory Disclosure System', *Virginia Law Review* 70 (1984): 717.
79 Clark, 'Agency Costs versus Fiduciary Duties': 78.
80 Eugene F. Fama, 'Agency Problems and the Theory of the Firm', *Journal of Political Economy* 88 (1980): 295.
81 Law Commission and the Scottish Law Commission, *Company Directors*.
82 Paul G. Mahoney, 'Mandatory Disclosure as a Solution to Agency Problems', *University of Chicago Law Review* 62 (1995): 1054.
83 Companies Act, 1985, § 232, in connection with Sched. 6, paras 15–28.
84 Ibid.
85 Ibid.
86 Companies Act, 1985, § 317.
87 Laurence C.B. Gower, *Gower's Principles of Modern Company Law* (London: Sweet and Maxwell, 1997): 614.
88 *Hely-Hutchinson v. Brayhead Ltd* [1968] 1 QB 549; [1967] 3 WLR 1408; [1967] 3 All ER 98 (Court of Appeal); and *Guinness plc v. Saunders* [1990] 2 AC 663; [1990] 2 WLR 324; [1990] 1 All ER 652 (House of Lords).

89 *North-West Transportation Co. Ltd v. Beatty* (1887) 12 App. Cas 589, 593 (Privy Council).
90 John H. Farrar and Brenda Hannigan, *Farrar's Company Law* (London: Butterworths Law, 1998): 424.
91 *Cook v. Deeks* [1916] 1 AC 554 (Privy Council); *Regal (Hastings) Ltd v. Gulliver* [1942] 1 All ER 378.
92 Richard Smerdon, *A Practical Guide to Corporate Governance* (London: Sweet and Maxwell, 1998): 168–173.
93 § 92, Décret No. 67–236 du 23 mars 1967 (JO 24 mars 1967) (hereinafter Decree No. 67–236).
94 Georges Ripert and René Roblot, *Traité de droit commercial* (1996): 933, LGDJ Tome 2, 15ème édition.
95 Yves Guyon, *Droit des Affaires* (1992): 398, Tome 1, 7th ed., Paris: Economica.
96 Yvan Balensi, *Les Conventions Entre les Sociétés Commerciales et Leurs Dirigeants* (1975): 114.
97 § 103(2) of Law No. 66–537.
98 Yves Guyon, *Droit des Affaires* (1992): 431.

Chapter 7

Economic analysis of the corporate debt restructuring mechanism in India

Aishwarya Mohapatra, Rumani Sheth and Suriti

Background note

About the CDR mechanism in India

The Corporate Debt Restructuring (CDR) Scheme was introduced by the Reserve Bank of India (RBI) in 2001 to act as a solution to a company in organizing its outstanding debts. It was meant to act as a tool for corporates to deal with financial difficulties 'because of factors out of their control and due to internal reasons'.[1] The objective of the CDR framework is to have in place a timely and transparent mechanism for restructuring of the corporate debts of viable entities facing problems, which are outside the purview of the Board for Industrial and Financial Reconstruction, Debt Recovery Tribunal and other legal institutions, *the benefit of all concerned.*[2] In particular, the aim was to preserve those viable corporate entities that are affected by certain internal and external factors and to minimize the losses to the creditors and other stakeholders through an 'orderly and coordinated restructuring programme'.[3]

The CDR mechanism consists of three groups, namely the CDR Standing Forum, the CDR Cell and the CDR Empowered Group.

The CDR Standing Forum: The general body for this system consists of the representatives of all participating banks and financial institutions.

CDR Core Group: It is formed from within the members of CDR Standing Forum to assist the Standing Forum in convening the meetings and taking decisions relating to policy, on behalf of the Standing Forum. The CDR Core Group lays down the policies and guidelines to be followed by the CDR Empowered Group and CDR Cell.

The CDR Empowered Group: It comprises all the executive director–level representatives of financial institutions and concerned banks, and decides whether the restructuring of the company is prima facie feasible and the enterprise is potentially viable in terms of the policies and guidelines evolved by the Standing Forum.

- When found feasible, the CDR Cell will then proceed to lay down the detailed Rehabilitation Plan. The CDR Standing Forum and Empowered Group are to be assisted by the CDR Cell in every function.[4]
- Legally, the basis of CDR is the Debtor–Creditor Agreement (DCA) and the Inter-Creditor Agreement (ICA), which lay down the terms and conditions of the final debt restructuring between the debtor and the creditor, or between creditors as determined.[5]
- All banks/financial institutions in the CDR system are required to enter into the legally binding ICA with necessary enforcement and penal provisions; if 75% of creditors (by value) agree to a debt restructuring package, the same would be binding on the remaining creditors.
- Debtors are required to execute the DCA. The DCA has a 'stand still' agreement which is legally binding for a period of 90/180 days, whereby both the debtor(s) and creditor(s) agree to stand still and commit themselves to refrain from taking recourse to any legal action during the period.[6]

Economic factors considered for approval of CDR mechanism

There are many factors that are considered by the CDR Empowered Group while looking into debt restructuring. The eligibility criterion for corporates to opt for the CDR mechanism is that they have to have multiple banking accounts/syndications/consortium accounts, engaged in any type of activity, with outstanding fund-based and non-fund based exposure of Rs 10 crore and above by banks and institutions.[7] The Empowered Group decides on the acceptable viability benchmark levels on the following illustrative parameters, which are applied on a case-to-case basis, depending on the merits of each case:[8]

- Debt service coverage ratio
- Break-even point (operating and cash)

- Return on capital employed
- Internal rate of return
- Cost of capital
- Loan life ratio
- Extent of sacrifice

CDR is divided into two categories on the basis of risk in the accounts. The categories are subject to separate sets of conditions.

- The first category, Category I, is applicable only to those situations where the accounts are of 'standard' and 'sub-standard' nature and it has to be so classified by 90% of the creditors.
- To fall under Category II, accounts must be applicable to 'doubtful accounts', and a minimum of 75% of creditors (by value) and 60% of creditors (by number) should satisfy themselves of the viability of the account and consent for such restructuring. This is noteworthy since to be classified as a good debt, 90% of creditors must agree, but the threshold for being called a bad debt is set at a comparably lower percentage, 75, even if all the creditors must comply with the decision of 75% and agree to restructure a debt against their will.

Failures of the CDR mechanism

Government intervention

Many experts are of the view that government intervention in CDR has a lot of drawbacks. Increased litigation, the endeavour to endure the economic crisis in an attempt to survive till the end through macroeconomic recoveries and proliferation in unproductive 'zombie' companies are some of them, as these companies require constant bailouts in order to operate. In spite of these, they agree that it is somewhat necessary for reformatory macroeconomic policies to solve the problem of imbalances in the economy. At the same time, government intervention will have to balance out a lot of distortions like the inefficiencies associated with debt restructuring as it tends to preserve commercial entities which are non-profit making in the present and also have almost no possibility of being a successful business entity in the future. This refers to the idea that it promotes irresponsible risk-taking. The enduring lesson from experience is that a little government intervention has invigorated and bolstered CDR. However, direct government intervention raises the possibility of substantial fiscal costs if resolutions in non-performing loans are subsidized. Government intervention will undermine credit culture by changing the clause's financial contracts forcibly through government funds post facto. To address the problem, it is necessary to determine where exactly the problem lies: one must try to disentangle whether banks are unwilling to lend or whether firms and households are unwilling to borrow. It has been seen that this differs hugely from market to market and evolves over time.

The focus of policy in the crisis containment phase should be to establish a predictable and foreseeable macroeconomic path, which would necessarily include thorough renovation and recovery of the banking system. Three approaches to corporate debt restructuring have been identified and compartmentalized by different degrees of government involvement. One of the approaches involves a market-based approach in which private sector debtors and creditors are left to analyse the terms of the burden sharing on an individual basis, which basically would rely on the solutions present in the market from the interplay of demand and supply. This was present in Hungary, Poland, Korea, Malaysia and Thailand in the last decade of the 20th century. Even though this approach is essentially market-oriented, the government would still have an important role through implementing legal reforms to implement prompt restructuring. In order to understand this better, we must look at the Thailand Financial Crisis at a closer level. It was a part of the bigger Asian financial crisis, a period of financial crisis that plagued East Asia from July 1997 and raised extreme concern of a worldwide economic meltdown due to financial contagion (a scenario where financial distress of the economy is contracted in a manner similar to the transmission of a medical disease: starting out with few shocks that go on to debilitate the entire system). On 15 May 1997, the Thai baht was hit by massive speculative attacks. On 30 June 1997, the Thai prime minister stated the official position that the baht would not be devalued. This was the incident which kick-started Asian financial crisis as the Thai government failed to defend the baht. In turn, the baht followed the fixed currency regime in which a currency is pegged to another one to ascertain its value: the Thai baht was pegged to the US dollar, which in turn was the main component against international speculators. The International Monetary Fund (IMF) unveiled a rescue package in 1997 after the Thai government was compelled to float the US-Baht currency; but later on increasing tax revenues allowed the country to balance its budget and repay the IMF debt.[9]

1 The second approach is an across-the-board approach involving direct government intervention, which determines the method and distribution of burden that is shared among necessary parties. Using this approach, the necessary solutions are usually applicable 'across the board' to all economic agents in the pre-specified category, regardless of their respective factors. This was present in Chile and Mexico in the 1980s. In the event of collapsing growth rates and surging inflation in Mexico, the 'Baker plan' was implemented in 1982, proposed by the US Treasury secretary Baker. In return for economic reforms, high-debt countries would get new entrance to medium-term new loans, in addition to rolling over or amortization of old loans. New loans had to come from both commercial creditors and the official lending institutions. In June 1983, the 'Paris Club', representing creditor governments, rescheduled Mexico's sovereign debt owed to major creditor countries. However, inflation then skyrocketed and investment fell. In September 1989, the 'Brady Plan' was agreed, legitimizing the concept of debt relief. By now, it was believed that US banks could withstand projected losses on Latin American debt. The Brady Plan forced them to do so. Essentially, the plan was to make debt relief acceptable to bank creditors by also providing a small but secure amount for the initial claim which did not get serviced in the end. So, we see that several forms of debt restructuring were thus applied.[10]
2 The last approach is an intermediate approach which relies on individual dealings and negotiations, and is supported by governmental financial incentives, regulatory reforms and formulation of public entities to invigorate debt restructuring. This was present in Mexico and Indonesia also in the 1990s.

The London Approach

This approach involves a set of non-binding principles released by the Bank of England in the 1970s. The so-called London Approach has impacted the development of government-sponsored guidelines for multi-creditor out-of-court debt restructurings. English banks developed this approach initially as a set of illustrations and guidelines to ease attempts to restructure distressed debts, at the same time maximizing their value. It further grew from the understanding that creditors would probably realize better returns through collective efforts to support a coordinated salvage the distressed corporate entity, instead of compelling it into insolvency. Consecutively, countries facing this problem in the late 1990s turned to this very approach to settle out of court. For instance, in Indonesia, Korea, Malaysia and Thailand, this approach was modified by augmenting the role of government agencies to provide incentives for restructurings.[11] The London Approach is criticized on the issues of management difficulties when it comes to large diversified commercial entities.

The authors are of the opinion that Asset Management Companies (AMCs) have been used to spur the restructuring of corporate debt with a view to maximize asset recovery and support rehabilitation of viable corporate entities and to support the rehabilitation of the banking sector by culling out bad assets and thus allowing banks to focus on their core business. AMCs can also be public, private and hybrid in nature, which has been elaborated as follows:

1 Public AMCs: Government-sponsored AMCs have given varied results; this has largely been due to public and market objectives that are usually at odds with each other. There are concerns related to independence, freedom from political interference and accountability. A suggestion is to include sunset clauses, which are clauses that provide for an automatic repeal of sections of law once a specific date is reached. Public AMCs should be preferred when the size of the debt is too high compared to the capacity of the private sector.
2 Private AMCs: Private AMCs are found to be most effective when the reforming structures are coordinated in such a manner so as to maximize their value. Cases where banks establish their own private AMCs are assessed with caution by regulators because many a times they align their accounts and balance sheets in such a manner that negative issues are covered, which gives a very positive image from the front which is actually false in reality. Understandably, in some cases, funding of large amounts sometimes remains strained.

3 Hybrid AMCs: An intelligent way to combat the aforementioned problems is to combine the structures of both public and private AMCs. They also utilize both public and private resources and expertise. A few examples are the Industrial Revitalization Corporation of Japan and the International Finance Corporation's Distressed Assets Recovery Program, which raised funding and expertise for asset recovery efforts from both public and private sources.[12]

The RBI set up the CDR mechanism in 2001 to facilitate restructuring debts of viable corporates outside the normal process. The Indian mechanism is based on the London Approach, as described earlier.[13] Comprehensive guidelines for both institutional and non-institutional CDR were issued in 2008. Later on, in 2012, master guidelines were issued. CDR guidelines were further issued in May 2013. Reserve Bank's efficient guidelines on restructuring of advances have developed slowly from simple instructions directing the rescheduling of the loans to disaster-affected people in the 1970s to comprehensive guidelines on restructuring of loans to large corporate houses under multiple banking arrangement. India's stance clearly reveals that it believes in an interventionist approach. In the authors' viewpoint, this needs to be looked into, as it includes problems like excessive leveraging and deficient project appraisals for cash-flow analyses. P. Chidambaram, former finance minister, had suggested that the higher capital requirements and asset quality emphasized in the Basel III norms had its origin somewhere in the economic problems faced in advanced economies, which has brought us here today.

Administrative loopholes in the CDR mechanism

Analysis of regulation: justifying CDR as an economic process and the public actors in the CDR mechanism as economic institutions

Typically, as an institute of social welfare the intentions of the CDR are well placed. To ensure timely and transparent mechanism for restructuring of the corporate debts and for the benefit of all stakeholders, such steps are indispensable.[14] In particular, the aim is to preserve those viable corporates that are affected by some internal and external factors so as to minimize the losses to the creditors and other stakeholders through a systematic restructuring programme. However, as with any other welfare-oriented institution, the CDR mechanism suffers from inefficiencies due to involvement of governmental red tape and misuse by stakeholders who hold sufficient leverage to use this red tape to their advantage.

One aspect is that the entities involved in advising recasts are nationalized banks, such as the State Bank of India. The CDR Empowered Group (EG) is entrusted with the task of considering whether a company's debt restructuring is prima facie feasible and the potential viability of the concerned enterprise in terms of the policies and guidelines evolved by the Standing Forum.[15] It is however submitted that there is a high amount of subjectivity involved in taking this decision. These are certain broadly spelt-out illustrative parameters such as debt service coverage ratio, break-even point (operating and cash), return on capital employed, internal rate of return, cost of capital, loan life ratio and extent of sacrifice. The EG examines the enterprise's viability and rehabilitation potential to approve the restructuring package under question. Such examination takes place within a time frame of 90 days or a maximum of 180 days within reference.[16] The EG decides on the acceptable viability benchmark levels on these illustrative parameters, which are applied on a case-to-case basis depending on the merits of each case. There have been many reports of debts being restructured for those entities that do not have the required assets to back these loans. In 2012, concerns regarding impairment in asset quality of Indian banks came forth.[17] Until the global financial meltdown of 2008, many banks rapidly expanded their loans backed by high economic growth of the pre-2008 period. The situation, however, has worsened in the past two years as a sharp economic slowdown and high interest rates led to many ambitious businesses defaulting on their borrowings.[18] Gross non-performing assets (NPAs) of domestic banks scaled to 4.2% of total lending by the end of September 2013 from 3.6% six months before.[19] The largest chunk of the bad debts is held by state-run banks, which accounts for two-thirds of loans, and 80% of the bad assets. On 5 March 2014, the former finance minister P. Chidambaram reviewed the performance of state-run banks and said that controlling bad loans was their biggest challenge.[20]

Moreover, only the consent of 75% of creditors (by value) and 60% (by number) is required for a restructuring to take place. Also no specification is provided regarding giving of reason for acceptance of such restructuring.

Rules versus standards

Indeed, the questions arise as to why there is such a sharp rise in the NPAs. More specifically, questions arise as to why the rise is so sharp in state-run banks. It is submitted that the problem is not just with the functioning of the banks but the policy in place which leaves too much subjectivity, and the behaviour of the banks to unsteady borrowers is only a reflection of the policy and the existence of high levels of graft at every stage.

To substantiate this, the author relies on an essay by Eric Posner,[21] who writes that

> when the legislature enacts a rule, it specifies in advance the particulars of some action, and whether that action will be penalized. When the legislature enacts a standard, it delegates to a court the authority to determine whether an action, after being committed, will be penalized. Rules state that you may not do A, B & C; a standard typically says that you may not behave 'unreasonably', or 'negligently' or 'unconscionably' leaving it to the concerned authority to determine whether an action meets these criteria.[22]

It is evident that the process of debt restructuring in India is a standard, and not a rule, as there is neither a legislative mandate nor a set of fixed criteria for approving debt restructuring.[23] Eric Posner, emphasizing on the rule of law, writes that due to the wide discretionary space available for enforcing of standards and stigma as the reason for compliance, they are over-complied with, but in practice are hardly enforced strictly, thus at times overriding the rule of law and promoting inefficiencies. This is precisely what is happening in the case of CDR where there is on paper overcompliance of standards, but enforceability, as is evidenced, is constantly declining.

Theories of inefficiencies in bureaucratic set-ups

Economics provides for sources of inefficiency in the government bureaucracy. This gives some answers with regard to the enforcement aspect and the lack thereof in the CDR mechanism.[24]

Theory of undersupply

The premise of this theory is that insufficient incentives allow the chief officers to spend undue time pursuing their own private interests and neglecting the tasks assigned to them. For example, if an officer's prestige increases with the number of subordinates he or she has, the chief officer is likely to maximize number of subordinates and engage in exhibition of 'discretionary behaviour', thus resulting into overstaffing.

Theory of oversupply

According to this theory, the chief officer seeks to maximize the budget for his or her department or subunit. This is possible because of the fact that the legislative bodies may sometimes lack information about the conditions of supply. This misuse by the department of the willingness to pay higher than the optimal efficiency level results in an inefficient output in the form of an inflated budget. This is atypical in many state-run units. Another phenomenon is incremental budgeting, which is also popular. This means that the funding agency and the delegates therein are fully aware of the proposal of inflated budgets. However, the departments succeed due to the fact that delegates need to handle a large number of claims, so that they are not able to check each claim in detail. Given their limited capacity, they prefer to use rules of thumb. It is to be noted that this phenomenon of incremental budgeting is witnessed in the case of banks which have been reported to go lax on project appraisals.[25]

Procedural failures

Services provided by bureaucrats are typically administered on a first-come, first-served basis. Where the number of clients in a queue increases more rapidly than the number of slots available to deal with them, demand for the service at hand is controlled by rationing by waiting. This is one phenomenon witness in the licenses issued for the 2G spectrum, which ultimately came under a lot of heat due to inefficiency in their allotments.

Corruption

A very important observation is that bribery frequently causes more bribery. It is also observed that it is more prevalent where valuable information has not yet been disclosed by an authority. Bribery inordinately leads to market imperfections. Another reason of festering of corruption is low enforcement, which, as mentioned earlier, is more prevalent when standards are the governing tool rather than a certain rule. Leading to an unfettered and deliberate exercise of power for illegal purpose becomes less costly and hence more prevalent.

Information asymmetry

The problem of the pervasiveness of information problems in the economy makes it impossible for government to make informed policy judgements.[26] The strength of the theory of asymmetric information is that it can explain both the failure of legal norms to effectuate the intended results and the reason for initial misspecification. Public interest view on the other hand signifies that both the legislative and executive branches consider the improvement of general welfare in both the design and implementation of legal norms. Therefore, they will follow advice by impartial experts on how to meet the standards of Pareto optimality, where private activities fail to accomplish this task. Note that performance of a public interest on behalf of legislators and the executive branch possibly entails a correction of subjectively driven individual actions. It is for this reason that the public interest is associated with paternalism. While the intentions of paternalism may be well placed, it does not always translate into Pareto optimality. To illustrate, legal norms can be the outcome of successful lobbying or rent seeking, thus privileging effective interest groups over the less organized citizenry.[27]

It is submitted that this is the exact state of affairs in India in regard to CDR. Recent measures include constitution of independent oversight committees that will vet the CDR applications.[28] This committee will consist of an expert from the legal field, investigative agencies and a finance professional to make sure that there will not be any scope for allegations. It intends to have no government representative or any serving banker. This is no doubt a refreshing step in the wake of recent overlending witnessed by banks; however, it does not absolve the mechanism of the evils of lobbying or rent seeking that is prevalent presently. Going to the CDR committee will be non-mandatory for a bank and the committee will act as a purely advisory body, helping the bank vet a particular case.[29] This is a paternalistic measure, which, as substantiated earlier, may be well intentioned but does not do much in achieving optimal Pareto efficiency since the process could be highly influenced by successful lobbying and rent seeking.

Rent seeking

An average of a three-pronged survey conducted by *The Economist* revealed that the gains from rent seeking over the past decade peaked at about $80 billion. That is equivalent of 7% of the stock market's value today. Calculated assumption of the politicians' and officials' average cut at 5% to 15% revealed that total bribes would amount to $4 billion to $12 billion.[30]

The Austrian solution

The Austrian benchmark for normative analysis is the facilitation of the market process. 'The efficiency of the economic system is judged by the extent to which it encourages individuals to pursue their own goals efficiently.'[31]

The typical starting point for a theory of the functions of the state is found in the insight that market mechanisms fail as a means of coordination. However, the multiplicity of roles played by various actors in the markets in the present day validates the principle of subsidiarity.[32] This principle states that problem solving should be left to the smallest subunit of society which is best capable of managing the issue at hand (which could be a family, a private club or a community, but at times ought to be the EU Council in Brussels). Thus, the theory of market failure alone cannot serve as an exhaustive justification for the intervention by the state, especially in the wake of huge inefficiency created in the form of high NPAs, losses due to graft, corruption and rent seeking and most of all a gnawing absence of a solution to combat these serious issues.

As has been pointed out, creation of more supervisory bodies on any functionality of the CDR mechanism will not lead to desired results as long as the body continues to be advisory and most of all not entirely free from governmental elements. However, such a situation in the present structure of the CDR mechanism is impossible because the committees that will be appointed to supervise the banks while reviewing debt restructurings will constitute experts from various fields, but not independently so. It is likely that they represent successful lobbies of either banks or huge corporates that want to continue drawing benefits from the CDR pile. The conflict between private interests and public interests is inevitable and bound to creep in later if not so from the beginning.

The Market Process Approach. As F.A. Hayek very famously put,

> The economic problem of society is . . . not merely a problem of how to allocate 'given' resources – if 'given' is taken to mean given to a single mind which deliberately solves the problem set by these 'data'. It is rather a problem of how to secure the best use of resources known to any of the members of society, for ends whose relative importance only these individuals know. Or, to put it briefly, it is a problem of the utilization of knowledge which is not given to anyone in its totality.[33]

This is the main criticism against governmental intervention and favourable to the market process, which promotes individual autonomy and economic freedom.

> The unavoidable imperfection of man's knowledge and the consequent need for a process by which knowledge is constantly communicated and acquired is . . . an essential part of the phenomena with which we have to deal. . . . To assume all the knowledge to be given to a single mind in the same manner in which we assume it to be given to us as the explaining economists is to assume the problem away and to disregard everything that is important and significant in the real world.[34]

Austrian economists continue to advocate that the market process is the best way to address these problems of information asymmetry and the conflicts that may arise due to the conflict of interests between public and private interests. Theories have developed which explain that the price system can be thought of as a sort of information pooling and processing device – a device for somehow overcoming the complexity implied by dispersed information. Prices act as information signals between people.[35] After providing this background, the next section attempts to put this idea into practice for the purpose of the CDR mechanism that is currently in place in India.

Corporate debt restructuring – an Austrian solution for India, government intervention – can it be reduced?

It is surprising that the doctrines of Austrian economics that are quite prevalent in the Western economic literature do not feature so prominently in the Asian subcontinent. In fact, several times, they are termed as being merely abstractions and academically sound but not practicable. However, it is to be brought to note that the same ideas find sound resonance in the economic foundations of the policies in the United States;[36] Posner in an article finds that societies committed to individual autonomy and economic freedom are also ones with a high commitment for the rule of law.[37]

After the repeated highlighting throughout the write-up of the present follies in the CDR mechanism in India, the alternative given in the following paragraphs may seem too simplistic. However, it is this simplicity which may be the reason of its efficient functioning. Of course, the authors plead the absence of technical knowledge of the financial intricacies; however, this model will definitely be more economically sustainable and legally executable.

The alternative mechanism is in total absence of centralized institutions. A case-by-case, market-based approach has been used in which private sector debtors and creditors are generally left to determine the nature, scope and terms of the burden sharing on a case-by-case basis and principally relying on market solutions.[38] Such an approach was adopted in Hungary and Poland in the 1990s, Korea, Malaysia and Thailand in the late 1990s.

A good start would be by enactment of a legislation which takes corporate debt restructuring out of the hands of state-run banks and encourages private money lenders to engage in debt restructuring as a trade. The legislation would be a rule and not a standard specifying the factors which, if present, must allow debt restructuring, but such a list will not be exhaustive and would leave options for other restructurings between parties. In the case of non-compliance, strong judicial sanctions can be imposed.

While this approach is essentially market-oriented, the government would still have an important role through implementing legal reforms to encourage timely market-driven restructuring.[39] And individual cases of restructurings can be helped out directly by the government by providing gratuitous payments, if so desired. The other important change would be to allow corporate entities to declare themselves bankrupt in order to seek the financial options available in the market. The lender can then decide, based on financial considerations, whether he or she wants to restructure the debt. In the event that he or she decides *not* to restructure the debt, he or she must specify the reasons. Also, establishment of credit rating agencies that will rate every entities' financial assets will enable private lenders to take the decision regarding restructuring the debt. Such a practice is prevalent in Hong Kong,[40] where most restructurings take place by way of informal workouts, compositions and arrangements essentially made by agreement of the parties concerned.[41]

Conclusion

As *The Economist* observes, in its 15 March 2014 issue,[42] 'Corruption produces bad decisions; concern over corruption produces indecision.' It reports that loans to industries with graft problems have infected the largely state-run banking system; at least a tenth of its loans are sour. A big problem in India is that these loans are being carried on in the books of nationalized financial institutions; other loans are being carried by institutions that are being recapitalized by the government.[43] It is a submission that the CDR mechanism, howsoever timely or transparent it may be (which is not the case as has been pointed out several times before in this chapter), deigns to restructure debts of entities facing problems and with a lower threshold of caution than should be used.[44] And this bailing out is done by nationalized banks whose ultimate source of funds is the citizenry of India. It is thus a case of redistributive approach facilitated by government intervention through either financial institutions or various standards in place.

However, economists have been known to advocate *against* such a redistributive approach to private law. This is for four main reasons. One is that redistribution by private legal rights relies on crude averages. In the present case, it would mean the presumption that the nationalized banks of the country are capable enough to efficiently redistribute such amounts as required for restructuring of these entities which may be financially troubled. This presumption is not evidenced by any exact data. Second, the distributive effects of reshuffling private rights are hard to predict. Translated into the CDR situation, this means that it is very difficult to determine the number of entities that could have been efficiently restructured and that have, in fact, been given the benefit of the CDR mechanism. Third, the transaction costs of redistribution through private legal rights are typically high. And fourth, redistribution by private law distorts the economy, that is a responsible entity with certain financial stability is dis-incentivized to continue as such, because ultimately an entity with not sufficient credentials for continuing operation is bailed out from the amounts put as deposits in nationalized banks with insufficient guarantee of returns. It is thus the authors' view that debt restructuring, as it stands today, can be turned into an efficient financial tool using the alternative model that has been suggested. If adopted, it would go a long way in absolving the mechanism of the leakages and the graft, features that are so inherent in public institutions.

Notes

1 Reserve Bank of India, 'Corporate Debt Restructuring', accessed 11 September 2014, http://www.rbi.org.in/scripts/NotificationUser.aspx?Id=440&Mode=0.
2 Ibid., 2: 'Objective'.
3 Ibid., 2: 'Objective'.
4 Ibid., 3: 'Structure'.
5 Ibid., 4.2: 'Legal Basis'.
6 Ibid., 4.3: 'Stand-Still Clause'.
7 Reserve Bank of India, 'Revised Guidelines on Corporate Debt Restructuring (CDR) Mechanism', accessed 8 November 2014, http://www.rbi.org.in/upload/notification/pdfs/67158.pdf.
8 Corporate Debt Restructuring Mechanism, 'Corporate Debt Restructuring Mechanism', accessed 18 August 2014, http://www.cdrindia.org/empgroup.htm.
9 George G. Kaufman, Thomas H. Krueger and William C. Hunter, *The Asian Financial Crisis: Origins, Implications and Solutions* (Springer, 1999).
10 Sweder Van Wijnbergen, 'Mexico and the Brady Plan', *Economic Policy* 6 (1991): 12.
11 Gerald E. Meverman, 'The London Approach and Corporate Debt Restructuring in East Asia'. World Bank, accessed 11 September 2014, http://www1.worldbank.org/finance/assets/images/DL_2_3_chapter10.pdf.
12 Nomura Research Institute Ltd, 'Japan's Asset Management Business 2012/2013', accessed 11 September 2014, http://www.nri.com/global/opinion/jamb/JAMB2012.pdf.
13 Reserve Bank of India, 'Corporate Debt Restructuring – Issues and Way Forward (Address by Dr. K. C. Chakrabarty, Deputy Governor, Reserve Bank of India at the Corporate Debt Restructuring Conference 2012)', accessed 11 September 2014, http://rbi.org.in/scripts/BS_SpeechesView.aspx?Id=716.
14 Ibid.
15 'CDR Empowered Group, Corporate Debt Restructuring Mechanism', accessed 11 September 2014, http://www.cdrindia.org/empgroup.htm.
16 Ibid.
17 Shashidhar M. Lokare, 'Re-Emerging Stress in the Asset Quality of Indian Banks: Macro-Financial Linkages', Reserve Bank of India, Press Release Dated 7 February 2014, accessed 20 March 2014, http://rbi.org.in/scripts/PublicationsView.aspx?id=15720.
18 Anand Adhikari, 'Gathering Storm', *Business Today* (30 March 2014).
19 Reserve Bank of India, 'Advisory Panel on Financial Stability Assessment and Stress Testing – Volume III', 23 March 2009, accessed 20 March 2014, http://www.rbi.org.in/Scripts/PublicationReportDetails.aspx?UrlPage=&ID=545.

20 Manoj Kumar, 'State Banks Face Bad Loans as Biggest Challenge: Chidambaram', *Reuters*, 5 March 2014, accessed 11 September 2014, http://in.reuters.com/article/2014/03/05/india-banks-loans-idINDEEA2406X20140305.
21 Eric A. Posner, 'Standards, Rules and Social Norms', *Harvard Journal of Law and Public Policy* 21 (1997): 101–117.
22 Ibid.
23 Reserve Bank of India, 'Corporate Debt Restructuring'.
24 Wolfgang Weigel, 'The Law and Economics of Public Sector', in *Economics of the Law: A Primer* (London and New York: Routledge Taylor & Francis Group): 144–145.
25 Press Trust of India, 'Corporate Debt Restructuring Biased towards Privileged Customers: Chakrabarty', *The Hindu Business Line* (11 August 2012), accessed 11 September 2014, http://www.thehindubusinessline.com/industry-and-economy/banking/corporate-debt-restructuring-biased-towards-privileged-customers-chakrabarty/article3754180.ece.
26 Wolfgang Weigel, 'The Private Interest Perspective', In *Economics of the Law: A Primer* (London & New York: Routledge Taylor & Francis Group): 301.
27 Ibid., 118.
28 Press Trust of India, 'Finance Ministry Asks Banks to Have Independent Corporate Debt Restructuring Oversight Panel', *NDTV Profit News* (7 June 2013), accessed 20 March 2104, http://profit.ndtv.com/news/industries/article-finance-ministry-asks-banks-to-have-independent-corporate-debt-restructuring-oversight-panel-323105.
29 Ibid.
30 'A Bad Boom', *The Economist* (15 March 2014), accessed 20 March 2014, http://www.economist.com/news/briefing/21598967-graft-india-damaging-economy-country-needs-get-serious-about-dealing-it.
31 Weigel, 'The Private Interest Perspective': 301.
32 Treaty of Rome, Article V (a); Roman Catholic Encyclica Quadragesimo Anno of 1931.
33 Friedrich Hayek, 'The Price System as a Mechanics for Using Knowledge', *American Economic Review* 35 (4) (1945): 519–530.
34 Ibid., 91.
35 Peter Lewin, 'Efficiency of the Market Process: An Evaluation of Three Recent Austrian Contributions', December 1995, accessed 20 March 2014, http://www.utdallas.edu/~plewin/effic.pdf.
36 Information Clearing House, 'The National Security Strategy of the United States of America', accessed 11 September 2014, http://www.informationclearinghouse.info/article2320.htm.
37 Posner, 'Standards, Rules and Social Norms'.
38 Thomas Laryea, *Approaches to Corporate Debt Restructuring in the Wake of Financial Crisis*, IMF Position Paper, accessed 20 March 2014, http://www.imf.org/external/pubs/ft/spn/2010/spn1002.pdf.
39 Ibid.
40 Chwee Huat Tan, *Financial Source Book for the South East Asia and Hong Kong* (Singapore: Singapore University Press, 2000): 184.

41 Norton Rose Fullbright, 'Asia Restructuring and Insolvency Briefing: Hong Kong', accessed 20 March 2014, http://www.nortonrosefulbright.com/knowledge/publications/18774/asia-restructuring-and-insolvency-briefing-hong-kong.
42 Weigel, 'The Law and Economics of Public Sector': 144–145.
43 Charles Adams and Michael Pomerleano, eds., *Managing Financial & Corporate Distress: Lessons from Asia* (Washington, DC: Brookings Institution Press, 2000).
44 Reserve Bank of India, 'Corporate Debt Restructuring'.

Chapter 8

Economic analysis of the dispute resolution mechanism under the Companies Act, 2013

Amrita Mohan

Background note

The economic analysis of corporate law dates back to the collaboration between a law professor and an economist: Berle and Means.[1] They identified the separation of ownership and control, with public corporations owned by a dispersed group of shareholders, none of whom owned enough shares to have the incentive to rigorously monitor managerial behaviour.[2] From agency problems, Ronald Coase[3] developed the theory of a firm, which explains the transactions within firms and between firms. Subsequently, Oliver Williamson filled in the gaps left by Coase,[4] by focusing on asset specificity. Jensen and Meckling's[5] contribution must be acknowledged, as they coined the idea of firm as a nexus of contracts.

In India for several decades the most prominent legislation that governed companies was the Companies Act of 1956. However, the act required several changes, and the introduction of the Companies Act, 2013, has completely changed the face of corporate law. Two major highlights in this regard are the establishment of the National Company Law Tribunal and the introduction of class action suits as a tool for creditors and shareholders to pin the companies' liability. The Companies (Second Amendment) Act, 2002, provides for the setting up of a National Company Law Tribunal (NCLT) and Appellate Tribunal (NCLAT) to replace the existing Company Law Board and Board for Industrial and Financial Reconstruction set up under the Sick Industrial Companies Act, 1985.[6] However, the Companies Act, 2013, contains provisions for the establishment and functioning of the NCLT. The setting up of NCLT was based on the recommendations of the Justice

Eradi Committee on Law Relating to Insolvency and Winding Up of Companies.[7] The committee examined not only the Companies Act, 1956, but also the other pertinent laws having a bearing on the subject, such as Sick Industrial Companies (Special Provisions) Act, 1985, Recovery of Debts Due to Banks and Financial Institutions Act, 1993 and the suggestions of the United Nations and International Monetary Fund Report – 'Orderly and Effective Insolvency Procedures – Key Issues'.[8] A class action is a lawsuit where a person sues a group of people, a group of people sues another group of people or a group of people sues a person. It is a procedural device enabling one or more plaintiffs to file and prosecute litigation on behalf of a larger group or class, wherein such class has common rights and grievances. This concept has been a prevalent legal right in most jurisdictions like the United States and the United Kingdom; however, in India it has been statutory recognition through the Companies Act, 2013. Section 245(1) of the Companies Act, 2013, permits the members, depositors or any class of them to proceed with a class action suit if they are of the opinion that the management or affairs of the company are being conducted in a manner that is pre-judicial to the interests of the company or its members or depositors. Class action suits, a highly commendable governance measure, are decisive to maintaining stability in the sector.

In this chapter, the author has discussed only from the victim's point of view and has not dealt with the incentives of the lawyer to handle class action suits. Further, the author has tried to evaluate the efficiency solely on established economics tools without delving too much into the constitutional controversies of the subject matter. The first part of the chapter deals with the economic analysis of the tribunal by employing microeconomic tools to evaluate its projected efficiency. The aim of this research is to rationalize the efficiency of the newly introduced provisions to evaluate if they lubricate the system or cause further hurdles. Presently, company law disputes are adjudicated through several forums like the Company Law Board, high courts and the Supreme Court. The establishment of a single tribunal to adjudicate all company law disputes holds the key to shaping the corporate sector growth in India. The latter part of the chapter deals with the idea of class action suits evaluated through the lens of property rights in economics.

Establishment of the NCLT: does it yield efficient outcomes?

The concept of substance-specific procedures evolved from the Delaware model of corporate law. It brought about the establishment of specialized tribunals to resolve corporate governance disputes.[9] The Delaware model is revered because it stands as a reason for the high attraction value of Delaware as a jurisdiction to invest in.[10] Post the enormous success of this model, specialized tribunals for adjudicating business-related disputes came into being. This concept has travelled far and wide across continents to finally reach India. Presently, disputes in company matters are divided between the High Court (HC) and the Company Law Board (CLB). Disputes relating to reduction of capital, mergers and acquisitions and amalgamation and winding up were with the HC, and the power of rectification of register, complaints regarding refusal to transfer/transmit securities, rectification of register of members and complaints of oppression and mismanagement were handled by the CLB. The NCLT has the powers of the CLB and High Court, and an appeal from an order of the tribunal has to be filed with the Supreme Court.[11] This consolidation would considerably reduce the litigation duration, reduce jurisdictional disputes among various adjudicatory bodies and provide a one-stop solution to all corporate disputes. Disputes relating to it have been legally transplanted into the New Companies Act, 2013, which proposes to establish a separate tribunal called the National Company Law Tribunal, whose sole jurisdiction is to resolve all disputes relating to company law. The debate in India has largely centred on the constitutional validity of such tribunals.[12] This chapter also seeks to analyse the economic efficiency of such tribunals given the current legal scenario in India.

Considering the efficiency argument

The traditional legal systems have always emphasized on accuracy over cost benefits. The detailed layout of procedure in courts aims to target solely on the accuracy, while the cost of time delays is not accounted for.[13] In their defence, the courts have upheld the principles of fair and free trial to all at any cost nevertheless. This accuracy is assumed to be fundamental in the adjudication systems through its clear procedural and substantive rules.[14] Norms of justice may dictate that these costs are unavoidable, while an economic analysis does not yield accurate results if all costs are not weighed upon while quantifying the benefits. The aim of an adjudicatory system through an economic analysis lens should be to seek and achieve optimum cost–benefit ratios by simplifying the procedure and establishing clear-cut rights and duties, thereby reducing social costs. There exists a dichotomy at some level between the goals of justice at any cost and economic cost–benefit analysis.

The Indian judicial system is overburdened with severe backlog of cases. As of July 2009, 53,000 cases are pending with the Supreme Court, 40 lakh with high courts and 2.7 crore with lower courts. This is an increase of 139% for the Supreme Court, 46% for high courts and 32% for lower courts from their pendency numbers in January 2000.[15] The primary reasons stated for such delay are high vacancy and poor judges-to-population ratios. Without enough courtrooms, the current backlog of cases simply cannot be accommodated. One way to mitigate this is to create additional courts. The problem then arises as to the appointment of additional judges for these courts. With the lackadaisical attitude of the government in filling up vacancies[16] and low supply of judges in the market,[17] additional courts would only add on to the problem. In such a scenario, specialized tribunals seem to address the situation. There would be no need to appoint new judges per se. These tribunals would have experts of their respective field analysing the dispute at hand along with judicial members to provide the legal reasoning. The Companies Act, 2013, postulates a good mix of judicial and technical members to effectively and efficiently adjudicate the disputes.[18]

Efficiency argument proposes that, to achieve efficient outcomes, a same level of output must be produced at a lower cost or a higher output must be generated with the same cost inputs.[19] Establishment of a singular tribunal as opposed to appointing more judges would produce higher yields with the same or lesser cost of input. The reason is that judges with specialized knowledge about the sector would dispose the cases faster as opposed to those who do not have specialized knowledge. Justice Malimath Report,[20] among others, has suggested that specialized tribunal must be established to deal with some matters pertaining to tax, services and labour, separately justifying it on the grounds that specialization provides consistency, certainty and speedy and quality judgements.[21] The Draft NCLT Rules provide for more than 16 benches within the tribunal, with specialized technical members as well as judicial members, keeping in mind speedy justice delivery mechanism and accuracy. These draft rules have not been notified yet, hence keeping the establishment of the tribunal in abeyance.

Pareto efficiency is the allocation of resources efficiently so as to make at least one person better off without causing detriment to another. The opposers to the establishment of NCLT argue that the detriment would be to the independence of the judiciary if non-judicial members are allowed to perform judicial tasks. Another opposition is that the separation of powers forms the basic structure of the Indian Constitution, which would be violated if members of the executive took over judicial posts. Here Pareto efficiency would be reached as the act envisages a tribunal filled with judicial members, a president who would be a retired high court or Supreme Court judge along with technical members. A more efficacious output is reached with no actual harm to the independence of the judiciary as the role of these technical members is not to usurp the powers of judiciary but to supplement them with their specialized knowledge. This is juxtaposed with the present system where the CLB is short of staff for several years and has at least 2,500 pending cases related to various aspects of company law.[22] Further, the Supreme Court in *R. Gandhi v. Madras Bar Association*[23] has clarified that it cannot be assumed that constitution of tribunals and transferring judicial functions are per se breach Rule of Law, Independence of Judiciary and Separation of Powers, as the constitution contemplates judicial power being exercised by both courts and tribunals.[24] While the apex court laid down certain amendments and caveat for the establishment of the NCLT and NCLAT, the question of violation of doctrine of separation of power was answered in negative. Therefore, efficient outcome of speedy and accurate judgement is attained with no actual harm done.

Expertise in complex areas of law

In certain subject areas, even the most competently contested case may be poorly suited for a generalized court. Complex tax, patent, competition law and highly regulated technical areas strain the capacity of the wisest of the wise judge unless he or she has spent a career immersed in that field. These complex laws are a reflection of the complex nature of today's society; if there is delay, uncertainty or inconsistency, it imposes real social costs. It is asserted that the costs of educating these generalized judges are a wasteful allocation of resources. This can be seen in the light of the various advantages of having specialization in dispute resolution:[25]

1 Experienced judges would not need to be educated about how a particular dispute fits into the broader corpus of law.
2 Specialist judges could resolve questions faster, and perhaps more 'correctly', without having to learn the relevant law, or requiring counsel to teach them.
3 Moreover, specialist judges could devote more time to individual matters than is now possible, since they would have smaller dockets, unencumbered by other business, such as criminal cases, which must take priority.
4 Limiting certain kinds of litigation to a single specialized tribunal would assure uniformity and predictability in the law and thus allow lawyers to settle more disputes without resort to the courts at all. Normative Coase is strengthened as a result of higher private settlement.

The opponents argue that separation of powers would be violated if the executive has powers in appointment, tenure and removal of judges and technical members. The Supreme Court while upholding the constitutionality of the NCLT and NCLAT[26] instructed the legislative to correct provisions, which give excessive powers to the executive in the matters of the tribunal. The Supreme Court clarified that an assumption that those members of the executive with great experience in the corporate sector would automatically be temperamental and impartial judicial administrators is misplaced. Hence, the court clarified that there must always be judicial members in the tribunal, whereas the presence of technical members can be obviated if the matter does not require any technical aspects to be adjudicated. The court further went on to state that even though the matter is shifted from the courts to tribunals, on the ground of pendency and delay in courts, and the jurisdiction so transferred does not involve any technical aspects requiring the assistance of experts, the tribunals should normally have only judicial members.[27]

Cost–benefit analysis of lengthy litigations

The rationale for the plaintiff spending on litigation even where net litigation costs are high is to attempt a gainful settlement that is over and above the cost incurred. The defendant will spend so long as this lowers his or her expected total outlays. The effects of each litigant's expenditures will generally depend on what the other does and the two will often be spending to rebut one another.[28] Delay in adjudicating disputes imposes a cost on the litigating party as well as the state. First, utility analysis would suggest that there is a disutility associated with a remedy over time.[29] Timely remedy is crucial in installing faith among the public in the judiciary. Second, the enormous amount of time spent on every case by the courts would mean that several other pressing cases would not even be brought to court. Hence, the opportunity cost of hearing every case is higher than the expected output. Opportunity cost is the highest-valued alternative foregone in the pursuit of an activity. The infamous example of guns versus butter is analysed here.

Figure 8.1 – With every additional unit of butter sought to be produced, the units of guns forgone increase. This works under the

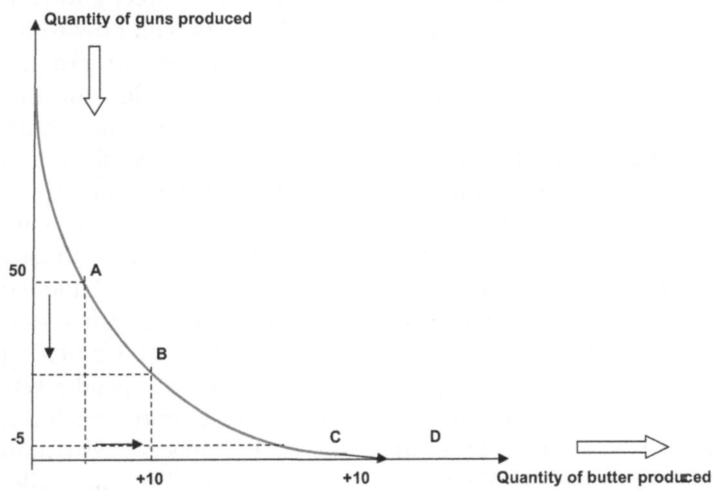

Figure 8.1 Cost–benefit analysis of guns versus butter

Source: Isan Gunawan, 'Academic Investigation: Digital Divide in Indonesia and How It Affects Its Production Possibility Frontier', http://blogs.swa-jkt.com/swa/10301/2012l0/29/academic-investigation-digital-divide-in-indonesia-and-how-it-affect-its-production-possibility-frontier/.

assumption that there are limited resources available, which could be used for the production of either guns or butter. For an addition of +10 units of butter, –50 units of guns are forgone. This continues to happen until point D, where only one commodity, that is butter, can be produced with no corresponding units of butter. This is a direct result of the law of increasing opportunity cost.

Similarly, the cost of adjudicating a company law matter happens at the cost of hearing other cases. With given supply of judges, only select cases reach the courts for adjudication. Generally, judges are generalists and not specialists in corporate and company matters. Hence, additional time is required for them to understand the issues with the help of various experts and evidences. The rationale of the new tribunal is to bring in people who have specialized knowledge in the field of company and corporate matters. This would automatically speed up the dispute resolution because of efficiencies of specialization of work. The pressure of more numerous and complex lawsuits cannot be solved simply by adding more judges, however; for even if the necessary resources could be found, uniformity is difficult to maintain as more judges make more decisions creating conflicts for higher courts to resolve.[30] The fact that judicial resources are scarce, and cannot be expanded infinitely, presents a familiar problem: how to make the best use of a limited commodity. Economic theory provides a typical answer: division of labour through specialization of the court system. Yet conventional wisdom resists this answer, arguing that specialized courts would produce inferior results at a cost unacceptable to our system of justice. Rather than increasing the judges-to-population ratio for corporate matters, these matters could be transferred to specialized tribunals, thereby efficiently allocating resources. There is a high opportunity cost of allocating resources as they could be allocated among several other sectors such as defence, health and education. Suppose 100 crore is the budget of Country X in a given year; it could either spend 30 crore on the judiciary or build schools all over the country. Such a cost can also be avoided by establishing such a specialized tribunal. The latter schemes might suffer due to increased resource allocation towards recruiting judges who may or may not be adept in resolving technical company law matters.

The NCLT Draft Rules and Section 422 of the New Companies Act, 2013, state that every application or petition presented before the tribunal and every appeal filed before the Appellate Tribunal shall be disposed of expeditiously and every endeavour shall be made to dispose of within three months from the date of presentation or filing. The Tribunal or Appellate Tribunal shall record the reasons for not disposing the application or petition or appeal within this period. The president or chairperson may extend the period for not exceeding 90 days. Clear deadlines pin responsibility and put incentives in place to dispose the cases without unreasonable delay. Members of the tribunal would be disincentivized to delay the process as they would be held accountable to higher authorities if reasons are found to be insubstantial.

Normative Coase and normative Hobbes

Private exchange will ordinarily occur among rational people when the net benefit is positive. The Coase Theorem suggests that the law can encourage bargaining by lowering transaction costs. Lowering transaction costs thus 'lubricates' bargaining. Normative Coase Theorem states that one must structure the law so as to remove the impediments to private agreements. While Coase Theorem has a positive connotation towards achieving private agreements, the Normative Coase Theorem has a negative connotation. The Coase Theorem states that where there is a conflict of property rights, the involved parties can bargain or negotiate terms that are more beneficial to both parties than the outcome of any assigned property rights. Normative Coase is a derivative of this umbrella concept. Most company law disputes arise either between the company and its shareholders or between the company and its creditors. The function of the laws must be to lower transaction costs by allocating rights and duties, respectively. For example, under the Companies Act of 1956, the fiduciary duties of the directors and the independent directors were not clearly spelled out. The New Act, however, clearly defines the rights and duties of the directors. The 1956 Act places the directors in the fiduciary position with regard to the companies' affairs. The 2013 Act, Section 166, stipulates a list of duties of directors and has in a sense codified the common law concept of fiduciary duties. This lubricates private exchange by lowering transaction costs. When conflicts arise during negotiations, clearly defined rights and duties help in identifying the claims and positions of the parties. This concept will not be detailed by delving into, as it is beyond the scope of the chapter. However, the author needs to highlight this crucial aspect the new act brought about to establish how the proposed tribunal is a mixture of both normative Hobbes and Coase Theorems.

While normative Hobbes Theorem states that one must structure the law so as to minimize the harm caused by failures in private agreements.[31] The costs of bargaining with a vast number of dispersed shareholders create a lot of information asymmetry, thereby increasing transaction costs. The function of law must be to provide for alternative smoothening of the litigating process to reduce the harm caused by failure of bargaining. One notable contribution is a mediation and conciliation panel for mediation between the parties during the pendency of any proceedings.[32] The parties may approach the tribunal, and a panel of experts would be appointed in furtherance or the tribunal may take suo moto action. This increases the prospects of a private agreement under the shadow of law. This flexibility cannot be attained with the same effect when courts are adjudicating. The courts do refer the parties to mediation; however, this is usually prevalent only in family matters.

Successful specialized tribunals have evolved to expedite decisions when delay is especially costly and where major policy choices are not required. While most cases litigated are payment claims to shareholders and its creditors, a speedy settlement would add to the utility of the remedy. With prolonged delay, the value of money falls in most cases. Though the court may award interest in cases of delay, the creditor or shareholder severely loses out in terms of value of money.

Introduction of the idea of class action suits under the new act

Efficiency of class action suits

The class action is a device by which parties too numerous to be brought before the court individually may nevertheless be bound by a proceeding in which their interests are represented through the efforts of one of the named parties.[33] These suits provide an effective mechanism for bringing claims to judgement where the cost of doing so by means of individual suits would be prohibitive, in that the litigation expenses would far exceed the value of whatever damages could be recovered.[34]

Class actions are one of the most potent tools available that enable vindication of claims which would otherwise not be litigated.

Litigants assert their rights only in a court of law only when their net benefits are projected to be positive. Small claims are often not litigated because of high costs of litigation. In a world of corporate scams, standardized corporate practice, governance malfunctions and fragmented and dispersed shareholding, there is a high possibility of several individuals to be harmed in identical ways. From an individual's standpoint, the benefits may be minute; however, the aggregate amount would be substantial. No claim is trivial, in social standpoint; class actions address this problem by aggregating individual claims together into a single lawsuit, which can support costs of litigation.

The economic advantages to instituting a class action suit is first economy: deciding a certain issue in a proceeding that binds all concerned with it avoids re-litigation of the same questions in a multitude of suits.[35] The second function of class treatment is that of enforcement of substantive law policies, the very purposes of which may be frustrated by inconsistent adjudication. Moreover, the class action device will tend to promote the fuller enforcement of those policies whenever it allows wrongful conduct to be brought before the court when it would otherwise go un-redressed.[36]

The Companies Act, 2013, introduces the concept of class action suit, which was missing from the erstwhile Companies Act, 1956.[37] The class action suit has become a global occurrence. It allows a large group of people with common grievance to sue or be sued collectively. It acts as a device that allows one or more plaintiffs to file a suit on behalf of a large number of people with similar or common rights and interests. Class action suits not only help in reducing the cost of the litigation by collective action but also save a lot of time of the court. Through class action it is possible to litigate small claims; normally a poor person cannot afford an expensive lawyer against a big corporation, which can do it easily, but in the case of collective claims, aggregate amount may be large enough to appoint a highly efficient lawyer. The class action owes its groundwork to US experience. It is one of the most compelling legal tools available to stakeholders in the United States.[38] In India instead of the term 'class action', the term 'representative suit' has been used. Order 1, rule 8, of the Code of Civil Procedure, 1908, talks about collective suit, where numerous persons have the same interest in one suit.

Satyam scam popularized class action suits in India. Ramalinga Raju, founder of Satyam, confessed to misstating the revenues and accounts, which led to the fall of the company's stock. The fraudulent act involved fabricated interest income, hidden debts, fake invoices and fictitious employees. Economists can only wonder if the shareholders have any incentive at all to monitor the company or that the information asymmetry is manifold. The US shareholders filed a class action suit and claimed $125 million from the company, but due to absence of any class action provision in Indian law at that time, the Indian shareholders were not able to claim any compensation.[39]

Property rights of class action suits

Public and private good

By proposing to place victims as owner of 'property rights' over a specific litigation, whose costs outweigh the benefits, we can construe class action as a scheme that follows an analogous judicial path to that described for property, aggregating the individuals' rights when their exercise on the judicial market is limited by contingencies which make the net benefit of the action negative. Contingencies arise from fragmentation and co-ordination costs, from the small size of individual damages and from asymmetry of information between plaintiff and defendant.

The productive efficiency of a static character concerns the overall production of 'justice', on the demand and supply sides, since on the judicial market both jointly concur to its production.[40] It produces 'judicial economy', which is done through aggregation of small claims on the demand side, which produces economies of scale in litigation that cause individual costs to decrease with increasing number of plaintiffs.[41] On the supply side, there is likewise a reduction in costs if the aggregation permits overall savings in resources compared to multiple individual actions, provided though that the savings afforded by aggregation are not offset by an increase in the number of lawsuits.[42]

There is a second tier to the efficiency argument; class actions integrate different interests to achieve a particular goal. It introduces a set of three incentives to all the interested parties, a profit for the attorney, redressal of harm for the victims and deterrence for the wrongdoer, thereby reducing the social costs. The role of class actions must be to balance these individual interests to integrate with that of the company. For the attorney, the interest is in the nature of a private good, who takes on the role of instituting a collective action which is directed at redressing the harm done to the victims.[43] Through the attorney, the suit is initiated; this acts as an inducement for victims to approach the courts in anticipation of higher net benefits. The potential class recovery is large enough to cover a reasonable attorney's fee. Thus, it becomes profitable for lawyers to specialize in class action litigation, and the lawyers' fee is large enough for them to search out potential class claims and bring suit on behalf of the class. Thus, the existence of the class action device can create a market for private enforcement of the law. This further reinstates access to justice and enhances deterrence. Though the redress is individual, it can be produced only as a club good. Finally, the deterrence effect as a result of transfer of the cost of wrongdoing from the victim to the wrongdoer makes it a public good because of the social benefits of higher deterrence achieved.

Club good

Plaintiffs are organized into a 'class' that translates to a 'club' in economic theory. This means a 'group of individuals who derive mutual benefit from sharing one or more of the following: production costs, attributes of the members, or goods characterised by excludable benefits'.[44] The result is that there is production and consumption of specific goods that that would not otherwise be produced: the club good is an excludable but non-rivalrous public good for the club members. According to this theory, it is congestible, in the sense that an increase in the number of members will at some point negatively affect their benefits.

In such class actions, the club good reinstates access to justice and the resultant redress of the wrong, which is then naturally shared out among the individual members. The compensation is ultimately private, but its collective production is a club good. Collective litigation and damages are non-rivalrous for the victims once the lawsuit has been started, but excludable through certification by the judge.[45] Excludability is crucial; on the one hand, it is required to place proper incentives to club members, thereby eliminating free-rider problem;[46] and on the other hand, excludability distinguishes the judicial function from regulations as the courts decide whether a particular person falls under the aggrieved class. There is an assumption that flows here: there is a failure of regulation, so that any equivalence between regulation and litigation cannot be envisaged without necessarily implying a negative outcome also for the latter.

There are two kinds of clubs: one is opt-in class action, wherein the category of potential victims is partly determined by the injurer, subsequently shaped and refined by the judge who certifies that the said persons could take part in the litigation.[47] Under this kind of action, there is a ceiling on the number of members. It is useful in eliminating congestion, which is a typical problem in clubs. Opt-out provides for a further fine-tuning, which benefits the victim's choices. Each member of the class has a residual right to express his or her will by opting out, thereby exiting the collective litigation. This solution preserves the voluntariness requirement that generally characterizes membership of a club, and would otherwise be of necessity violated.[48]

The effects of class action suits are wide; it permits the adjudication of meritorious claims that would otherwise not be litigated in a given legal system.[49] Legal systems initially recognized class actions as a remedy for tort claims. Even today, jurisdictions around the world employ class action as a juridical tool to protect victims through raised compensation. Many scholars have expressed their concern[50] with extending the scope of class action to financial and securities frauds.[51] Critics have maintained that class action since its inception has had a broader political agenda, extending its scope to areas like civil rights, health protection, consumer protection and environmental questions.[52] The debate now rages between the firms and consumers/shareholders; it has altered the balance of power and helped in effective resource allocation. The legislator's incentives behind implementing class action must be guided by sound economic and policy principles rather than purely politically vested interests.[53]

Therefore, a judgement binds everybody in that particular class; it extinguishes all claims included in the class and not just those of the named parties. This means that every person falling within the class is considered an absent class member and thus included de jure in the lawsuit, unless there is a specific opt-out request, as stated earlier.[54] Clubs can be used as a method to pursue cost-sharing arrangements and produce economies of scale.[55] In India, opt-in method is adopted. This limits the scope of the free-rider problem, as only those with genuine claims would be willing to incur the litigation costs.

Alternative to class action

Government regulation and self-regulation are the possible alternatives to class action suits. Government regulation is not feasible at all times because of high public expenditure and pressure on public finance. The Satyam scam, among others, is a mirror reflection of the failure of regulations and legislations to keep up with the advancement of technology and advance fraudulent corporate practices. Class action suits are present to protect the victims after the injury is caused, by ensuring just compensation. This produces a higher deterrence effect than individual claims, whereas a violation of a regulation would in most cases result in a penalty which the company pays off without owning up to the responsibility pinned on it. Proponents of self-regulation argue that the market will evolve its best practices by self-regulation. However, self-regulation may be ineffective, as the industry may not be motivated to discipline its members, or may not be sufficiently coherent or organized to assure that its members will comply with self-regulation.[56]

Policy implications: analysis of Indian procedural rigours

Creating this market alternative to regulatory enforcement requires procedural law to authorize class actions, a supply of experienced and entrepreneurial plaintiffs' lawyers, a way to finance the litigation and substantive law that recognizes consumers' claims and does so in such a way that it will be efficient to litigate hundreds, thousands or even millions of claims together.[57] First, the procedural law in India is found in The Code of Civil Procedure, 1882, and the substantive or enabling provision is found in Section 245 of the New Companies Act, which reads:

> Such number of member or members, depositor or depositors or any class of them, as the case may be, as enumerated, may file an application before the Tribunal, if they are of the opinion that the management or conduct of the affairs of the company are being conducted in a manner prejudicial to the interests of the company or its members or depositors, to restrain the company from oppression or mismanagement.

The new act states that the class can sue the directors or auditors or any expert/advisor affiliated with the company. The new act not only enables victims to secure higher compensation but also empowers shareholders to seek from the tribunal any or all of the following:

- To restrain the company and its directors from acting on such resolutions.
- To restrain the company from committing an act which is ultra vires or in breach of the articles.
- To declare a resolution altering the company's memorandum or articles of the company as void, if it was passed by suppression of any material or misstatement of any facts or obtained.
- To restrain the company from acting contrary to the provisions of the act or any other law in force.
- To restrain the company from taking any action against the resolution passed by the members.
- To claim damages or compensation or any other suitable action from or against (i) the company or its directors for omission or any wrongful act; (ii) audit firm including the auditor of the company for misleading or any unlawful act; and (iii) any advisor or expert for misleading or fraudulent act.
- To seek any other remedy deemed suitable to tribunal.

This enormous vesting of powers can pose several instabilities within a corporate structure. The directors may not be incentivized to undertake risk for the benefit of the company if the fear of being sued is so high. The courts must hence scrutinize the claims before initiating the trial. Frivolous and malicious claims must be segregated from genuine meritorious ones. The provision lays down criteria based on which the tribunal must evaluate a claim like whether members or depositors are acting in good faith, if there is any evidence as to the involvement of any person other than directors or officers of the company, whether cause of action is such which can be pursued by the member or depositor and considering the evidence as to the views of the members or depositors who have no personal interest in the matter being proceeded.

The legislation provides for safeguards like a minimum of 100 shareholders or owner of share capital of a certain threshold value or depositors of not less than 200. This ensures that only genuine claims arise, as the transaction and co-ordination costs to institute a class action suit are high; hence, unless the grievance is substantial, the shareholders or depositors alike would not initiate a suit against the company. This is, however, not without its limitations: the possibility of the minority shareholders holding the company to a ransom to get favourable policies or to satiate vested interests, and misuse class action suits. Moreover, class action suits are representative in nature rather than group litigation, and individual claimants receive a small portion as damages, while the attorney walks away with a sizeable amount. Critics of class actions say that attorneys sometimes file frivolous lawsuits just to earn a quick settlement.[58]

It was the J.J. Irani Committee that first recommended the class action suit in 2005. Had it been incorporated then, the Indian shareholders of Satyam Computers might not have suffered and would have been compensated passably. It goes without saying that the class action suit provided in the Companies Act, 2013, is the result of Satyam Computers' scam and will be a boon to the shareholders who now will be able to keep a check on companies' malpractices and sham schemes. Being a US concept, the class action has developed with time as a tool in the hands of investors and has for some time now been part of many countries, including the United Kingdom and Singapore. Class action suit is the need of the hour, and its introduction might open the floodgates of class action suits against the companies. Though legally transplanted into the Indian system, class actions in India do not suffer from agency problems as seen in United States,[59] like contingency fee to be paid to the attorneys, litigation costs not borne by the losing party and several other substantive legal provisions,[60] thus incentivizing the plaintiffs and their attorneys to file frivolous suits. India has, to a great extent, avoided these agency problems by providing safeguards to the defendant as well.

Conclusion

The author recognizes that certain limitations are prevalent in the present study. First, this being an arm-chair research, certain practical nuances arising out of the dispute settlement mechanism in the Companies Act, 2013, may not be identified and discussed in the chapter. Second, the concept of establishing a specialized tribunal has been discussed by employing cost–benefit analysis and efficiency argument. The author concedes that quantifying cost of delivering justice trivializes it to a greater deal than intended by the author. Third, the author has not dealt with every provision in the company law which facilitates private bargaining but has stuck on to two most relevant subject matters with respect to dispute settlement.

The establishment of the NCLT and NCLAT has simplified the dispute settlement procedures in India. Prior to the Companies Act, 2013, the presence of several tribunals and boards cluttered the justice delivery system while imposing huge costs on the state. Specialized tribunals though efficient in their disposal have procedural defects, which have led to parties challenging the awards for violation of principles of natural justice in several cases. While specialization intends to ease the burden on courts, it may lead to multiplicity of cases if adjudged without applying judicial mind to it. While the presence of judicial members in the said tribunal cannot be obviated, the presence of technical members in adjudging all matters before the tribunal is recommended. It would be Pareto efficient as costs of delay can be mitigated if sector-specific technical members provide their insight into the case. Tribunals have in the past indicated speedy disposal of cases within a prescribed time frame, which would otherwise take eons to settle. Class action suits, popularly known as representative suits in India, would greatly benefit minority shareholders in matters of oppression and mismanagement of the company. On the flip side, it would possibly dis-incentivize the management to make bold business decisions. In the light of the several corporate frauds that have shaken India in the recent past, class action suits create right incentives and disincentives. A litigant's costs of litigation are an area often undervalued in India, which therefore is the primary reason for many causes of action losing their way before they open the doors of justice. Class action suits incur reasonable justice administration costs, while benefitting many marginal victims who would otherwise not seek a remedy. It is to be seen if this concept proves beneficial to the company's long-term stability or leads to frequent hostility between the stakeholders.

Notes

1 Adolf A. Berle and Gardiner C. Means, *The Modern Corporation and Private Property* (New York: Macmillan, 1932): 123.
2 Claire A. Hill and Brett H. McDonnell, 'Introduction: The Evolution of the Economic Analysis of Corporate Law', *Research Paper Series, University of Minnesota Law School Legal Studies* 12 (21) (2012): 1–16.
3 Ronald H. Coase, *The Nature of the Firm*, Reprinted in *The Economic Nature of the Firm: A Reader* 4 (16) (1937): 72–73.

4 Michael Jensen and William Meckling, 'Theory of the Firm: Managerial Behavior, Agency Costs, and Ownership Structure', *Journal of Financial Economics* 3 (4) (1976): 305–360.
5 Ibid.
6 The Companies (Amendment) Act, 2002, No. 1 of 2003, accessed 8 September 2014, http://lawmin.nic.in/legislative/textofcentralacts/2003.pdf.
7 PBI (Press Information Bureau), 2000, *Justice Eradi Committee on Law Relating to Insolvency of Companies*. http://pib.nic.in/focus/foyr2000/foaug2000/eradi2000.html.
8 Grover Purushottam, 'National Company Law Tribunal – A Single Window Institution for Corporate Justice', accessed 15 July 2014, http://www.icsi.edu/WebModules/Programmes/PCS/7PCS/BG%20PCS-6-Grover.pdf.
9 Jeffrey W. Stempel, 'Two Cheers for Specialization', 61 Brooklyn Law Review 67 (1995): 72
10 Saundra Torry, 'Quayle and Bush Administration Take on Civil Justice Reform', *Washington Post* (3 February 1992); Max Boot, 'Chorus of Reformers Adds New Pitch', *Christian Science Monitor* (25 January 1994).
11 Section 10 GF, The Companies (Second Amendment) Act, 2002, accessed 8 September 2014, http://lawmin.nic.in/legislative/textofcentralacts/2003.pdf.
12 *SP Sampath Kumar v. Union of India* (1985) 4 SCC 458.
13 Steven Shavell, 'Economic Analysis of Litigation and the Legal Process', *Harvard Law School John M. Olin Center for Law, Economics and Business Discussion Paper Series Paper*, 404, Chapter 9, p. 6 (2003).
14 Louis Kaplow, 'The Value of Accuracy in Adjudication: An Economic Analysis', *The Journal of Legal Studies* 23 (2) (1994): 307.
15 PRS Legislative Research, 'Text of Speech – Addresses by the Chief Justice of India at the Joint Conferences of Chief Ministers and Chief Justices, 2006, 2007 and 2009', accessed 15 July 2014, http://www.prsindia.org/administrator/uploads/general/1251796330~~Vital%20Stats%20-%20Pendency%20of%20Cases%20in%20Indian%20Courts%2026Aug2009%20v10.pdf.
16 Pradeep Thakur, 'Over 300 Posts of Judges in High Courts Vacant', *Times of India* (24 December 2012), http://timesofindia.indiatimes.com/india/Over-300-posts-of-judges-in-high-courts-vacant/articleshow/17736747.cms.
17 Indian Development Foundation, 'Judicial Impact Assessment: An Approach Paper', accessed 8 September 2014, http://lawmin.nic.in/doj/justice/judicialimpactassessmentreportvol2.pdf.
18 National Company Law Tribunal Rules, Draft Rules, Companies Act, 2013, accessed 15 July 2014, http://www.taxmann.com/datafolder/News/CHAPTER%20XXVII%20-%20NCLT.pdf.
19 Robert Cooter and Thomas Ulen, *Law and Economics* (Delhi: Pearson Education, 2012).
20 Ministry of Home Affairs, 'Committee on Reforms of Criminal Justice System: A Report under Government of India (2013)', accessed 4 September 2014, http://www.mha.nic.in/hindi/sites/upload_files/mhahindi/files/pdf/criminal_justice_system.pdf.

21 Ibid., 136.
22 Sangeeta Singh, 'Ministry to Appoint 3 New Members to CLB', *Live Mint* (11 December 2011), http://www.livemint.com/Politics/7Q6GUscPWsog6hZFZhZfRK/Ministry-to-appoint-3-new-members-to-CLB.html.
23 *Union of India v. R. Gandhi, President, Madras Bar Association* and *Madras Bar Association v. Union of India*, accessed 15 July 2014, http://judis.nic.in/supremecourt/helddis3.aspx.
24 Vyapak Desai and Vivek Kathpalia, 'Supreme Court Upholds the Constitutionality of National Company Law Tribunal', *India Law Journal* 3 (3) (2010), accessed 16 July 2014, http://www.indialawjournal.com/volume3/issue_3/article_by_vyapak_desai.html.
25 H. Friendly, 'Federal Jurisdiction: A General View', *New York University Law Review* 8 (28) (1973): 153–171.
26 Desai and Kathpalia, 'Supreme Court Upholds the Constitutionality of National Company Law Tribunal'.
27 Ibid.
28 A. Mitchell Polinsky and Steven Shavell, 'Economic Analysis of Law', *Discussion Paper No. 536 12/2005Harvard Law School* (2005), accessed 16 July 2014, http://www.law.harvard.edu/programs/olin_center/papers/pdf/Shavell_et%20al_536.pdf.
29 Francisco Cabrillo and Sean Fitzpatrick, *The Economics of Courts and Litigation* (Gloucestor, UK: Edward Elgar, 2008).
30 Michael J. Kastenncier and Robert W. Remington, 'Court and Access to Justice: A Legislative Perspective', *Harvard Journal of Legislation* 16 (1979): 301, 307–309.
31 Robert Cooter, 'The Cost of Coase', *Journal of Legal Studies*11 (1) (1982): 1–33.
32 Section 442(1), Companies Act, 2013, accessed 2 April 2014, http://www.mca.gov.in/Ministry/companies_act.html.
33 'Developments in the Law-Class Actions', *Harvard Law Review* 89 (1976): 1318.
34 Richard Posner, *Economic Analysis of Law* (New York: Wolters Kluwer Law, 1977).
35 FED.R. CIV.P. 23, Advisory Comm. Note, 39 F.R.D. 69, I02–I03 (1966); *Taliaferro v. State Council of Higher Education*, 372 F. Supp. I378, I387 (E.D. Va. I974); Note, In Rem Validity – A Two-Sided Coin, 59 GEO.L.J. 73, 85 (0970).
36 'Defendant Class Actions', *Harvard Law Review* 91 (3) (1978): 630–658.
37 Section 245, Companies Act, 2013, accessed 4 April 2014, http://www.mca.gov.in/MinistryV2/companiesact.html.
38 Janet Cooper Alexander, 'An Introduction to Class Action Procedure in the United States', accessed 3 August 2014, http://www.law.duke.edu/grouplit/papers/classactionalexander.pdf.
39 Manan Dua, 'Class Action Suit in the Companies Act 2013 – The Investor Activism', *CLA* 119 (2014): 1.
40 Jürgen G. Backhaus, Alberto Cassone and Giovanni B. Ramello, *The Law and Economics of Class Actions in Europe: Lessons from America* (Gloucestor, UK: Edward Elgar Publication, 2012).

41 Roger Bernstein, 'Judicial Economy and Class Action', *The Journal of Legal Studies* 7 (2) (1978): 349–370.
42 Ibid.
43 Kenneth W. Dam, 'Class Actions: Efficiency, Compensation, and Conflict of Interest', *The Journal of Legal Studies* 4 (1) (1975): 47–73.
44 Cornes Richard and Todd Sandler, *The Theory of Externalities, Public Goods, and Club Goods* (London: Cambridge University Press, 1996): 347.
45 C. Silver, 'Class Actions – Representative Proceedings', In *Encyclopedia of Law and Economics*, edited by B. Bouckaert and De Geest G. Cheltenham (Northampton: Edward Elgar, 1999): 194–240.
46 Cornes and Sandler, *The Theory of Externalities, Public Goods, and Club Goods*: 347.
47 S. Issacharoff, 'Class Action Conflicts', *University of California at Davis Law Review* 30 (1997): 805–833.
48 Cornes and Sandler, *The Theory of Externalities, Public Goods, and Club Goods*.
49 D.L. Rodhe, *Access to Justice* (New York: Oxford University Press, 2004).
50 A. Klement and Zvika Neeman, 'Incentive Structures for Class Action Lawyers', *The Journal of Law, Economics and Organization* 20 (1) (2004): 102–124.
51 D. Porrini and G.B. Ramello, 'Class Action and Financial Markets: Insights from Law and Economics', *Journal of Financial Economic Policy* 3 (2) (2011): 140–160; T.S. Ulen, 'An Introduction to the Law and Economics of Class Action Litigation', *European Journal of Law and Economics* 32 (2) (2010): 185–203.
52 D.R. Hensler, Moore B. Dombey, E. Giddens, J. Gross, E. Moller and M. Pace, eds., *Class Action Dilemmas: Pursuing Public Goals for Private Gain* (Santa Monica, CA, and Arlington, VA: Rand Publishing, 2000).
53 Porrini and Ramello, 'Class Action and Financial Markets'.
54 Dam, 'Class Actions'.
55 Cornes and Sandler, *The Theory of Externalities, Public Goods, and Club Goods*.
56 Janet Cooper Alexander, 'An Introduction to Class Action Procedure in the United States', *Stanford Centre on Conflict and Negotiation*, accessed 25 July 2014, http://law.duke.edu/grouplit/papers/classactionalexander.pdf.
57 Ibid.
58 Barbara J. Rothstein and Thomas E. Willging, *Managing Class Action Litigation: A Pocket Guide for Judges, Federal Judicial Centre* (2010), accessed 25 July 2014, http://www.fjc.gov/public/pdf.nsf/lookup/ClassGd3.pdf/$file/ClassGd3.pdf.
59 Steven T. Cotrreau, 'The Due Process Right to Opt Out of Class Actions', *New York University Law Review* 73 (1998): 480, http://www.nyulawreview.org/sites/default/files/pdf/NYULawReview-73-2-Cottreau.pdf.
60 Umakanth Varottil, 'Shareholder Activism and Class Action Lawsuits', *IndiaCorpLaw Blog*, 1 June 2009, http://indiacorplaw.blogspot.in/2009/06/shareholder-activism-and-class-action.html.

Part IV

Game theory and law

Chapter 9

An economic analysis of cybercrimes

Esha Goel and Kundhavi Suresh

Background note

Cybercrime has become one of the biggest challenges for law enforcement agencies. The ease with which it is committed, its invisibility and the disregard for geographical boundaries have put this crime in the list of the most dangerous and untraceable crimes.[1] Investigation, collection of evidence and prosecution are close to impossible. The growth of the Internet might have a lot of advantages, but it has brought with it the menace of untraceable and undetectable criminal activities. The European Commission explains that computer-related crimes are committed across the cyberspace and does not stop at the conventional state borders.[2] Technology gives the ability to loot and inflict harm upon the entire world with little risk of apprehension and allows for experimenting with new varieties of criminal endeavours.[3] Cybercrime is a global phenomenon, sometimes having its effect on the entire national or international community. Beginning from viruses that attack financial records or the stock market[4] to a false message that causes a nuclear reactor to shut off[5] or a dam to open[6] to a blackout of the air traffic control system that results in airplane crashes,[7] cybercrimes can cause severe and widespread economic or physical damage.[8]

It is interesting to note that there is no accepted definition of cybercrime. A few efforts have been made to define the term, but they fail to encompass the magnitude of the offence.[9] For example, the UN manual on the prevention and control of computer-related crime provides the following definition:

> Computer crime may involve activities that are traditional in nature, such as theft, fraud, forgery and mischief, all of which are generally subject everywhere to criminal sanctions. The

> computer has also created a host of potentially new misuses or abuses that may, or should be criminal as well.[10]

According to Pavan Duggal, cybercrime referred to all the activities done with criminal intent in cyberspace or using the medium of Internet. These could be either the criminal activities in the conventional sense or activities, newly evolved with the growth of the new medium. Any activity, which basically offends human sensibilities, can be included in the ambit of cybercrimes.[11] In particular, cybercrime can be described as 'the use of a computer-based means to commit an illegal act'.[12] It can also be described as 'any crime that is facilitated or committed using a computer, network, or hardware device'.[13]

Many economic offences such as fraud, theft, industrial espionage, sabotage, extortion and invasion into privacy also fall within the ambit of cybercrime. At its most severe, cybercrime will border on terrorism, encompassing attacks against human life and against national security establishments, critical infrastructure and other vital veins of society. Terrorism encompasses actions intended to provoke a state of terror in the general public, a group of persons or particular persons.[14] Cyber offences take the form of hacking, phishing, email bombing, cyberterrorism, viruses, contaminants, pornography and so on.

Cyberspace and the theory of market for lemons

The first question that comes into one's mind is, how does a market over the Internet vary from other markets? We see that the primary difference is with respect to transaction costs.[15] An Internet market due to lower transaction costs also attracts a large number of market participants. But the problem of information asymmetry poses a threat. Information asymmetry is a situation where one party to a transaction has more information compared to the other. Considering the anonymity and probability of deception over the cyberspace, one can only imagine how often one will be faced with a situation of information asymmetry. What happens when there is information asymmetry? In 1970, George A. Akerlof, in his seminal work on the 'Market for Lemons',[16] showed that adverse selection could be a possible reason to bring about market failure.[17] The basic argument that he put forward is that in a market for used cars, there is an asymmetry of information between the buyers and sellers, which leads to uncertainty of the quality of the car and correlative price averaging where the price of a good car may also be determined on the basis of the price of the bad cars due to lack of information. Like a market for lemons, a market for cybercrimes may thus emerge. We see that like in the market for used cars there is a huge amount of information asymmetry that exists in the cyber world.[18]

Buyers and sellers are not aware of the actual quality of the car and then they aversely select cars, thereby driving good cars out of the market and leaving behind bad cars. It is assumed that sellers are aware of the quality of the goods they are offering. For the sake of understanding, a value R is assumed below which the buyers cannot differentiate the quality of goods. Sellers can sell goods between quality Qm, which is the maximum quality, and $(Qm - R)$, which is the minimum quality, and buyers will be unable to differentiate between the same. For the purpose of creating potential for a transaction to occur, it is assumed that the buyers value the goods more than the sellers. The sellers are assumed to view the good of quality q at q dollars, and buyers are willing to pay an amount of dQ dollars, where $d > 1$. We also assume uniform distribution of the quality of the car between $Qm - R$ and Qm. In a case where all the goods have been sold, the average quality would be $(Qm - R + Qm)/2$. But sellers with goods having quality more than p will decide not to sell. The expected quality of the goods will be between $Qm - R$ and p: $\text{Qe} = (p + Qm - R)/2$. This 'quality supplied' is shown in Figure 9.1. (At any price above Qm, all the goods are sold and the expected quality is $Qm - R/2$; supply is vertical.) Buyers are willing to pay $p = d\text{Qe}$ for a good having the average quality of Qc. Solving for q, we get the 'demand' for quality, $\text{Qe} = p/d$, as shown in the graph. Setting demand equal to supply and solving for p gives an equilibrium price of

$$p^* = \frac{Qm - R}{\frac{2}{d} - 1}$$

provided that

1 $d > 1$
2 $Qm > R$
3 $R > 2Qm\,(1 - 1/d)$

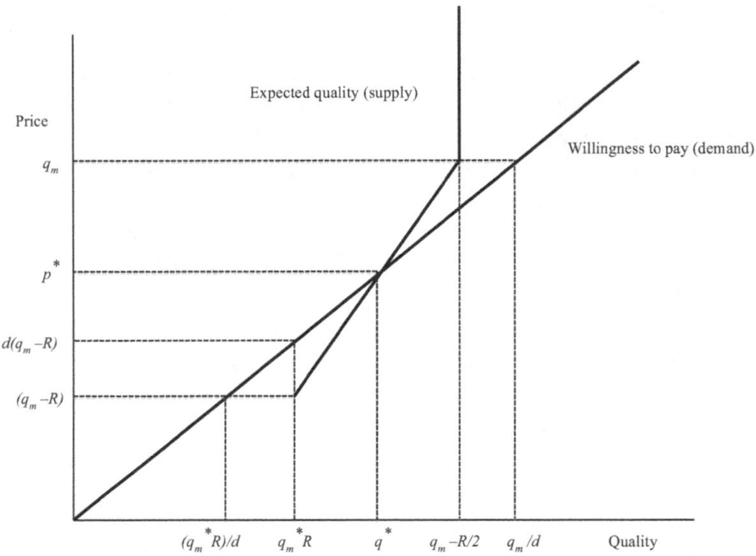

Figure 9.1 Demand–supply in cyberspace market

Source: John H. Huston and Roger W. Spencer, 'Quality, Uncertainty and the Internet: The Market for Cyber Lemons', *The American Economist* 46 (2002): 50–60.

At a price above p^*, the quality required by buyers to substantiate the price is greater than the average quality provided by sellers. At a price below p^*, the quality required by buyers to substantiate the price is less than the average quality provided by sellers. The first inequality demands that buyers value the product more than sellers do. If d falls below 1, then the demand curve rotates downward and, as a result, does not intersect supply. Since in that case buyers value the product less than sellers, no items are exchanged. The second inequality requires that R must be less than Qm. If $R = Qm$, then buyers cannot distinguish between even the very worst and very best goods. In the model, supply crosses demand at a price of zero. This is the extreme case of Akerlof's model in which the worst goods drive out all goods of higher quality. The model predicts that as long as demand intersects supply in its upward sloping range, that is as long as the third inequality holds, price will be less than Qm. This provision is violated if either R is too small or d is too large. A smaller R implies better-informed consumers who can distinguish finer gradations of quality. If $R < 2q_m\,(1 - 1/d)$, then consumers are well informed to avoid the lemon problem, and a price above *Qm* is generated. At the extreme, if $R = 0$, customers know precisely what quality is being offered. The second and third inequalities combined imply that $Qm > 2Qm\,(1 - 1/d)$. Solving for *d* generates the constraint that $d < 2$. If *d* is above 2, buyers value the product so much more than sellers that even at $p = Qm$, the price where all the sellers are willing to sell their products, buyers are still willing to buy, and thus the lemon problem does not come into play. If either *R* is too small or *d* is too large, demand intersects supply along the vertical section above *Qm*, and the interesting aspects of informational asymmetry are assumed away.[19]

Thus, we see how asymmetry of information could be a problem with respect to the cyberspace. The probability of sale of bad goods is very high in the cyber market, thus leading to many activities of crime and fraud.

Economic analysis of hacking

Hacking is commonly associated with unlawful intrusion into secured Internet resources of an individual. In the digital age, hacking has posed a huge menace.[20] Most organizations such as banks, schools, companies and hospitals store and organize information on electronic media. Hence, a large part of confidential and sensitive information such as credit card numbers, social security numbers, bank account details and telephone numbers is available on the virtual web, which then imposes the same to the risk of theft, manipulation or viewing.[21] Access to such information requires basic and easily available equipment such as a personal computer and Internet connection. The increasingly computer-based world is increasingly vulnerable to malevolent computer hackers. The costs of uncontrolled hacking can be very high. The most obvious costs to a target occur when a hacker causes malicious system damage or steals proprietary information. Malicious hackers can create large costs in the form of lost or stolen data, work product and profits, and may also inhibit business growth through unfair competition or sabotage. Society bears these costs indirectly by paying higher prices for goods and services. Society also might bear the cost directly in cases where taxpayers' money is lost[22] or a public service is disrupted. Malicious hackers can also create large human costs in the form of systematic disruptions of critical services, international espionage, terroristic threats or harassment and cyberstalking of individuals. The oft-cited worst-case scenario is an 'electronic Pearl Harbor', in which terrorists systematically disrupt public resources such as telephones, power and air traffic control.[23]

On its part, India protects individual information from the wrath of hacking under penal provisions of the Information Technology Act, 2000, which include imprisonment and fine. Unauthorized access attracts civil and criminal liability under the act. The act provides an extremely broad definition of hacking[24] and transcends generally accepted perceptions of the act. Consequently, a wide variety of activities that are not normally associated with hacking per se can be read into the provision, for example data theft, data diddling or cyber fraud.[25] Section 66 of the act lays down the following ingredients required to constitute the offence of hacking:

1 The accused must either:
   a intend to cause wrongful loss or damage, or
   b know that he is likely to cause wrongful loss or damage to the public or any person.
2 The accused must either:
   a destroy, delete, or alter any information, or
   b diminish the value or utility of any information, or
   c affect injuriously by any means any information residing in a computer resource.

Consequently, a wide variety of activities that are not normally associated with hacking per se can be read into the provision, for example data theft, data diddling or cyber fraud.[26] The following paragraphs highlight the economic efficiency of the law and also discuss the incentives and disincentives for committing the crime of hacking.

Kinds of hackers

In order to create effective deterrence against hacking the nuanced distinction between 'hacking' and 'cracking' was developed.[27] The word 'hacking' is derived from the word 'hack', which referred to a shortcut or easy method of writing code generally. A technical definition of hacking according to the Digital Guards database[28] is 'unauthorized use, or attempts to circumvent or bypass the security mechanisms of an information system or network'. Darlington[29] believes hacking is not limited to accessing data or information but also includes an attack on the privacy of all people. Almost all different opinions agree on the illegality of hacking. 'Cracking' is the name given to malicious (i.e. criminal) hacking.[30] The more dangerous trend is that of cracking, which is a form of hacking just motivated by material factors such as the lure of financial benefit, or free telephone calls, and access to sensitive and marketable information, or denial of service attacks where a person actively participates to sabotage a system or inflict damage upon it.

The offender's perspective

In summary, there are two kinds of hackers: hackers who engage in this activity for fame or, for some non-monetary incentive, and those who carry on the practice for profit motives. Before proceeding to compute a supply–demand curve for the market related to hackers, we must begin with an evaluation of the costs of hacking since it will largely determine the nature of the supply curve. Hackers must bear moderate initial fixed costs of hacking such as investing in a telephone line, a computer and a modem. For more sophisticated attacks, fixed costs may also include training in basic programming and computer languages. As far as the variable costs are concerned, two components come to mind: electricity and time invested by the hackers. The number of other hackers is an important factor in determining the supply curve for 'hacks' to what we call the 'hackers market'. The demand side of the market is unusual in the sense that there is no demand, as such, for hacks. For fame-driven hackers, the demand arises from the fact that the more hacks that are conducted, the more the information that is out in the open, the happier the hacking community is. On the other hand, crackers (malicious hackers) rely on the demand for propaganda activity, or other members with the same financial end. The demand-side difference in the two kinds of activities is clear – the fame-seeking hacker market does not pay for more hacking with a higher price except for additional fame on the completion of new hack. It could be termed that the fame-driven community has a 'reaction function', which specifies how much the hacker community reacts with fame to a particular hack. We may at least conclude that there is positive slope since there is likely to be more applause with more hacks and less applause with less hacks.

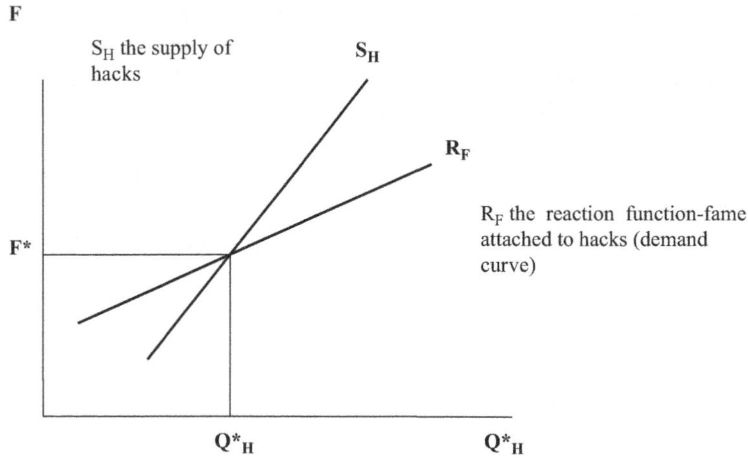

Figure 9.2 Fame-driven hacking markets

Source: Peter T. Leeson and Christopher Coyne, 'The Economics of Computer Hacking', *Journal of Law, Economics and Policy* (1) (2) (2005): 511–532.

In Figure 9.2, the hacker's supply curve is less elastic than the community's fame reaction, which would imply that the hackers represented are less responsive to changes in the fame than the hackers' community when they react to such hacks. In a case where the demand curve is more elastic than the supply curve, the situation may be reversed. In such a situation, the law must take into account that the response of the hacking community to hacks is more closely related to the fame than the producers of hack. This dichotomy presents a unique opportunity to use these variables to implement a policy to reduce the quantity of hacking in the fame-driven industry.

The variables for cracking (hacking with a profit motive) are completely different and, interestingly, simpler in the case of profit-driven hacking. The criminal behaviour can be expected to comply with behavioural models for all other types of crimes. The producers seek money, and the supply demand for hacking is expressed in traditional price/quantity space and price equilibrates the behaviour of suppliers and consumers. The market has a positively sloping curve and negatively sloped demand curves. Hackers will provide a larger quantity of hacking if they are paid more and less if they are paid less. It's therefore like a normal demand–supply curve (Figure 9.3).

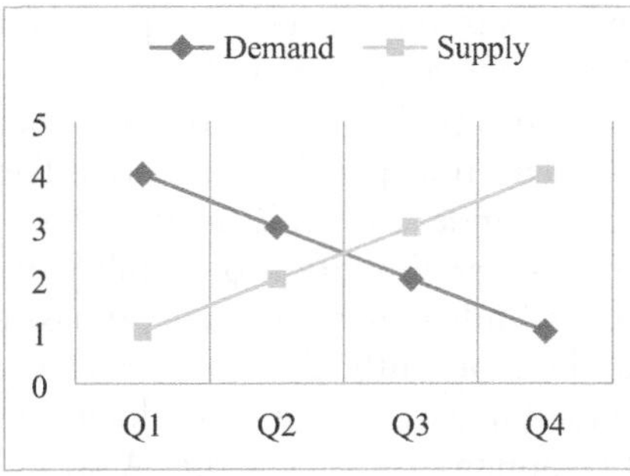

Figure 9.3 Profit-driven hacking markets

Source: Peter T. Leeson and Christopher Coyne, 'The Economics of Computer Hacking', *Journal of Law, Economics and Policy* (1) (2) (2005): 511–532.

Social perspective: incentive to disincentivize

The societal effects of hacking are found on three distinct levels based on the group they affect. First, individuals are affected on account of loss of money, privacy and sensitive information such as credit card details.[31] At the organizational level, it impacts private as well public organizations, causing huge losses in the form of loss of profits, business loss and operation hurdles, sometimes even bankruptcy.[32] At the national level, hacking attacks of severe nature have the capacity to stall, freeze and even irreparably damage a nation's essential infrastructure.[33]

Efficiency analysis of current law

The Indian legal framework in dealing with cybercrime is more or less encompassed within the Indian Penal Code and most important the Information Technology Act, 2000. The following are the salient features of relevant provisions, which address hacking.

Section 43

This section prescribes a civil compensation for contravention in cases of unauthorized access,[34] introduction of a virus,[35] denial of service attacks[36] and abetment of unauthorized access.[37] The law therefore creates a disincentive in terms of commission of the acts.

In so much as the legal response is not in terms of penalty receivable by the state but is in the form of compensation payable to the victim, it would be fair to assume that the purpose is compensatory. This would call for the application of concepts such as those applicable for the compensation payable for torts. The statutory limit for the compensation under the act is set at *1 crore*. The application of it reveals that first the limitation of liability at 1 crore may be sufficient to curb fraudulent acts on a general basis, but critical system damage may be more difficult to repair. Hence, enough deterrence is not provided in cases of attacks, albeit honest, which have destructive and crippling effects of large. A straightforward compensation sufficiency test will reveal that costs such as the lost business due to downtime, goodwill loss and investigative costs cannot in all cases be adequately covered within the framework of the statutory cap. Adding the most unique and undesirable effect of anonymity associated with computer attacks, the disincentive is severely diluted and would not provide effective deterrence.

Section 43A

This provision provides for compensation in cases where the body corporate dealing in information acts negligently in maintaining reasonable security practices and makes it liable for failure to do the same. On an overall system efficiency perspective for the maximization of social welfare and reduction of social cost, this provision is sound as it imposes the cost/obligation to take preventive measures on the persons in the best position to take the measures at the minimum overall cost. The rationale behind this provision is beyond reproach, yet it suffers from the same limitation of liability under Section 43.

Section 66

This critical section provides for the criminalization of all acts referred to in section 43 when committed either dishonestly or fraudulently. The penalty is Rs 5 lakh or three-year imprisonment or both. Section 66 criminalizes only conduct that is dishonest or fraudulent and therefore leaves open the possibility that certain acts committed even with clear intent remain outside of penal sanctions. However counterintuitive, this provision in our opinion is sound insofar as it excuses hacking in the purest sense, and preserves the societal benefits of such activities and criminalizes only the nefarious forms of hacking such as email bombing, phishing and other acts of unauthorized access.

The subjective intentions, or a state of mind, of the accused criminal are a pervasive consideration in the criminal law. The concept of intent can be said to serve three economic functions: identifying pure coercive transfers, estimating the probability of apprehension and determining whether the criminal sanction will be effective (cost-justified) in controlling undesirable conduct.[38] In special application to the distinction between hacking and cracking, we must adopt a modified approach. First, we can safely presume that the act of unauthorized access or denial of service hardly, if ever, arises out of unintentional conduct. Strictly applying *punish intentional acts* will wipe out the distinction between acts of hacking in the harmless way vis-à-vis acts of hacking with intent to damage or destroy. This would have two potential negative impacts. First, any societal benefit arising out of the hacking in terms of improvement of system design and so on would no longer be available as the sanction would be too severe. Second, once a person gains unauthorized access, there will be no disincentive to refrain from inflicting actual damage to the system.

The provision on the whole is sound in identifying the critical ingredient of fraud and dishonesty, which imposes different hurdles – civil compensation for acts with low risk of societal harm compensated and possible penal sanctions for grossly offensive conduct.

Economic analysis of cyberterrorism

Computer-related acts in support of terrorism offences are included in the content-related cybercrime category. The recent United Nations Office on Drugs and Crime publication 'The Use of the Internet for Terrorist Purposes'[39] observes that computer systems may be used for a range of acts that promote and support terrorism. These include propaganda (including recruitment, radicalization and incitement to terrorism), financing, training, planning (including through secret communication and open-source information), execution and cyber attacks.[40] Cyberterrorism may be defined as a 'premeditated, politically motivated attack against information, computer systems, computer programs, and data which result in violence against noncombatant targets by subnational groups or clandestine agents'.[41] Such an attack can take many forms,[42] like hacking into air control systems, nuclear power plants, hacking pharmaceutical company's computers and changing the formula of essential drugs causing mass deaths.[43] Thus, we see that cyberterrorism is the convergence of terrorism and cyberspace. It is generally understood to mean unlawful attacks and threats of attack against computer networks and the information stored therein when done to intimidate or coerce a government or its people in the furtherance of political or social objectives.[44] The Federal Bureau of Investigation has defined cyberterrorism as 'the unlawful use of force or violence against persons or property to intimidate or coerce a govt, the civilian population, or any segment thereof, in furtherance of political or social objectives through the exploitation of systems deployed by the target'.[45]

A hacker's perceived cost–benefit structure is inclusive of a comparison of benefits and costs to make decision about engaging in a crime by a cyber-criminal.[46] A cybercrime is committed if

$$M_B + P_B > O_{CP} + O_{CM}.P_A.P_C \tag{1}$$

where
M_B = the monetary benefits of committing the crime;
P_B = the psychic benefits of committing the crime;
O_{CM} = monetary opportunity costs of conviction;
O_{CP} = psychic costs of committing a cybercrime;
P_A = the probability of arrest;
P_C = the probability of conviction.

The product term on the right hand side $O_{CM}\, P_A\, P_C$ in Equation (1) is the expected penalty effect. Equation (1) portrays how costs and benefits of committing a crime can influence a criminal.[47] Thus, we see that if the monetary benefit and psychological benefit are high, then the crime is committed.

The question that arises now is, how can cyberterrorism be combated and what is the most economically efficient solution? The investigation of cyberterrorism often demands intrusive or coercive search, surveillance or monitoring activity by intelligence or law enforcement agencies.[48] While legislating, human rights should also be kept in mind.[49] An appropriate decision analysis compares the marginal costs of security measures with the marginal benefits in terms of fatalities and damages averted. The decision problem is to maximize the net benefit (benefits minus the costs), or the net present value:[50]

$$\textit{Net benefit} = p_{(attack)} \times C_{(loss)} \times \Delta R - C_{(security)} \qquad (2)$$

where

$p_{(attack)}$: The *probability of a successful attack* is the likelihood that a successful terrorist attack will take place if the security measures were not in place.

$C_{(loss)}$: The *losses sustained in the successful attack* include the fatalities and other damage, both direct and indirect, that will accrue as a result of a successful terrorist attack.

ΔR: The *reduction in risk* is the degree to which the security measure foils, deters, disrupts or protects against a terrorist attack.

$C_{(security)}$: The *costs* are those of providing the risk-reducing security measure required to attain the benefit.

A security measure is viewed as cost effective or efficient if the net benefit exceeds zero.[51] Overall risk is consequent to the results of various individual scenarios, which is weighed against the probability of its occurrence. This is known as the probabilistic risk modelling. The equilibrium amount of terrorist may be achieved by reducing the marginal benefits to terrorists. The marginal rate of substitution will be reduced for all other activities for terrorism, as shown in Figure 9.4.[52]

In a way, terrorists behave rationally, having to choose between legal activities and terrorist activities in order to promote their political goals.[53] Figure 9.5a and b shows the decision faced by terrorists with regard to the effect of deterrence depending on the identified incentives. The budget constraint depends on the expected cost of terrorism and all other activities. The slope of terrorist's budget constraint is the negative of the ratio of the expected costs of terrorism and other activities. The cost of terrorism consists of material resources and collecting information as well as the time required to prepare the attacks. Moreover, expected costs also reflect the danger involved in actually carrying out the act as discussed earlier, including probability of being caught and punishment expected. The terrorists derive utility from both legal and terrorist activities. The shape of the indifference curve depends on the preferences or the motivation of the terrorists. Highly intrinsically motivated terrorists, or fanatics, are convinced they are doing

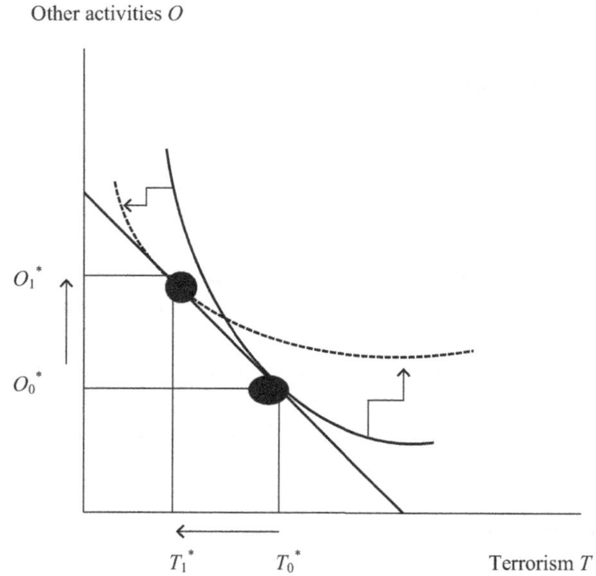

Figure 9.4 Reducing the activities of terrorists

Source: Frey and Luechinger (2003).

the right thing, irrespective of incentives from outside. In this case, the indifference curve is very steep. Such an indifference curve could also be explained by inter-temporal utility considerations. But terrorism is often undertaken to achieve a particular political goal rather than as an end in itself. The shape of the indifference curve is therefore determined by not only the preference of the terrorist but also the effectiveness of terrorism in promoting a political goal. The tangency between the indifference curve and the budget constraint identifies the equilibrium extent and intensity of terrorism T*. It is also seen that terrorists systematically react to externally offered incentives.[54] Deterrence policy raises the cost of terrorist acts by increasing the risk of apprehension and by punishing the perpetrators more severely. But deterrence policy does not solely depend on the incentives of the potential terrorists. It also seeks to prevent terrorist acts by making them more difficult to undertake. A deterrence policy is therefore in many cases able to raise the perceived cost of terrorism. Figure 9.5a and b shows that the budget

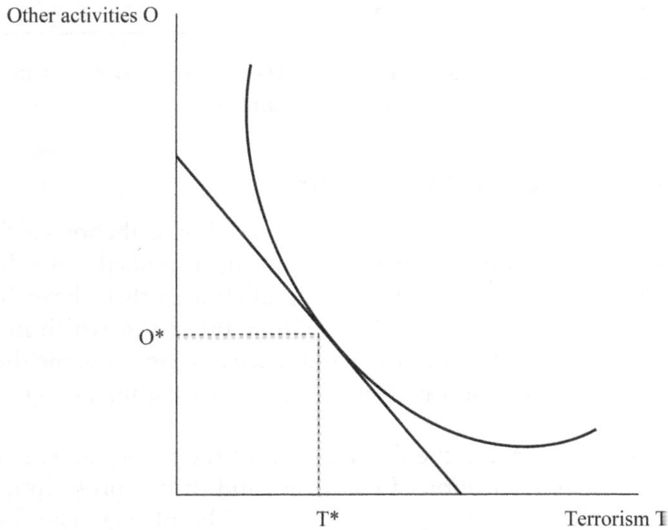

Figure 9.5a Decision calculus of a prospective terrorist

Source: Bruno S. Frey and Simon Luechinger, 'How to Fight Terrorism: Alternatives to Deterrence', *Defence and Peace Economics* 14 (4) (2003): 237–249.

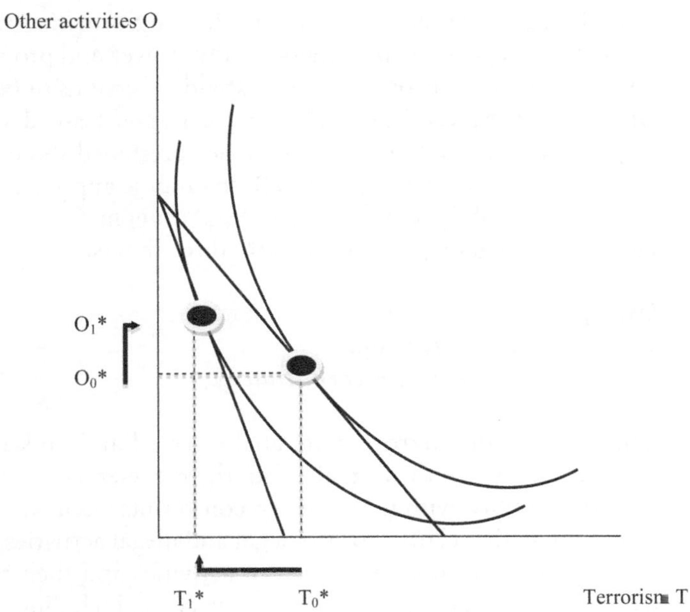

Figure 9.5b Increasing the cost of terrorism

Source: Bruno S. Frey and Simon Luechinger, 'How to Fight Terrorism: Alternatives to Deterrence', *Defence and Peace Economics* 14 (4) (2003): 237–249.

constraint rotates inwards along the terrorism axis, resulting in a smaller equilibrium amount of terrorism.

Game theory and cyberterrorism

The theory of games has been widely used as a theoretical basis for strategic reasoning.[55] Some strategists have applied game theory directly to the problems of strategic analysis; others have based their reasoning on theories of bargaining processes, which in turn have sprung from developments and reorientations of game theory. In either case, the result is strategic reasoning within a game-theoretic framework.[56]

The key elements in the development of the theory of games are (a) the formal description of the games and (b) the proscription or description of how the game is or should be played. The former involves the formalization of the rules of the game. The rules provide a formal description of the bare bones context within which the action must take place. They describe the nature of the transaction, the attributes of the players and the elements of uncertainty. The latter provides normative or behavioural solution theories dealing with how the game should be or is played. The normative theories deal with concepts such as fairness, equity, power and property rights. The behavioural theories contain extended versions of *homo economicus* or, more recently, models of capacity, constrained, optimizing agents, that is individuals who are not presumed to be able to calculate and evaluate without limit. Both of these approaches to solution theory are of direct relevance to legal thought.[57]

To characterize a game, we must specify three things:

1 *players*,
2 *strategies of each player* and
3 *pay-offs to each player for each strategy.*

Rationality implies that terrorists are goal oriented and rank their strategies according to their goals and their preferences. They maximize their utility within budgetary constraints because their actions depend on the relative costs of legal and illegal activities, the relative gains between these two types of activities and their total resources available. Terrorists consider their costs, including risk, time and likelihood of confrontation with the authorities or their

Table 9.1 Strategies for the state and the terrorists

Terrorist			
State		Target 1	Target 2
	Target 1	2	–1
	Target 2	–3	4

Source: Sarita Azad, 'Defence against Terrorist Attacks: Game Theory Can Help', IDSA Comment, accessed 3 November 2014, http://www.idsa.in/idsacomments/DefenceagainstTerroristAttacksGameTheorycanHelp_sazad_030111.

supporters. Terrorists change their strategies when the constraints are changed, and they refrain from behaviour that prohibits the fulfilment of their goals.[58]

Probability of the outcome determines the strategy. Let us assume a game theory model between terrorists and the government, where they are the two players and there are two targets. The terrorists are likely to attack both targets but not at the same time. Considering the fact that defence measures to combat terrorism are expensive, the government can defend only one of the targets. A game theory model chooses the best strategy for the government and the strategies and pay-offs may be determined by using empirical data. Suppose there is a situation where, at a particular instance, the terrorists decide to attack the first target and the state also defends the same target; we notice that there is a pay-off of 2 for the state as it can combat the attack. But if the state defends target 2 while the terrorists attack the first target, then the state will incur a negative pay-off of –1. Similarly, if the state defends target 2 and the terrorists attack target 2, then there is a pay-off of 4, but if the terrorists attack target 1, then there is a negative pay-off of –3 and so on. The respective payoffs can be seen in Table 9.1.

Assuming that the state defends target 1 at probability p_1 and target 2 at probability p_2, the state gains

$$2p_1 - 3p_2$$

But if the terrorist group chooses target 2, the state will get

$$-p_1 + 4p_2$$

In order to maximize the state's utility, the simple linear programming problem is to maximize u such that

$$u \leq 2p_1 - 3p_2$$

$$u \leq -p_1 + 4p_2$$

Assuming $p_1 + p_2 = 1$, the values of p_1 and p_2 can be calculated as 7/10 and 3/10, respectively. This implies that if the game is played ten times, the state should choose to defend target 1 and target 2 seven and three times, respectively, in order to maximize its response. It is to be noted that in real-life situations there can be n number of targets instead of the simple choice of two. Also, the numerical value of pay-offs would be entirely dependent on the importance of the targets. To sum up, game theory is based on mathematical formulations, mirroring the real-life choices. By postulating that the players think ahead not just to their immediate consequences but also to the others, it can provide a framework to think about defending against terrorist attacks.[59]

Conclusion

The explosive growth of the Internet has led to the emergence of a computational network that covers the globe, with a staggering number of users connected at any given time to each other, browsing World Wide Web, sending messages, transferring files and searching for information on a range of topics that defy classification. Although this phenomenal growth has created exciting opportunities for information access, economic transformation and interactivity on a global scale, it has also revealed that the Internet is not immune to the problems intrinsic to any public good, as congestions sometimes threaten to render it useless.[60] We see that the number of cybercrimes has also been increasing on a large scale, and the chapter provides an economic analysis of two specific cybercrimes, namely hacking and cyberterrorism.

A search of news databases during any given month also turns up tales of incidents of cybercrime around the world.[61] It is clear that hacking, once considered a novelty, has now become commonplace.[62] This increasingly prevalent phenomenon is also costly, in terms of both cleaning up after a successful hack attack[63] and preventing one by maintaining up-to-date security. Hacking, with respect to its prohibited behaviour and its uncertain and potentially large costs, bears similarities to other criminal phenomena such as drug use, vandalism and trespass that have been with us for centuries; but hacking has drawn special attention because it involves the cyberspace, which is universal and has emerging specialized regulation. Hacking has gone from being an exotic crime understood and practised by a relatively small group to a common problem faced by targets at all levels and practised by many segments of the populace. It goes hand in hand with cyberterrorism. Despite the difficulty of designing one-size-fits-all solutions, criminal law still forms an economically effective basis for regulation because it embraces the underlying principle that unauthorized entry into a computer, like unauthorized entry into a home, amounts to taking valuable privacy and should be prohibited. Care must be taken in choosing solutions so that small businesses and individuals are not forced to choose between overinvesting in security or leaving cyberspace, and so that quality security products and services will continue to be available on the market. As the government pursues policies designed to gather information on hacking threats, the law will likely continue to evolve based on new findings made in an increasingly cooperative public/private environment.

Taking a look at politics and a theory of rational choice, we see that the trend has been to use deterrence to fight terrorism. It is argued by some that a rational choice approach offers a wider range of anti-terrorism policies.[64] Apart from deterrence, terrorist attacks could be made less attractive to terrorists or opportunity costs could be reduced to combat terrorism. Game theory claims predictive power for future events, extrapolating both from laboratory experiments of the behaviour of non-terrorists playing non-naturalistic games and from post hoc analysis of real-world incidents.[65]

Notes

1 Atul Jain, *Cyber Crime: Issues and Threat* (New Delhi: Gyan Publishing House, 2005).

2 Marc D. Goodman and Susan W. Brenner, 'The Emerging Consensus on Criminal Conduct in Cyberspace', *UCLA Journal on Law and Technology* 6 (2) (2002): 3.

3 Model Code of Cybercrime Investigative Procedure, Article VII, accessed 3 November 2014, http://www.cybercrimes.net/MCCIP/art7.htm.

4 Duncan B. Hollis, 'Why States Need an International Law for Information Operations', *Lewis & Clark Law Review* 11 (2007): 1042.
5 Vida M. Antolin-Jenkins, 'Defining the Parameters of Cyberwar Operations: Looking for Law in All the Wrong Places?', *Naval Law Review* 51 (2005): 140.
6 Barton Gellman, 'Cyber Attacks by al Qaeda Feared: Terrorists at Threshold of Using Internet as Tool of Bloodshed, Experts Say', *Washington Post* (27 June 2002), accessed 3 November 2014, http://www.informationclearinghouse.info/article4475.htm.
7 'Air Traffic Control: Weak Computer Security Practices Jeopardize Flight Safety', U.S. General Accounting Office, 1998, accessed 3 November 2014, http://www.gao.gov/products/AIMD-98-155.
8 Oona A. Hathaway, Rebecca Crootof, Philip Levitz, Haley Nix, Aileen Nowlan, William Perdue and Julia Spiegel, 'The Law of Cyber Attack', *California Law Review* 100 (2012): 817.
9 Amita Verma, *Cyber Crimes & Law* (Allahabad: Central Law Publications, 2009).
10 'UN Manual on the Prevention and Control of Computer-Related Crime 1994', accessed 3 November 2014, http://www.uncjin.org/Documents/irpc4344.pdf.
11 Pavan Duggal, *Cyber Law – The Indian Perspective* (New Delhi: Saakshar Law Publications, 2002).
12 Hathaway, Crootof, Levitz, Nix, Nowlan, Perdue and Spiegel, 'The Law of Cyber Attack'.
13 Sarah Gordon and Richard Ford, 'On the Definition and Classification of Cybercrime', *Journal in Computer Virology* 2 (2006): 13.
14 Goodman and Brenner, 'The Emerging Consensus on Criminal Conduct in Cyberspace'.
15 Thompson S.H. Teo and Yu Yuanyou, 'Online Buying Behavior: A Transaction Cost Economics Perspective', *Omega* 33 (5) (2005): 451–465.
16 George A. Akerlof, 'The Market for "Lemons": Quality Uncertainty and the Market Mechanism', *Quarterly Journal of Economics* 84 (1970): 488–500.
17 Jonathan Levin, 'Information and the Market for Lemons', *RAND Journal of Economics* 32 (4) (2001): 657–666.
18 Jason A. Cody, 'Derailing the Digitally Depraved: An International Law and Economics Approach to Combating Cybercrime and Cyberterrorism', *Michigan State University – DCL Journal of International Law* 11 (2002): 231.
19 John H. Huston and Roger W. Spencer, 'Quality, Uncertainty and the Internet: The Market for Cyber Lemons', *The American Economist* 46 (2002): 50–60.
20 Peter T. Leeson and Christopher J. Coyne, 'The Economics of Computer Hacking', *Journal of Law, Economics and Policy* 1 (2) (2005): 511.
21 Robert J. Sciglimpaglia Jr., 'Computer Hacking: A Global Offense', *Pace Yearbook of International Law* 3 (265) (1991): 201.
22 Mary M. Calkins, 'They Shoot Trojan Horses, Don't They? An Economic Analysis of Anti-Hacking Regulatory Models', *Georgetown Law Journal* 89 (2000): 171.

23 Tim Weiner, 'The Man Who Protects America from Terrorism', *The New York Times* (1 February 1999), accessed 3 November 2014, http://www.nytimes.com/1999/02/01/world/the-man-who-protects-america-from-terrorism.html?pagewanted=all.
24 Information Technology Act, 2000, § 43, 66.
25 Chaitanya Ramachandran and Karan Lahiri, 'Hacking as an Offence in India: Section 66 of the Information Technology Act 2000 – Resolving Ambiguities in Light of European and American Law', *Centre for Teaching Learning and Research* 13 (1) (2007): 33–38.
26 Ibid.
27 Ahmad Nehaluddin, 'Hackers' Criminal Behaviour and Laws Related to Hacking', *Centre for Teaching Learning and Research* 15 (7) (2009): 159–165.
28 Digital Guards database, 2001, accessed 2 March 2014, http://www.digitalguards.com/Glossary.htm.
29 Roger Darlington, 'Crime on the Net', 2001, accessed 15 July 2009, http://www.rogerdarlington.co.uk/crimeonthenet.html.
30 Nehaluddin, 'Hackers' Criminal Behaviour and Laws Related to Hacking'.
31 'The History of Policing', *Encyclopaedia Britannica*, accessed 3 November 2014, http://208.154.71.60/bcom/eb/article/2/0,5716,115162+1+108569,00.html.
32 Marc D. Goodman, 'Why the Police Don't Care about Computer Crime', *Harvard Journal of Law and Technology* 10 (1997): 468–469.
33 Rivka Tadjer, 'Detect, Deflect, Destroy', *Internet Week* (13 November 2000), accessed 3 November 2014, http://www.internetweek.com/indepth/indepth111300.html.
34 Information Technology Act, 2000, § 43(a).
35 Ibid., § 43(c).
36 Ibid., § 43(f).
37 Ibid., § 43(g).
38 Stephen Shavell, 'Criminal Law and the Optimal Use of Nonmonetary Sanctions as a Deterrent', *Columbia Law Review* 85 (6) (1985): 87.
39 'The Use of the Internet for Terrorist Purposes', *UNODC* (2012), accessed 3 November 2014, https://www.unodc.org/documents/frontpage/Use_of_Internet_for_Terrorist_Purposes.pdf.
40 Ibid.
41 Mark M. Pollitt, 'Cyberterrorism – Fact or Fancy?', *Proceedings of the 20th National Information Systems Security Conference*, 285 (1997) (quoted in Dorothy E. Denning, *Activism, Hacktivism and Cyberterrorism: The Internet as a Tool for Influencing Foreign Policy*), accessed 3 November 2014, https://www.rand.org/content/dam/rand/pubs/monograph_reports/MR1382/MR1382.ch8.pdf.
42 John Arquilla, 'The Great Cyberwar of 2002', *Wired* (1 February 1998), accessed 3 November 2014, http://www.wired.com/wired/archive/6.02/cyberwar_pr.html.
43 Research-papers.com, 'Cyber War', accessed 3 November 2014, http://www.research-papers.com/papers/tech2.shtml.
44 Maneela, 'Cyber Crimes: The Indian Legal Scenario', *US–China Law Review* 11 (2014): 570.

45 Praveen Dalal, 'Cyber Terrorism and Its Solution: An Indian Perspective', *ICFAI Journal of Cyber Law* 4 (1) (2005): 70.
46 Gary Becker, 'Crime and Punishment: An Economic Approach', *Journal of Political Economy*, 76 (2) (1968): 169–217.
47 S. Aguilar-Millan, J.E. Foltz, J. Jackson and A. Oberg, 'The Globalization of Crime', *Futurist* 42 (6) (2008): 41–50.
48 'The Use of the Internet for Terrorist Purposes'.
49 Richard Posner, *An Economic Analysis of Law* (New York: Aspen Publishers, 1998): 237–270.
50 Mark G. Stewart and John Mueller, 'Terrorism Risks and Cost-Benefit Analysis of Aviation Security', *Risk Analysis* 33 (2013): 895.
51 OBPR, *Best Practice Regulation Handbook, Office of Best Practice Regulation* (Canberra: Australian Government, 2010).
52 Bruno S. Frey and Simon Luechinger, 'How to Fight Terrorism: Alternatives to Deterrence', *Defence and Peace Economics* 14 (4) (2003): 237–249.
53 M.I. Lichbach, 'Deterrence or Escalation? The Puzzle of Aggregate Studies of Repression and Dissent', *Journal of Conflict Resolution* 31 (2) (1987): 266–297.
54 T. Sandler and J.L. Scoot, 'Terrorist Success in Hostage Taking Incidents: An Empirical Study', *Journal of Conflict Resolution* 31 (1) (1987): 35–53.
55 A.L. Burns, 'From Balance to Deterrence: A Theoretical Analysis', *World Politics* 9 (1957): 494–529; D. Ellsberg, *The Crude Analysis of Strategic Choice*, originally published as P-2183 (Santa Monica, CA: Rand, 1960); D. Ellsberg, 'Theory of the Reluctant Duelist', *American Economic Review* 46 (1956): 909–923; M. Kaplan, 'The Calculus of Nuclear Deterrence', *World Politics* 11 (1958): 20–43.
56 Alan Coddington, 'Game Theory, Bargaining Theory, and Strategic Reasoning', *Journal of Peace Research* 4 (1) (1967): 39–45.
57 Martin Shubik, 'Game Theory, Law and the Concept of Competition', *University of Cincinnati Law Review* 60 (1991–1992): 285.
58 Todd Sandler, John T. Tschirhart and Jon Cauley, 'A Theoretical Analysis of Transnational Terrorism', *American Political Science Review* 77 (1983): 36–54.
59 Sarita Azad, 'Defence against Terrorist Attacks: Game Theory Can Help', *IDSA Comment*, accessed 3 November 2014, http://www.idsa.in/idsacomments/DefenceagainstTerroristAttacksGameTheorycanHelp_sazad_030111.
60 Bernardo A. Huberman and Rajan M. Lukose, 'Social Dilemmas and Internet Congestion', *Science* 277 (5325) (1997): 535–537.
61 Mary M. Calkins, 'They Shoot Trojan Horses, Don't They?'
62 Gary Amold, 'Bullock Gets Entangled in "The Net"', *Washington Times* (28 July 1995); Thomas R. King, 'Movies: Director Goes On-Line to Push "Sneakers"', *Wall Street Journal* (28 August 1992); Robert Trigaux, 'Hackers: The Underbelly of Cyberspace', *St. Petersburg Times* (14 June 1998); Kenneth Turan, 'An Apocalypse of Kinetic Joy: Imagination Is Overpowered in "The Matrix", a Wild Thriller in Which Reality May or May Not Be Virtual', *L.A. Times* (31 March 1999).

63 Michael Lee, Sean Pak, David Lee and Aaron Schapiro, ‘Comment, Electronic Commerce, Hackers, and the Search for Legitimacy: A Regulatory Proposal’, *Berkeley Technology Law Journal* 14 (1998): 844.
64 Frey and Luechinger, ‘How to Fight Terrorism’: 237–249.
65 Jeff Victoroff, ‘The Mind of the Terrorist’, *Journal of Conflict Resolution* 49 (2005): 3–42.

Chapter 10

Economics of child labour

Gayathree Devi Kalliyat Thazhathuveetil

Background note

Child labour is a widespread phenomenon across the world and is observed in different forms in both developed and developing nations. The International Labour Organization defines the term 'child labour' as work that deprives children of their childhood, their potential and their dignity, and that is harmful to physical and mental development. It refers to work that is mentally, physically, socially or morally dangerous and harmful to children and interferes with their schooling by depriving them of the opportunity to attend school or obliging them to leave school prematurely or requiring them to attempt to combine school attendance with excessively long and heavy work.[1] It is estimated that around 215 million children work throughout the world today.[2]

There is no doubt that child labour is physically, mentally and psychologically taxing on young children; a child is as human as an adult and holds the right not to be exploited for economic purposes. Therefore, child labour is a social evil that ought to be condemned. However, does child labour adversely affect the nation's economic progress? Generally, the impact of child labour on the developed world is negligible, but child labour is seen across the world as a predominant feature of developing countries. The reason attributed towards such a presumption is that child labour stems out of poverty, which plagues developing nations the most. Poverty, as an extreme human condition, has always evoked immense social interest,[3] and its validity, as a causative factor of child labour, is unquestionable. While poverty is not the sole cause of child labour, it is a major and the most worrisome cause, at least in developing countries.[4] This chapter reviews literature on child labour, analyses child labour as an economic compulsion of poor families in developing countries and also answers the question whether child labour is an isolated individual/household decision or a decision necessitated by ineffective implementation and enforcement of government policies. The second section seeks to understand child labour as a variant of the Dictator Game. The third section analyses parental decisions from the angle of altruism. The fourth section considers the question of child labour having serious economic implications, in addition to the 'given' social implications. The last section considers the dichotomy between official documents and NGO's claims about child labour rates in India and argues against the effectiveness of the Child Labour (Prohibition and Regulation) Act, 1986.

Agency and Dictator Game

In social sciences, the term 'agency' fundamentally refers to the capacity of individuals to act independently and to make their own free choices. Agency forms the crux of the theory of *homo economicus*, that is the economic human, which proposes that a rational actor is inherently self-interested and such an actor independently and freely chooses only that alternative which would maximize his or her benefit or utility.[5] The rational choice theory stems from this understanding of man. Therefore, the significance of 'agency' and 'rationality' cannot be undermined in appreciating how actors bargain and make rational choices in the labour market. However, the question is whether children can be treated as real agents. An important assumption of the rational choice theory is that a rational decision maker should be able to rank outcomes in order from least preferred to most preferred.[6] Emile Durkheim, a French sociologist, pointed out that 'childhood is essentially a period in which the individual, in both the physical and moral sense, does not yet exist'.[7] This rationalization is universally acknowledged – a child lacks the cognitive faculties to make decisions regarding allocation of time between work and schooling. There is no *infans economicus* responding to market signals.[8] Generally, parents bond the labour of their children; they make market decisions on behalf of their children.

This situation may be understood as a variation of the Dictator Game. The Dictator Game is a game in experimental economics where one player, the dictator, decides on how to divide a fixed amount of money between himself and a recipient.[9] The game is in fact a one-person task of the dictator; the recipient is entirely passive. The recipient simply receives whatever amount the dictator decides on. Unlike an Ultimatum Game, the Dictator Game provides for the automatic implementation of the dictator's decision, without the recipient being able to decide whether to accept it or not. Therefore, it does not amount to a 'game' per se because there is no bargaining; it is more of a decision theory. At the household level, the parents/household head is the dictator, whereas the child is the recipient. Let us assume that the child's leisure is a variable divisible between labour and schooling. The dictator (parent) decides how to divide the child's times, and the recipient (child) passively accepts this decision. If the parent decides that the child ought to effectively enter the labour market and contribute to the family income, the child does so. The child is incapable of bargaining with the parent; thus, the parent ensures that the child responds to labour market signals.

Parental altruism and Rotten Kid Theorem

The idea of narrow self-interest has stood the test of time and forms the fundamental assumption of practically every experimental study in the field of economics. If one were to assume that a rational person always seeks to maximize his or her utility, then in a Dictator Game, the dictator ought to assume complete possession of the divisible commodity. A 'rational' dictator ought to not leave anything for the recipient. However, Dictator Games present strong evidence for other-regarding behaviour[10] and suggest that consciousness of 'fairness' or 'justice' is an influencing factor.[11] For instance, Forsythe *et al.*[12] find that 70% of the dictators actually do not grab the entire pie for themselves, leaving the receiver with on average 24% of the total amount. In fact, Dictator Games were originally thought of as an elegant way to identify the altruistic component of behaviour.[13] In the Dictator Game, the dictator decides what part of the commodity ought to be given to the recipient. As such, any giving by the dictator is attributed to altruism.

Although economics, as a subject matter of study, tends to focus more on self-interested actors, the concept of 'altruism' is not entirely ignored. In fact, Adam Smith noted as follows:

> How selfish soever man may be supposed, there are evidently some principles in his nature, which interest him in the fortune of others, and render their happiness necessary to him, though he derives nothing from it except the pleasure of seeing it. . . .

> The greatest ruffian, the most hardened violator of the laws of society, is not altogether without it.[14]

In many experiments, including Prisoner's Dilemma, public goods and bargaining experiments, subjects are often found to act benevolently towards each other.[15] In fact, altruism or unselfish behaviour is an important facet of family economics and explains household games and decisions.

The decision to send a child into the labour market is generally made by parents. Thus, when we consider the issue of child labour in the light of literature on altruism, on the face of it, it may appear as though every parent who sends his or her child into the labour market is non-altruistic. In fact, this view was popular with social reformers of the 19th century and is considered as the basis of child labour laws in England.[16] Authors like Parsons and Goldin proceeded on the assumption of parents being non-altruistic in their analysis of child labour.[17] The justification given is that child labour takes an immense physical, mental and psychological toll on young children and it would be impracticable to assume that a parent sending his or her child into the labour market is unaware of this. However, contemporary economists tend to disagree with this simplified argument.[18] Under normal circumstances, poverty pushes parents to make the choice of child labour. When extreme income and borrowing constraints form the basis for parental decisions, how justified is it be to call them egoistic?

Let us consider the two-period model of child labour proposed by Baland and Robinson.[19] In the first period, parents decide how to allocate their child's time between child labour and human capital accumulation. Thus, if a poor household head/parent decides to send the child into the labour market in the first period, there would be an increase in the household income and consumption in the first period. On the other hand, if the head/parent decides to send the child to school, the child would be in a position to increase his or her income and consumption in the second period, but fails to contribute to the household income in the first period. Thus, the choice is between increasing present income and consumption of the household or increasing the child's future consumption. Unless current income is sufficient to meet the family expenditure and the child's education expenses, it becomes impossible for a poor household head/parent to invest in improving the child's future consumption. Therefore, in dire situations, a poor household sacrifices the future welfare of the child in favour of the present benefit to the household in the form of child wages and reduced schooling costs.[20] Therefore, at a micro-level, child labour is a rational decision as long as the poor household head/parent seeks to increase family income for household subsistence.

However, the question still remains whether such a poor household head/parent, who is not bearing the future costs of the child labour decision but is taking advantage of it in the present, is altruistic. A significant theory that may be applied to answer this question is Gary Becker's Rotten Kid Theorem. Becker asserts that if a family has a head who cares sufficiently about all other members to transfer general resources to them, then redistribution of income among members of the household would not affect the consumption of any member, as long as the head continues to contribute to all.[21] The major conclusion is that if a head exists, other members also are motivated to maximize their family income and consumption, even if their welfare depends on their own consumption alone.[22] Thus, if a household head/parent is altruistic, the child's consumption will not be affected and the child will have an incentive to maximize family income. Therefore, parental altruism may be understood as the presence of child consumption in the utility function of the parent. As Bhalotra puts it, 'If the parent is altruistic parental consumption cannot be increased without increasing child consumption simultaneously'.[23]

Therefore, generally, even parents who send their children into the labour market are altruistic, as long as the family income is being apportioned in such a way that the child's welfare is not ignored. In fact, the presumption in favour of parental altruism is not affected even in cases where the children are engaged in hazardous work, because very often, asymmetry of information leads to such decisions. However, parental altruism need not be true in all cases. For instance, where the parents are economically well off and yet send the child into the labour market, or where parents are unemployed and hence send their children into the labour market as their income-earning substitutes, altruism cannot be assumed as these instances are merely exploitative. In such cases, reverse altruism comes into play, that is parents are egoistic actors, whereas children are altruistic actors.

Welfare economics

In simple terms, welfare economics is that branch of economics that seeks to optimally allocate resources in such a manner that social welfare is ensured. Welfare economics evaluates institutions in terms of whether they make people better or worse off. At the micro level, different optimal or rational preferences may exist in terms of allocating resources, and it is near-impossible to satisfy all individual preferences. Therefore, in order to ensure maximum social welfare, welfare economists typically apply the concepts of Pareto optimality and Pareto improvement and decide whether an institution is efficient or not.

A social state is Pareto optimal if and only if no one's welfare (defined in terms of their preferences) can be raised without reducing the welfare of someone else. If the economy is not at a Pareto optimum, there is some inefficiency in the system.[24] While the Pareto criterion analyses whether individual preferences are satisfied, the branch of welfare economics applies this very criterion to the entire economy and checks whether social preferences are satisfied. Thus, as far as an individual is concerned, Pareto efficiency is obtained when the marginal benefit of an action exceeds its cost. Welfare economics understands this very criterion in the sense that economic efficiency is satisfied when the marginal social benefit of an institution exceeds its marginal cost. There is no denial that child labour is an inefficient choice from the perspective of human rights; the child suffers physically, mentally and psychologically on account of a choice that his or her parents make. But is child labour economically inefficient? The answer to this question lies in the short-run and long-run impacts of child labour.

As mentioned earlier, studies reveal that child labour is predominant in poor households. Poor household heads/parents generally choose to send their children into the labour market because child wages form an additional source of family income and help in household subsistence. Therefore, an obvious short-run impact of child labour is an increase in household income. When this short-run effect is considered in isolation, child labour may seem like a rational choice. If the child is to be sent to school, the household will have to bear the cost of education in addition to the child's subsistence expenses. Therefore, child education creates negative utility for the parents. If, on the other hand, the child is sent into the labour market, in addition to the accrual of child wages, the child's subsistence expenses are not incident upon the parents. Although parents may act rationally by sending their children to work in order to increase their probability of survival, they may not perceive the long-run negative implications of child labour for their own family.[25] In most cases, parents make the decision of sending their children into the labour market based on the misconceived notion that child labour and schooling are perfect substitutes. However, this fallacious belief creates negative utility for the whole family in the long run. Child labour undoubtedly presents monetary benefits in the short run; however, the returns to work experience decline monotonically.[26] The benefits of going to school are mainly long term and will flow mainly to the child, rather than the parent. Yet, as has been found in a number of studies, the private returns to education are greater than the returns to child labour.[27] Education generally provides an opportunity to take up intellectual jobs, which tend to be high paying as compared to agricultural or industrial labour.

In addition, at a macro level, child labour impacts the long-run growth and development of the economy. The nexus between schooling and human capital accumulation is close, and therefore, to the extent that child labour impedes school attendance, it reduces human capital accumulation in the country, which negatively impacts the labour productivity, economic growth and economic development of the country. Further, the widespread availability of child labour has a detrimental effect on adult labour. When child labour increases and becomes a competitive market, child wages increase. Accordingly, adult wages may fall and child labour may become more profitable than adult labour.[28] This provides an incentive to adults to increase their fertility rates. Those adults who are willing to send their children into the labour market can maintain status quo, as far as household income is concerned. However, what about those adults who do not engage their children in labour? Their wages and household income fall. Thus, widespread child labour makes child labour necessary for every family's survival.

Furthermore, increased incidence of child labour leads to depressed technological growth. Child labour is generally in the interests of firms, since it provides them with a cheaper source of labour than adults. This may lead to replacement of mechanical labour with manual labour, as it is a cheaper alternative. Accordingly, firms begin to reduce fixed capital investments, which reduce the overall growth of the nation. Therefore, as can be seen, while an individual act (token) of child labour may be Pareto improving when we consider its consequences for a single poor family, the practice of child labour may make other families worse off by changing the range of options that are open to them. The benefit accruing to a single household is at the cost of the nation's growth. Therefore, child labour is Pareto inefficient and forces the economy into a Pareto inferior position.

Child Labour (Prohibition and Regulation) Act, 1986

The most common policy response to the practice of child labour is the imposition of a prohibition on the same; it is assumed that such a prohibition would lead to an increase in school attendance (since schooling and child labour are considered to be largely substitutable), in addition to increasing adult wages (assuming that children displaced adults in the labour market). Governments generally do not seek to ban all forms of child labour. The idea of the 'Worst Forms of Child Labour', which stems from Article 3 of the International Labour Organization's Convention No. 182,[29] guides most governments in banning only those forms of child labour that are hazardous in nature. The said article prohibits all forms of slavery or practices similar to slavery, use/procuring/offering of a child for prostitution or illicit activities and work which is likely to harm health, safety or morals of children.

Drafted along the same lines, the Child Labour (Prohibition and Regulation) Act, 1986, is a landmark legislation that seeks to reduce the incidence of child labour in India. The 1986 Act imposed a minimum age restriction – persons up to age 14 were ineligible to work in certain industries and occupations. The prohibited occupations include transport of passengers, catering establishments at railway stations, ports, foundries, handling of toxic or inflammable substances, handloom or power loom industry and mines.[30] The processes banned for children include beedi making, manufacturing of matches, explosives, shellac, soap and so on, construction, automobile repairs and production of garments. However, agriculture and family-run businesses are not banned from hiring children for their work.[31] The law merely places limitations on how many hours children may work in an industry or occupation and also specifies during which hours of the day children may work.[32] The only exception is child labour in household enterprises.

Nonetheless, this law's effectiveness in curbing child labour is debatable. The International Confederation of Free Trade Unions' report reveals that in the past 25 years, officially recognized child labour in India has increased from 10.7 million to 17 million – and these figures are known to be underestimates. In contrast to the official figures, independent studies reckon the figures to range from 44 million to 100 million.[33] This being the case, it ought to be analysed whether the present prohibition has the welfare impact it endeavours to create.

The Basu and Van Model[34]

The basic economic model created by noted economists Kaushik Basu and Pham Hoang Van explains the perverse consequences of a child labour prohibition. This model assumes that there is a single-sector economy and families in the said economy send their children into the labour market only when the household income is insufficient to meet subsistence consumption levels. Child labour and adult labour are assumed to be perfect substitutes. Consider that child labour is prohibited in this economy and firms that flout the prohibition are forced to pay a fine. The firms push the burden of these fines onto the children, by reducing child wages. This leads to a fall in the household income, and they are forced to send more children into the labour market to bring the household income back to the level of subsistence consumption. Firms also prefer to employ children instead of adults, as child wages are lower than adult wages. Therefore, a ban on child labour would only lead to an increase in child labour in countries where poverty is prevalent.

In Figure 10.1, assume that the child labour market is at an initial equilibrium position 'E', with equilibrium wages 'P' and equilibrium

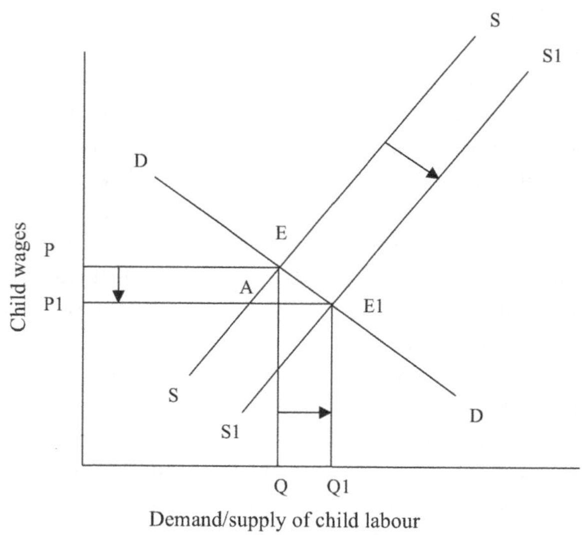

Figure 10.1 Child labour market

Source: Akanksha Agarwal, 'Child Labour in India', *Indian Labour Journal* 54 (11) (2013): 1103.

child labour demand/supply 'Q'. Firms flouting the Child Labour Ban pay fines and reduce child wages from 'P' to 'P1'. Accordingly, the new labour market equilibrium falls to position 'A'. This forces households to increase the supply of child labour, whereby the supply curve shifts from 'S' to 'S1'. Accordingly, new equilibrium is found at 'E1', with 'P1' wages and 'Q1' number of child labourers. As is evident from the figure, there is an increase in the number of child labourers in the economy from 'Q' to 'Q1'. In India, child labour is widespread in the agricultural sector, followed by the manufacturing sector, and hotels and restaurants.[35]

The Child Labour (Prohibition and Regulation) Act, 1986, does not ban the use of child labour in the agricultural sector, but only in the manufacturing sector. Therefore, let us assume that there is a two-sector economy (i.e. the agricultural sector and the manufacturing sector), wherein a fine is imposed on the manufacturing sector for flouting the child labour ban. Thus, child wages drop in the manufacturing sector to offset the increased fine. Two cases arise in such a situation. One possibility is that child wages in the manufacturing sector continue to be higher than child wages in the agricultural sector. In such a situation, children do not have an incentive to move to the agricultural sector. Poor families seek to employ more children, and firms prefer this since their production cost decreases. In this case, there is an overall increase in child labour in the economy. Due to this increase in labour supply, adult wages also fall. Therefore, poor families continue to be poor, and both adults and children are working in the manufacturing sector at a low wage rate. The second possibility is that wages in the agricultural sector are higher than wages in the manufacturing sector. In this case, as soon as child wages drop in the manufacturing sector, children are induced to move to the agricultural sector. Accordingly, labour supply in the manufacturing sector decreases, due to which adult wages increase. In return, household income also increases. If this rise in income is sufficient to send the child to school, the ban achieves its goal. However, if this rise is insufficient to reduce the number of working children, the agricultural sector will simply see more child labour, with low child wages.

Statistical data shows that almost 85% of the working children are engaged in agriculture.[36] Therefore, the latter scenario seems to be true in India – the ban has increased adult wages in the manufacturing sector; however, the increase is not sufficient to reduce child labour. Hence, the ban on child labour proves to be ineffective.

Conclusion

Child labour is a phenomenon true for both developed and developing nations. However, the nexus between poverty and child labour cannot be denied; therefore, child labour is predominantly observed in developing nations. We observe that child labour is generally a household decision made by the household head/parent to meet household subsistence consumption. Contrary to the popular belief that only egoistic parents force their children into the labour market, it is seen that even altruistic parents may be forced into making the child labour decision, owing to income and borrowing constraints. Asymmetry of information regarding the industry/occupation may also lead to parental decisions. While child labour may seem like a rational choice in the short run, it adversely affects the household income and also takes its toll on the nation's economic progress in the long run. The general policy response to child labour is a ban on the most hazardous forms of child labour, such as prostitution, drug trafficking, mining and industrial work. However, as observed in an earlier section, the ban imposed on child labour in India through the Child Labour (Prohibition and Regulation) Act, 1986, proved to be ineffective because it failed to increase adult wages to the extent of reducing the number of working children.

Considering that child labour has serious long-term implications for a nation's economy, the government cannot afford to let the economy operate under an ineffective policy. A ban is very much plausible and can be effective to curb child labour. However, India is a nation where a considerable proportion of the population lives in abject poverty. Therefore, to expect that the practice of child labour can be tackled by a solitary policy is naïve. In a country like India, poverty is almost always the sole cause for child labour. Therefore, what our economy requires at this stage is a perfect policy mix that aims at reducing both poverty and child labour, and perfect enforcement of this policy mix. Access to education is definitely the most significant policy in the mix. With the coming into force of Article 21A of the Indian Constitution, in 2010, India became one of the 135 countries to make education a fundamental right of every child between 6 and 14 years. Free education ensures that the parents need not worry about schooling costs. Therefore, parents who can manage the household, without the child's contribution to the household income, are indifferent towards the child going to school. This policy, therefore, can improve school attendance.

However, there is a need to reduce both the direct costs and opportunity costs of education. The free education policy cuts down the direct costs of education. The simultaneous operation of policies like the Mid-Day Meals Scheme and Anganwadis will reduce the opportunity costs of education and further incentivize parents to send their children to school, because such policies reduce the child's consumption burden on the parents. In fact, the Mid-Day Meals Scheme, which was introduced in the 1960s with the objectives of protecting children from classroom hunger, increasing school enrolment and attendance or reducing child labour, has indeed reduced the number of child workers.[37] Another policy introduced by the Indian government to target child labour is the Anganwadi Scheme. Sometimes, both the parents are in the labour market, and the elder sibling cannot go to school because he or she is left to take care of the younger ones. This is a common form of child labour in India, where even though the elder child is not effectively contributing towards the family income, he or she is prevented from going to school. Anganwadis have played a significant role in curbing such child labour. Poverty increases the incidence of child labour. Poverty also reduces the family's ability to borrow. The lack of credit facilities makes it further costly for poor families to forego present income by sending their children to school. Therefore, poverty alleviation schemes, which generally provide employment to adults for a fixed number of days, ought to be continued, so the incidence of child labour is reduced.

The current policy mix of free education, poverty alleviation programmes, Mid-Day Meals Scheme, Anganwadis, public distribution system, subsidy schemes and so on can definitely curb both poverty and child labour. Nevertheless, the implementation of these schemes has been discouraging, considering that the number of child labourers in the country is startlingly high. Simultaneous implementation of all these programmes alone can reduce the incidence of child labour. Ineffective implementation of this policy mix and improper enforcement of the child labour ban are the reasons why child labour continues to plague the nation. Therefore, as seen, child labour is not an individual/household decision; it's a consequence of an inefficient welfare state. Unless the welfare state takes positive steps towards effective implementation and enforcement of its policies, household decisions will continue to favour child labour.

Notes

1 'What Is Child Labour', *International Labour Organization*, accessed 22 August 2014, http://www.ilo.org/ipec/facts/lang--en/index.htm.
2 'World Day against Child Labour – 12 June', *UN News Center*, accessed 7 October 2014, http://www.un.org/en/events/childlabourday/background.shtml.
3 Prof. B.B. Pande, 'Review of Poverty and Human Rights – Sen's Capability Perspective', Polly Vizard, ed., *Journal of National Human Rights Commission* 5 (2006): 191.
4 Guy Thijs, 'Child Labour – Trends and Challenges in Asia', 1997, accessed 7 October 2014, http://www.ilo.org/public//english/standards/ipec/conf/lahore/lahoretrends.pdf.
5 James H. Davis, F. David Schoorman and Lex Donaldson, 'Toward a Stewardship Theory of Management', *The Academy of Management Review* 22 (1) (1997): 20.
6 Robert Cooter and Thomas Ulen, 'An Economic Theory of Contract', In *Law and Economics* (New Delhi: Pearson Education, 2004): 219.
7 Emile Durkheim, 'Characteristics of Childhood', In *Essays on Morals and Education 1919*, translated by H.L. Sutcliffe, edited by W.S.F. Pickering (London: Routledge, 1979): 150.
8 Jane Humphries, 'Cliometrics, Child Labor, and the Industrial Revolution', *Critical Review* 13 (4) (1999): 269–283.
9 G.A.M. van de Pol, 'The Dictator Game: Gender Differences in Behaviour under Social Pressure', accessed 7 October 2014, http://thesis.eur.nl/pub/16157/Master-Thesis-Geerten-van-de-Pol-2014-Final.pdf.
10 Alexander K. Koch and Hans-Theo Normann, 'Giving in Dictator Games: Regard for Others or Regard by Others?', accessed 22 August 2014, http://econ.ucdenver.edu/beckman/tiffany/koch-southern.pdf.
11 Daniel Kahneman, Jack L. Knetsch and Richard H. Thaler, 'Fairness and the Assumptions of Economics', *The Journal of Business* 59 (4) (1986): S285.
12 Robert Forsythe, Joel L. Horowitz, N.E. Savin and Martin Sefton, 'Fairness in Simple Bargaining Experiments', *Games and Economic Behavior* 6 (1994): 347–369.
13 D.J. Zizzo, 'Do Dictator Games Measure Altruism?', 2011, accessed 22 August 2014, http://www.uea.ac.uk/documents/166500/0/CBESS-11-15.pdf.
14 Adam Smith, *Theory of Moral Sentiments* (Québec: Presses De L'Université Laval, 1961).
15 James Andreoni and John H. Miller, 'Analyzing Choice with Revealed Preference: Is Altruism Rational?', In *The Handbook of Experimental Economics Results*, edited by Charles R. Plott and Vernon L. Smith (Amsterdam: Elsevier, 2008): 4–54.
16 V. Bhaskar and Bishnupriya Gupta, 'Were American Parents Really Selfish? – Child Labor in the 19th Century', accessed 7 October 2014, http://www2.warwick.ac.uk/fac/soc/economics/staff/bgupta/childapr06.pdf.

17 Donald O. Parsons and Claudia Goldin, 'Parental Altruism and Self-Interest: Child Labor among Late Nineteenth-Century American Families', *Economic Inquiry* 27 (4) (1989): 637–659.
18 Bhaskar, and Gupta, 'Were American Parents Really Selfish? – Child Labor in the 19th Century'.
19 Jean-Marie Baland and James Robinson, 'Is Child Labour Inefficient?', *Journal of Political Economy* 108 (4) (2000): 667.
20 Judith Sommer, 'How Altruism Affects the Relationship between Poverty and Child', accessed 22 August 2014, http://www.wiwi.hu-berlin.de/professurenen/vwl/fw/dissertations/Seminararbeiten/Development_Economics/Wintersemester_2007__2008/Judith_Sommer_How_Altruism_affects_the_Relationship_between_Poverty_and_Child_Labour.
21 Gary Becker, 'A Theory of Social Interactions', *Journal of Political Economy* 82 (6) (1974): 1067.
22 Theodore C. Bergstrom, 'A Fresh Look at the Rotten Kid Theorem – And Other Household Mysteries', *Journal of Political Economy* 97 (5) (1989): 1138.
23 Sonia Radhika Bhalotra, 'Parent Altruism, Cash Transfers and Child Poverty', *Bristol Economics Discussion Papers* (2004): 4 (Discussion Paper Number 04/562).
24 Richard Just, Darrell Hueth and Andrew Schmitz, *The Welfare Economics of Public Policy: A Practical Approach to Project and Policy Evaluation* (Edward Elgar Publishing Ltd, 2004), accessed 22 August 2014, http://www.aru.org.bo/capacitaciones/diplomados/Edward_Elgar-The_Welfare_Economics_of_Public_Policy-A_Practical_Approach_to_Project_and_Policy_Evaluation.pdf.
25 Rosaana Galli, 'The Economic Impact of Child Labour', *International Institute for Labour Studies Discussion Paper 128*, accessed 22 August 2014, http://www.ilo.org/inst/publication/discussion-papers/WCMS_193680/lang--en/index.htm.
26 Jamie Gordon, 'The Economic Implications of Child Labour – A Comprehensive Approach to Labour Policy', accessed 22 August 2014, https://econ.duke.edu/uploads/assets/dje/2008/Gordon.pdf.
27 Kathleen Beegle, Rajeev Dehejia and Roberta Gatti, 'Why Should We Care about Child Labor?: The Education, Labor Market, and Health Consequences of Child Labor', *Journal of Human Resources* 44 (4) (2009): 2.
28 International Program on Elimination of Child Labour, International Labour Organization, 'Child Labour Wages and Productivity: Results from Demand-Side Surveys', 2007, accessed 7 November 2014, http://www.ilo.org/ipecinfo/product/viewProduct.do?productId=7065.
29 International Labour Organization, 'ILC87 – CONVENTION 182', accessed 7 October 2014, http://www.ilo.org/public/english/standards/relm/ilc/ilc87/com-chic.htm.
30 Part A, Schedule, The Child Labour (Prohibition and Regulation) Act, 1986.
31 Part B, Schedule, The Child Labour (Prohibition and Regulation) Act, 1986.
32 The Child Labour (Prohibition and Regulation) Act, 1986, § 7.

33 International Confederation of Free Trade Unions, 'No Time to Play: Child Workers in the Global Economy', accessed 7 October 2014, http://library.fes.de/fulltext/netzquelle/01312.html.
34 Kaushik Basu and Pham Hoang Van, 'The Economics of Child Labour', *The American Economic Review* 88 (3) (1998): 412–427.
35 Akanksha Agarwal, 'Child Labour in India', *Indian Labour Journal* 54 (11) (2013): 1103.
36 Sharmistha Self and Richard Grabowski, 'Agricultural Technology and Child Labour: Evidence from India', accessed 7 October 2014, http://cola.siu.edu/economics/_common/documents/discussion/agtech-child-labor.pdf.
37 Government of India, Ministry of Human Resource Development, Department of School Education and Literacy, *Report of 5th Joint Review Mission on Mid Day Meal Scheme* (Assam, 2013), accessed 7 October 2014, http://mdm.nic.in/Files/Review/Fifth_Review/Assam/Report_Assam_JRM_Final.pdf.

Part V

Regulatory economics and markets

Chapter 11

The limits of democracy

An economic analysis of countermajoritarian institutions

Lalit Panda

Background note

Judicial review is a part of most constitutional democracies and is a countermajoritarian institution that works alongside with majoritarian ones. As a result of this, it is often criticised for its shortcomings in ensuring social welfare. The chief allegation is that its action to invalidate the working of democratically elected representatives is a usurpation of the will of the majority on the basis of rules and inclinations that are incapable of providing for good governance. It is the intention of the author to assess this allegation through the lens of law and economics, specifically whether judicial review as a concept could be found to meet a criterion of efficiency. This will be done by attempting to place the democratic process into a framework that assesses its tendencies for its ability to bring about an equilibrium at the point of maximum utility. While this may appear to be counter to most prevalent views of the nature of democratic action, it is this very framework that can best assess the process for efficiency and assess where judicial review may find a legitimate place and purpose.

The following section reviews the existing literature on the subject of the working of democracy and of judicial review that has been done along the lines of law and economics. Here, the author intends to sift through the extensive literature on public choice so as to distinguish the assumptions it takes up in its analysis of democracy and of political activity in general. It will be found that the present work will deviate on certain fundamental points in its view of democratic action. This deviation may appear to some to not reflect certain realities of politics, but the intention is not to shroud the analysis in romance but to instead point to certain conclusions that appear only in specific instances in politics. These instances are those that are most removed from economic actions and would therefore be more likely to be considered of a political nature.

On the basis of this idea, an economic framework of analysis is built up in the third section by examining the relationships between rights that are mutually exclusive choices or, as the author calls them, situations of intractable conflict. It further examines the relationship between the votes of two conflicting interest groups and the rights of each interest group that comes to be protected. In doing so, it will be apparent that the analysis is one that is from the perspective of the government making a proposal to the different interest groups, consuming and producing the rights at the same time so as to derive the highest possible utility in the form of votes. This will be found to be an analysis removed from the traditional situations that bring in majority cycling. This is not to say that it obviates the possibility of cycling but that instead it considers a situation where it is not immediately relevant.

Certain conclusions regarding the deficiencies of democracy are highlighted in the third section, and it is proposed that judicial review is intended to address these same deficiencies. The fourth section proceeds to lay out certain specific prescriptions on the basis of the conclusions already made. These prescriptions are intended to bring out what is best in judicial review and allay the fears of its critics, especially in relation to the Indian Constitution. The author considers such activity to be wholly within the physical and legal possibilities of a constitution and is optimistic of the legitimacy of judicial review on the same grounds. The fifth section provides the conclusion.

Relevant views on democracy and judicial review

Scholarship analysing political institutions with economic tools regularly works to explain the working of democracy and the mechanisms by which voters bring certain governments into power, not to mention the different proposals put forward by political parties and the preferences that voters have among the said proposals. The field has come to be known as public choice and has seen seminal work by such economists as Kenneth Arrow, Duncan Black, Anthony Downs, James Buchanan and Gordon Tullock. Work on the functioning of a democracy has come to show how different rules of collective decision-making could compare the rankings of different candidates pairwise in the preference orderings of different voters. This could often result in the problem known as 'majority cycling', which essentially results from the failure of majority voting in meeting a logical requirement of transitivity and which also means that political parties that wish to destabilise the government in power can *always* put forward a proposal that would meet majority approval.[1]

An example of this can be seen should we consider three voters, A, B and C, ranking their preferences for candidates I, II and III, for a particular public post open for elections. Each of these voters not only chooses his or her most preferred candidate, but also, as per the ordinal analysis of economic preferences, ranks all three candidates in the order that he or she prefers them for the post. Now let us consider a situation where voter A prefers II to I to III, voter B prefers III to II to I and voter C prefers I to III to II. In this particular set-up of preferences, we may assess who is the most popular candidate for the post under election. Here, we see that candidate II has a majority preferring him or her for the post over I. Both A and B have ranked him or her higher. Thus, II should be elected over I. Similarly, candidate I is preferred over III by a majority of voters A and C. But now we come to the problem – candidate III turns out to be preferred over candidate II, as a majority of B and C have ranked him or her higher. This means that candidate II is preferred over I, candidate I is preferred over III, but candidate III appears to be preferred over II. This clearly violates the logical principle of transitivity and means that none of the candidates in the election can be considered to provide the voters with maximum utility. Their voting will become irrational. This would understandably result in a situation where political equilibrium at a point of maximum utility would become impossible. It is also to be noted that the fields of public choice and social choice regularly reject the cardinal measurement of utility (and interpersonal comparability of utility) as a significant way in which to carry out their analyses and instead opt for preference orderings in the ordinal sense.[2]

The problems of majority rule decision-making came to be addressed by Duncan Black, who pointed out that majority cycles came about because in a certain logical ordering of the candidates, some voters might have 'double-peaked preferences'.[3] Now this was by no means a far-fetched possibility in actual politics.

No group of individuals who agree on a set ordering of candidates on the basis of some political variable would necessarily have all individuals preferring one candidate and all others in descending order of preference to the left and right on the spectrum. They could well mean multiple-peaked preferences. James Buchanan and Gordon Tullock, in their work *The Calculus of Consent*, had further ideas to put forward in the form of their acceptance of cycling as a reality with benefits (cycling would ensure that minorities would never be permanently side lined and could always be included in the formulations of future proposals[4]), and also in the form of prescriptions as to when voting rules should be shifted away from simple majority to supermajority and unanimity.[5] This was part of their overall suggestion that the rational individual would pursue the choice of forming a constitution with other individuals with whom he or she may have to make collective choices.[6] Given that a rule of simple majority would necessarily mean the imposition of a number of externalities on those groups that do not agree to the proposals the majority would carry out, and given also that any rule requiring unanimity would be fraught with high transaction costs in arriving at a unanimous decision (and given also that external costs fall and decision-making costs rise with the increasing unanimity of a decision), the individual would bargain with all other individuals to find the optimal level of unanimity for a particular decision that would ensure that external and transaction costs are minimised. Thus, for instance, where high external costs are likely, one would choose a rule of supermajority.

Buchanan and Tullock, in their analysis of the role of the constitution, stress greatly on unanimity as a rule that plays a very significant role. They do, however, mention countermajoritarian institutions thus:

> While it is clear that something akin to the doctrine of inalienable rights, institutionally embodied in constitutional provisions limiting the authority of legislative majorities, can easily be reconciled with our construction, we should emphasize that this doctrine is not central to our construction. The fact that much of our construction can be reconciled with a strain of orthodox democratic theory, and vice versa, should not obscure the profound differences between our approach and the one which has been implicit in much political theory and philosophy, both ancient and modern. The most basic difference lies in the incorporation into our models of the economic meaning of the unanimity rule.[7]

We may look also at other works regarding countermajoritarian institutions in alternative frameworks. Tom Ginsburg's paper on the design of constitutional courts[8] must be highlighted in its explanation as to how and why courts and their levels of independence come to be at the time they are being designed and formed. However, this work looks closely at the political situation of the constituent powers and the dominance of one or more political parties in the determination of whose interests the court will come to serve. He finds that independent courts are born from deadlocked constituent politics, where parties require such a court as an insurance in the event that they do not succeed in retaining majority. Similarly, other analyses have stressed on the influence of political variables on the decision-making of constitutional courts. One such work examines the role of independence and assertiveness in a court under a newly formed democracy after transition from an authoritarian government.[9] Another discusses the predictability of decisions of such courts in the light of party alignment and supposed advancement of ideological goals.[10] Here, they use certain datasets to good advantage and find that the influence of politics on courts is complex and does not constitute an immediate reflection of certain attitudes or alignments. Significantly, Landes and Posner have also forwarded a number of pertinent arguments that situate the problem of judicial independence within an interest group analysis (where the groups 'buy' legislation).[11] However, they base their justification on the suggestion that independent judges could be valued because they could provide some assurance of temporal stability for 'legislative bargains', the idea being that a legislature must be given the ability to lock itself into deals that future legislations cannot undo easily. There also exist a number of game-theoretic approaches to the subject matter that are not immediately relevant to the present analysis.[12]

On the other hand, there is a vast amount of literature in political theory and constitutional law that goes towards defending or refuting the need for constitutional courts and understanding how their countermajoritarian status may be counter to the ideals of democracy.[13] While both the defenders and the critics have put forward extensive views that are too voluminous to represent here, this chapter intends to provide a fresh look at the economic justifications for judicial review that does not link it with political bargaining and the interests of legislators but instead bases it directly on its utility to a population. There is also significant debate and constant uncertainty as to the extent of the powers of judicial review and when they are exercisable and when not. Critics point out a number of instances when such courts have engaged in what may be called 'judicial overreach' or 'judicial activism'. Constitutional courts also have a number of tools with which to approach and deal with unconstitutional actions. How does it choose between its prospective tools? These too have to be understood, and law and economics must give certain prescriptions as to when and how judicial activity is to be aligned so as to best ensure efficient outcomes.

A defence of judicial review

The foremost reason for which judicial review comes under attack is its supposed role in undermining the process of democratic decision-making in which the choice of a collective is made according to the will of the majority by a simple majority rule of voting. Those who defend the constitutional courts often do so by considering it as a solution to the principal-agent problem that lies at the heart of democracy.[14] However, this chapter intends to create a framework in which judicial review can be analysed for the immediate results it gives to social welfare and how this objective of maximising social welfare can be best achieved. Figure 11.1 is a rough representation of how democracy functions.

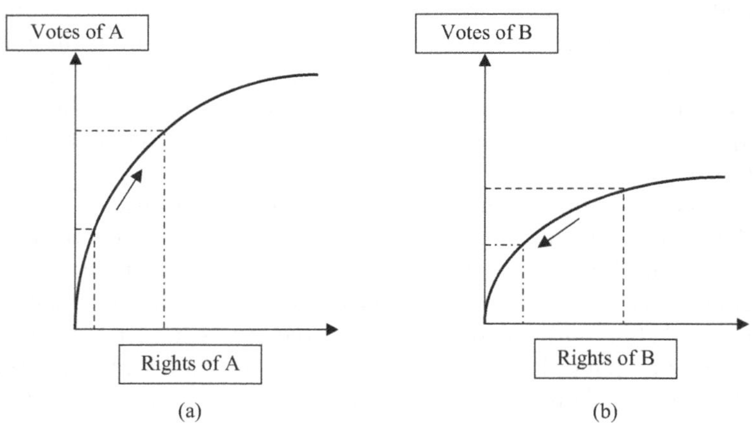

Figure 11.1 Functioning of democracy

Source: Author's own compilation.

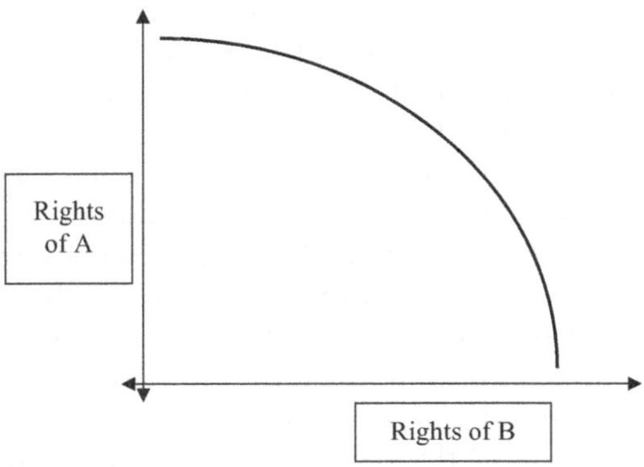

Figure 11.2 Relationship between rights of interest groups

Source: Author's own compilation.

Figure 11.1a and b shows two relationships that are themselves controlled by a third relationship shown in Figure 11.2. Figure 11.1a and b shows the relationships between the rights of interest groups A and B, respectively, protected by a particular legal framework and the votes cast by the interest group in favour of the political party or representative supporting that legal framework. For example, in Figure 11.1a, the graph shows the direct relationship between the rights of A protected by the legal framework and the votes cast in favour of the party supporting that framework. Here, we are analysing a situation in which the rights of interest groups A and B are in conflict and cannot coexist. If the party in question proposes to protect A's rights to a certain extent, there will be a concomitant number of votes from interest group A. If it proposes more protection, more voters will be won over. (Those not voting because enough protection has not been proposed may be voting for other parties for other reasons or not voting at all.) The votes cast will increase at a decreasing rate. Two reasons are given for this: first, the population of any interest group must necessarily be limited. Thus, the increase in votes will simply stop after a point. Second, it may be possible to derive a concept of *diminishing marginal inclination towards group welfare*. Here, it should be understood that as more and more rights are given to A, more members of the interest group who had been holding out their votes for a better and more satisfactory level of rights would decide to cast their votes in favour of the proposer of a legislation. This should not be confused with the situation of more active voters coming out to vote first and less active ones coming forth later (less active voters would be less concerned once they have already derived certain rights and would not come out to vote at all if the rights that satisfied them were already elicited by the votes of the more active voters). The changes in rights and votes should be seen as disparate quantities that are measured from election to election and not during one election. We must also consider the fact that there are differing preference arrangements within the interest group that do not match the aggregate arrangement. Thus, those who are satisfied after the protection of a lower-order right will continue to be part of the body of voters already won over for the next election and will not be part of the additional voters coming in at each new election. Fewer and fewer new voters will switch votes each election. (One problem may be that less active voters who had come forth to vote when they had minimal rights may fall into passivity and not feel the need to go to the polling booth when their rights stand at a secured position. It is assumed that such a fall into passivity does not occur.)

A further explanation must be given – here, the rights of A and the rights of B are being assumed to be in direct conflict. Thus, the protection of a certain quantity of the rights of A would necessarily mean that a certain quantity of the rights of B is being restricted. This is the nature of the situations that this analysis is studying – ones of irreconcilable conflict. Buchanan and Tullock's emphasis on 'political exchange' and political bargaining (the operation by which two or more interest groups conflicting on two or more different fronts each compromise on the one they value less so as to gain an upper hand in the one they value more) towards a surplus through external benefits is not within the framework of this analysis as they look only at rights that do in fact conflict without the possibility of reconciliation. It is not the purpose of this chapter to consider the role of law in furthering the formation of agreements between individuals and between interest groups through logrolling in legislatures. It considers, in full pessimism, all interests to be in conflict with the interest of some other (whether this other exists or is a future entity) and disregards the possibility of the existence of self-regarding interests or rights. Such politics is towards the minimisation of external costs. It is not that Buchanan and Tullock do not consider this but that they have actively worked to take on the other kinds of situations:

> Much political discussion seems to have proceeded as follows: 'If the interests of two or more individuals conflict, unanimity is impossible. Some interests must prevail over others if action is not to be wholly stifled.' This line of reasoning seems quite plausible until one confronts ordinary economic exchange. Note that in such an exchange the interests of the two contracting parties clearly conflict. Yet unanimity is reached. Contracts are made; bargains are struck without the introduction of explicit or implicit coercion. In this case, no interest prevails over the other; both interests are furthered. Our continued repetition of this simple analogy stems from our conviction that, at base, it is the failure to grasp fully the significance of this point that has retarded progress in political theory.[15]

In the view of this author, it must be accepted that 'ordinary economic exchange' is not always possible or plausible and the incompatibility of certain of our human interests (along with the restriction of some interests without any direct reward to the restricted party) must be something we must live with. Politics exists for this reason, and any attempt to have it swallowed up by economics for sheer faith in the coincidence of exchange would be misguided. Certain non-negotiables do exist in the minds of men. Now to understand how the rights of A and the rights of B are related, see Figure 11.2.

Here it may be observed that there is an inverse relationship between the rights of A and the rights of B, which would mean that any change in the protection (or restriction) of the rights of A will *necessarily* mean a proportionate but not necessarily equal change in the restriction (or protection) of the rights of B. So this would mean that when there is any change in the rights of A in Figure 11.1a, there will also be a simultaneous change in the rights of B in Figure 11.1b. Both will yield different numbers of votes from A and B and the intensity of the preference that each has for its rights being different, the elasticity of the curves will differ.

A further note must be added on the measurement of rights on the x-axis of the graphs in Figure 11.1. Here, the author has employed a system of arranging different 'rights' or appreciable and divisible interests on the axes in the order of the quantum of utility that they give to the interest group as a whole and pegged to the different cardinal values of the utility. Thus, an important point to note would be that the x-axis takes full account of the intensity of preferences. Thus, if the right to free speech on the Internet, the right to a free press and the right to assembly are next to each other on a spectrum or axis, the distance between the first two will not be the same as the one between the second and the third and will instead reflect the appropriate cardinal utility derived from the rights. This arrangement of rights may not match the traditional arrangements of rights on liberal-conservative dimensions or necessarily the graded levels of liability in the judicial-legal framework. However, it is suggested that any arrangement derived from the conflation of the utility levels of individuals for different rights should form the appropriate spectrum for all such analyses.

Given the complex ordinal analyses that have been undertaken in other studies of public choice, the present framework may seem somewhat simple. However, it has been employed because of a few important reasons. First, the author believes that there is sufficient reason to believe that there is meaning to the interpersonal comparison of utility and the addition of their cardinal values. He derives this faith from ideas from neurological studies in the past decade.[16] Second, it may be possible to conflate multiple-peaked and multidimensional preferences on the x-axis, with the rights being ordered as per the aggregate utility being derived from the preferences of different individuals. Multiple peaks are factored through the reordering of interests on an axis as per their total utility instead of a preconceived political spectrum. Multiple dimensions enter the analysis as and when they are relevant to a conflict situation. Third, the framework is structured not to look at choices between parties and proposals and is instead made out to explain how a single party would arrive at a proposal to maximise votes. There would be no cycling in the decision-making of a party or government making a proposal because even if there were three or more interest groups, transitivity would be assured by the progression of the quantum of votes from one interest group to the other in pairwise analyses of the same contentious right. Thus, if for a particular right on the pairwise conflict spectrums between interest groups A, B and C, B yields 10 votes over C's 8 and if for the same right, A yields 12 over B's 10, then there is no possibility of C turning around and yielding more than 12 votes for the same right in its pairing against A, unless, of course, if C is somehow sensitive against the right going to A more than it is against the right going to B. It would therefore be profitable to consider situations involving three and more interest groups to be *simultaneous* three-way (or multiple-way) analyses. If C considers the threat of A and B gaining the rights simultaneously, then whatever sensitivity it has towards the usage of the right by A would manifest itself simultaneously with whatever threat it feels towards the right being appropriated by B. Thus, the maximum votes would come from C for that right and the government would opt to give C the right to maximise its votes. (The consequent loss of votes from A and B is not to be added up to derive some kind of net loss of votes – C's right is the most efficient for the government as it cannot give the right to two conflicting interest groups at the same time and thus gain advantages over the highest voting group. The conflation of two groups' rights is held to be physically impossible here, and by all possibility, logrolling and bargaining is assumed to not exist.)

From here, let us now examine how fundamental democratic actions take place on this framework. In Figure 11.1, we may assume a certain quantum of rights of A and the corresponding quantum of rights of B to be the starting position. This position is indicated by the dashed lines indicating the relevant points in Figure 11.1a and b. However, let us assume that the rights of A and B that have been protected are at such a position as to yield a certain number of votes that is lower than the highest possible level of votes. This may be because the government/party has been protecting more rights of B than it needs to and is getting fewer votes than it could if it did not instead switch to protecting some of A's votes. This being the case, the rational government will work to maximise its votes by reducing the number of rights it has granted to B and instead protecting the corresponding rights of A that are freed up. This is illustrated by the arrows in Figure 11.1a and b, showing the change in the legal position from the points indicated by the dashed lines to the one indicated by the dashed and dotted lines. In Figure 11.1a, we see that the increase in the rights of A has resulted in a quick rise in the votes that A is willing to yield. And in Figure 11.1b, we see that the rights of B that are being restricted result in a fall in the votes being given by B but that this fall is not by much. It is indicated by the nature of the graphs that the increase in votes of A will be at a decreasing rate and the decrease in the votes of B will be at an increasing rate. The government will shift the rights structure only so long as the increase in votes from B is higher than the decrease in votes from A. Thus, it is apparent that the point at which the government will stop changing the rights will be at the point when the rate of decrease of the rights of A equals the rate of increase of the rights of B, that is the point at which it receives maximum votes.

The preceding discussion is a simplified analysis for understanding how democratic action works towards a stable rights structure. However, the pertinent question to ask here would be, does it result in the highest possible level of utility for society? Is it the optimal method by which to arrive at an efficient society? We must keep in mind that conflict between interest groups A and B includes within the members of the interest groups all those who are interested in the position of rights even in the slightest. Given that the position of rights in one particular conflict could have an effect on the outcomes of other conflicts on the basis of how the conflicts are defined and whether they can be wholly demarcated with logical consistency, the population affected could be quite large. To understand the possible effects of the position of rights under democracy, see Figure 11.2, which shows the relationship between the rights of A and the rights of B. The rights are in conflict with each other, but the graph is meant to show how far they can coexist if concessions are made by one towards the other. Given the physical impossibility of complete coexistence, we derive a graph not unlike a production possibility frontier. The relationship is indirect, which means that the more one of the rights is protected, the less the other can possibly be protected. The concavity towards the origin is because of the special way in which the rights are arranged on the axes. The equal units on the axes are indeed utils. But non-uniform points on the axes represent the improvement of utility derived from different coherent rights sequenced so that the first rights to be protected and the last to be restricted are always the most precious or utility-providing rights. This is in line with a general principle that if, in a situation of conflicting rights, one is to try to provide certain rights to interest group A by withdrawing them from B, one would do so by withdrawing the least precious rights first, in the hope that one may satisfy A without doing too much harm to B in the process.

However, one important difference in this analysis, as against the Production Possibility Frontier (PPF), is that when allocating rights between the interest groups, one does not look at the opportunity cost of each right (as one would in the case of the products on the PPF) but one would instead simply look at the rights in terms of the utility they provide. The units on the two axes in Figure 11.2 are utils in themselves and, maximising them being our goal, we need not weight each util according to the corresponding importance it may have as one would weight the products on the PPF. In Figure 11.2, we may simply proceed to maximising the total utility by finding the point at which the rate of change of the rights of one interest group becomes equal to the rate of change of the other. It would appear that these would only be conflicts that occur in the allocation of rights after achievement of Pareto efficiency.

Now the central thrust of this chapter is the following. The preceding analysis makes it apparent as follows:

1 The point of equilibrium in the working of a government lies at the point of maximum votes but the point of economic efficiency would be at the point of maximum utility. It would appear that democratic action can under no circumstances guarantee the maximisation of utility through majoritarian institutions.
2 Countermajoritarian institutions would therefore operate at their best when they are structured to meet those specific situations when democratic action fails to ensure such maximum utility.[17] In the representation of Figure 11.1, countermajoritarian action would essentially freeze democratic restructuring of rights and prevent it from proceeding beyond a point where it is becoming inefficient. We may therefore move to make certain general observations as to what may be certain general trends in instances of the failure of democracy so that we may make prescriptions as to how a countermajoritarian institution like a constitutional court of judicial review *should* operate. Whether it does in fact do so in many instances today and whether it is capable of doing it is subject to debate.[18] Below are certain generalised conditions under which democracy fails in the economic sense (in relation to the analyses of intractable rights examined earlier).
3 High information costs and insufficient awareness of voters as to how their vote will affect their own rights.[19] This would essentially mean that there has been a failure in constituting the interest groups accurately, and some from interest group A may in fact want to be part of B or form a different group C if given the right information. This lack of information could be (a) a genuine failure in the analysis of the situation by both the voters and the government, (b) a failure on the part of one interest group in assessing the effects of a change in the rights of another interest group on their own rights either because of a spillover effect due to the logical consistency in the application of precedent uniformly across different conflict situations or because of social mobility[20] resulting in changes in the

membership of interest groups or (c) an instance of information asymmetry between the voters and the government and a resultant principal-agent problem.[21]

4 Intensity of preference of the interest group not assessed by democracy,[22] resulting in the possibility either that majority rule gives an inefficient outcome despite minority utility trumping majority utility or that intense preferences are especially vulnerable to harmful spillover effects across conflict situations.
5 Lack of voting responsiveness of certain interest groups to restriction in their rights.
6 Lack of responsiveness of successive governments to an inefficient rights structure or of the same government which continues in power through logrolling and political exchange.

It would thus be the primary objective of a countermajoritarian institution to address the first two problems. In our analysis, we will be looking specifically at judicial review as the specific mode of creating countermajoritarian collective actions. Thus, it is proposed that choices in relation to the use of judicial review should be made on the basis of how far it (a) mitigates the effects of democratic action that has been taken with less than necessary information and high spillover effects and (b) operates to protect intense preferences.

It may be debatable as to whether there is merit in protecting *all* intense preferences. This is not the intention behind the earlier prescription. It is intended that those intense preferences should be especially targeted for protection, which have especially high spillover effects across the jurisprudence of differing conflict situations and political dimensions. This would be a combination of both (a) and (b). This form of understanding of judicial review is very much in line with the traditional conception that matters of 'constitutional importance' are above those of ordinary legal importance. What may not be immediately clear is that this view makes fundamental rights a mere quantitative and not a qualitative improvement on normal legal rights. In other respects, they are the same.

Calibrating the Indian Constitution

We will now be working to put forward certain specific prescriptions regarding the Constitution of India on the basis of the general conclusions we arrived at in the previous section. Three essential prescriptions are put forward: one, constitutional courts in India should more regularly seek authentic and relevant statistical data on matters of fundamental rights; two, interactions between the legislature and the judiciary in matters of judicial review should follow a mode of 'constitutional dialogue'; and three, constitutional reform should aim at the reduction of what I call 'textual-jurisprudential asymmetry'. Further prescriptions regarding the tools of judicial review are also made.

As mentioned earlier, strong objections continue by a number of groups as to the legitimacy of judicial review either in all situations or in some situations where critics say it has no role. An important part of the faith and reliance of the modern world on democracy comes from traditional experience that when given a choice to formulate policy or rules, the policy maker is invariably waylaid by bias towards making policy that benefits himself or herself or those close to whom or someone from whom he or she may derive benefit. Democracy acts as a check, but it also acts as a strong indicator of the wisdom of many individuals. If a million people approve of a particular course of action after having considered it, does that not easily hold more say than the decision of 5 or 15 black-clad old men whose minds are filled with legalese? However, as discussed in the preceding section, it is clear that there must be some countermajoritarian institutions as part of a democracy to fill its treacherous gaps. If judicial review is to be one of those institutions, it must fill those gaps as best as it can. Part of our central premise in this chapter is that the constitutional court should actively be involved in the democratic process, especially when there appears to be a lack of information about a particular policy. And in such instances, the best course of action it can take is to call for a fact-finding commission to be constituted to gather data and analyse it so that this can be overseen and checked by the court. This rigorous scientific method of working with empirical data is often the best alternative courts can provide as an improvement upon the idea of the wisdom of the masses. We must take note, of course, that cases involving fundamental rights are considered by courts without regard to the numbers behind them. If a single individual's fundamental rights are being violated, he or she may move the court to stall the machinery of democracy – courts here operate with a legal analysis that assesses the jurisprudential and social spillover of the restriction of that one person's rights on the rights of many others, and here, the court does not need the backing of numbers. However, there are other instances when they do need numbers to make a decision, and here, they should be ready to work with them. With this in mind, it can operate to counter information costs and asymmetry and do so especially in the cases of those conflicts that are most likely to ignore intense preferences. This is because fundamental rights have been framed and drafted to provide protection, especially in those circumstances when interests are so intense that restricting them results in damage to society's fabric. They create inclusive institutions that have been found through experience to engender necessary stability and productiveness.[23]

Let us now turn to the problem of constitutional dialogue. The author has already made clear that he considers the role of judicial review to be one that involves the modulation of rights structures away from the outcomes that democracy would create in certain specific circumstances of intense preferences, low information and high spillover. To do so, however, its mode of action is that of the invalidation of actions and legislations. Such activity is patently incapable of accurately arriving at positions of higher utility. Just because an action by the legislature would have become inefficient if carried through all the way does not mean that it could not provide great benefit if carried through part way. To ensure that such situations do not occur, the legislature must come forward with a legislative sequel or response to the judicial invalidation that takes into account the judiciary's interpretation and creates a new legislation away from the flaws pointed out in the old. This concept of constitutional dialogue has been popularised in Canadian constitutional law, where researchers have found evidence that their legislatures consistently replied to judicial invalidation,[24] thus making the actions of the constitutional court more bearable where it has allegedly made harmful decisions. Thus, while the responsiveness of legislatures to invalidation is essential, to engender such responsiveness, it is necessary that the judiciary operate to leave room for improvements upon previous democratic missteps and that the constitution and the formulation of the rights be made so as to allow the courts to leave such room. Such acts of conscious concession, trial and error, can bring the position of the law more accurately to its most efficient resting place. One may consider the constant back and forth between the Supreme Court and the Parliament over the development of the Basic Structure Doctrine[25] or over reservation in education[26] and public services.[27] It may be hoped that such back and forth has resulted in more structuring of the law.

We may turn from here to the matter of the different tools of invalidation that may be used by a constitutional court in review. The most basic method is to strike down the entire legislation, whereas if the invalidity is not such an extensive corruption, it may only be necessary to sever the offending provisions and strike those down. Hogg *et al.* are fundamentally in favour of this approach to review. Though on the surface it may seem more confrontational in eliminating altogether the legal intention of the legislature, it may be that striking down as opposed to activist interpreting allows the legislature to come back to the policy in question and reframe the legislation in a way appropriate to the legislature's own intention.[28] Thus, instead of the court applying its mind and modifying the legislation towards its own objectives (or the objectives that is 'sees' the legislature to have), the legislatures themselves get a chance to continue towards their own policy goal according to the method that they desire. The specific methods that do involve modifications are reading in and reading down the provisions within the act. Reading in involves the judicial interpretation of a particular legislation so as to add in words into the text that would save it from becoming unconstitutional. Reading down involves the interpretation of particular words or phrases within the legislation so as to reduce the scope of the plain meaning of the text to a more limited sense. Of the two, Hogg *et al.* clearly prefer 'reading in' and consider that to be a part of the tool of striking down itself. They consider the express addition of certain words to have the effect of spurring the legislature from coming out with an amendment to bring the text back to the legislature's intention if the court has caused it to depart from the same.[29] They claim, however, that since 'reading down' is purely an interpretation and involves no addition of words, it does not elicit the same reaction from the legislatures.

In the opinion of this writer, it would not seem appropriate to make any distinction at all between reading down and reading in because both are purely interpretive and cannot effectively change the words of the text though they each change the legal effect of the text in exactly the same way. There is no reason to believe that the legislature is more likely to respond with an amendment to reading down than it will to reading in. There are a host of cases that have been decided by the Indian Supreme Court and the old Federal Court, which effectively illustrates how the operation of reading down modifies the words of the text in a way that could altogether distort the legislative objective. The courts have in varying contexts read the word 'property' to exclude agricultural land so as to save a legislation without competence,[30] read the laws on sedition to apply only to 'acts involving intention or tendency to create disorder or disturbance of law and order or incitement to violence',[31] read provisions on imprisonment of death row convicts to exclude solitary confinement and custody in irons,[32] read the word 'sale' to exclude transactions without a previous contract of sale,[33] read provisions regarding the natural guardian of a minor to allow the mother to be guardian after the absence and not necessarily the death of the father,[34] read the words 'affairs of the temple' to include only secular affairs,[35] read the words 'imported into the city' to mean 'imported into the municipal limits for purposes of consumption, use or sale only'[36] and eliminated liability for simply being a member of a banned organisation.[37]

The claim by Hogg *et al.* that these modifications would not elicit a legislative response the way a striking down would has some merit in the sense that altogether confounding the legislative intent is more likely to catch the legislature's attention than a simple modification of the policy in the legislation in the light of the judiciary's understanding of the legislature's intention. It should be noted here that the action of reading down has been, nonetheless, undertaken more often by the Supreme Court of India than it has been in Canada. Even if we were not prejudiced by the fact that review cases take place more often here than in Canada, there still remains the fact that judicial policy requires reading down to be considered before a court can resort to striking a legislation down altogether:

> Before declaring the statute to be unconstitutional, the Court must be absolutely sure that there can be no manner of doubt that it violates a provision of the Constitution. If two views are possible, one making the statute constitutional and the other making it unconstitutional, the former view must always be preferred. Also, the Court must make every effort to uphold the constitutional validity of a statute, even if that requires giving a strained construction or narrowing down its scope.[38]

How can one reconcile this view that courts ought to interpret laws in a way that makes them constitutional (interpretations that could well go contrary to the legislative intent) with the view that striking down a law allows the legislature to undertake its own remedy to unconstitutionality? One view is, of course, that interpretations that result in modifications should be undertaken only when there is ambiguity in the text. It would appear from court practice, however, that reading down is used in cases of unambiguous infringement of rights or drafting negligence. This may lead us to a proposition that the position regarding this tool is different in India, where legislatures do not respond as easily to judicial action (thus causing the courts to be reluctant in striking down laws and thus withdrawing benefits and provisions of necessity), and Canada, where review is more rare and legislatures take it upon themselves to follow through on the legislative objectives of their original legislations by coming out with a legislative 'sequel'. Reading down may indeed be a viable course for Indian courts.

One final prescription comes in the recognition of a certain peculiarity in the working of most constitutions, and an aggravated form of this is the Indian Constitution. It is what the writer calls textual-jurisprudential asymmetry. In the opinion of the writer, all statutory texts come with certain legal effects that derive from the meaning of the words in the statute. Most interpretation being plain-meaning reading of the text, departure from the same is difficult to undertake and the courts are firmly anchored to the legislative position of the law. This 'anchoring', however, is not available in as strict a form in the case of judicial precedent and reading of the same by a court in later cases or in the purposive interpretation of legislative texts. What is identified in instances of judicial freedom and flexibility is the possibility of judicial overreach. The author makes it clear that he is not against all forms of judicial activism or the flexible interpretations necessary for the adaptive evolution of law. However, it is necessary to realise that textual-jurisprudential asymmetry, or the gap that forms between the available text on a particular rights structure and the possible interpretations that a court may take of it (or has taken of it), is quantitatively assessable and that where it is most stark, it needs to be hemmed in by legislative or constitutional reform. Thus, either the legislature must hem in the growing jurisprudence by legislating or making constitutional amendments that invalidate the judgements, or it must legislate to recognise and incorporate the judgement in available texts. In relation to the Indian Constitution, the author finds stark instances of asymmetry in the matters of the interpretation of 'life' in Article 21, in the interpretation of the powers of the Supreme Court under Articles 141 and 142 (this question is pending to be referred to a constitutional bench[39]), in the interpretation of decisions regarding judicial appointments (a matter that may be resolved by the proposed National Judicial Commission) and in the Basic Structure

Doctrine itself. All of these are instances of large layers of jurisprudence being built up on the foundation of little or no textual backing. The risk of such activity is that (a) it could all be uprooted rather quickly if the legislature decided to invalidate it and (b) it could engender in the actions of the courts the very form of judicial overreach that critics of judicial review complain of. These are very real and grave threats to the Indian political, social and legal fabric. Constitutional reform alone can work to allay the fears.

Conclusion

The author began this chapter in the hope that an analysis in law and economics would best be able to explain the nuances and provide prescriptions for the problems that are alleged to be caused by judicial review.

We began by examining the relevant text available on the subject and found the law and economics treatment of the same to be meagre. To further the analysis, a specific economic framework was chosen, which was meant to best look at the context in which courts worked. It will be found that the insistence of the author on matters of intractable conflict or 'mutually exclusive choices' was made so as to best bring out the peculiarities of legal and political workings. Otherwise, analysis of the same may be done through the lens of exchange and bargaining as well, concepts that have been well studied previously. In our analysis, we came upon the conclusion that the operation of democratic activity did not ensure the maximisation of social welfare and it failed to do so in very specific instances. To allay the problems inherent in democracy, it is apparent that countermajoritarian institutions are a necessity. For these to work at their best, their actions should be directed to fill the gaps that democracy leaves – an essential but supplementary role. This is the central thrust of this chapter.

Towards creating applications of the earlier proposition, it became necessary to point out the general trends as to when democracy tends to fail in providing optimal results. High information costs, high socio-legal spillover of rights restrictions and intense preferences were seen to be the signs of inefficiency. It was further postulated that constitutional rights have no qualitative difference as against legal rights but that the difference is only a quantitative one. Thus, towards finding prescriptions regarding the same in the Indian Constitution, we worked to sort out those instances where judicial review by the Supreme Court of India tended to deviate from the requirement of filling democratic gaps.

It was found that an essential problem with judicial review is that it takes a sledgehammer at those matters where a small mallet would suffice. To keep the working of the court accurate, it seems necessary for it to have accurate and relevant empirical data. It is also necessary that it has a responsive and accommodative parliament to work with so that the position of the law can best be calibrated via a two-way dialogue. Finally, it was found that a certain institutional and textual environment is necessary for a constitutional court to work with accuracy, and this may be lacking in certain parts of Indian constitutional law. It has been prescribed therefore that textual-jurisprudential asymmetry be kept limited to that extent as is necessary beneficial judicial flexibility. Just as legislatures require bounds within which to work so as to ensure stable results, a judiciary too should function under certain fundamental guidelines so that extreme actions are avoided and an unstable legal framework is not erected. It is hoped that the article has done justice to its objectives.

Notes

1 Kenneth Arrow, *Social Choice and Individual Values* (New York: Wiley, 1951): 3; James M. Buchanan and Gordon Tullock, *The Calculus of Consent: Logical Foundations of Constitutional Democracy* (Ann Arbor: University of Michigan Press, 1962): 240; Robert Cooter, 'Constitutional Consequentialism: Bargain Democracy versus Median Democracy', *Theoretical Inquiries in Law* 3 (2002): 8–9.
2 Arrow, *Social Choice and Individual Values*: 9–11.
3 Duncan Black, 'On the Rationale of Group Decision-Making', *Journal of Political Economy* 56 (1) (1948): 13.
4 James M. Buchanan, 'What Is Public Choice Theory?', *Imprimus* 32 (2003): 1–7.
5 Buchanan and Tullock, *The Calculus of Consent*: 51–58.
6 Ibid., 63.
7 Ibid., 184.
8 Tom Ginsburg, 'Economic Analysis and the Design of Constitutional Courts', *Theoretical Inquiries in Law* 3 (2004): 49.
9 Nuna Garoupa, Veronica Grembi and Shirley Ching-ping Lin, 'Explaining Constitutional Review in New Democracies: The Case of Taiwan', *Pacific Rim Law & Policy Journal* 20 (1) (2011): 1–40.
10 Nuna Garoupa, Fernando Gomez-Pomar and Veronica Grembi, 'Judging under Political Pressure: An Empirical Analysis of Constitutional Review Voting in the Spanish Constitutional Court', *Journal of Law, Economics and Organization* 29 (2013): 519.

11 William Landes and Richard Posner, 'The Independent Judiciary in an Interest-Group Perspective', *Journal of Law and Economics* 18 (1975): 875.
12 Georg Vanberg, 'Legislative-Judicial Relations: A Game Theoretic Approach to Constitutional Review', *American Journal of Political Science* 45 (2001): 346.
13 Alexander Bickel, *The Least Dangerous Branch* (Monterey, CA: Bobbs-Merrill, 1962); Tom S. Clark, *The Limits of Judicial Independence* (New York: Cambridge University Press, 2011); Philip Hamburger, 'A Tale of Two Paradigms: Judicial Review and Judicial Duty', *George Washington Law Review* 78 (2010): 1162; Christopher Wolfe, ed., *Judicial Activism: Bulwark of Freedom or Precarious Security?* (New York: Brooks/Cole Publishing Company, 1991); Robert H. Bork, *The Tempting of America* (Free Press, 1997); Ronald Dworkin, *A Matter of Principle* (Oxford: Oxford University Press, 1985); Mark Tushnet, *Taking the Constitution Away from the Courts* (Princeton, NJ: Princeton University Press, 2000).
14 David S. Law, 'A Theory of Judicial Power and Judicial Review', *The Georgetown Law Journal* 97 (2008): 723.
15 Buchanan and Tullock, *The Calculus of Consent*: 184–186.
16 Veit Stuphorn, 'Neuroeconomics: Cardinal Utility in the Orbitofrontal Cortex?', *Current Biology* 16 (15) (2006): R591–R593; Daniel Kahneman, 'Experienced Utility and Objective Happiness: A Moment-Based Approach', In *Choices, Values and Frames*, edited by D. Kahneman and A. Tversky (New York: Cambridge University Press and the Russel Sage Foundation, 2000): 673–692.
17 Cass R. Sunstein, 'On the Costs and Benefits of Aggressive Judicial Review of Agency Action', *Duke Law Journal* 38 (1989): 522–537.
18 D.H. Cole and P.Z. Grossman, 'Protecting Private Property with Constitutional Judicial Review: A Social Welfare Analysis', *Review of Law and Economics* 5 (2009): 233.
19 Ilya Somin, 'Political Ignorance and the Countermajoritarian Difficulty: A New Perspective on the Central Obsession of Constitutional Theory', *Iowa Law Review* 89 (4) (2004): 1287–1371.
20 Thomas Piketty, 'Social Mobility and Redistributive Politics', *The Quarterly Journal of Economics* 60 (3) (1995): 551; Daron Acemoglu, Georgy Egorov and Konstantin Sonin, 'Political Economy in a Changing World', *NBER Working Paper No. 19158* (2013).
21 Landes and Posner, 'The Independent Judiciary in an Interest-Group Perspective'.
22 Robert A. Dahl, *A Preface to Democratic Theory* (Chicago: University of Chicago Press, 1956): 48–50, 90–124.
23 Daron Acemoglu and James Robinson, *Why States Fail: The Origins of Power, Prosperity and Poverty* (UK: Random House, 2012).
24 Peter W. Hogg and Allison A. Bushell, 'The Charter Dialogue between Courts and Legislatures (or Perhaps the Charter of Rights Isn't Such a Bad Thing After All)', *Osgoode Hall Law Journal* 35 (1997): 75; Peter W. Hogg, Allison A. Bushell Thornton and Wade K. Wright, 'Charter

Dialogue Revisited – Or "Much Ado about Metaphors"', *Osgoode Hall Law Journal* 45 (1) (2007): 1.

25 *Shankari Prasad v. Union of India* (1952) SCR 89; *Sajjan Singh v. State of Rajasthan*, AIR 1965 SC 845; *IC Golak Nath v. State of Punjab*, AIR 1967 SC 1643; *RC Cooper v. Union of India*, AIR 1970 SC 564; *Kesavananda Bharati v. State of Kerala*, AIR 1973 SC 1461; *Minerva Mills v. Union of India* (1980) 3 SCC 625; *Waman Rao v. Union of India* (1981) 2 SCC 36; *IR Coelho v. State of Tamil Nadu*, AIR 2007 SC 861.

26 *Chamapkam Dorairajan v. State of Madras*, AIR 1951 SC 226; *TMA Pai Foundation v. State of Karnataka* (1994) SCC (2) 195; *PA Inamdar v. State of Maharashtra* (2005) 6 SCC 537; *Ashok Kumar Thakur v. Union of India* (2007) 4 SCC 361; *Islamic Academy of Education v. State of Karnataka* (2003) 6 SCC 697; *Sudha Tiwari v. Union of India* (2011) (2) ADJ 819.

27 *Indra Sawhney v. Union of India* (1992) 3 SCC 217; *M Nagaraj v. Union of India* (2006) 8 SCC 212.

28 Peter W. Hogg, Allison A. Bushell Thornton and Wade K. Wright, 'Charter Dialogue Revisited': 10.

29 Ibid.

30 *In Re* Hindu Women's Right to Property Act, AIR 1941 FC 12.

31 *Kedar Nath Singh v. State of Bihar*, 1962 AIR 955.

32 *Sunil Batra v. Delhi Administration*, AIR 1978 SC 1675.

33 *New India Sugar Mills v. Commissioner of Sales Tax*, AIR 1963 SC 1207.

34 *Githa Hariharan v. Reserve Bank of India*, AIR 1999 SC 1149.

35 *Govindlalji v. State of Rajasthan*, AIR 1963 SC 1638.

36 *Indian Oil v. Municipal Corporation, Jullundher*, AIR 1993 SC 844.

37 *Sri Indra Das v. State of Assam* (2011) 4 SCR 289.

38 *Government of Andhra Pradesh v. P. Laxmi Devi*, 2008 (4) SCC 720.

39 *University of Kerala v. Council of Principals of Colleges of Kerala & Ors.*, SC Civil Appeal No. 887 of 2009, Order of 11 November, 2009.

Chapter 12

Economic analysis of competition law

Aanchal Kapoor

Background note

Economics has had a huge effect on competition law. Earlier, the courts made efforts to protect the competition and not competitors. Courts now act as protectors of smaller firms to an economic standard of antitrust liability, which focuses entirely on antitrust market effects. There has been a shift from the per se rules to the rule of reason analysis. Two new trends have emerged due to the change in understanding of competition law. The first trend is the increased relevance of economic efficiencies, and the second one is the necessity to demonstrate anti-competition market effects. Competition law is about economics and economic behaviour.[1] It is necessary that an economic assessment of terms like 'market definition' and 'market power' is done so that it becomes easier to understand competition law in those terms. The study of markets is primary to the study of competition law. The main object of this field of law is to ensure that there is continuous competition between suppliers and that consumers/buyers benefit from such competition. The application of competition law involves identifying markets and assessing whether this competition is working well. The study of economics involves how markets work. By understanding economics, we can know how markets operate and know whether the behaviour of firms will result in a competition that is likely to benefit consumers. Today, economics is an essential tool to access market power and to determine the boundaries of market.

What is competition law?

Even though 'competition' is not defined in law, it is understood to mean the process of rivalry in order to attract more customers or to enhance profits. Competition law deals with market failures on account of restrictive business practices in the market.[2] The history of competition law is traced back to the enactment of the Sherman Act in 1890 in the United States.[3] Competition in the market is all about competing for quality, price and resources, leading to a market oriented towards consumer rights, fair trade and efficient resource allocation development of small businesses, and incentives for innovation and dispersion of economic power. The benefits arising out of competitive markets are perceived to promote economic development.[4]

What is meant by economic analysis of law?

Economic analysis of law is the application of economic methods to the analysis of law. Various concepts are used to explain the effect that economics has on law. Major issues are related to goods and services; therefore, economics has been closely associated with both money and (monetary) prices. Since the 1960s, economists have applied their analytical tools to study non-market behaviours that are traditionally in the domains of political science, sociology, law and other disciplines. It is through this endeavour that economics has emerged as not a particular subject matter but as a unique analytical approach.[5] When we talk about cartels, there are various economic approaches that are available to help detect cartels. They can be classified as the *structural* approach, *conduct* approach and *performance* approach. An economic analysis can help identify the critical factors that may aggravate this fragility and prompt cartel participants to come forward and report their activity. These approaches can be useful in merger control.

Pre-Chicago school economic framework

The pre-Chicago School in the case of horizontal issues adopted a framework known as 'structure, conduct and performance'.[6] This proved that there was a direct relationship between industry concentration and economic performance. This paradigm found that there was a positive relationship between industry performances, and it also established that industries categorized as having high level of entry barriers tended to have higher rates of return. However, the aim of the analysis was to protect small businesses. In the case of vertical issues, antitrust economics relied on the leverage theory as the anti-competitive paradigm. This theory held that if a seller had a monopoly of one product, he or she could and would monopolize its indispensable complements as well, so as to get additional monopoly profits.[7] Before the antitrust economics revolution started, the court took a very restrictive stance towards all vertical restraints. It held that most vertical contractual agreements that placed a restraint on downstream price and non-price competition were per se illegal.

Chicago School of economic analysis

This school challenged the theoretical and empirical basis of assumed direct relationship between industry concentration and performance in horizontal issues. The argument was that collusion depended on a number of factors other than industry concentration. Particularly, heterogeneity of products, importance of non-price competition and other factors made it less probable that collusion would succeed in an industry. Although industry factors are important, it will be easier to detect cheating, if there is a conspiracy where market shares are fixed instead of prices. On monitoring the deviations, one will easily get to know of cheating. The offsetting effects associated with product heterogeneity and non-price competition characteristics must be taken into account.

A hypothesis showed that smaller returns earned higher rates of return than smaller firms in non-concentrated markets, which would have been the case if small firms benefitted from market prices that were held to be of higher competency effects.[8] The Chicago School was the basis of the US Department of Justice 1982 Merger Guidelines.[9] The earlier merger policy did not take efficiencies into account,[10] but this school advocated that the merger policy should take into account efficiencies. Prior to this, potential efficiencies from mergers were not only not accepted as a defence, but some courts actually held that a merger could be made illegal if it made firm more efficient and thereby disadvantaged smaller competitors.[11]

There was a significant impact on antitrust law of vertical restraints by criticism of the weak economic analysis both underlying the established anti-competitive arguments against vertical arrangements and providing a more sophisticated economic understanding of the potential pro-competitive efficiency motivation for vertical arrangements. It has been argued that tying was unlikely to increase a firm's profits because there was a single potential monopoly profit in a vertical chain of production. Therefore, a monopolist could maximize profits solely by charging a monopoly price for the tying good on which it had market power. A monopolist could not collect twice for its market power by using a vertical restraint to leverage its monopoly power into other markets.[12] The analysis implies that if a profit-maximizing monopolist imposes restrictions on its customers, such as tying the sale of a product to another product which it sells at prices greater than the existing competitive prices, the monopolist would have to reduce the price of its tying product.

Post-Chicago extensions

In the case of horizontal issues, development in post-Chicago understanding of antitrust law was the way to understand the dynamic game-theoretic oligopoly models. Many models were developed in which it was observed how the oligopolistic interaction led to the adoption of complex strategies in which the firms changed their behaviour depending on the market outcome of the previous periods. The repeated interaction between firms increases the ability to punish cheaters. This model further suggested that an individual firm's decisions to deviate from collusive agreement are likely to be more costly than what was believed in the Chicago School. Collusive agreements can be identified because industry participants will repeat the exercise of explicit collusion and tacit coordination. The repeated multi-period interaction increases the ability of firms to punish those firms that deviate from both explicit cartels and implicit or tacit coordinated understandings. Moreover, firms in an oligopolistic industry take into account the expected reaction of their rivals to their competitive behaviour, and hence, equilibrium may exist above perfectly competitive levels without any evident or explicit communication.

Later around the early 1990s, the focus of merger analysis shifted from mergers as the primary theory of economic harm to unilateral effects. In a differentiated produce industry, even if there is no explicit or implicit coordination between firms, it may be profitable for a merging firm to unilaterally decide to reduce its output and significantly raise the price. This will be the case if pricing of a merging firm's products is constrained primarily by competition from a product of the merging partner, so that removing the constraint provides the firm with an economic incentive to increase prices.[13] In addition, unilateral effects models typically speculate a simpler form of oligopolic interaction, wherein each firm assumes that the competitors will not change their behaviour in response to their own actions.

The shift to unilateral effects was theorized in the 1992 Merger Guidelines,[14] which describe several different mechanisms by which a merger in a differentiated products industry may lessen competition through unilateral effects, including conditions where competition is localized or firms are capacity constrained.[15] Merger enforcement by antitrust agencies and the courts also shifted their focus to unilateral effects.[16] The statistical analysis underlying unilateral effects merger simulation models is complex, but unilateral effects models are based on simple and restrictive assumptions.

Market definition and market power

Market definition

The analysis of competition policy starts by defining what the 'relevant market' is. The definition of market helps to identify the sources of competition that are likely to restrict or minimize the effects of the exercise of market power. The relevant market as evaluated in terms of competition law is different as compared to market categorization used in industry reports or markets the firms perceive themselves to be occupying.[17] It is also necessary to understand what a competitive market is when we are doing an economic analysis of competition law. It is a market where there are many firms producing the same commodity and there are many purchasers for the same. In such situations, each producer believes that he or she has no control over the prevailing price of the commodity because he or she supplies such a small fraction of it. Likewise, each consumer believes he or she has no control over the price because he or she buys a small fraction. Assuming that there is free entry and exit, this is what economists refer to as long run.

In an imaginary world of 'perfect' competition, a market will definitely produce an efficient result. Efficiency has a particular meaning in economics. An efficient position is one in which the only way to make anyone better off is to make someone else worse off.[18] This refers to a situation in which no more mutually advantageous bargains or contracts can be made. In any situation in which A can be made better off, with B being no worse off, it will be efficient for that transaction to take place. Such a situation is referred to as one of *Pareto optimum*. This theoretical ideal permits an examination of the extent to which observed market structures diverge from 'perfect competition' and the resulting harm.[19] To attain a perfect competition, there must be very large, tending to infinite, numbers of producers and consumers.[20] The product is homogeneous so that there are no significant differences between one producer's product and the next.[21] Both producers and consumers are perfectly informed about the market and are motivated by the desire to maximize profits and satisfaction.[22]

'Economic substitutability' is a key concept in the description of a relevant competition policy or antitrust market. In other words, it is the willingness of customers to accept one product instead of another product. Due to the availability of close substitutes for a particular good, a monopolist will lose his or her monopoly market power. If the new player already supplies a technologically similar good, so that only small investments and modifications are required, competition policy speaks of 'supply-side substitution'. If, on the other hand, the new player is not active in any of the related industries, competition policy classifies this constraint as 'entry'; this is because the new entry is typically not an immediate constraint; it is generally not taken into account at the stage of market definition, but as part of the evaluation of competitive effects.[23]

The concept of substitutability is often applied through the methodology of the small but significant non-transitory increase in price (SSNIP) or 'hypothetical monopolist' test. This approach starts with the narrowest conceivable market, and an evaluation of the following question is necessary at this juncture, that is, could a hypothetical monopolist over the goods in that market implement an SSNIP? In practice, an SSNIP is often interpreted as being a 5% to 10% price increase.[24] In case the answer to the SSNIP question is 'yes', then the said market is considered to be a relevant market. However, if, on the other hand, there are sufficient substitutes to undermine the profitability of such a price rise, the said market would be broadened to include other substitute products, beginning with the closest substitute.[25]

This broader set of products would comprise a second candidate market that would be subject to an SSNIP analysis. This procedure is iterated until one has defined a relevant market.[26]

The starting point for the SSNIP test should be the competitive price level. This is particularly relevant for situations where there are allegations of market power abuse. If the current price is above the competitive level, the SSNIP test that is carried out from the prevailing price would tend to define the relevant market too widely.[27] That is because, if the prevailing prices were already at supra-competitive levels, even a monopolist would find it unprofitable to implement a further price rise. This point is generally known as the 'cellophane fallacy', after the overly broad market definition that was drawn by the US Supreme Court in its 1956 *Du Pont* decision,[28] which involved cellophane packaging. The *Cellophane* case dealt largely with determination of market in the product sense, in which it explored the effect of substitute wrapping materials on cellophane sales. The majority of the bench held that cellophane was not a market in itself but it was part of a greater 'flexible wrapping paper' market, and since it comprised 20% of this latter market, it could not possibly be said to 'monopolize' it.

Relevant market

After already identifying the relevant market through the various tests mentioned, such as the SSNIP test, the next step would be to establish the dominance of the supplier in the relevant market so identified. The relevant product market and the relevant geographic market are the two aspects of relevant market.

Relevant product market

Relevant product market is the smallest set of close substitutes. There are two aspects to determine substitutability of products: demand-side substitutability, shift of demand to competing product on price rise; and supply-side substitutability, shift of production to meet demand.[29]

Factors to be considered while determining relevant product market are as follows:

1 Physical characteristic of product
2 End use of product
3 Price
4 Consumer preference – empirical evidence
5 Classification of industrial products

Relevant geographic market

Relevant geographic market can be defined as the area in which products are available at approximately the same price, given transport costs and any increase in demand can be met from other relevant markets in neighbouring geographical areas profitably.[30]

Factors to be considered are as follows:

- Shipment cost – very important
- Regulatory trade barriers – octroi/sales tax
- Local specification requirements – language display
- National procurement policy – only local (state-level or national) suppliers permitted
- Adequate distribution facilities – perishable products

A relevant market helps to define the market share of a producer and determine the dominant undertaking in the relevant market. We can use the Microsoft case in the United States[31] to understand this concept of relevant market and whether it had been abusive. In this case, according to the facts stated before the court, Microsoft had a monopoly in the PC desktop OS market. The same was revealed by the large share it held in Intel-compatible PC OS. Next, there was a very high entry barrier and there was no other viable option available to customers.

Network effects explained 'barriers to entry'. As there were more Windows users, it meant a large installed base, which in turn motivated independent software vendors (ISVs) to write more applications for Windows. Due to higher number of applications available for Windows, it motivated more consumers to choose Windows, and this acted like an 'endless loop' and created, augmented and enhanced the dominant position of Windows, thereby creating an entry barrier to new competitors. Developing new applications is characterized by two important features: 'economies of scale' and 'sunk costs'. As the costs involved in developing a certain program/application can be used for that particular development activity and are expended in the process, it is a sunk cost. Further, as is well known, the 'marginal cost' of producing an additional copy of a program is zero; thus, the industry is characterized by economies of scale; this implies that greater the number of users, more desirable is a given application. Considering this particular feature of the industry, the developers want to make programs for the predominant OS and in the present case it being Windows OS; developers have an incentive to write more and more programs for the same, which in turn attracts more users to the system. This is the 'network effect'. As for the other systems, one can use these applications only if the application is 'portable'.

The court recognized the fact that even though Microsoft had to incur costs to attract ISVs to continue writing newer applications for its OS, these costs were nonetheless insignificant vis-à-vis 'overwhelming' entry barriers faced by new entrants trying to enter the market which was already dominated by Microsoft.[32] Empirical evidence was cited with respect to barriers to entry. The court further held that others failed to successfully compete with Microsoft even after putting enormous efforts and costs. Even reverse engineering was unviable because other systems could not support Intel OS.[33] In the end, a 'leveraging infringement' was observed, consisting of Microsoft's use of its dominant position on the client PC operating systems market to extend that dominant position to two adjacent markets, namely the markets for work group server operating systems and the market for streaming media players.[34]

Market power

The key concern of competition law is with acquisition of market power, that is when a firm can profitably raise prices above marginal cost.[35] A firm that has market power can raise price without losing sales. The US Supreme Court has defined market power as the 'power to force a purchaser to do something that he would not do in a competitive market'. The existence of such power is ordinarily inferred from the seller's possession of a predominant share in the market.[36]

The conditions necessary to acquire market power are as follows:

- Availability of substitutes
- Number of competitors
- Market share
- Barriers to entry
- Threat to potential competitors

The size of a firm's market share is an important indicator for the existence of market power.

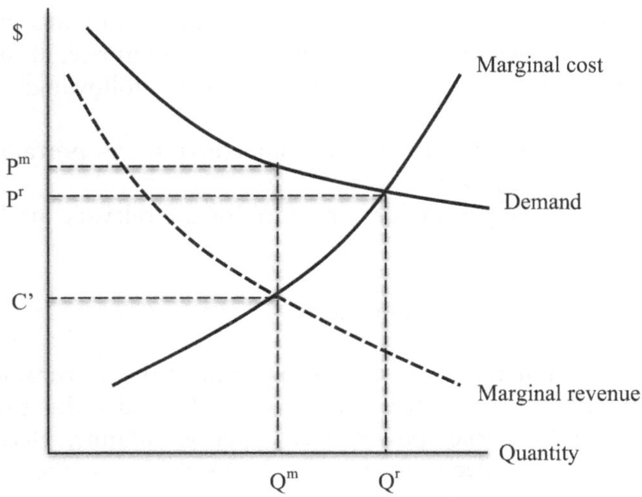

Figure 12.1 Marginal cost, marginal revenue and demand under monopoly market

Source: William M. Landes and Richard A. Posner, 'Market Power in Antitrust Cases', *Harvard Law Review* 94 (937) (1981): 939.

A simple economic meaning of the term 'market power' is the ability to set price above marginal cost.[37] Under perfect competition, price equals marginal cost, so if a firm's price is above its marginal cost, the implication is that the firm does not face perfect competition, that is it has at least some market power.[38]

A monopolist is shown setting price at the point on his or her demand curve where marginal cost equals marginal revenue rather than, as under competition, taking the market price as given. At the profit-maximizing monopoly price, P^m, price exceeds marginal cost, C', by the vertical distance between the demand and marginal cost curves at the monopolist's output, Q^m, that is by $P^m - C'$, as depicted by Figure 12.1.

Market power is a pivotal concept underpinning the competition and access provisions of competition legislation. Prohibitions against misuse of market power involve a complex combination of legal and economic principles, an understanding of which gives considerable insight into many other aspects of the legal framework governing competition. Market power is more likely to exist if an undertaking or a group of undertakings has a persistently higher market share.

Abuse of dominance and economic analysis

The Competition Act, 2002, defines dominant position in a market in terms of a place of strength enjoyed by an enterprise, in the relevant market in India, which enables it to do the following:

- Operate independently of the competitive forces prevailing in the relevant market.
- Affect its competitors or consumers or the relevant market in its favour.

There are two types of dominance:

1 Single dominance: This entails that competitive constraints are not sufficiently effective and therefore the undertaking enjoys substantial market power over a period of time. Here, the undertaking's decisions are largely insensitive to the actions and reactions of competitors, customers and consumers. The EU Commission considers the existence of market power to result in the capability of firms to profitably raise the prices.[39] This direct effect of dominance causes an indirect effect, that is exclusionary conduct by dominant firms that harm competitors and, thus, result in higher prices to consumers. In this context, note that harm to competitors represents a necessary but not a sufficient condition for harm to consumers.[40]
2 Collective dominance: This means that the firms collectively possess market power. 'For collective dominance to exist requires that there exist a group of firms that: (a) do not face significant competitive constraints from other firms outside the group; and (b) these firms are able to adopt a mode of parallel behaviour that reduces the effectiveness of competition between themselves' (Paha 2013). Under these circumstances, it is possible that prices would be increased above the competitive level. However, one must note the thin line of difference that exists between collusion and collective dominance.

Abusive conduct is of two broad types, that is excessive pricing and foreclosure. When a dominant firm raises prices above competitive level, it is known as excessive pricing. In competition law, a firm is said to be dominant if it has large market power, and in economics it is said that a firm with market power also holds the ability to raise prices above the competitive level, and with this we can draw a conclusion that excessive pricing is the most intuitive form of abuse. To prove excessive pricing, one needs to compare the observed level of prices and prove the profitability of the price rise. Observing a firm charging a price above its costs does not indicate that this firm exercises market power but can simply be a result of its productive efficiency.[41] Disentangling the effects of market power and productive efficiency is a difficult task that requires analysing the industry as a whole rather than focusing on a single firm alone. One may also, in this approach, compare prices across regions, across firms, across similar products and across periods to see if there is an abuse of dominance. If excessive pricing is found, then it implies that any authority should insist that the firm in question lower its price to a level that is not excessive. The term 'anti-competitive foreclosure' describes a situation where effective access of actual or potential competitors to supplies or markets is hampered or eliminated as a result of the conduct of the dominant undertaking whereby the dominant undertaking is likely to be in a position to profitably increase prices to the detriment of consumers.[42]

EU can be concerned with behaviour where firms intentionally lower their price below its competitive level. In case of price-based exclusionary conduct, a dominant firm may set prices below costs and thus drive a competitor out of the market. If the excluded firm had previously posed a competitive constraint on the dominant undertaking, the exclusion is likely to result in higher prices. In order to detect such behaviour, the commission will engage in analysing prices and costs. Setting prices below average variable costs 'indicates that the dominant undertaking is sacrificing profits in the short term and that an equally efficient competitor cannot serve the targeted customers without incurring a loss'.[43] Setting prices below average total costs 'indicates that the dominant undertaking is not recovering all the fixed costs of producing the good or service in question and that an equally efficient competitor could be foreclosed from the market'.[44]

Abuse of dominance in India

In India, after economic reforms and liberalization of the economy, a need to review the competition law was felt. The new Competition Act, 2002, was thus enacted. According to Section 18 of the act, 'Subject to the provisions of this Act, it shall be the duty of the Commission to eliminate practices having adverse effect on competition, promote and sustain competition, protect the interest of consumers and ensure freedom of trade carried on by other participants, in markets in India.'[45] Accordingly, under the act, the commission is empowered to take action against anti-competitive agreements like cartels and abuse of dominant position, which further includes predatory pricing and unfair or discriminatory conditions of prices.

Abuse of dominant position by an enterprise is a serious violation under the Indian Competition Act.[46] Section 4 of the act specifically states that 'no enterprise shall abuse its dominant position. It also states that there shall be an abuse of dominant position if an enterprise imposes unfair or discriminatory conditions or prices in the purchase or sale of goods or provision of services or if it limits or restricts production of goods or provision of services or technical and scientific development or it denies market access, etc.' The dominance of an enterprise is to be judged by its power to operate independently of competitive forces or to affect its competitors or consumers in its favour.[47] Hence, an enterprise with a share of say less than 25% of the market could possibly be determined to be the 'dominant' if it satisfies the preceding criteria; on the other hand, an enterprise with higher market share may not be considered as dominant if it does not meet the criteria mentioned in the act.[48] The act also lays down a number of factors that the commission needs to take into consideration in determining whether an enterprise enjoys a dominant position, such as market share, size and resources of the enterprise; size and importance of competitors; economic power of the enterprises; vertical integration of the enterprises; and entry barriers, which would involve a fair amount of economic analysis.[49] The definition under Section 4 of the Competition Act seems to be helpful for the purposes of delimiting actions that shall constitute dominance; however, such a definition cannot be dealt as exclusive of any economic considerations.[50] Come to think of it, it is an absurd proposition economically that a firm may act independent of its consumers. The demand curve mandates that any enterprise act in consonance with its consumers.

In economics jargon, we can say that demand curve of a firm indicates the number of units of any commodity a firm may sell at a particular price. Typically the downward curve, as shown in Figure 12.2, indicates that a firm shall sell more units of a certain commodity at a lower price.[51] It is not generally possible for a firm to sell more units of a commodity at a raised price. This is equally applicable to both dominant and non-dominant firms. Keeping in mind this economic consideration, the legal definition in Section 4 and Hoffman case[52] can have such a classification, that is a dominant firm would be one that could raise its prices higher than a non-dominant firm without considerable effect to its demand; an example for the same would be a company involved in the gasoline market or any other essential goods for that matter, where consumers may not significantly reduce consumption in case of price rise.[53]

Power to *behave to an appreciable extent independently of its competitors, and ultimately of its consumers*, seems economically incoherent; therefore, the essential focus on determining dominance must be the *ability to prevent effective competition*.[54] Practically, dominance will essentially be the ability of any firm to price its goods above market price and still get the desired demand or have comparatively lower impact on demand.[55] Thus, a firm enjoying monopoly in a market can be said to be in a dominant position.

In case the Competition Commission of India finds that an enterprise has abused its dominant position, then penalties will be imposed and other such actions as the commission deems fit will be taken. It can impose a penalty of not more than 10% of the turnover of the enterprise. It can pass a 'cease and desist' order, and

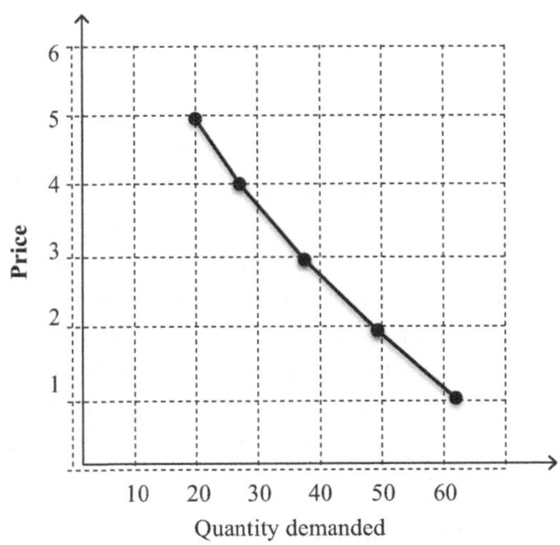

Figure 12.2 Demand curve

Source: NetMBA-Economics, The Demand Curve, http://www.netmba.com/econ/micro/demand/curve/.

pass such other orders as may be considered appropriate.[56] It can also recommend to the central government for division of dominant enterprise. Thus, the Competition Commission of India has the power to inter alia direct the enterprise to disclose information to its competitors, or it can recommend division of an enterprise, if these are considered appropriate to the case.[57]

Predatory pricing

It is a practice of driving rivals out of business by selling at a price below the cost of production.[58] A company that engages in predatory first lowers the price in order to drive out its competitors and scare off potential entrants and then raise the price when rivals exit the market.[59] At times such firms incur short-term losses in order to gain long-run gains. During the period of predation, the predating firm loses much more money than an equally efficient rival. It is important that the predatory firm meet all its demands at the low price in order to maintain the low price, but the rival is free to reduce its output in order to minimize its losses. And after this, there are chances the predation might not exceed. Predatory pricing is an investment in future monopoly, as sacrifice of today's profits for tomorrow.[60]

If the price is lowered by one firm and the number of units it has to sell in order to drive its rival out of business, the incumbent produces at a higher marginal and average cost than its rival and suffers losses. Consumers gain during this period of predation because they are able to purchase the product at a lower price. In case of *Indian Oil Corporation Ltd & Ors. v. Reliance Industries Ltd & Ors.*,[61] the contention was that appellants were selling the petroleum products at lower prices, that is below the international prices, and that the respondents were suffering market revenue loss as they were required to sell their products at a higher international price. This price for the appellants had been set by the Ministry of Petroleum and Natural Gas, and the case examined whether the price fixed by the ministry was to be considered as predatory pricing. The court dismissed the appeal and declared that there was no evidence of price-fixing.

Legal standards of predation

Many courts have adopted rules proposed by Areeda and Turner. A firm's pricing is predatory if its price is less than its short-run marginal cost. The logic behind this test is that no firm ever profitably chooses to operate where price is less than short-run marginal cost unless it is motivated by strategic concerns. They further suggest using average variable cost as a proxy for short-run marginal cost[62] if data limitations prevent the determination of short-run marginal costs. They also recognize that pricing below average total cost is not proof of predatory behaviour.[63] One can say that predatory pricing suits could be strategy by a less efficient firm to protect its market position. The evidence in a predatory pricing case of a lowering of price that inflicts losses on rivals is exactly what one expects when a more efficient firm competes in market. This point made by the author can be supported by Easterbook,[64] who suggested that the courts should not consider cases of predatory pricing until the firm has been driven out of business or the predator has increased the prices.

Overview of cases

In *Re United Brands Company*,[65] the court opined that in order to determine the dominant position, it is important to define the relevant market first, from both a product and geographic perspective.[66] Hence, only when the relevant market is own can one assess the position in which a particular company is in. In *Hoffman-La Roche*,[67] the court held that 'substantial market share' is essential but it is not the final determinant of a dominant position. The court here was of the view that the other important factors that are to be taken into consideration are the relative market share of the incumbent and its competitors and the relationship between them, the technological advantage of the incumbent firm, a highly developed sales network and absence of potential competition.

Cartel and economic analysis

'Cartels are agreements between enterprises (including association of enterprises) not to compete on price, product or customers.'[68] The objective of a cartel is to raise the price above what the competitive level is; this in turn results in injury to the consumers and the economy. The end result of cartelization is higher prices, poor quality and less or no choice for goods/services.[69] *In simpler terms, a cartel agreement is between businesses wherein they agree not to compete with each other. Such agreements are secret, verbal and often informal.* Generally, there are two ways in which cartels can be detected. One way is to observe the means by which firms coordinate and observe the end result of such coordination. Detecting by observing the market impact of that coordination refers to suspicions emanating from the pattern of firms' prices or quantities or some other aspect of behaviour.[70] However, the question is, how can economic analysis help in detection of cartels? We need to understand how we can use economic data, that is prices, quantities, market shares, demand shifters, cost shifters, to discriminate between collusion and competition.

The process involves screening, verification and prosecution. The main purpose of screening is to identify markets where collusion is suspected. It is designed in order to identify industries for closer scrutiny. Verification entails systematically trying to exclude competition as an explanation for observed behaviour and to provide evidence in support of collusion. Screening may involve looking at price patterns, but verification requires controlling for the demand and cost factors and any other variables that are necessary in order to distinguish collusion and competition. The task of the prosecution is to develop economic evidence that is going to be sufficient to persuade the courts that the law has been violated.[71] A well-founded analysis quantifies the economic effect of a cartel on the market.[72] In reality, the 'successful' carrying out of cartel agreements is rare. Therefore, a quantitative assessment may prove that the actual economic effects on the market are marginal.[73]

Functioning of a cartel

Figure 12.3 and its explanation help in understanding how a cartel functions.

In the case of perfect competition in a market, products or services are provided at a price that equals marginal costs. By creating a cartel, in theory the producers can raise their price and consequently increase their profits. This approach will lead to reallocation of surplus between producers and consumers equivalent to area A representing the profit of the cartel members. A price increase usually results in a decrease of demand, and hence, less output is sold.[74] This deadweight loss is equal to triangle B. The loss of the consumers (A + B) surpasses the gains of the cartel members (B); thus, a cartel decreases total welfare, similar to a monopoly.

A deadweight loss is a loss of economic efficiency, which occurs only when the equilibrium for a good or service is not *Pareto optimal*. This

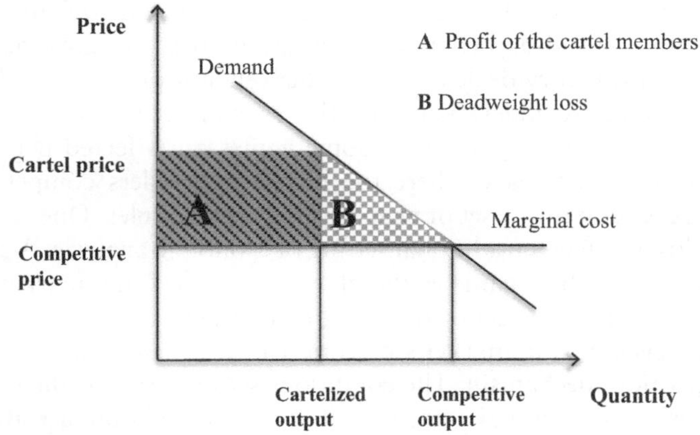

Figure 12.3 Functioning of cartel

Source: European E&M Consultants,'Cartels:The Economic Perspective', accessed 0 September 2014, http://www.ee-mc.com/uploads/media/Cartels_Economic_Perspective_03.pdf.

deadweight loss does not benefit the consumer or the producer. It also causes loss to the society. The main aim of a cartel is 'to increase the joint profits of its members to a level as close to that a monopolist would earn as possible.'[75]

Market conditions in a cartel

Prices above marginal costs are rather a result of fixed costs or product differentiations. Producers may be interested in establishing a cartel in order to achieve higher profits through increased, cartelized prices. However, each member of a cartel has an economic incentive to deviate from any cartel agreement.[76] The reason is that the cartel price is higher than the competitive price. For example, if an individual undertaking lowers its own price, then it will benefit an increase in demand for its own products at the cost of the other cartel members.[77] Due to the lower price, the deviating company will gain a competitive advantage, and this will further lead to increased market shares and the undertaking will achieve a price above the competitive level. This will then lead to increase in profits. A cartel can never be implemented under 'normal' market conditions as the undertakings are going to underbid one another repeatedly until the competitive price level is reached again.

Game can be defined as 'a contest, physical or mental, according to set rules, undertaken for amusement or for a stake'. Games are explicitly defined as behavioural situations that are governed by rules. Game theory deals neither exclusively nor primarily with the contests that are undertaken. This theory analyses the behaviour of 'players' in conflict situations. Some games are affected if played out in a market place where the buyers and sellers compete for resources subject to a set of property and trading rules. One can say that this is in fact a traditional setting of economic analysis. A cartel can be said to be a game as the players are sellers in a market and they have their own set of rules and regulations.

However, certain market structures can result in a failure of the competition mechanism. The conditions set out are that the undertakings reach a mutual agreement first and, in addition, are able to monitor this agreement. This is possible if the market is a transparent one; this is because only a few producers are active, producing a few, homogeneous products.[78] Constant conditions of supply and demand assist cartelization as well. On the other hand, the stability of a cartel reduces if new competition enters by means of market entries or because of extensive demand fluctuations. In such a case, a cartel member cannot know for certain if a decrease in demand has been caused by an alteration of demand of the consumers of the product that the cartel is producing or by a cartel member who is not following the agreement. Another important factor facilitating cartel agreements is the possibility of the cartel members to sanction undertakings that deviate from an agreement.[79] Only a serious, effective sanction mechanism makes a durable coordination feasible and deters cartels members from deviating due to a strong self-interest.[80]

The aforementioned situations are seen by the market players in competition. However, the analysis of the same is done by use of economic tools. Price wars that make a deviation financially unattractive are a type of punishment, and this may discipline the cartel participants. As stated earlier, a cartel agreement can be successful only if all important market participants take part in it. In case important producers are not members of the cartel and/or do not follow the agreement, cartel members might lose market shares and then this will not be profitable. Furthermore, cartel members always have an option or, say, an incentive to deviate from the price agreed to by everyone as this would entail higher profits for them. Hence, practically you cannot have successful cartels. Incentive to deviate is based on the rationality assumption that rational individuals would place their own interest above the interests of the entire cartel.

The EE and MC approach

There are two ways in this approach, one is the before-and-after method and the other is the yardstick method. The 'before-and-after' method compares the price curves before the agreements with the price curve during the period of the agreements. The price curves are deduced from the price–demand relationship by means of single regression analysis. The aim of cartel agreements is to raise or at least fix current prices.[81] The before-and-after method analyses the actual price development and is therefore appropriate to invalidate the allegation that prices have increased during the cartel period. Other factors influencing the price, like changes of demand or costs, technological developments or market entries of competitors, are not considered in this methodology. Thus, this tool can be used as a starter for further analyses.[82]

For example, we talk about a cartel that is formed between five companies selling salt. A, B, C, D and E are the said companies. A, B and E were selling 1 kg at Rs 50 and C and D were selling 1 kg at Rs 40. The companies decided to form a cartel. They fixed a price at Rs 55. This price was higher than what the companies had initially been selling at. Applying the before-and-after method we can see that there is in fact a factual price development and can therefore say the price increased during the cartel period. This way we can also say that application of simple economic tools that is looking at price has helped in detection of cartel.

Another approach is the 'yardstick' approach. In this method there is comparison of the price development in the period of the agreement with the price development of a comparable product or geographical market in which competition is evident. If the relevant product market is a regional one, the identical product market in another geographical region is normally used as the reference market. But it is also possible to use the development of the prices for different products in the same geographical region.[83] One important principle is that the market conditions of the reference market should be similar to the market conditions of the market under review. This assumption relates to important conditions of competition like cost structure, demand or number of competitors.

The methods used for the yardstick approach are trend analyses and price correlations. If the price correlation with the reference market is close to +1, it can be assumed that both markets have similar price developments and no effective cartel agreement exists. The most comprehensive approach uses the possibility of econometric modelling of markets to estimate the significance of different influencing factors on the price.[84] This method involves the calculation of a hypothetical price without the alleged cartel agreement during the period of the agreement using a market simulation model based on data before the period of the agreement. If the price equals or is close to the actual price that persisted during this period, it is proved that the alleged cartel agreements did not have any impact on the price setting. Econometric modelling is very meaningful as all relevant factors for the price setting are integrated. In addition, the modelling of the market permits the integration of game-theoretic approaches. Thus, by means of econometric modelling, the instability of cartels can be shown. However, econometric modelling of the market requires a higher work load. On the other hand, the econometric market modelling approach is well accepted by the antitrust authorities.[85]

Application of game theory

As mentioned earlier, even game theory can be applied. In game theory, the collusion agreements can be described using extensive forms. For example, two firms share the market; they have colluded and are maintaining high prices. Here, each of the firms can decide to stop the collusion and start a price war so that they can increase their market share or make a situation whereby the other firm will have to quit the market.

Nash equilibrium

The concept of Nash equilibrium came from John Nash. Nash equilibria are defined as the combination of strategies in a game in such a way that there is no incentive for players to deviate from their choice.[86] This is the best option a player can make, taking into account the other players' decision and where a change in a player's decision will only lead to a worse result if the other players stick to their strategy. Here, we can take the example, where there are four firms U, V, W and X selling toothpaste in the market. They collude and they mark the price of their product above competitive level. The collusion goes on for three years, but later V wants to deviate from this arrangement. If it deviates, then the other three will suffer losses, as V will sell its product at a lower price. Hence, the other players will be worse hit by this outcome.

Economic analysis of collusion

It is important to examine the difference between the legal and the economic concept of collusion.[87] From a legal perspective, collusion is a situation where market prices are close to monopoly prices. Motta defines collusion as a situation where 'undertakings set prices which are close enough to monopoly prices'.[88] From an economic perspective, for the existence of collusion it is not needed to establish coordination among competitors. Collusion from an economic perspective may occur in explicit collusion and in a tacit collusion situation.[89] This is not the case from a legal point of view, where coordination between firms in the form of an agreement or concerted practice, together with the object or effect of distortion, prevention or restriction of competition, is needed.[90]

The main motive behind formation of collusion is not only to have increased profit. There are several other factors that also play an important role. When we talk about markets that are characterized by price competition, there are chances that information will be shared, which could have negative consequences.

To see if the information exchange is restrictive or not, the EU Commission focuses its attention on the characteristics of the market on which the exchange takes place and also on the information exchange itself, such as the nature and type of information and the frequency of exchange.[91] According to Motta, despite the efficiency reasons for information exchange, it is unlikely that there will be a need for such an exchange in order to achieve these efficiencies.[92] Although information agreements (e.g. agreements among competitors to fix prices[93] or output, divide markets by allocating customers[94]) are seen as illegal, in particular in oligopolistic markets, there is no per se rule against the exchange of information. Those agreements that are not seen as per se illegal are then analysed under the rule of reason doctrine. They include agreements that might be considered per se illegal, under the condition that they are reasonably necessary to achieve pro-competitive benefits. Thus, there are situations where information exchange will have a larger welfare impact, for example when speaking about markets where concentration is not very large. Information exchange can improve investment decisions, and there are chances it could result in better quality or overall ability to respond to demand changes. It could be considered pro-competitive when firms are able to accurately manage demand and supply forecasts and therefore better allocate resources.[95] Finally, even without any governmental intervention, cartels are doomed to fail on their own from the time of their inception.

Cement cartel case in India

Let us now take a look at the cement cartel case in India. Steps taken included identifying the prime structural patterns of the cement industry and further analysing the traits such as price, transparency, entry and exit and concentration, which are conductive to collusion. In this case, the price analysis done by experts showed how the manufactures had increased their market power.

A critical event analysis was done, and this involved finding some events during the critical period, which may indicate the presence of a cartel in the industry. It has been noticed that the consumption of cement increases with the rise of per capita income in developing nations. The demand comes from housing sector, infrastructure and industrial construction and so on. Further, one needs to remember that input costs and profit margins are not influenced by the cement market players. The profit margins largely depend on the cement prices and the pricing power of producers. Intense competition can therefore erode profit margins, whereas collusive agreements can mean an increased price stability and also high profits for all.[96] In analysis of this sector it was necessary to define the product and the geographic market. It is easy to define the relevant market in both these terms. The cement market can be said to be separate market as it has no substitutes and is a preferred building material. Coming to the geographic market, it can be said that economically the product is sold in a small radius of production facilities, and therefore, there exists a regional market for the same. The players suspected to be in collusive agreement included the top cement producers of the country, and it is suspected that the Cement Manufacturers Association (CMA) was the agent for facilitating exchange of information vital for the collusion to sustain.[97] It was alleged that the cement cartel had been in existence since 2000.[98]

The author will now like to briefly examine the primary factors for collusion.

Price development

As stated earlier, the analysis of price is an important tool to predict the presence of cartels. For this, we need to see the increase in price without corresponding increase in costs, which is an indication of the expanding market power of the producers. Next, see if there is a decrease in seasonal variation in price series during the critical time period as compared to non-cartel period.[99] The wholesale price index was used to detect the change in price.

A sudden change in price trend was seen since 2000. The trend was said to be steeper after 2000. Some might be of the view that price increase is not evidence enough to prove collusion; however, analysing input costs would help one prove the collusion. If there has been no such increase in price of the input costs, then it would imply rise in market power of producers.[100] When we look at prices and market power, it is worth noting that the price of cement shot up more swiftly as compared to the input costs. This change is yet another indication of increase in market power. Without there being a change in costs, price increases indicate changes in market power and hence show changes in profitability, which is said to be the main reason for any sort of collusive agreement.[101]

This now leads us to look at the seasonal variation. A study of the quarterly cement prices starting 1994 to 2009 revealed a change in seasonal pattern since 2000. This acts as proof that the producers used their market power to reduce the fall of prices during such months or time periods when there is less demand and increase the price when the demand is high.

Transparency

This is important for the inception and sustenance of collusion. The cement industry in India has a CMA. This is like a regulating body and it regulates prices. Yet there were allegations that CMA indulged in collusive behaviour. Majority data that is collected by CMA with respect to price and demand is exchanged only between members, that is cement producers as against consumers. Cement being a homogeneous good with little differentiation, exchange of data on sales, production and capacity of each firm helps the firms form collusive contracts and easily detect deflections.[102]

Entry behaviour and concentration

For collusion, another trait can be seen, that is high market concentration and barriers to entry. Collusion is more likely if the number of firms in the industry is less. Effectiveness of a collusive agreement can be ensured only if there is a barrier to entry. Many researchers have concluded that there is high concentration in the cement industry. This makes the entry of new players difficult. Further, the other reason contributing to this is its capital intensive nature and the long gestation period. It is also difficult to get rights in order to obtain various inputs like limestone, and this, therefore, causes further hindrance to new players. We can take the example of Sanghi Cements, which entered the Gujarat market in 2004. Its entry affected the already-existing Gujarat players. Sanghi Cements at first reduced its prices to establish itself in the market. There were price wars, and only months later there was normalization in the prices.

Now if we do an event analysis, it will help us know whether there was any sort of collusion. It is claimed that the alleged collusion started in 2000 due to a demand depression. This poor performance was the result of a supply–demand mismatch. A slowdown in demand since 1997 left the industry with huge surplus capacity, leading to falling prices and shrinking profit margins.[103] When the alleged collusion began, the prices started to rise. They rose by 25%. This clearly indicated a collusive agreement because a sudden increase in price during a low demand scenario is unheard of.[104] Price decline may result from actions of outsiders as well. For instance, a new entry in the industry may destabilize the cartel. Price wars may continue till market shares are not readjusted, and the new entrant either is accommodated into the market or is driven out.[105] We can take a look at the Sanghi Cements case mentioned earlier. The pricing power was in the hands of the producers. This was because the demand and supply equation was balanced. In such situations, it is difficult to find evidence of collusion as players claimed that rising prices were the result of a tight demand–supply situation and not because of collusion as there was utilization to full capacity. But as new capacities added began to be functional in early 2009 and capacity utilizations dropped, collusion among market players became more apparent. Since February 2009, it has been noticed that the cement companies throughout India increased their prices in successive jumps.[106] These increases were unjustified as capacity utilization had come down. This indicated the presence of collusive agreements between producers to raise prices to establish a higher base price for when prices began to decline in the upcoming business downturn. This is how economics was used in detection of cartels in the cement industry in India.

To conclude it can be said that there has been an increase in the integration of markets, the cross-border activities of firms.[107] The increase in price in cartels is because of removing or reducing competition. The negative effect of cartel leads to a loss of social welfare, and as a result of this the price increases. Further, it also damages the wider economy. Detecting and taking enforcement action against firms involved in cartels is one of the main enforcement priorities for antitrust authorities around the globe,[108] and this can be done with the help of economists. With this the author has been able to prove her hypothesis that economic and economic tools do help in the detection of cartels.

Mergers and economic analysis

Merger is a union of two or more businesses for better, efficient and effective functioning. Businesses merge for various reasons. There are chances market players might object to any merger transaction, as it could lead to a monopoly or else create barriers to entry and such similar anti-competitive practices.[109] Shareholders are likely to object to mergers due to which there is reduction of share value or share effectiveness or transaction. Similarly, individuals can also oppose to such transactions, which can lead to higher market prices, decrease in quantity or quality of goods and other analogous practices.[110] Hence, a merger transaction could adversely affect competition, and therefore, merger control is required. There are essentially two types of mergers, horizontal mergers and non-horizontal mergers, which are also known as vertical mergers.

Horizontal mergers involve companies that operate at equal levels of the supply chain, producing substitute goods. Substitutes are those products where an increase in the price of one good induces an increase in demand for the other.[111] A non-horizontal merger or vertical merger, in contrast, involves companies that operate at different levels of the supply chain, for example a merger between a wholesaler and its retailer, or a manufacturer and its input supplier.[112] The author has discussed horizontal and non-horizontal mergers simultaneously in this chapter. A merger can have either of the following effects on competition.

- Coordinated effects: This addresses whether the merger will raise the likelihood that firms in the relevant market will jointly increase the prices.
- Unilateral effects: This addresses whether there will be an incentive to the merged firm to raise prices on its own even if the competitors are not raising their prices in response.

Unilateral effects

Unilateral effects arise when the merged group is able to profitably reduce value for money, choice or innovation through its own acts without the need for a co-operative response from competitors.[113]

Economic methods in evaluating unilateral effects

A horizontal merger is said to give rise to unilateral effects if the merged firm finds it profitable to increase price irrespective of the reactions of the remaining competitors. To establish any theory of unilateral effects, the restricting output is central to it; due to increased price, the merged firm has to accept that there will be a reduction in the volume of sales.

Key principles of unilateral effects

There will be a rise to unilateral effects in a merger if the merged entity thinks that it will be profitable post-merger to increase price acting unilaterally, namely independent of its competitors. The cost of price increases or equivalent output restrictions arises from the loss of the margins that would have been earned absent the loss in sales.[114] It can be said the larger the post-merger market share of the merged entity, the more likely the merger is, ceteris paribus, to give rise to unilateral effects.[115]

Under the dominance test, combined market shares above 40% were usually seen as providing a threshold below which no competition concerns were raised. But, with the change in merger test, the threshold is now 25%. This change is because the market shares significantly understate the competitive constraint that exists pre-merger between the merging parties. Where the products are highly differentiated, market share is not a good indicator of the likely competitive effect, since some products are 'closer' competitors.[116] Closeness is when firms sell homogeneous products or in markets that are characterized by bidding for tenders. Hence, it is important to assess whether market shares overstate or understate magnitude of competitive restraint.

The following are used to evaluate unilateral effects.

Estimating diversion ratio: The ratio between two competing firms measures the percentage of lost sales following a price increase by firm that is captured by another. This statistic helps see the closeness between the firms. If the ratio is high, then it means that the merger will result in significant unilateral effects.

Taking the help of an illustration; suppose Pantaloons and Westside are two brands of comparatively cheaper clothing, and Tommy Hilfiger and United Colors of Benetton are more expensive in the Indian market. When United Colors of Benetton increases its price, some consumers will shift to another brand. Assume that those consumers switch from United Colors of Benetton to the following:

- 65% switch to Tommy Hilfiger
- 15% switch to Westside
- 15% switch to Pantaloons
- 5% switch to other brands

In this case, the diversion ratio between Tommy Hilfiger and United Colors of Benetton is 65%, while with the other two brands it is 15%. This shows that more consumers think Tommy Hilfiger is a closer substitute to United Colors of Benetton. Hence, if these two brands were to merge, then the shift would not be too big to the other brands.

Conducting merger simulations: This uses standard economic tools to compare predicted prices before and after the proposed merger. Three steps are involved, namely estimating a demand system based on the pre-merger information, which is in fact similar to the econometric method described for estimating diversion ratio. The second step is solving the supply function based on specific oligopoly competition model (that is a market featuring a small group of competitors) and the pre-merger supply information such as marginal costs and margin. The third and final step is calibrating the post-merger equilibrium prices and quantities, which is often done by adjusting market shares to reflect the post-merger situation. This is usually applied in branded consumer mergers. When there is enough data, a merger simulation can provide direct estimate of the magnitude of unilateral effects. The selected model may not reflect other important aspects of competition in the industry, which are often rich and diversified.

Using the Gross Upward Pricing Pressure Index: The Gross Upward Pricing Pressure Index (GUPPI) test, also referred to as the upward price pressure test, is a tool that economists have refined in recent years to provide a quantifiable measure of a firm's post-merger incentive to raise prices.[117] The GUPPI, described in the Horizontal Merger Guidelines (without using the term 'GUPPI'), has been adopted by other jurisdictions, including the European Union. It provides a simple benchmark to evaluate the magnitude of the merger's impact on the buyer's incentives to increase prices.[118]

It further takes into account two factors, that is the firm's margin on the product that it sells and the diversion ratio of its customers to the merging partner. Assume that firm A is acquiring firm B. Firm A sells product 1 at price P1 and firm B sells product 2 at price P2. Although the formula for the GUPPI can be quite complicated in certain situations, in its most basic version, the GUPPI for product 1 is calculated using the following formula: GUPPI = (diversion ratio from product 1 to 2) × (profit margin of product 2) × (P2/P1).[119]

If the diversion ratio, the margin and the price ratio are high, then GUPPI will also be high.

Coordinated effects

A merger is said to give rise to coordinated effects concerns when the consequent change in market structure,[120] including the reduction in the number of firms and the greater combined market share held by the merging party, better enables the merged firm and at least one of its remaining competitors to reach and sustain a tacit agreement not to compete effectively with one another and thereby raises prices.[121] This price increase is termed 'coordinated effects' since they result not only from the actions of the merged entity but also from the realization among a number of firms that the returns to competing less vigorously with one another are higher than competing vigorously.[122]

Coordinated effects rely on one or more of the remaining competitors also restricting their output when the merged entity restricts its output.[123] When a company decides to enter into an acquisition or merger with a competitor (commonly referred to as a horizontal merger), the transaction is reviewed by the authorities. The key concern in reviewing a deal is whether the transaction is likely to reduce competition and harm consumers, also known as causing competitive harm.[124]

Empirical analysis is fundamental in assessing merger effects as analysing data is often the most efficient as well as immediate way to validate or refute contradictory claims and opinions made by parties who have opposite interests.[125] The utilization of mass trading in merger control is not restricted to leading experimental examination. In fact, economics is now closely embedded within merger control as it provides the essential conceptual framework to analyse the functioning of the markets and to assess merger effects.[126] The adoption of the horizontal and non-horizontal mergers guidelines provides evidence that DG Competition has placed sound economic thinking at the heart of competition enforcement.[127] The analysis of mergers has moved away from structural presumptions that increased concentration will necessarily result in anti-competitive conduct, towards a more complex analysis that incorporates predictions of competitive effects using tools of modern economic analysis.[128] Significantly, both rule of reason analysis and current merger analysis require an evaluation of pro-competitive efficiencies that may result from firms' agreements, unilateral conduct or proposed transactions.[129]

There are various tools that are relied on for economic analysis of competitive harm and evaluate the likelihood of increased prices post-merger. Market concentration metrics, such as market shares and Herfindahl-Hirschman Index levels, are often the starting point of predicting a merger's likely competitive effects.[130] These metrics are most helpful in markets where the products are homogeneous. However, concentration measures do not always properly capture different degrees of competition among differentiated products, in cases such as consumer products like cars or smart phones, where there are many brands but the products differ in terms of physical attributes and features.[131] As a result, especially in differentiated product markets, economists tend to put less weight on concentration measures and investigate other factors that consider interactions among different market players.[132]

Economists are engaged to evaluate a horizontal merger's competitive effects, by both the antitrust agencies and the transacting parties, to apply a range of analytical tools to the available evidence. The economic analysis of competitive harm in every merger takes into account the relevant market's unique features, market participants and competitive dynamics.

Role of the relevant market in merger

Under the new significant impediment to effective competition (SIEC) test, market definition plays a vital role in the competitive assessment of mergers. Defining relevant market continues to provide a useful filter for determining whether a more detailed assessment of the merger is required. Mergers that have companies with low market shares in a properly defined relevant market cannot give rise to competition concerns and, therefore, do not require a detailed assessment.

The definition allows an assessment of the market structure, which includes calculation of market shares and how these are affected by the merger. Qualitative and quantitative evidence is assessed in this framework for the purpose of market definition. In case of qualitative evidence, it is useful to gauge which are the alternatives that the customer would consider suitable as a starting point for the market definition exercise.[133] The Horizontal Merger Guidelines state that mergers where the post-merger entry would have a limited market share are unlikely to impede effective competition. This is the case when market share of the merging parties is not more than 25%. Where the combined market share of the merging parties is more than 50%, the situation becomes problematic.

It is important to recognize the Horizontal Merger Guidelines as they state that these thresholds provide an initial indicator of the likelihood of competition concerns and do not give rise to assumption of either the existence or the absence of competition concerns. Entry is another point that has to be looked into. The Horizontal Merger Guidelines state, 'When entering a market is sufficiently easy, a merger is unlikely to pose any significant anti-competitive effect.' This is because no firm has a dominant position; it is a situation of almost 'perfect competition'. Hence, assessing new entrant is important. One can say that where competition between existing firms is vigorous, one would not expect to see entry taking place even if barriers to entry were low. There can be two types of entry: 'hit and run' and the 'long-term entry'.

In the first one, there is sudden entry and the exit can happen anytime if the company sees that the profit opportunity is lost. In the second one, firms incur sunk costs and entry will be undertaken by firms that aim to remain in the market in the long term. What really matters in such situations is whether entry is likely to prevent rise in prices post the merger.

Buyer power is also a pertinent point. This refers to the ability of buyers to take actions to alter the structure of the supply market. The Horizontal Merger Guidelines say that the power can be exercised by threatening to resort to alternative sources of supply. In such cases, it is necessary that there is a difference between genuine sources of power from mere appeals to the fact that customers are large. The European Commission in a case has particularly argued that buyers do not possess buyer power because they are less concentrated than their upstream suppliers. The main pro-competitive effect of vertical mergers consists in the elimination of double mark-ups. However, vertical mergers may also give rise to foreclosure concerns. A vertically integrated firm might harm its rivals in the downstream market by a refusal to supply important inputs (input foreclosure). The vertically integrated firm might also refuse to purchase inputs from its upstream competitors (customer foreclosure). These aspects are detailed in turn after providing a short introduction to non-horizontal mergers and the European Commission's non-horizontal merger guidelines.

A non-horizontal merger can give rise to competition concerns if the merged entity has a significant degree of market power in at least one of the markets concerned. Here, also in order to assess the market share and levels of concentration, it is a necessary pre-condition to define relevant market. A proper assessment needs to be done of the buyer power and include not only concentration of buyers in the observation but also if these buyers have the potential to influence the terms of supply.

Merger efficiencies

The underlying reason behind competition is to ensure that there is optimal allocation of existing resources and achieve efficient market outcomes. Ignorance of economies by competition law and competition enforcement agencies would prejudice the very object of preserving competition.[134] Efficiencies serve public interest and are beneficial to the society at large.

ICN Merger Guidelines Workbook[135] reads:

> Efficiencies include cost savings, more intensive use of existing capacity, economies of scale or scope, or demand-side efficiencies such as increased network size or product quality. They might also encompass pro-competitive changes in the merged entity's incentives, for example by capturing complementarities in R&D activity, which in turn might increase incentives to invest in product development in innovation markets.

Mergers can be strategic in nature, perhaps bringing together a company great at marketing with another whose skills lie in product design or engineering. Perhaps companies may simply realize that by joining production efforts, they can produce output more efficiently than they could as separate companies. Joint production can create synergies, allow the exploitation of economies of scale and facilitate the better use of expertise. For each of these reasons, mergers may create production efficiencies and actively reduce costs. 'When those cost reductions are passed on to consumers, they may offset the negative effect of the loss of a competitor on market prices and output.'[136]

In modern competition policy, it is widely accepted that efficiencies may have a potential countervailing positive effect in the post-merger world so that the merging parties may resort to an efficiency defence. Efficiency can be classified as productive efficiency, allocative efficiency, dynamic efficiency and transactional efficiency. Economies of scale and scope are part of the productive efficiency. 'Economies of scale' refers to benefits yielded out of larger units of production with existing capital assets. The benefits of this include optimal utilization of captive plants and reduction in cost incurred out of operations and investment in fixed assets.[137]

When related activities are carried out simultaneously, the benefits of economies of scope can be reaped. In other terms, production of two different but related products and production and distribution are done by the same person.[138] A market is said to achieve allocative efficiency when the market processes lead society's resources to be allocated to their highest-valued use among all competing uses.[139] This can occur when production is allocated to highest-value buyers.[140] For example, in the case of a vertical merger between the makers of a compressor used in a refrigerator and the makers of a refrigerator, a lot of packing material and resources on transportation would be saved and be available to society for use elsewhere. This is also a clear case of enhancement in allocative efficiencies as a result of a merger.

Gains that are achieved out of innovation are called dynamic efficiencies. Innovations result in better quality, novel products and better technologies. A merger of two small firms may empower the merged firm to invest more in research and development and innovate. However, merger between innovative firms may monopolize the scarce intellectual properties in the hands of the resulting entity.[141] Vertical mergers act as transactional efficiencies. It helps to reduce the price raise due to opportunistic behaviours and hold-ups. We can take the example of a merger between a monopoly wholesaler and a monopoly retailer that reduces the price mark-up by the retailer, which in turn leads to the possibility of reducing the price of products sold.[142]

Even though efficiencies are used as a defence in case of mergers and are also a mode of approving mergers, firms should not use this as a way of consummating anti-competitive mergers. The specificity factor raises two questions. One is whether the efficiencies are a result of the merger and whether this efficiency can be achieved in any other manner.

Taking the example of American Airways and US Airways merger, the said merger is said to have a negative impact on competition. It will not result in merger efficiencies to the consumer; in fact, it will result in fewer seats, and a rise in price, all of which will be detrimental to the consumer's interest.

Figure 12.4 shows Williamson's model on effects of merger. To understand this, let us assume that there are two firms, each with a significant market share, and they operate in a concentrated market. A horizontal merger takes place between the two firms. The figure explains the impact on price and allocation pattern.

D is the customer's demand for the product. The average cost of production and price of the product before the merger are given by P_1 and AC_1, respectively. Q_1 denotes the quantity demanded when the price was at P_1. In the pre-merger market scenario, it may be noticed that price is equal to cost ($P_1 = AC_1$).[143]

The merger further increases the market concentration and places the resultant entity in a dominant position. As a result of dominance, the resultant entity achieves pricing power and scale benefits. While the pricing power leads to increased price, scale benefits reduce the average cost of production. The increased price and decreased cost are given by P_2 and AC_2, respectively. As a result

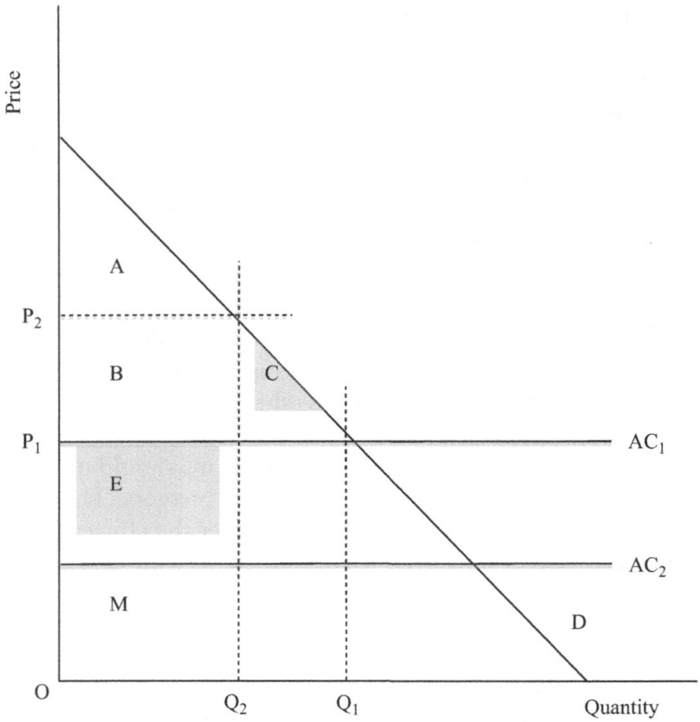

Figure 12.4 Williamson's model on effect of merger

Source: Kaushal Sharma, Shankar Singham and Sriraj Venkatasamy, 'Economies (Efficiencies) – An Essential Consideration in Merger Analysis', accessed 15 October 2014, http://www.cci.gov.in/images/media/presentations/Final_Efficiency_Article01-Feb-2011.pdf.

of increased price, the quantity demanded gets reduced from Q_1 to Q_2.[144] From the discussion, it is clear that the merger had led to increase in price, reduction in demand and reduction in cost of production. These consequences put together have impact on competition, consumers, stakeholders and society as a whole. Quantification of the differences in price, demand and cost in view of the merger and their impact on the different sects of the society forms the basis of welfare trade-offs.[145]

A non-horizontal merger between two suppliers may create the incentive and ability to foreclose rivals for two reasons. One is that the merged firm may be able to leverage market power from one market into another.[146] In simple terms, the market can reduce competition in another market too, and this will result in an increase in price, which will be detrimental to the consumers. A vertical merger can foreclose firms, thereby reducing competition in a number of related markets. The second reason is in relation to conglomerate effects; foreclosure in related markets may be used to protect market power rather than to leverage it into related markets. By tying and bundling of related products, the merged firm may be able to deter entry into the market in which it has market power.

Economies of scale and merger

Let us consider a situation wherein attractive economies of scale are available and one party to the proposed merger currently fails to achieve those economies.[147] To know whether or not the economies of scale are merger specific, there are two conditions that must hold, namely a merged firm will in fact achieve those economies and the previously pre-merger firms would not do so absent a merger. If the economies of scale are very attractive, it is more likely that a merged firm would in fact seek them, but it is also likely that individual firms would try to expand absent a merger.[148] For example, in the SBC/Ameritech merger, the parties had argued that it was important to provide facilities-based service to large multi-location customers and that this was an efficiency of the merger.[149] Under imperfect competition, scale efficiencies can be merger specific, but the same logic limits the scale efficiencies to those insufficiently attractive to have been realized pre-merger.[150]

To answer the question whether simple economies of scale are a merger efficiency, it is pertinent to note that antitrust agencies should be fairly sceptical of efficiency claims that are based on simple scale economies. Such scale economies can be achieved unilaterally, without a merger, and through this consumers are likely to benefit. The reason for scepticism is if consumer welfare is the standard instead of overall economic efficiency, then if simple scale economy efficiencies are in fact merger specific, then there exists a reason to doubt that they will both be large enough and sufficiently passed through which consumers will benefit.[151]

In 1998, FTC challenged the proposed mergers[152] of leading drug wholesalers on an efficiency defence based on simple scale economies. There were four parties, and they merged forming two parties. The companies would purchase medicines from the manufactures and sell it to hospitals, pharmacies and so on; they would also stock and deliver the goods. The combined market share reached almost 80%, and both sets defended the merger saying that it was expected that they will achieve significant efficiencies from their consolidation. The claimed efficiencies were related to the basic economies of scale:

- Saving through consolidation of warehouses along with an associated reduction in inventories.
- Savings based on volume buying from drug manufacturers.
- Savings in corporate overhead.

FTC argued that the claimed efficiency would not reach the consumer, they were inflated and most of the efficiencies could be achieved without a merger.

The judgement came in favour of the defendants. Hence, economically the competition among drug wholesalers in this case will tend to force the individual firms to achieve available economies of scale. Consumers stand to reap the gains from the competitive struggle.[153] To conclude, it can be said that the delaying of time at which any single firm gains efficient scale is the very essence of competition in the presence of newfound scale economies.[154] The fact that economies of scale are a merger efficiency has been proven, and hence, the hypothesis has also been proven.

Conclusion

Economics helps in the better understanding of competition law. It is necessary that lawyers study the subject economic analysis of law as it helps in breaking down subjects such as this to help understand law. The author has been successful in proving that economics helps in detection of cartels and that economies of scale are a merger efficiency. The simple tools of economics such as demand, supply, price and market help understand the complex nitty-gritty of competition law. The competition policy exists in order to protect consumers and ensure freedom of businesses and to engage in economic conduct free from abuse by dominant firms. This will then contribute to economic development but also in determination of dominant firm or if a group is highly subjective and complex.[155]

The aspects of competition law such as abuse of dominance, cartels and mergers are inter-related topics. Where on the one hand the formation of a cartel can also mark dominance in a market, on the other hand, a merger between two firms of the same market can also result in dominance. The example of De Beers, where a merger later resulted in a cartel formation, is a classic example of how the various aspects of competition law are related. The use of econometric analysis is very helpful in market definition and also in case of mergers. It is suggested that modelling and estimation of the structure of demand are necessary to understand the system. The uses of theories like the game theory and Nash equilibrium should be used more often in economic analysis of law. Articulation of the theory can make clear thinking by laying bare key assumptions and reasoning steps, and by structuring the collection of evidence.[156] The analysis helps to focus the attention of decision makers on the connection between the economic theory of the case and the evidence and clarify what is in dispute and what evidence could help test them.

The objective of this chapter to define market in terms of competition and economics has been fulfilled. The dynamics of what a market is is essentially alike; however, the way markets work in economics and competition is different, thereby making the study of markets together necessary in both aspects. It is also necessary to note that the advances in the use of economic analysis in the application of antitrust law were also the consequence of a change in the view about the paradigm of competition relevant for the application of the law.[157] Further, in cases of mergers, having a merger simulation will have a substantial value. Developing counties such as India deal with varied problems. Some are distinct in their characteristics like high entry barrier (as in the case of cement) and public sector monopolies; the practices of abuse of dominant positions, cartelization and anti-competitive mergers are very much prevalent in India. Hence, there is a potential harm to economies. This chapter has looked into the international and national scenarios. The study of the international scenario is necessary because it will help combat and understand the competition issues in our country.

Notes

1 M.M. Sharma, 'Role of Economics in Competition Law', accessed 14 August 2014, http://www.vaishlaw.com/article/Role of Economics in Competition% 20Law-MM Sharma.pdf.

2 A. Kumar, 'Competition Law at a Glance', accessed 23 March 2014, http://cci.gov.in/images/media/articles/competition_lawglance_20080409115746.pdf.

3 Paul Cook, 'Competition and Its Regulation: Key Issues', *Annals of Public and Cooperative Economics* 73 (2002): 541–558.
4 Kumar, 'Competition Law at a Glance'.
5 Bingyuan Hsiung, 'Economic Analysis of Law: An Inquiry of Its Underlying Logic', *Erasmus Law and Economics Review* 2 (1) (2006): 1–33.
6 Hugo L.C. Hazersloot, 'Traditional Industrial Economics and Purchasing: A Theoretical Application of the SCP-Paradigm on Decision Points in Purchasing', accessed 12 October 2014, http://www.utwente.nl/mb/ba/education/ba-thesis-2013-2/hazersloot.pdf.
7 Richard A. Posner, 'The Chicago School of Antitrust Analysis', *University of Pennsylvania Law Review* 127 (4) (1979): 925–948.
8 Hsiung, 'Economic Analysis of Law'.
9 William J. Kolasky and Andrew R. Dick, 'The Merger Guidelines and the Integration of Efficiencies into Antitrust Review of Horizontal Mergers', *Antitrust Law Journal* 71 (207) (2003), accessed 10 October 2014, http://www.justice.gov/atr/hmerger/11254.htm#N_1_.
10 Oliver E. Williamson, 'Economies as an Antitrust Defense: The Welfare Tradeoffs', *American Economic Review* 58 (1969): 18.
11 *U.S. v. Philadelphia National Bank*, 374 U.S. 321 (1963); *FTC v. Procter & Gamble Co.*, 386 U.S. 568 (1967).
12 Jean Tirole, 'Market Power and Regulation, Compiled by the Economic Sciences Prize Committee of the Royal Swedish Academy of Sciences', accessed 5 November 2014, http://www.nobelprize.org/nobel_prizes/economic-sciences/laureates/2014/advanced-economicsciences2014.pdf.
13 US Department of Justice, '1982 Merger Guidelines', accessed 14 August 2014, http://www.justice.gov/atr/hmerger/11248.htm.
14 Carl Shapiro, 'The 2010 Horizontal Merger Guidelines: From Hedgehog to Fox in Forty Years', *Antitrust Law Journal* 77 (2010): 49.
15 Ibid.
16 Jonathan B. Baker, 'Why Did the Antitrust Agencies Embrace Unilateral Effects?', *George Mason Law Review* 12 (2003): 31.
17 Paul Hofer, Williams Mark and Wu Lawrence, 'Principles of Competition Policy Economics', *The Asia-Pacific Antitrust Review* (2004), accessed 10 August 2014, http://www.nera.com/extImage/03Economicssjc4-7.pdf.
18 Universita Degli Di Parma, 'Introduction to Competition Law', accessed 10 August 2014, http://www.unipr.it/arpa/defi/furse_ch01.pdf.
19 Ibid.
20 Sandra Marco Colino, *Competition Law of the EU and UK* (Oxford: Oxford University Press, 2011).
21 Ibid.
22 Universita Degli Di Parma, 'Introduction to Competition Law'.
23 Hofer, Mark and Lawrence, 'Principles of Competition Policy Economics'.
24 Ibid.
25 Ibid.
26 Ibid.
27 Ibid.
28 *United States v. E.I. du Pont de Nemours & Co.*, 351 U.S. 377 (1956), 76 S.Ct. 994.

29 Amitabh Kumar, 'Economics of Competition Law', *Paper Presented at the Seminar on 'Competition Policy and Law' organized by PHD CCI*, Chandigarh, accessed 6 October 2005, http://www.competition-commission-india.nic.in/speeches_articles_presentations/3-Economics_32.pdf.
30 Presentation by Augustine Peter, 'Abuse of Dominance and Combinations', accessed 11 October 2014, http://www.competition-commission-india.nic.in/Advocacy/workshop12062007/F-2-Abuse_of_Dominance_LMA_11_06_07.pdf.
31 *United States v. Microsoft Corp.*, 253 F.3d 34 (2001).
32 Ibid.
33 Ibid.
34 'Competition Law SMP and Dominant Positions', Competition Law SMP and Dominant Positions, *UK Essays*, accessed 17 March 2014, http://www.ukessays.com/essays/economics/competition-law-smp-and-dominant-positions-economics-essay.php.
35 Presentation by Amitabh Kumar, 'Economics of Competition Law'.
36 *Lee v. Life Insurance Co. of North America*, 829 F. Supp. 529 (1993).
37 William M. Landes and Richard A. Posner, 'Market Power in Antitrust Cases', *Harvard Law Review* 94 (937) (1981): 939.
38 Ibid.
39 European Commission, 'Communication from the Commission – Guidance on the Commission's Enforcement Priorities in Applying Article 82 EC Treaty to Abusive Exclusionary Conduct by Dominant Undertakings', OJ 2009, C-45/7, accessed 27 August 2014, http://www.hartpub.co.uk/updates/korah/AbusiveExclusionaryConduct.pdf.
40 Ibid.
41 Johannes Paha, 'The Economics of Competition (Law)', accessed 19 August 2014, https://wiwi.uni-giessen.de/dl/down/open/goetz/c995a5eea02570e0a0fb84b138cb7c10ffefe98e46e7a3d38fecdc6ab7608b186f6fe09496567428b0fb0f321e4c8c5b/Paha_2013_The_Economics_of_Competition_Law_3.0.pdf.
42 Ibid.
43 European Commission, 'Communication from the Commission'.
44 Ibid.
45 Section 18, Competition Act 2002.
46 Competition Commission of India, 'Abuse of Dominance in the Indian Competition Law', accessed 10 September 2014, http://cci.gov.in/images/media/articles/abuse_20080409115506.pdf.
47 Ibid.
48 Competition Commission of India, 'Abuse of Dominance in the Indian Competition Law'.
49 Ibid.
50 Shaurya Sahay, 'Abuse of Dominance: Predatory Pricing', accessed 10 September 2014, http://cci.gov.in/images/media/ResearchReports/AbuseofDominancePredatoryPricing.pdf.
51 Ibid.
52 *Hoffmann-La Roche & Co AG v. Commission of the European Communities*, Case 85/76 dated 13 February 1979.

53 Sahay, 'Abuse of Dominance: Predatory Pricing'.
54 Ibid.
55 Ibid.
56 Competition Commission of India, 'Abuse of Dominance in the Indian Competition Law'.
57 Ibid.
58 Herbert Hovenkamp, *Federal Antitrust Policy: The Law of Competition and Its Practice* (St. Paul, MN: West Publishing Co., 1994).
59 C. Scott Hemphill, 'The Role of Recoupment in Predatory Pricing Analyses', *Standard Law Review* 53 (1581) (2001): 1582–1585.
60 *A.A. Poultry Farms, Inc. v. Rose Acre Farms, Inc.*, 881 F.2d 1396, 1401 (7th Cir. 1989).
61 *Indian Oil Corporation Ltd & Ors. v. Reliance Industries Ltd & Ors.*, 2009 ELR (APTEL) 954.
62 Michael A. Salinger, *The Legacy of Matsushita: Has This Thing Called Economics Gotten Way Out of Hand?*, accessed 30 September 2014, http://www.ftc.gov/sites/default/files/documents/public_statements/legacy-matsushita-has-thing-called-economics-gotten-way-out-hand/060929matsushitaloyola_0.pdf.
63 Philip Areeda and Donald F. Turner, 'Predatory Pricing and Related Practices under Section 2 of the Sherman Act', *Harvard Law Review* 88 (4) (1975): 697–733.
64 Frank H. Easterbrook, 'Predatory Strategies and Counterstrategies', *The University of Chicago Law Review* 48 (1981): 263–337.
65 *United Brands Company v. Commission*, Case 27/76 Judgement dated 14 February 1978.
66 Ibid.
67 *Hoffmann-La Roche & Co AG v. Commission of the European Communities*, Case 85/76 dated 13 February 1979.
68 Shivani Anand, 'Identifying Cartels Using Economic Evidence: A Case Study of Indian Cement Industry', accessed 10 November 2014, https://www.researchgate.net/publication/242777915_IDENTIFYING_CARTELS_USING_ECONOMIC_EVIDENCE_A_CASE_STUDY_OF_INDIAN_CEMENT_INDUSTRY.
69 'Cartels under Competition Act 2002', *Advocacy Booklet*, Competition Commission of India.
70 Joseph E. Harrington Jr., 'Detecting Cartels', accessed 10 September 2014, https://www.competitionpolicyinternational.com/assets/Uploads/Detecting-Cartels.pdf.
71 Ibid.
72 European E&M Consultants, 'Cartels: The Economic Perspective', accessed 10 September 2014, http://www.ee-mc.com/uploads/media/Cartels_Economic_Perspective_03.pdf.
73 Ibid.
74 Ibid.
75 John M. Connor, 'Global Cartels Redux: The Amino Acid Lysine Antitrust Litigation', In *The Antitrust Revolution: Economics, Competition, and Policy*, edited by J. E. Kwoka, Jr, and L. J. White (New York: Oxford University Press, 1996): 252–276.

76 'Definition of Cartels', accessed 14 September 2014, http://www.lawteacher.net/criminal-law/essays/definition-of-cartels.php.
77 European E&M Consultants, 'Cartels: The Economic Perspective'.
78 Ibid.
79 Ibid.
80 Ibid.
81 Ibid.
82 Ibid.
83 Ibid.
84 Ibid.
85 Emily Clark, Mat Hughes and David Wirth, 'Study on the Conditions of Claims for Damages in Case of Infringement of EC Competition Rules: Analysis of Economic Models for the Calculation of Damages', *Ashurst-Study* (2004), accessed 10 November 2014, http://ec.europa.eu/competition/antitrust/actionsdamages/economic_clean_en.pdf.
86 'Nash Equilibrium', accessed 3 October 2014, http://www.policonomics.com/nash-equilibrium/.
87 Rastislav Funtia, 'Legal and Economic Analysis of Cartels, Their Enforcement and the Leniency Program', *DANUBE: Law and Economics Review* 2 (2012): 35–47.
88 Massimo Motta, *Competition Policy: Theory and Practice* (Cambridge: Cambridge University Press, 2004).
89 'Nash Equilibrium', accessed 3 October 2014, http://www.policonomics.com/nash-equilibrium/.
90 Ibid.
91 Directorate General for Competition, European Commission, 'Issues Raised in Discussions with the Carrier Industry in Relation to the Forthcoming Commission Guidelines on the Application of Competition Rules to Maritime Transport Services', *Information Note, Directorate General for Competition*, accessed 10 September 2014, http://ec.europa.eu/competition/consultations/2006_maritime_guidelines/issues_paper_shipping.pdf.
92 Motta, *Competition Policy*.
93 *United States v. Trenton Potteries Co.*, 273 U.S. 392 (47 S.Ct. 377, 71 L.Ed. 700).
94 *Palmer v. BRG of Georgia, Inc.* 498 U.S. 46 (1990).
95 Motta, *Competition Policy*.
96 Anand, 'Identifying Cartels Using Economic Evidence: A Case Study of Indian Cement Industry'.
97 Ibid.
98 S.D. Naik, 'Cement: No Time for Quick Fixes', *Economic & Political Weekly* (23 June 2001), accessed 10 November 2014, http://www.epw.in/journal/2001/25/editorials/cement-no-time-quick-fixes.html.
99 Anand, 'Identifying Cartels Using Economic Evidence: A Case Study of Indian Cement Industry'.
100 Ibid.
101 Frank Maier-Rigaud and Hans Friederiszick, 'Triggering Inspections Ex Officio: Moving beyond a Passive EU Cartel Policy', *Journal of Competition Law and Economics* 4 (1) (2007): 89–113.

102 Anand, 'Identifying Cartels Using Economic Evidence: A Case Study of Indian Cement Industry'.
103 Ibid.
104 Ibid.
105 Ibid.
106 Ibid.
107 Funtia, 'Legal and Economic Analysis of Cartels, Their Enforcement and the Leniency Program'.
108 Ibid.
109 Tejas K. Motwani, 'Analysis of Merger Control under Indian Competition Law', accessed 1 October 2014, http://citeseerx.ist.psu.edu/viewdoc/download?doi=10.1.1.467.5673&rep=rep1&type=pdf.
110 Ibid.
111 Simon Bishop, Andrea Lofaro, Francesco Rosati and Juliet Young, 'The Efficiency-Enhancing Effects of Non-Horizontal Mergers', *RBB Economics Report for Enterprise and Industry DG* (Brussels, 2006), accessed 1 October 2014, http://ec.europa.eu/DocsRoom/documents/3667/attachments/1/translations/en/renditions/native.
112 Ibid.
113 'Unilateral Effects', accessed 2 October 2014, http://www.internationalcompetitionnetwork.org/uploads/library/doc561.pdf.
114 'RBB Comments on the Proposed Creeping Acquisitions Law in Australia', accessed 2 October 2014, http://archive.treasury.gov.au/documents/1583/PDF/RBB_Economics.pdf.
115 Ibid.
116 Ibid.
117 Dr Elizabeth Xiao-Ru Wang, 'Economic Tools for Evaluating Competitive Harm in Horizontal Mergers', *Charles Rivers Associates*, accessed 2 October 2014, http://www.crai.com/uploadedFiles/Publications/Economic-Tools%20for-Evaluating-Competitive-Harm-in-Horizontal-Mergers.pdf.
118 Ibid.
119 Ibid.
120 Simon Bishop, 'Creeping Acquisitions – The Way Forward, RBB Economics LLP', accessed 5 October 2014, http://archive.treasury.gov.au/documents/1583/PDF/RBB_Economics.pdf.
121 Ibid.
122 Ibid.
123 Ibid.
124 Dr Wang, 'Economic Tools for Evaluating Competitive Harm in Horizontal Mergers'.
125 Directorate for Financial and Enterprise Affairs, Competition Committee, 'Economic Evidence in Merger Analysis', *Working Party No. 3 on Co-operation and Enforcement* (2011), accessed 1 October 2014, http://ec.europa.eu/competition/international/multilateral/2011_feb_economic_evidence.pdf.
126 Ibid.
127 Ibid.
128 'Antitrust Law and the "New Economy"', *University of North Texas Libraries*, accessed 11 October 2014, http://govinfo.library.unt.edu/amc/report_recommendation/chapter1.pdf.

129 Ibid.
130 Dr Wang, 'Economic Tools for Evaluating Competitive Harm in Horizontal Mergers'.
131 Ibid.
132 Ibid.
133 Directorate for Financial and Enterprise Affairs, Competition Committee, 'Economic Evidence in Merger Analysis'.
134 Kaushal Sharma, Shankar Singham and Sriraj Venkatasamy, 'Economies (Efficiencies) – An Essential Consideration in Merger Analysis', *CCI*, accessed 7 April 2014, http://www.cci.gov.in/sites/default/files/presentation_document/Final_Efficiency_Article01-Feb-2011.pdf.
135 International Competition Network, ICN Merger Working Group: Investigation and Analysis Subgroup, 'Merger Guidelines Work Book', *Fifth Annual ICN Conference in Cape Town*, 2006, accessed 10 November 2014, http://www.internationalcompetitionnetwork.org/uploads/library/doc321.pdf.
136 Peter J. Davis and Eliana Garcés, *Quantitative Techniques for Competition and Antitrust Analysis* (Princeton, NJ: Princeton University Press, 2010): 395.
137 International Competition Network, ICN Merger Working Group: Investigation and Analysis Subgroup, 'Merger Guidelines Work Book'.
138 Sharma, Singham and Venkatasamy, 'Economies (Efficiencies) – An Essential Consideration in Merger Analysis'.
139 Kolasky and Dick, 'The Merger Guidelines and the Integration of Efficiencies into Antitrust Review of Horizontal Mergers'.
140 Ibid.
141 Ibid.
142 Ibid.
143 Kaushal Sharma, Shankar Singham and Sriraj Venkatasamy, 'Economies (Efficiencies) – An Essential Consideration in Merger Analysis', accessed 15 October 2014, http://www.cci.gov.in/images/media/presentations/Final_Efficiency_Article01-Feb-2011.pdf.
144 Ibid.
145 Ibid.
146 David Rosenbaum, *Market Dominance: How Firms Gain, Hold, or Lose It and the Impact on Economic Performance* (Praeger, 1998).
147 Joseph Farrell and Carl Shapiro, 'Scale Economies and Synergies in Horizontal Merger Analysis', *Anitrust Law Journal* 68 (2001): 685–710.
148 Ibid.
149 Ibid.
150 Ibid.
151 Sharma, Singham and Venkatasamy, 'Economies (Efficiencies) – An Essential Consideration in Merger Analysis'.
152 FTC v. Cardinal Health, 12 F. Supp. 2d 34.
153 Sharma, Singham and Venkatasamy, 'Economies (Efficiencies) – An Essential Consideration in Merger Analysis'.
154 Ibid.
155 G.R. Bhatia, 'Assessment of Dominance: Issues and Challenges under the Indian Competition Act, 2002', accessed 4 October 2014, http://www.

manupatrafast.com/articles/PopOpenArticle.aspx?ID=8de19f8a-5bbd-42b6-a96a-692a0f376625&txtsearch=Subject:%20Commercial.

156 Jonathan B. Baker and Timothy F. Bresnahan, *Economic Evidence in Antitrust: Defining Markets and Measuring Market Power*, accessed 5 November 2014, http://web.stanford.edu/~tbres/research/buccirossi_01_ch01_001-042.pdf.

157 Alberto Pera, *Changing Views of Competition, Economic Analysis and EC Antitrust Law*, accessed 3 October 2014, http://www.clubeconomia.it/pdf/ecj1.pdf.

Chapter 13

An economic analysis of Indian pharmaceutical pricing policy

Drugs (Prices Control) Order, 2013

Prateek Kumar and Shreya Ramakrishanan

Background note

Medicines account for 20% to 60% of health spending in low- and middle-income countries, compared with 18% in countries of the Organisation for Economic Co-operation and Development. Up to 90% of the population in developing countries purchase medicines through out-of-pocket payments, making medicines the largest family expenditure item after food.[1] High prices of medicines might force people to forego treatment or go into debt. Initiatives to stimulate availability and access through manufacturing innovations, procurement mechanisms, or supply chain improvements require management of pricing to have sustainable impact. The Millennium Development Goal targets 'in cooperation with pharmaceutical companies, [to] provide access to affordable, essential drugs in developing countries' and also recognizes the pharmaceutical sector as an essential realm for government action and intervention. The market of pharmaceuticals is an imperfectly competitive market by definition. An imperfectly competitive market is one that shares most of the characteristics of a perfectly competitive market, for example free entry and exit of firms and the presence of many firms, but has one important monopolistic element: firms produce differentiable output rather than the homogeneous output produced by perfectly competitive firms. Thus, imperfectly competitive firms distinguish their output by brand names, colours, sizes, quality, durability and so on.[2] Roger J. van den Bergh and Peter D. Camesasca note that 'competition policy should not seek to achieve the ideal of perfect competition, but should, instead, formulate criteria for judging to what extent an industry is *workably competitive*' (emphasis added).[3] Therefore, analysing the nature of the pharmaceutical market in India in the light of the 'structure-conduct-performance paradigm: criteria' established by Scherer and Ross[4] for judging whether an industry is workably competitive can be of some guidance. The analysis of pharmaceutical market and industry in India as per the Scherer and Ross criteria is given in Table 13.1.

It is thus evident from the analysis presented in Table 13.1 that the pharmaceutical industry in India is not workably competitive.

Table 13.1 Analysis of pharmaceutical market as per the Scherer and Ross criteria

Criteria	*Whether satisfied (and reason)*
A. *Structural criteria*	
The number of firms must be at least as great as economies of scale will permit.	Satisfied
There must be no artificial restraints in entry or mobility.	Satisfied
The products on offer must have moderate and price-sensitive differences in quality.	No. The products have moderate difference in quality but are mostly not price-sensitive.
B. *Conduct criteria*	
Competitors must be subject to a degree of uncertainty as to the extent to which price initiatives will be followed.	Satisfied
Firms must pursue their objectives independently without reciprocal agreements.	Satisfied
No unfair trade practices or exclusion measures must be used.	Satisfied
Inefficient suppliers and customers must not be constantly protected.	Satisfied
Advertising must be informative and not misleading.	Satisfied
There must be no harmful, persistent price discrimination.	Satisfied
C. *Performance criteria*	
Firms' production and distribution process must be efficient and must not waste resources.	Satisfied

Criteria	*Whether satisfied (and reason)*
Production levels and product quality (differentiation, product life, safety, reliability) must accord with customers' wishes.	Satisfied
Profits must reach just the right level to ensure investment, efficiency and innovation.	No. The pharmaceutical industry is not able to generate revenues for investment in innovation and so on.
Price levels must encourage rational choice, steer markets towards equilibrium and prevent the reinforcement of cyclical instability.	No. The extremely high prices of the branded drugs show that the price level has not encouraged rational choice.
Opportunity to introduce superior technical products and processes must be exploited.	Satisfied
Advertising expenditure must not be excessive.	Satisfied
Success must go to the sellers who respond best to consumers' wishes.	No. The sellers who sell the pharmaceutical products at lower prices have lower profit margins and may have lesser profit too.

Source: F. M. Scherer and David R. Ross, *Industrial Market Structure and Economic Performance* (Boston: Houghton Mifflin, 1990), 5 and authors' own analysis for preparing table.

Factors responsible for the failure of pharmaceutical market in India

- The demand for medicines is largely prescription driven, and the patient has very little choice in this regard.
- Marketing strategy and advertising: The pharmaceutical manufacturers create a brand value through advertising; they ensure deep-rooted availability of their high-cost products and give greater sales margin to final selling agents, incentivizing them to make only their products available at their shops and sell them even where cheaper options are prescribed.
- Severe information asymmetry: Most of the consumers are unaware of the technical similarities of compositions of different medicines and depend solely upon the prescription of the doctor and the advice of the medicine shopkeeper. This lack of knowledge about the availability of cheap drugs makes market penetration easier for the branded drug makers despite their higher price for the same quality product.

- Pharmaceutical products are in the nature of necessary goods for which the patient has no choice but to spend, and buying pressures of time constraints also force consumer to accept high-cost medicines.

And even if market failure alone may not constitute sufficient grounds for government intervention, but when such failure is considered in the context of the essential role that pharmaceuticals play in the area of public health, which is a social right, such intervention becomes necessary, especially when exploitative pricing makes medicines unaffordable and beyond the reach of most and also puts huge financial burden in terms of out-of-pocket expenditure on health care.[5]

Explaining the pharmaceutical market's strategic game

The market situation of the pharmaceutical market in India can be explained as a form of strategic game using the game theory and Prisoner's Dilemma. The players in this game are the pharmaceutical companies who have a brand value (Manufacturer 1: M1) and hence sell generic drugs at comparatively higher prices than the pharmaceutical companies who do not have a brand value (Manufacturer 2: M2) and who are the other players. Each of these players has two strategies – decrease the prices or increase the prices. The pay-offs for the strategy are in the form of increased sales and increased market share and greater profits. Assumptions raised for the explanation are as follows:

- The cost of production for both M1 and M2 is same, and hence, it can be taken as 0 for easier calculation of profits.
- The selling price of M1 drugs is 10 and M2 drugs is 2 in current market.
- Market consists of ten consumers, of whom two consume M1 drugs and eight consume M2 drugs.
- Increase and decrease in prices is taken at 50% of the selling price; hence, on increase, the price of M1 becomes 15 and of M2 becomes 3, whereas on decrease, the price of M1 becomes 5 and of M2 becomes 1.

In this illustration, it must be noted that an increase in the prices of M1 will not change its market share as its consumers have a specific choice or no choice but to use its product. However, the decrease in the prices of M1 will make its product more competitive and attract double market share, thereby selling the product to four instead of two consumers. It will, however, still have lesser market share than M2 due to its higher cost and social inequality. On the other hand, an increase or decrease in the prices of M2 will not change its market share as the other product is still much costlier than M2 drugs and all people who cannot afford M1 are already buying M2 drugs.

Using the preceding assumptions, the following calculations can be made:

- When M1 increases its prices from 10 to 15, its market share remains same and its profit increases to 30.
- When M1 decreases its prices from 10 to 5, its market share doubles to 4 and its profit remains at 20.
- When M2 increases its prices from 2 to 3, its market share remains the same and its profit increases to 24 if coincided with an increase in the price of M1, else its profit increases to 18 if coincided with a decrease in the price of M2.
- When M2 decreases its prices from 2 to 1, its market share remains the same and its profit decline to 8 irrespective of any change in the price of M1.

These calculations can be represented in the form of the pay-off matrix in Figure 13.1.

Thus, the preceding analysis makes it clear that M1 and M2 will always increase their prices to further their goal of profit maximization in this particular market. Therefore, the game theory suggests Adam Smith's 'invisible hands of market', which suggests that the self-regulating behaviour of markets will not be able to force the prices of these pharmaceutical products to come from P1 to P2 (as shown in Figure 13.2) which is the price at the point of market equilibrium at point E. Thus, in the absence of Adam Smith's 'invisible hand', it becomes the responsibility of the government to bring down the prices from P1 to P2, which is the theoretical justification of governmental intervention in price determination in the pharmaceutical industry.

Legal background of pharmaceutical pricing in India

The Constitution of India (Article 245) empowers both the central Parliament and the state legislative assemblies to make laws on

		M2	
		Price increase	**Price decrease**
M1	Price increase	24 30	8 30
	Price decrease	18 20	8 20

Figure 13.1 The pharmaceutical sector's pay-off matrix

Source: Author's own analysis.

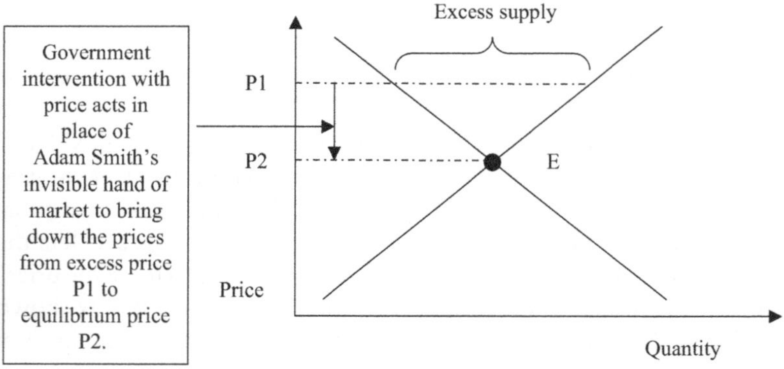

Figure 13.2 Government intervention as an alternative to market forces to attain market equilibrium price

Source: Price Floors and Price Ceilings, Experimental Economics Center, Georgia State University, http://www.econport.org/content/handbook/Equilibrium/Price-Controls.html.

the subjects of 'price control' and 'drugs', which are enlisted in the Concurrent List of the VII Schedule of the Constitution that entails the distribution of specific subjects to the centre and the states in the Indian federal system. In exercise of this power, the Parliament of

India had passed the Essential Commodities Act, 1955. Under Section 3 of the said act, the government of India has passed the Drugs (Prices Control) Orders (DPCO) from time to time to regulate the prices of medicines in the country. The National Pharmaceutical Pricing Authority (NPPA) was established vide the Resolution No. 33/7/97-PI.I dated 29 August 1997 and passed by the Ministry of Chemicals and Fertilizers, Government of India, inter alia, to fix prices and notify the changes therein, if any, of bulk drug and formulations, monitor the prices of decontrolled drugs and formulations and oversee the implementation of the provisions of the Drugs (Prices Control) Orders.

An analysis of competing price mechanisms in India

The most popularly used and recommended pricing mechanisms for pharmaceutical sector are the cost-plus pricing and external reference pricing mechanisms. Cost-plus pricing is a method for setting retail prices of medicines by taking into account production cost of a medicine together with allowances for promotional expenses, manufacturer's profit margins and charges and profit margins in the supply chain.[6] WHO categorically recommends that 'countries generally should not use cost-plus as an overall pharmaceutical pricing policy'.[7] The WHO Guideline has arrived at the following benefits and downsides of the cost-plus pricing method:[8]

Benefits of cost-plus pricing

- Based on the experience of the panel members, it was suggested that cost-plus pricing might stabilize medicine prices in unregulated settings.
- The method might reduce out-of-pocket payments in an unregulated market.

Downsides of cost-plus pricing

- Application of cost-plus pricing to medicines requires significant technical and human resources, particularly to obtain and validate reliable estimates of component prices such as active pharmaceutical ingredients (APIs).
- Formulae used by countries to calculate cost-plus prices can be manipulated to the advantage of manufacturers and disadvantage of patients.

'External reference pricing' (ERP; also known as international reference pricing) refers to the practice of using the price of a pharmaceutical product (generally ex-manufacturer price, or other common point within the distribution chain) in one or several countries to derive a benchmark or reference price for the purposes of setting or negotiating the price of the product in a given country.[9] WHO has recommended the following with respect to ERP formula:[10]

- Countries should consider using ERP as a method for negotiating or benchmarking the price of a medicine.
- Countries should consider using ERP as part of an overall strategy, in combination with other methods, for setting the price of a medicine.
- In developing an ERP system, countries should define transparent methods and processes to be used.
- Countries/payers should select comparator countries to use ERP based on economic status, pharmaceutical pricing systems in place, published actual versus negotiated or concealed prices, exact comparator products supplied and similar burden of disease.

The WHO Guideline has arrived at the following benefits and downsides of the ERP method:[11]

Benefits of ERP

- May be simpler than some other methods for price setting.
- Allows international comparisons and benchmarking.

Downsides of ERP

- The choice of countries as reference countries may lead to inflated prices.
- If ERP is used as the only method for price setting, entry of new products may be delayed and price manipulation may result.
- ERP use may result in higher-priced generic products.
- It may be deceptively 'simple' and result in locally inappropriate prices, if incorrect reference countries selected and/or the comparator prices are not the real prices paid.
- Published prices may not reflect actual prices as these may be negotiated or conceal rebates, according to the legal systems

in place. Countries need to know whether published prices are actual or special prices.

- Data sources for comparator prices may be difficult to verify.

In the light of the fact that India faces unique health care challenges with its huge population pressure and stage of economic development and environmental conditions, it may be very difficult to obtain reliable data from any comparator country, given the fact that the countries that India could be compared to in terms of its health care statistics are not in a position to provide such data as to facilitate India to implement the ERP mechanism for pharmaceutical pricing. Therefore, it will be seen later in this chapter that India has used a unique formula to arrive at a domestic reference price ceiling under the recent National Pharmaceutical Pricing Policy, 2012 (NPPP).

Past attempts at pharmaceutical pricing

The Report of the Hathi Committee (1975) was the first important landmark in the development of the Indian Pharmaceutical Pricing Policy, as it emphasized the achievement of self-sufficiency in medicines and of abundant availability at reasonable prices of essential medicines. The DPCO, 1979, specified 342 medicines under price control. The number of medicines was reduced to 74 under DPCO, 1995, which declared 'abundant availability on a continuous basis, at reasonable prices, of essential, life-saving and prophylactic medicines of good quality, is the corner stone of the new measures'.

Under DPCO, 1995, the price of bulk drugs was fixed by specifying a maximum rate of return to bulk drug manufacturers. The maximum retail prices were fixed using cost-plus methods and were determined by use of data submitted by companies and by comparing elements of cost of each company. The formula used was

$$RP = (MC + CC + PM + PC) \times (1 + MAPE/100) + ED$$

where RP is retail price, MC is material cost, CC is conversion cost, PM is cost of packing material, PC is packing charges, MAPE is maximum allowable post-manufacturing expenses and ED is excise duty.

The WHO review of the Indian Pharmaceutical Pricing Policy (DPCO, 1995) indicated that between 1996 and 2006 the rise in prices of all medicines was 39.93% and for price-controlled medicines it was 0.02%.[12] The coverage and nature of price control of drugs in India has varied over several price control regimes, altering the following three main components:

1 The scope of price control, that is which drugs are covered under it.
2 Within these drugs that came under the price control regime, for each of the drug, whether the price of the bulk drug or the final formulation would be controlled.
3 The method for determining the price.

The 1994 Drug Policy was introduced in the backdrop of liberalization of economy, doing away with industrial licensing and allowing foreign investment. Here, the scope of price control was determined by the market share of companies vis-à-vis the total market sales turnover of various drugs. By the application of this standard, a list of 74 bulk drugs was identified, and these drugs as well as the formulations based on these drugs (currently about 1,577 in number) were brought under the price control regime.[13] Hence, it is pertinent to note that both the bulk drug and its formulations came under the ambit of price control. The method of determining the prices was based on the cost of production and post-production expenses.

In 2000, in keeping with fast-paced economic liberalization, foreign direct investment in the pharmaceutical sector was increased to 100% under the automatic route.[14] Vide the Drug Policy, 2002, the turnover limit for deciding the drugs that fall under the price control regime was increased from Rs 4 crore to Rs 25 crore. This policy was challenged in the Karnataka High Court, which issued a stay on its implementation. However, the stay was vacated subsequently by the Supreme Court in 2003. The Supreme Court directed the central government to ensure that essential and life-saving drugs do not fall out of the price control, which has the force of law.[15]

However, the Drug Policy, 2002, never came to be implemented, and the 1994 policy maintained status quo. The government of India formed a task force to explore options other than price control for achieving the objective of making available life-saving drugs at reasonable prices under the chairmanship of Mr Pronab Sen. The report submitted by the task force on 20 September 2005 highlighted the need for many organic changes in the pharmaceutical sector, including issues like regulation, investment, manufacture, supply and procurement.[16] With the aim to attain a balance between expansion of the pharmaceutical industry and provision of affordable and accessible medicines to consumers and to reconcile short-term interests with long-term goals and concerns,[17] the government of India came out with the DPCO, 2013, which implemented the NPPP, 2012, and provided the legal infrastructure to declare ceiling prices for drugs listed in the National List of Essential Medicines (NLEM) and also for regulating the prices of non-scheduled drugs in cases of extraordinary circumstances

Key features of the DPCO, 2013

The Department of Pharmaceuticals, Ministry of Chemicals and Fertilizers, government of India, notified the NPPP, 2012, on 7 December 2012. The NPPP was then adopted into the DPCO, 2013.[18] The new price control mechanism differs from the 1994 policy in respect of all the three components of a price control regime in the context of drugs. In a nutshell, it covers the 348 drugs mentioned in the NLEM, 2011, and introduced the market-based pricing mechanism for determining the price ceiling. Basically, it seeks to address the availability and affordability of essential drugs through the medium of price control, thereby following the directive passed by the apex court in *Union of India v. K.S. Gopinath & others*.[19] The criterion for determining what exactly constitutes essential drugs is solely the NLEM-2011, which is proving to be a point of contention.[20]

Principles forming the basis of the DPCO, 2013

Essentiality of medicines

According to the NLEM, 2011, 'Essential medicines are those that satisfy the priority healthcare needs of majority of the population.' The factors affecting this list are cost, safety and efficacy. Under the 2012 policy, the 'essentiality' criterion is sought to be met by relying solely on the list of medicines specified in the NLEM.[21] The rationale for following this method is that apart from complying with the Supreme Court directive, out of the 348 medicines listed in the NLEM-2011, only 34 drugs are included among the 74 drugs listed in the First Schedule of DPCO-1995.[22] This aspect is a change from the earlier regimes that focused on market share/dominance/

monopoly of pharmaceutical companies, in order to determine the scope and ambit of the price control regime. Under the 1994 policy, the scope of price control was determined by the market share of companies vis-à-vis the total market sales turnover of various drugs, and using this criteria, 74 drugs were identified.

Market-based pricing

Under market-based pricing, the ceiling price of a medicine covered by the NLEM-2011 would be the simple average price of all its brands that have more than 1% market share, that is

$$\frac{\begin{pmatrix}\text{Sum of prices of all the brands of the medicine having}\\ \text{market share more than and equal to 1\% of the total}\\ \text{market turnover of that medicine}\end{pmatrix}}{\begin{pmatrix}\text{Total number of manufacturers producing such brands}\\ \text{of the medicine}\end{pmatrix}}$$

This is a departure from the cost-based pricing method which was followed since 1979. Earlier, the prices were controlled at two levels. First, a ceiling limit was placed upon the profit that can be made on the bulk drug, that is the raw material or API, and second, a ceiling limit was placed on the price of the final drug, using the cost of manufacturing as a basis for calculation of the ceiling limit. Ceiling price of the final drug = cost of raw materials + costs of conversion + the maximum allowable post-manufacturing expenses of 100% (which includes the profit of the manufacturer and various distribution costs).

The rationale given for removing the earlier method is that since the ceiling limit of formulations was based on the 'lowest common denominator', the ceiling was low and clustered within a narrow band, neither allowing new players to enter the market (by posing as an entry barrier in the form of a low price ceiling due to which it was very difficult for new entrants in the market to recover the fixed and variable costs[23]) nor allowing the existing players any room for even minor innovations in manufacturing process or product delivery and so on, thereby stifling competition. As a result, there was stagnation in the production activity.[24] Another rationale given is that since the input material market is unregulated and its prices are largely dependent on market conditions and market forces, price determination in accordance with costing would be against the notion of competition as the failure to periodically revise the ceiling limit will hurt the industry by reducing its already-nominal profit margins and thereby strengthening the entry barrier.[25] By the introduction of the market-based pricing method, the ceiling limit has been made into a mathematical function of the prices of all the manufacturers (having more than 1% market share), thus taking into the account the highest to the lowest prices. The market based pricing method may lead to an increase or decrease of the ceiling limit. Where the ceiling limit would be raised, it would allow flexibility in pricing over a broader range, and allow new players to enter the market, and hence facilitate competition in the market,[26] which will later bring down the ceiling limit. In cases where it brings the ceiling limit down, it shows that a healthy level of competition already exists, which has been able to capture the demand of the market and will force the high-cost segment drug makers to compete in the turf of low-cost segment manufacturers, forcing them to reduce cost of production and glitches in supply chain and so on.

Price control only on formulations

The DPCO, 2013, has listed 348 final formulations for price control, whereas under DPCO, 1995, only 74 bulk drugs and their formulations were covered under the price control order. This is a significant departure from the previous price control regime. The rationale for moving away from limiting the prices of bulk drugs to limiting the prices of their formulations only is that the Bulk Drug/API may not fully reflect the 'essentiality' of the actual drug formulation. It is pertinent to note that only 47 bulk drugs out of the 74 notified in the First Schedule of the DPCO, 1995, are now under production, which means that manufacturers are using alternative bulk drugs to create same class of formulations, thereby avoiding the price regulation. Another reason cited was that pricing of both the bulk drug and the formulation is more complex, and time consuming, while only the formulations have a direct impact on the consumers.[27]

Illustrations explaining the impact of the pricing regime change

For the purpose of convenience, let us assume B_1 and B_2 are two bulk drugs and F_1, F_2 and F_3 are three final formulations. Let P_1 denote the price ceiling under the old regime and P_2 denote the price ceiling under the new regime. The different situations that can occur due to the change in scope of the two regimes, and the impact of each situation on the price, are given. Also, illustrations are given for some situations. If the old regime covers a bulk drug, B_1, and a final formulation made out of that bulk drug, F_1, and the new regime covers the same final formulation F_1, then the following situations can arise:

A. The companies actually comply with the old ceiling limit by selling their drugs at prices lower than this ceiling, then:

- The new price ceiling P_2 will be lower than the earlier limit P_1. This will result in gain for the consumers.
- If the brand values of all companies are actually lower than the earlier ceiling, then:
  P_2 will be lower than P_1.

This will result in gain for the consumers.

Illustration I

S. No.	Name of formation	Strength	Unit	Ceiling price under new regime	Ceiling price under old regime
1.	Gentamicin injection	40 mg/ml	1 ml	2.18	
	Conventional pack				2.8
	Temper proof pack				2.72
2.	Dexamethasone injection	4 mg/ml	1 ml	2.51	3.24

B. If the companies still sell at prices higher than the earlier ceiling P_1, then:

- If the brand values of companies selling this medicine are too high, and there are too many companies selling at this very high cost, then:
  P_2 will be much higher than P_1.

This will result in gain for the pharmaceutical companies.

Illustration 2

S. No.	*Name of formation*	*Strength*	*Unit*	*Ceiling price under new regime*[28] *(P_2)*	*Ceiling price under old regime*[29] *(P_1)*
1.	Co-trimoxazole (trimethoprim + sulphamethoxazole) tablets	160 + 800 mg	One tablet	1.28	0.10
2.	Carbamazepine tablets	200 mg	One tablet	1.37	
	St.				0.1096
	Bl.				0.1074

- If the brand values are not too high or are high for too few companies, then:
  P_2 will be slightly higher than P_1.

This will result in slight loss for consumers.

Probability: there is a high probability of its occurrence, as the other three are rare and extreme situations.

Illustrations 3

S. No.	*Name of formation*	*Strength*	*Unit*	*Ceiling price under new regime (P_2)*	*Ceiling price under old regime (P_1)*
1.	Doxycycline tablets	100 mg	One tablet	0.94	
	Each tablet contains doxycyclineHCl/ hyclate				0.336
	Each tablet contains strip/ blister doxycycline monohydrate				0.696
2.	Streptomycin sulphate injection	0.75 g	Each pack	7.91	7.86
3.	Griseofulvin tablets	250 mg	One tablet	1.45	

(Continued)

Illustrations 3 (Continued)

S. No.	*Name of formation*	*Strength*	*Unit*	*Ceiling price under new regime (P_2)*	*Ceiling price under old regime (P_1)*
	St.				1.236
	Bl.				1.212
4.	Ranitidine injection	25 mg/ml	1 ml	1.43	1.17
5.	Dexamethasone tablets	0.5 mg	One tablet	0.19	0.15 (for strips, not jars)
6.	Salbutamol sulphate tablet	2 mg	One tablet	0.14	0.122
7.	Ciprofloxacin hydrochloride injection	200 mg/ 100 ml	1 ml	0.16	
		2 mg/1 ml	1 ml		0.15
8.	Co-trimoxazole (trimethoprim + sulphamethoxazole) suspension	40 + 200 ml/ 5 ml	1 ml	0.24	
	100 ml bottle with M. Cup		1 ml		0.13

If the old regime covers a bulk drug B_1 out of which two final formulations can be made – F_1 and F_2 – both of which are under the ambit of the old regime, but only F_2 is under the ambit of the new regime, then:

Assumption: F_1 and F_2 are of the same therapeutic class.

A. The companies actually comply with the old ceiling limit by selling F_2 at prices lower than this ceiling, then:

- The new price ceiling P_2 for F_2 will be lower than the earlier limit P_1.

This will result in gain for the consumers.

B. If the companies still sell at prices higher than the earlier ceiling P_1 for F_2 (assuming the brand values of companies are little high), then:

- P_2 will be slightly more than P_1 for F_2 and F_1 will no longer have a ceiling limit. This will result in slight loss to the consumers, who do not need to be bothered much about the lack of regulation of F_1 since both formulations serve the same purpose; hence, the loss suffered will be equal to the slight increase in price of the regulated formulation only.

Illustration 4: Only Penicillamine capsules 250 mg is covered by the new regime, while the old regime had various formulations of the bulk drug Penicillin.

If the old regime covers a bulk drug B_1 out of which two final formulations can be made – F_1 and F_2 – both of which are under the ambit of the old regime, but none of the final formulations find a place under the new regime, then:

- There will be no ceiling for both formulations, and prices could therefore increase. This will result in gain for the companies.

Probability: It is important to note two points:

1 There are 34 formulations common between the new and old regime, and there are 47/74 bulk drugs under the old regime, which are still under production. That leaves 13 formulations (assuming that a bulk drug can lead to one formulation only), which are under production, but which are not covered under the new regime.
2 Since 13/348 is a very small number, the probability of this situation actually occurring is also correspondingly much lower. However, the specific therapeutic necessity of these 13 bulk drugs and their formulations needs to be analysed along with the fact whether or not an alternative drug has been put under the pricing regime to make it available at affordable cost.

If the bulk drug is not covered by the old regime, but is covered by the new regime, in the form of a final formulation from the bulk drug, then:

- There will be a new ceiling for this particular formulation. This will result in gain for the consumers.

Probability: Since the new regime covers 108 + 348 final formulations, and only 47 bulk drugs, which are still under production and their final formulations are covered under the old regime, the chances of this situation actually occurring are more. Illustration: Pyrazinamide tablets and sodium valproate tablets are covered by the new regime and not the old one.

However, it will only be prudent to keep in mind that the aforementioned data has been chosen very carefully to make sure that it aligns with the possible situations and that in this exercise the impact of inflation on dilution of the value of money has not been taken into consideration for keeping the price values authentic and also to keep the data simple and comprehensible. If the cost inflation Index[30] is to be considered, then it may be noted that a marginal increase in the ceiling price for a medicine under the DPCO, 2013, may just be an appearance of increase, which may actually be a deduction in the ceiling if the devaluation of currency is kept in consideration. An example can be taken from the preceding data: the price ceiling for streptomycin sulphate injection was notified under the DPCO, 1995, in the year 2003 as Rs 7.86, which would amount to Rs 11.74 in 2013–14,[31] much higher than the new ceiling of Rs 7.91.

Criticisms of the DPCO, 2013

General criticisms

- Market-based method of pricing is not used for regulating the prices of other sectors.
- The ceiling price has no co-relation with the cost of production.
- The data of IMS Health, a private company, instead of a government or a neutral public agency, is being relied upon. Apart from being expensive, it is not accessible in the public domain.[32]

Economic criticisms

The NPPP will lead to increase in the ceiling price

The prices of branded drugs are high and unrelated to the cost of production, since they reflect the brand value, due to aggressive brand promotion, among other factors. As most brand prices are high, the profit of these companies are above normal profits, and since profits are to the tune of 200% to 4,000%,[33] the simple average taken of all the prices will surely be higher than the ceiling that would be prescribed under the cost-plus method. In most competitive markets, leading market players can reduce prices substantially while earning normal profits. In the health sector, competition works only at the early stages of a new drug brand.[34] Eventually, brands of the same medicine sell at totally different prices, and the difference between the highest and the lowest price is significant. Also, it is pertinent to note that most of the brands are priced in the higher ranges.

Hence, the final ceiling price determined by the applicability of the market-based method will be higher than the limit prescribed under the cost-plus method (in cases where the drug has an overlap between both the pricing regimes), although the prices of the branded drugs will be reduced. Hence, although the Supreme Court judgement seems to have been complied with, the criticism is that this relatively high price ceiling legitimizes higher prices and induces affordable brands to raise their prices as well. Hence, due to information asymmetry, aggressive stance of higher-priced brands and higher ceiling level, the lower-priced brands may raise their prices to compete with the profits of the higher-priced brands.

The increase in prices may not be reflected in increased investment on R&D

The rationale for allowing more profits to these companies is that they invest more in R&D and have better quality of final drugs. However, the criticism is that the supernormal profits earned by companies manufacturing highly priced brands do not necessarily reflect in their investments into R&D and high-quality standards. This argument is supported by two facts:

1 Even approved companies, which are exporting drugs, are doing so at vastly different and often very competitive prices.
2 The top 30 Indian companies spent an average of 7% of their net sales on R&D in 2011–12.[35] The lowest-priced brands are therapeutically similar to higher-priced brands of the same generic medicine.

The NLEM is not an exhaustive list of essential drugs

The NLEM, 2011, consists of 348 drugs. However, it is not an exhaustive list of essential medicines as it has included only one medicine of a particular category in its list. Given the different levels of efficacy of different medicines and their side effects, it may not bring justice to all poor consumers as some patients will still be forced to buy the non-NLEM medicines prescribed by doctors. There are many life-saving essential drugs required for the treatment of severe ailments that are yet not covered by the NLEM. For example, in the case of medicines needed for treatment of bronchial asthma, only salbutamol is included in the current NLEM. Other essential medicines such as theophylline, doxofylline, montelukast and zafirlukast are missing from this list. Many of these are useful in life-saving, tertiary-care situations, which may also at times occur at the primary-care level.[36]

The NLEM drugs cover only Rs 16,000 crore of the total domestic market of Rs 68,000 crore,[37] which means only about 25% of it; hence, 75% of the market remains uncovered by the NPPP. However, the DPCO, 2013, states that if the prices of non-scheduled drugs increase by more than 10% in a year, the government will force the manufacturer to fix the prices at a maximum of 10% of the price.[38] Hence, even though 75% of the market remains uncovered by the NPPP, it cannot increase prices indiscriminately.

The policy could be avoided by making inessential formulations from essential bulk drugs

As non-NLEM drugs are mostly fixed dose combinations (FDCs), they vary between 40% and 60% of the number of formulations.[39] This 75% includes drugs of the same therapeutic class. Therefore, in order to avoid the policy framework, there can be migration from formations under the list to FDCs or other drugs of the same class, which are not covered by the list but are a variation of the bulk ingredient. In other words, companies would be allowed to make inessential formulations from essential bulk drugs.[40] Companies could misuse this provision by decreasing production of single-ingredient essential medicines and manufacturing instead inessential or irrational combinations using these essential APIs. The remedy suggested is to put all drugs of the same therapeutic class under the price ceiling.

However, the NPPP states that if a manufacturer of an NLEM drug launches a new drug by combining the NLEM drug with another NLEM drug or a non-NLEM drug or by changing its strength and dosages, the manufacturer is required to seek approval from the government.[41] Therefore, it may not be very easy to circumvent the policy. However, the basis for granting price approval has not been stated and it may be granted on irrelevant considerations.

The ceiling price linkage with inflation may lead to inappropriate increase in the ceiling

The NPPP states that the prices of the NLEM-2011 medicines will vary annually, with increase or decrease of wholesale price index (WPI) as notified by the Department of Industrial Policy and Promotion. The criticism levelled against this is that WPI affects only conversion costs, and not the cost of the bulk ingredient or API, which actually forms a majority of the cost of manufacturing the final drug.[42] Hence, any reduction in overall prices would be exceeded within two years due to inflation, and the ceiling prices would be increased due to increase in WPI.[43]

Criticisms by the pharmaceutical industry

Price fixation of non-scheduled drugs

Paragraph 19 of DPCO, inter alia, authorizes the government, *in extraordinary circumstances*, if it considers necessary so to do *in public interest*, to fix the ceiling price or retail price of any drug for such period as it deems fit. The NPPA has expressed the view that there exist huge inter-brand price differences in branded-generics/off-patent drugs, which is indicative of a severe market failure, as different brands of the same drug formulation, including the off-patent drug, which are identical to each other in terms of active ingredient(s), strength, dosage, route of administration, quality, product characteristics and intended use, vary disproportionately in terms of price. The different brands of the drug formulation may sometimes differ in terms of binders, fillers, dyes, preservatives, coating agents and dissolution agents, but these differences are not significant in terms of therapeutic value.[44]

The NPPA had fixed the price of 108 non-scheduled formulation packs of 50 anti-diabetes and cardiac medicines showing extreme inter-brand price differences, acting under paragraph 19 of DPCO, 2013, vide internal guidelines issued on 29 May 2014. It had decided that, to start with, inter-brand price variation would be examined in respect of single-ingredient formulations in eight therapeutic groups, namely anti-cancer, HIV/AIDS, anti-TB, anti-malaria, cardiovascular, anti-diabetics, anti-asthmatic, and immunological (sera/vaccines); and wherever the maximum retail price of the brand(s) of medicine of a particular formulation exceeds 25% of the simple average price, the same would be capped at the 25% level.

The NPPA had invoked the *extraordinary circumstances* clause by relying on the fact that there is very high incidence of diabetes in the country, which affects around 61 million persons, and the figure is expected to cross 100 million by 2030 as per the projection of the International Diabetes Federation; and it is estimated that every year nearly 1 million people in the country die due to diabetes.[45] Aggrieved from the issuance of the notification fixing the prices of these 108 non-schedules drugs, various pharmaceutical industry associations have challenged the vires of the notification in Bombay High Court[46] and Delhi High Court[47] on the ground that there did not exist an extraordinary circumstance that called for the intervention of the regulator. The courts have thus far shown an inclination to favour the sectoral regulator, which can be seen from the fact that the Delhi High Court declined to grant stay order over the NPPA notification, thereby allowing NPPA to continue with price control until the matter is finally decided judicially. The Supreme Court of India also favoured the NPPA move to force American pharmaceutical giant, Pfizer, to slash its prices (as it could not have increased it more than 20% in a year) when the apex court granted stay over the Bombay High Court decision that favoured the plea of Pfizer.[48]

However, the pharmaceutical industry has pointed out that NPPA's interpretation of Para 19 is 'erroneous' as inter-brand differences in branded-generics/off-patent drugs are not indicative of a 'severe market failure'. Also, different brands of the same drug formulation cannot be considered 'inter-changeable' as there are bound to be differences in quality. The argument is that larger companies would spend far more on quality control mechanisms than their smaller counterparts and hence all brands of the same formulation cannot be considered 'identical'.[49] Taking cognizance of the issue, the government of India directed the NPPA to take back the move to fix prices of these 109 drugs, and the NPPA had withdrawn the internal guidelines of 29 May 2014.[50] Since the withdrawal of the guidelines, the prices of a number of drugs are reported[51] to have registered a significant increase. For example, the prices of Glivec – an anti-cancer drug patented by Novartis – shot up to Rs 1 lakh from the earlier Rs 8,500, while that of its generic version Veenat by Natco rose to Rs 11,500 from Rs 8,500. Similarly, the price of Plavix, used to treat heart diseases and blood pressure, reportedly rose to Rs 1,615 from its earlier price of Rs 147.

Anti-competitive effect of price fixation

An industry expert was quoted as having termed the NPPA's stance of fixing the price ceiling of drugs as 'anti-competitive' as it will force companies in the highest price bracket to lower their prices, thus encroaching on the mid-segment, which in turn will migrate to the lowest-price band.[52] It is argued that this will trigger a fight for survival at the lowest-price segment, which will put small and medium enterprises (SMEs) players under severe stress. As SME is the soft underbelly of any manufacturing industry, a shrinking SME base will in time erode the competitiveness of the entire industry. Thus, it is argued that NPPA's stance will slowly cripple the pharmaceutical industry in India.

Impact on dynamic efficiency and quality manufacturing

The industry has raised its concern over the imposition of the ceiling prices on 348 essential drugs under NLEM, by adopting a simple average price formula, stating that it has been to the industry's disadvantage and will deter investments in (a) research, thereby crippling even the minimal effort that was being taken by the industry to achieve invention and innovation in the production of new products and production processes; and (b) high-quality manufacturing and distribution.[53] Kiran Mazumdar-Shaw (CMD, Biocon) has suggested that 'computation of price ceilings should be based on an equitable formula which ensures like-for-like comparisons and factors the quantum of investments. If return on investment is denied, any such price formulae will erode huge value for this all-important sector and make business unviable'.[54]

Economic analysis of the DPCO, 2013

The preceding analysis of the NPPP makes it abundantly clear that the NPPP will have the following impact on the pharmaceutical sector:

- It will put larger number of drugs under the price control regime.
- The market-based pricing mechanism will increase the price ceiling, thereby allowing the low-cost drug manufacturers to sell their products at higher prices.

- The prices of high-cost drugs from manufacturers with good brand value will decrease.
- The prices of low-cost drugs from manufacturers with little brand value may increase.
- The consumer of the low-cost drugs will lose more money, but it will be balanced out with the availability of many other drugs at cheaper prices due to the NLEM.
- The consumer of high-cost drugs will gain with its price reduction.

Gain distribution analysis: consumer versus manufacturer

In the situation under Drug (Price Control) Order, 1995, as fewer drugs were regulated, the manufacturers gained from excessive high prices of the unregulated drugs and had abnormal profits. This was an inefficient system (as per the Pareto criterion) as the manufacturers of the drugs gained at the cost of the consumers. However, the loss of the consumers was less than the total gain of the manufacturers, as the consumers suffered no loss so far as the manufacturers gained normal profit and the loss of the consumers was only the gain of the manufacturers over and above normal profit. Therefore, if assumptive values are given to the situation to facilitate the analysis, the gain of the manufacturers under the DPCO, 1995, was 25 (5 normal and 20 abnormal) and the loss of the consumers was 20 (only to the extent to which the manufacturers gained abnormal profits). Let this be situation A in which the gain distribution between consumer and manufacturer is A (–20, 25).

Under NPPP, more number of drugs falls under the umbrella of price regulation; however, the ceiling limits are being decided by the market-based mechanism, which is leading to a higher ceiling. The loss of profits of the manufacturers of the high-cost drugs is taken over by the manufacturers of the low-cost drugs, and since this loss–gain adjustment takes place within the same group (manufacturers) in our analysis, there is no loss to the manufacturers per se. The gain in the price of the drugs manufactured by low-cost drug manufacturers leads to a loss to the consumers which is balanced out by the reduction in the prices of the other, hitherto-unregulated drugs, which are manufactured only by high-cost drug manufacturers. However, the increase in the price of the low-cost drugs will be minimal, as the producers of these drugs have a very small market share and competitive factors will prevent any substantial price increase. Thus, the consumer will gain more by the decrease in the prices of the high-cost drugs than what he or she will lose by the increase in the prices of the low-cost drugs and will be a net gainer. Therefore, if assumptive values are given to the situation to facilitate the analysis, the gain of the consumers will be, say, Rs 15 due to the decrease in the cost of the high-cost and hitherto-unregulated drugs, and their loss will be, say, Rs 5 due to the increase in the cost of the low-cost drugs. Therefore, the consumer is at a net gain of Rs 10. The gain of the consumer will be the loss of the manufacturer, and the manufacturer will hence stand at a net loss of Rs 10. Therefore, the gain distribution in Situation A will change to B (–10, 15).

As the income of the low-cost drug manufacturers rises with the added revenue from increased prices of the low-cost drugs, they will enter the market of high-cost drugs. As the ceiling of the low-cost drugs would now be higher, the entry barrier would be removed (the extremely low ceiling under the DPCO, 1995, acted as an entry barrier as the drugs were sold at very cheap prices, which made it difficult for a new firm to enter the market as it would not be possible for it to recover the fixed and variable costs[55]) and new players will enter the market and increase the competition. The new players will continue to enter the market till the competition reaches the saturation point, and the prices prevailing in the market are almost at the level of cost of manufacturing in the case of the low-cost drugs. In the case of the high-cost drugs also, as new players enter that market, the competition will drive the prices even further down. Thus, the gain distribution will further change. The consumers' loss due to the previously increased prices of the low-cost drugs would no more exist, and the prices of the high-cost drugs will fall further. Due to optimum competition in the market, the drug manufacturers will make only normal profit. Therefore, the gain distribution would be as follows: C (0, 5).

Thus, the ultimate impact of the NPPP, in the long run, will change the gain distribution from Situation A (–20, 25) to C (0, 5). The economic rationality of the NPPP lies in the Kaldor–Hicks Efficiency Theorem, as can be seen in Figure 13.3, which states that where gainers gain more than losers lose, they may pay adequate compensation to the losers to ensure that the losers do not lose and still the gainers gain something.[56]

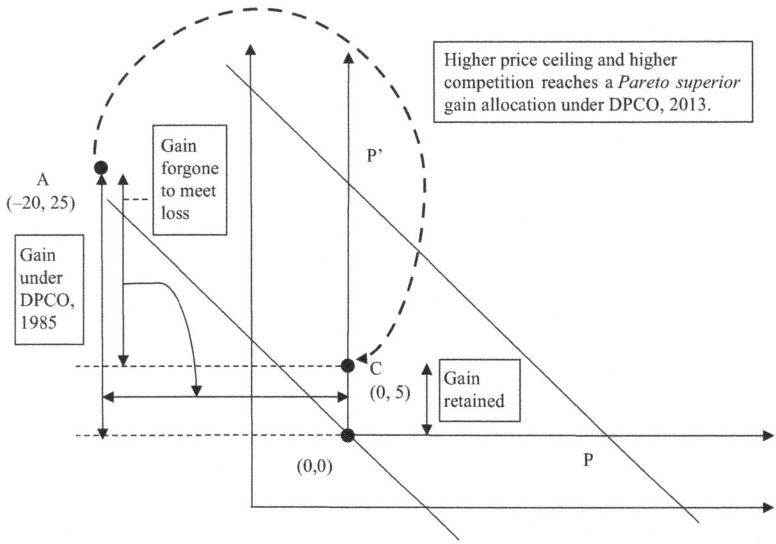

Figure 13.3 Application of Kaldor–Hicks efficiency to the NPPP/DPCO, 2013.

Source: Prateek Kumar, 'Economic Analysis of the Right to Fair Compensation and Transparency in Land Acquisition, Rehabilitation and Resettlement Act, 2013 (Chapter 6)', In *Economic Analysis of Law :An Indian Perspective*, edited by Bimal N. Patel, Ranita Nagar and Hiteshkumar Thakkar (LexisNexis, 2013): 143.

Conclusion

The preceding economic analysis leads to the conclusion that the DPCO, 2013, will lead to a better allocation of the gains between the consumer and the manufacturer in the long run, but it will take time to show concrete results as the complete impact of the DPCO, 2013, will be seen only when the competition in the pharmaceutical sector for both the low-cost and the high-cost drugs reaches the saturation point.

The driving down of the prices of the high-cost drugs below the ceiling limit would be very beneficial to middle-class people. The inclusion of larger number of drug formulations under DPCO, 2013, which cannot escape the clutches of the law will go a long way in ensuring availability of drugs at affordable cost for all sections of the society. Some of the suggestions include the following:

- Centralize procurement and decentralize distribution in order to achieve value for money.[57]

- The only rational, scientific ceiling price is one that has a clear-cut relation to the cost of raw material and cost of production. Therefore, the pricing mechanism should have a relation with the cost of production, and the market-based pricing mechanism is a farce.[58] The ceiling price, alternatively, can be a simple multiple of the cost of the API component in the formulation. The prices of APIs that go into a formulation can be 'discovered' by the excise duty returns (e.g. the ER-3 forms) filed online monthly by manufacturers, and by actors, at every stage up to the formulation manufacturer.[59]
- Put all drugs of the same therapeutic class under the price ceiling and expand the scope of NLEM to cover essential drugs exhaustively.
- Computation of price ceilings should be based on an equitable formula, which ensures like-for-like comparisons and factors the quantum of investments.[60]

Notes

1 'WHO Guideline on Country Pharmaceutical Pricing Policies', 2013, accessed 11 October 2014, http://cyber.law.harvard.edu/people/tfisher/Health/WHO_Guidelines.pdf.
2 Robert Cooter and Thomas Ulen, *Law and Economics* (Delhi: Pearson Education, 2012): 32.
3 Roger J. van den Bergh and Peter D. Camesasca, *European Competition Law and Economics: A Comparative Perspective* (London: Sweet and Maxwell, 2006): 71.
4 F.M. Scherer and David R. Ross, *Industrial Market Structure and Economic Performance* (Boston: Houghton Mifflin, 1990): 5.
5 'NPPA Order No. S.O. 1731 (E), F. No. 23(1)/2014/Div-III/NPPA', accessed 21 September 2014, http://www.nppaindia.nic.in/paragraph19/press10july14/so1731e-10-7-14.html.
6 National Pharmaceuticals Pricing Policy, 2012, accessed 11 October 2014, http://www.nppaindia.nic.in/NPPPNotification.
7 Ibid., 13.
8 Ibid., 12–13.
9 Ibid., 13.
10 Ibid., 16.
11 'WHO Guideline on Country Pharmaceutical Pricing Policies', accessed 11 October 2014, http://cyber.law.harvard.edu/people/tfisher/Health/WHO_Guidelines.pdf.
12 Ibid.
13 National Pharmaceuticals Pricing Policy, 2012.
14 Foreign Exchange Management (Transfer or Issue of Security by a Person Resident Outside India) Regulations, 2000, Notified Vide Notification

No. FEMA 20/2000-RB, dated 3 May 2000, accessed 11 October 2014, http://www.rbi.org.in/Scripts/BS_FemaNotifications.aspx?Id=174.

15 *Union of India v. K.S. Gopinath & Others*, SLP No. 3668/2003, Order dated 12 November 2003.

16 Report of the Task Force to Explore Options Other Than Price Control for Achieving the Objective of Making Available Life-Saving Drugs at Reasonable Prices, Submitted to the Department of Chemicals and Petrochemicals, Government of India, 20 September 2005, accessed 11 October 2014, http://www.pharmaceuticals.gov.in/sites/default/files/Dr.%20Pronab%20Sen%20Committee%20Report1_0.pdf.

17 Drugs (Price Control) Order, 2013, Department of Pharmaceuticals, Ministry of Chemicals and Fertilizers, Government of India, Notified on 15 May 2013, accessed 11 October 2014, http://www.nppaindia.nic.in/DPCO2013.pdf.

18 Ibid.

19 National Pharmaceuticals Pricing Policy, 7 December 2012.

20 S. Srinivasan and Anant Phadke, 'Pharma Policy 2012 and Its Discontents', *Economic & Political Weekly* 48 (1) (2013), accessed 11 October 2014, http://www.epw.in/system/files/pdf/2013_48/01/Pharma_Policy_2012_and_Its_Discontents.pdf.

21 National List of Essential Medicines, Ministry of Health and Family Welfare, Government of India, accessed 11 October 2014, http://mohfw.nic.in/WriteReadData/l892s/7364497513National%20List%20of%20Essential%20Medicine,%202011.pdf.

22 Drugs (Prices Control) Order, 1995, Department of Chemicals and Petrochemicals, Ministry of Chemicals and Fertilizers, Government of India, Notified on 6 January 1995.

23 van den Bergh and Camesasca, *European Competition Law and Economics*: 83.

24 Ibid.

25 National Pharmaceuticals Pricing Policy, 2012.

26 Ibid.

27 Ibid.

28 NPPA Order No. S.O. 1156 (E), dated 28 April 2014, accessed 11 October 2014, http://www.nppaindia.nic.in/ceiling/press28april14/so1156e-28-4-14.html.

29 Compendium of the Prices of Scheduled Drugs Fixed/Revised by NPPA, National Pharmaceutical Pricing Authority, Department of Pharmaceuticals, Ministry of Chemicals and Fertilizers, Government of India, 31 March 2011, accessed 11 October 2014, http://www.nppaindia.nic.in/index1.html.

30 Clause (v) of the Explanation to Section 48 of the Income Tax Act, 1961.

31 Cost-Inflation Index for assessment year 2003–04 was declared to be 463 by CBDT Notification No. 179/2003 [F.No. 142/11/2003-TPL], whereas the Cost-Inflation Index for assessment year 2013–14 has been declared as 939 by CBDT Notification No. 40/2013 [F.No. 142/7/2013-TPL].

32 Srinivasan and Phadke, 'Pharma Policy 2012 and Its Discontents'.
33 Ibid.
34 Sakthivel Selvaraj *et al.*, 'Pharmaceutical Pricing Policy: A Critique', *Economic & Political Weekly* 47 (4) (2012), accessed 11 October 2014, http://www.epw.in/system/files/pdf/2012_47/04/Pharmaceutical_Pricing_Policy_A_Critique.pdf.
35 Srinivasan and Phadke, 'Pharma Policy 2012 and Its Discontents'.
36 Ibid.
37 Ibid.
38 Drugs (Price Control) Order, 2013.
39 Ibid.
40 Selvaraj *et al.*, 'Pharmaceutical Pricing Policy'.
41 National Pharmaceuticals Pricing Policy, 2012.
42 The WPI for all commodities (base 2004–05 = 100) for 2010–11 was 143.2 and for 2011–12 was 156.13, accessed 11 October 2014, http://www.eaindustry.nic.in/wpi_data_display/display_data.asp.
43 Srinivasan and Phadke, 'Pharma Policy 2012 and Its Discontents'.
44 'NPPA Order No. S.O. 1731 (E), F. No. 23(1)/2014/Div-III/NPPA', accessed 21 September 2014, http://www.nppaindia.nic.in/paragraph19/press10july14/so1731e-10-7-14.html.
45 Ibid., 10 July 2014.
46 *Indian Pharmaceutical Alliance v. Union of India*, WPL/1942/2014, filed on 22 July 2014.
47 *Organisation of Pharmaceutical Producers of India v. National Pharmaceutical Pricing Authority*, WP(C) 4809/2014.
48 *Union of India v. Pfizer Ltd*, SLP (Civil) 9178/2014.
49 Viveka Roychowdhury, 'India's Loss, China's Gain', *Financial Express* (31 July 2014), accessed 11 October 2014, http://pharma.financialexpress.com/editorial/4204-india-s-loss-china-s-gain-20140815.
50 NPPA Notice F. No. 23 (01)/2014/Div-III(M&E)/NPPA, dated 22 September 2014, accessed 11 October 2014, http://www.nppaindia.nic.in/order/withdrawguideline-22–9-14.pdf.
51 Surabhi, 'Caught between Legal Basis and Industry Protests, NPPA Loses Pricing Powers', *Indian Express* (4 October 2014), accessed 11 October 2014, http://indianexpress.com/article/business/business-others/caught-between-legal-basis-and-industry-protests-nppa-loses-pricing-powers/.
52 Roychowdhury, 'India's Loss, China's Gain'.
53 'Kiran Mazumdar-Shaw Urges PM Narendra Modi to Cure Pharma Sector', *The Financial Express* (27 July 2014), accessed 11 October 2014, http://www.financialexpress.com/news/kiran-mazumdarshaw-urges-pm-narendra-modi-to-cure-pharma-sector/1274163.
54 Ibid.
55 van den Bergh and Camesasca, *European Competition Law and Economics*: 83.
56 Cooter and Ulen, *Law and Economics*: 42.
57 Srinivasan and Phadke, 'Pharma Policy 2012 and Its Discontents'.
58 Ibid.

59 Ibid.

60 Cost-Inflation Index for assessment year 2003–04 was declared to be 463 by CBDT Notification No. 179/2003 [F.No. 142/11/2003-TPL], whereas the Cost-Inflation Index for assessment year 2013–14 has been declared as 939 by CBDT Notification No. 40/2013 [F.No. 142/7/2013-TPL].

Part VI

Economic analysis of media laws

Chapter 14

Economic analysis of cross-media ownership

Aakanksha Parashar, Madhuja Barman and Chandni Patel

Background note

India is a democratic nation, and this is evident from the fact that the media in the country gets to enjoy a considerable freedom related to the publishing of news or broadcasting. Media, in reality, has turned out to be the fourth pillar in the bureaucratic set-up, backed by Article 19 of the Indian Constitution embracing the freedom of press. The freedom provided under the constitution ensures that media houses are free from unnecessary censorship but they are not absolute. The restriction on this freedom can be imposed if it comes under the purview of Article 19(2). Further, the media industry was not granted protection from the otherwise general rules applicable to industries, such as taxation and paid holidays rules.

In recent times, many are being criticized and severely punished for displaying their thoughts, as in the case of the famous cartoonist Aseem Trivedi, who was put behind bars when he represented a national symbol in a cartoonish manner.[1] These incidents prove the fact that any freedom can be exercised till it does not interfere with the rights of some other individual. Developed countries like the United States and the United Kingdom have positive regulations over their media houses, which allow them adequate freedom and regulate the publishing of controversial news that might incite emotions against government. Many a time, the media houses assume uncontrollable power in their hands, which can be fatal for the citizens as well as the government because they try to stir the trust which the citizens have reposed on the government, and if gone unchecked, then it can lead to a breakdown of the nation.

Media houses are horizontally and vertically integrating their own newspapers, news channels and other mediums of conveyance.

Horizontal and vertical integration yield two-fold results, where it helps in increasing the economies of scale but can also result in media pluralism. This chapter deals with the horizontal and vertical integration in media industry bringing out the favourable aspects of such integration, followed by the undesirable consequences. Finally, the conclusion summarizes with the help of various views and opinions regulating cross-media ownership in the Indian context.

Integration of media industry

In any business, two types of integration can prevail: vertical and horizontal. Vertical integration occurs when a company expands its business into areas that are at different points on the same production path, such as when a manufacturer owns its supplier and/or distributor. Such integration can help companies reduce costs and improve efficiency by decreasing transportation expenses and reducing turn-around time, among other advantages. The other type of integration called horizontal integration is the acquisition of additional business activities that are at the same level of the value chain in similar or different industries. This can be achieved by internal or external expansion. Because the different firms are involved in the same stage of production, horizontal integration allows them to share resources at that level.

The entertainment and media (E&M) industry broadly consists of four segments, that is television, print, radio and other media (e.g. Internet access, film, out-of-home advertising, music, gaming and Internet advertising). In the media sector, vertical integration occurs when a media company owns different businesses in the same chain of production and distribution. For example, 20th-century Fox owns the studios in Hollywood, in addition to the cinemas, the television channels and the DVD rental shops. It owns parts of chains so that it can make money from every part of it. 'Horizontal integration' or 'cross-media ownership' refers to the ownership/control by one entity, of different categories of media, which are print, radio and television, in a given market.[2] It is defined as single ownership of two or more related businesses (as a newspaper and a television station) that allows the owner to control competition.[3] Cross-media ownership is the ownership of multiple media businesses by a person or entity. These businesses may include print, television, radio and various online entities. When a person or entity owns any two of these media outlets, it is considered to be involved in cross-media ownership.

The era of technology has overhauled traditional media and made preponderous advancement. Media is making both horizontal and vertical transgression and is replete with such examples when it stretches itself in the field of distribution and broadcasting sectors. A group like the *Times of India* owns 40 different media and other businesses, so does *Hindustan Times*, *Ananda Bazaar Patrika*, *Jagaran*, *Malayala Manorama*, *Zee* and *Bhaskar* group. It is possible to visualize three types of accumulation of ownership interest in the media: cross-media owners across the various carriers such as television, radio or print; consolidation, including vertical integration among media operations of content, carrier and distributor within a media segment such as television or radio; and market share dominance in a given geography within each media segment.[4] Truly, the concept of cross-media ownership is a very debatable topic and brings in the perfect mixture of the concept of 'law and economics' within it.

Before analysing the economic aspect of media, it is imperative to examine the reason behind the importance of concentration of media. Harcourt and Verhulst (1998)[5] give five reasons:

1 *Cost cutting*: Mergers often mean cost cutting, staff layoffs that lead to closing media outlets and less investment in the content. This leads to standardization rather than diversification in media content.
2 *Entry barrier*: Due to media concentration, large market players have the ability to close the market to new entrants, independent producers. This would lead to either market monopoly or oligopoly. This situation is considered to be counter-competitive for media market because of the increased social costs. Hence, competition law is needed to prevent market concentration.
3 *Influence on public opinion*: Media gives an owner potential power to influence public opinion in its favour. Concentration of media hence restricts media pluralism.
4 *High costs*: The increased use of encryption technologies in the delivery of media content threatens to financially burden the public with high costs for popular viewing. A high cost for access could be established by gateway monopolies. The result could be the development of what has been termed as the 'information rich' and the 'information poor'.[6]
5 *Minority audiences*: The new channels seek to identify market niches to boost profitability. This often results in specialized

channels, which tend to be thematic and narrow-cast. Minority audiences could be overlooked in such process, and sometimes they might even be served by these channels.

Economic tools

Media and economies of scale

Over the past few decades, there has been a composite move to consolidate the media industries, that is print, television or film, where the majority of the sections of media will be controlled by fewer members so that the cost of production and distribution can be reduced and media can have bigger access to public.[7] The public gets drawn to certain shows when a well-known media house is heading it. In India, audiences get drawn to movie theatres when a film is produced by UTV production[8] or other such renowned production houses, and in certain scenarios, they do exercise monopoly.

In the economic context, it is believed that media industry is characterized by *high production cost* and *economies of scale*. However, empirical research has shown that sometimes films and programmes that attract a lot of audiences can also have high economies of scale. Samuelson, an American economist, believes that the cost that is incurred when the first edition of a television programme or film is produced is always higher, and later, the incremental cost to attract one extra consumer is less or nil. The same logic applies to content of such media also.[9] A lot of the costs also depend upon the talent of star who will be casted in the said show as he or she will charge a cost based on his or her capacity to draw audiences. Particular inputs, especially in the case of talent, are probably the main source of the relation between production costs and targeted audiences. The talents are identified based on demand and can serve to inform and orient supply. However, the initial stages of launching a programme are when a lot of production costs are incurred; however, a few weeks after the show is launched, the cost of production gets down to zero as there is no additional cost to attract that one extra additional unit of audience.

The rarity of talent should not be analysed as rarity of an ordinary factor. Stars *in themselves* are not rare; there are few of them because consumers' attention is rare and because the time they have to seek information for their consumption of experience goods is limited. The very small number of stars is often explained as 'winner takes it all' because mediocre talent is seen simply as an imperfect substitute for eminent talent, whereas demand is for the best.[10]

Broadcasting rights on content are negotiated at prices that depend on an audience estimated ex ante, and sometimes also on the audience ex post. However, if we exclude the case in which certain production factors are remunerated in relation to actual audiences, the *production costs* of programme content cannot be linked to the ex post audiences unless the production factors do depend on the expected audiences and unless there is a correlation between the expected audience at the time of production and the actual audience in the end.[11] There is extreme uncertainty when a show is going to be launched, and this uncertainty characterizes the media largely explaining the nature of relations between the demand targeted at the time of production and demand finally expressed and satisfied. If these two quantities were closely correlated, information goods would be normal goods. Costs in most cases depend on demand, and any production house should have the capacity to judge the taste of the audience, and to adjust the production ex ante, with precision. If expected demand and the final demand were not related, then the whole process would have been meaningless. In this case, there would have been no empirical relation between the audiences and production.

Information is an *experience good*, the usefulness of which is not ex ante, and a *network good*, which is more useful when consumed by others as well; the process of acquisition of information by potential consumers, from those who have already consumed, plays a very crucial role. In the Indian scenario also, when producing a show, the producers and channel heads have to keep in mind the tastes of the Indian audience, which is influenced by a lot of factors such as their customs and preferential content.[12] Thus, it can be seen that stars are very few and the money they charge is based on their talent quotient and their popularity index, and this increases the cost of production even though the media house is a big entity and each person is proficient in his or her work. However, the high cost of production is incurred at the initial stages, and once the show is released and gets its due publicity, it does not require to spend any additional cost on attracting new audiences; this publicity ensures the profit of the production house. On the contrary, if the programme is not up to the mark, then the falling television rating points indicate the same and the show is called off so that the cost of production does not keep on increasing and eat into the expected profit of the media houses.

However, the major problem faced is that now economies of scale do not matter in the digital realm. As seen in the case of digital newspapers, there are no costs of production and printing and if the quality is good, then they yield almost equivalent impact on the society. An example is the case of *Tehelka*, which previously was in print as it had its newspaper and magazine; however, it was accused of investigative journalism and received a lot of criticism and was removed from business. However, it has its online portal, which has an equal impact on the society, and this proves that such organizations do not have to incur any production cost, since their profits are magnanimous. When we look into literature and other such reading portals, today we have a lot of websites, which provide e-books on Amazon, and there are independent authors who directly publish in such websites. These strategies lead to dwindling profits for the publishers in the market. It is an established fact that the consumer would always be happy to pay the cost of transmission rather than the cost of production. With the change in the market structure, the established publishing houses are not able to match up with those who are present in the market due to their profit-maximizing incentive.[13] The most affected industry due to this change is the music industry, as consumers will pay only for the cost of production of any product till they have it in their reach and after they have obtained the information, they will not a pay a penny more than the cost of transmission. Producers and channels come out often with advertisements to avoid piracy; however, the consumers also like to cut down their costs, and thus, they do take the help of downloading sites to fulfil their desires.

The television industry and film industry are slower in catching up with the trend, as even though the distribution costs are negligent, the cost of producing high-quality videos is still borne by them. The entertainment industry continues to lobby politicians for more aggressive copyright enforcement and longer copyright periods. With copyright extensions being granted at every turn, it has in reality created a system of eternal copyright where it can continue to cream off fees for works that not only owed a lot to others when being created (e.g. Mickey Mouse) but also should have passed out of copyright years ago if such extensions had not been granted.[14]

Thus, the economic tool of economies of scale is clearly diminishing and diseconomies of scale have started. The cost of production has reduced, and people have started paying for only the cost of transmission, and this has led to closing of many media houses. For example, in Kolkata, the famous music store Music World was closed down as people have stopped buying CDs and music tapes and the business was running in losses.[15] These companies are too big and too slow to adapt to the digital revolution where their dominance through scale is being questioned by smaller outfits with a deeper focus on quality – but currently they have the law in their pocket to destroy the competition that way. If we want better-quality journalism, better-quality music, better-quality television – and everyone to get paid – then small independent firms are the future where competition is not decimated by economies of scale, and shareholders are not skimming off the top.[16]

Media and economies of scope

Economies of scope are to do with making savings and gaining efficiencies as more of a firm's output is consumed. Economies of scope refer to the savings and cost-efficiencies made possible 'by simultaneous production of many products by one firm'. Such economies would allow the producer to provide goods at cheaper rates rather than goods supplied separately by an individual firm. Economies of scope arise when there are some shared overheads, or other efficiency gains, available that make it more cost-effective for two or more related products to be produced and sold jointly, rather than separately. Savings may arise, for example, if specialist inputs gathered for one product can be reused in another.[17]

It also refers to reduction of total costs of producing products when a company controls more than one function where the total cost of producing two or more messages within the same business is less than producing them separately in two or more non-related businesses. Thus, if one company can publish a book, a newspaper and a magazine at a lower total cost than what it would cost for three separate businesses (a book publisher only, a newspaper-only business and a magazine-only business), then that company is experiencing economies of scope. There is considerable overlap in skills and talent needed to produce different types of media messages; there is great advantage to economies of scope within the mass media industries. Media businesses achieve these economies of scope through consolidation, such as mergers, acquisitions and joint ventures.[18]

Economies of scope are common within the media because the nature of media output is such that it is possible for a product created for one market to be reformatted and sold through another. For example, an interview with a politician that is recorded for broadcast within a documentary might also be edited for inclusion within other news programmes, either on television or on radio. The same television content can be repackaged into more than one product. The reformatting of a product intended for one audience into another 'new' product suitable for different audiences creates economies of scope. Whenever economies of scope are available to be exploited, diversification will be an economically efficient strategy because 'the total cost of the diversified firm is low compared with a group of single-product firms producing the same output'.[19]

Media industries are heavily reliant on technology and therefore are regularly affected by new advances in how media may be produced or distributed. Every major revolutionary step starting from printing and broadcasting to the spread of the Internet has brought upheaval and opportunity for market incumbents. Digitization had a deep impact on media industries and markets. It has helped in gauging the attention of the audiences, and consumption has increased and reshaped the media markets. It has brought with it a lot of commercial and creative possibilities. Digitization has affected production costs and has facilitated the introduction of automated content management systems which enable more efficient exploitations and management of content assets. But it has also introduced new hazards, including the greater threat of intermediation, that is lifting and reassembling of online content and other 'free rider' problems.[20]

Consolidation[21]

The major reason for consolidation by any media house or corporate bodies is to increase the economic hold over the market. There are *three* different consolidation techniques. First, it is the horizontal merger. This is when a media company buys another media company of similar nature, for example when one brand of newspaper buys another chain of newspaper. The major factors that motivate such mergers are removal of certain bottlenecks of input supplies, improved profitability, better customer service and achievement of economies in both scale and size.[22]

The second technique is the vertical merger. It is when one media company buys suppliers or distributors to create integration in the production and distribution of messages, for example book publisher buying a printing plant and some bookstores. This too increases economies of scope. Viacom owns cable television services such as MTV and Nickelodeon; in 1994, Viacom acquired Paramount Communications Inc., which is a film and television production company, and this represents a vertical merger. Vertical merger would facilitate to raise barriers to entry, facilitate collusion and provide with other facilities.[23]

The third technique is conglomerate merger. This is when a media company buys a combination of other media companies or companies or non-media houses, for example a film studio that buys a newspaper, radio station and so on. At one time, Paramount Communications owned Paramount Studio, which was one of the leasing producers of motion pictures, television shows and cable programming. The conglomerate merger increases both economies of scale and diversification. It followed a relatively straightforward adaptation of the horizontal merger where entry was only probabilistic. A somewhat higher market power threshold was appropriate, that is a challenge was unlikely unless market concentration was high.[24]

No single merger is appropriate for a media house, but there should be a mixture of all three to yield the maximum results in any situation. From a business point of view, cross-media ownership is very attractive because it achieves economies of scope and it can reduce risk by diversification across many different kinds of vehicles and audiences.

Media as public good

Economically, media deciphers goods as a public and a private commodity/good. *Private goods* are goods that are excludable in nature, that is the individuals who have paid for it shall only have access to it and can obtain utility out of it. The other people who do not pay for it do not use it. On the other hand, *public goods* are those goods that can be used by any individual or group of people and are not excludable. However, one of the most important characteristics of media or information which is produced is its *nonappropriability*, that is information is generally difficult and costly to produce but cheap to transmit.[25]

Media can be considered to be a public good, and each additional user incurs certain additional marginal cost. The users do not impose an additional cost on the media channels as the product that is circulated, that is news and the value of it, does not deplete because certain additional users may add to it. Cost of producing media in certain cases starts from production or post-production times, especially in the case of movies and films, where it is important to promote the movie so that the audience will be driven to the theatres and the cost of production will be incurred back. Therefore, it often makes sense that a good proportion of money is spent on advertising and promotion of the movie and other such allied activities.[26]

Media is considered to be a public good, and sometimes consumers try to 'free ride' by just paying for the cost of transmission. Sometimes, it so happens that consumers do not pay anything for the use of the media content, but they attain the full utility out of the media content that is being displayed. For example, when certain consumers watch cricket matches, news or any such content standing outside any showroom, they do not pay more than the cost of transmission; they lose out on the ease and comfort they would have achieved sitting in their homes and enjoying the same media content.[27] Excluding any person from obtaining media content is going to be expensive because the transmission of ideas is cheap.

It is difficult to exclude public from not using public good without adopting a method that is inexpensive. Thus, what the media personnel do is sign contracts with their employees that they would endeavour to *protect trade secrets*.[28] An employee of any media-related company is made to sign a contract that he or she would not distribute or transmit any information before it is officially released. Today, it is a common phenomenon that a song from the movie releases on YouTube or any such video-sharing site and people do not take the pain to buy a pack of CDs of the same. Thus, it proves that the cost of downloading from such sites is way easier and cheaper than spending a hefty amount on CDs. Trade secret protection ideally prevents the transmission of information and allows its producers to appropriate the value.

Advertising media content can pay off substantially as the producer has to spend negligibly on reaching new audiences, thus not sustaining production costs. For instance, Microsoft really became rich by producing a standard operating system for PCs; however, it marketed among the masses because even though the cost of production is high, the additional cost of reaching to new customers is negligent or is very low; thus, it is not harmful to reach any number of customers. In this manner, even though production of media can be costly, its promotion and advertising does help in recurring all the production cost.[29]

Oligopoly and anti-competitive market

Oligopoly is the most common type of market structure in which media firms operate.[30] The reason for firms having oligopoly structure is the prevalence of economies of scale. The economies of scale largely happen because the media industry is characterized by high initial production costs and low marginal reproduction and distribution costs.[31] Thus, due to economies of large-scale production, there is a fall in the cost, and this cost advantage associated with the size dictates that an industry is an oligopoly unless some form of market intervention or government regulation prevents the firms from growing to their most efficient size. And if there is no intervention by the government, then the existing firms will create barriers for entry of new firms, and the media industry will be dominated by a handful of large firms. Sometimes, the economies of scale act as a barrier to entry because any new firm that enters the market will be smaller than established firms and will suffer cost disadvantage.

Now that it has been established that the common type of market structure in which media firms operate is oligopoly, we try to understand how such market structure proves to be anti-competitive. Oligopoly market refers to a market where the companies are aware that the decisions each of them makes are interdependent of those made by other undertakings in the market.[32] In an oligopolistic market, the main focus of the firm is on the behaviour of the other firms. This has been explained in many models, of which the Bertrand model is one. The Bertrand model focuses on an oligopolistic market with just two sellers of equal size and efficiency that offer an identical product. These undertakings engage in caprice competition with the purpose of shifting customer demand from one to other. As per the model, in such a situation the price ultimately settles at the average variable cost level, allowing for practically no profits. Hence, in an oligopolistic market, the undertakings must focus on the conduct of its competitors and their reactions to each other's behaviour.[33] This seems to go against the policy of antitrust law, which supports price competition.

When cross-media ownership is allowed without the required regulations and control, a few entities can create oligopoly market over the entire industry. Political groups and leaders can apply pressure on or highly influence media personnel who can distort news or can give a biased opinion about any subject matter, which could prove dangerous for the public. However, it is not restricted only to political leaders; even corporate houses can provoke them to publish or say something that would be beneficial for them but is not the truth.

Connections between the machinery of government and the wider political system are unavoidable and exist in every country. Government and other allied machinery take a deep interest in the field of media, and politicians try to accommodate their wishes and desires in the influential media group and, simultaneously, the media can influence policy makers' decisions in such a manner that the social benefit which the public would have derived from the policies would diminish in a diminishing rate.[34] On the contrary, it can also happen that the media plays an important role in shaping the public opinion, which indirectly would have an impact on the policy maker's decisions. Kingdon in his book *Agendas, Alternatives and Public Policies* admits that the media may have an indirect influence on the policy agenda. To the extent that public opinion affects policy makers, media can have a part in shaping the policy agenda by influencing public opinion.[35]

Kingdon, on the other hand, posits that the only function of the media is to report the happenings in the government and not affect or influence it. Kingdon opined that the media's tendency to bring forth the most newsworthy material or dramatic story tends to increase the impact it can have on the policy decisions and other formulations. Those stories tend to come at the end of the governmental policy-making process rather than at the beginning. Kingdon argues that the media mostly reports on what the government does; it is actually the government that influences public opinion via media coverage, which then feeds back to the government, leaving the government as the key player in the end.[36]

Kingdon surmises that the media bears no leverage over policy makers and the decision-making process; surely, they do take notice of the news which is the talk of the nation and bring in laws and regulations necessary to regulate them, as part of the feedback mechanism. However, to rebut his arguments, there is evidence from all over the world how *investigative journalism* brought up issues that subsequently became a priority on the policy agenda and led to substantial political changes, without the government initiating any of it.[37] In India, when the 'Nirbhaya Rape Case' took place, it portrayed the monopoly that the media had over the nation, and the government was forced to bring amendments in criminal law. Therefore, all these developments prove that media has a monopoly over the political decisions made in the Parliament, and cross-media ownership is a step higher where the newspaper, radio and television are owned and influenced by a single producer or entity or small group of producers. It is indeed time to debate regulatory issues for cross-media ownership, and in the absence of an independent media regulator, the Telecom Regulatory Authority of India (TRAI) discussions have long-term implications for the critical and booming Indian media industry, says P.N. Vasanti, director of Centre for Media Studies, a New Delhi–based multidisciplinary research organization. The Hyderabad-based Administrative Staff College of India (ASCI) has pointed out that there are ample evidences which prove that there is cross-media ownership, and specific regulatory methods or tools should be adopted to reduce such concentration specially in the regional market.

Therefore, in an oligopoly market due to the interdependence of the undertakings, media favours a non-competitive market Due to the size of the undertakings, it manages to drive out the small undertakings, and this creates entry barriers. Also, the interdependence of the undertakings under oligopoly spares media the trouble to pay continuous attention to consumers. This result creates a problem for antitrust laws that aim to protect the consumer interest and promote healthy competition.

Media pluralism

Throughout the world, media pluralism is considered essential to democracy. A pluralistic media includes a variety of outlets with diverse ownership and viewpoints, independence and transparency and is generally believed to contribute to a press that honours the ideals of democracy and reflects diversity within society. Some economists, however, argue against media pluralism, holding that diverse viewpoints in the media may actually serve to divide rather than unite people.[38] They rely on some of the vices of media in the corrupt world, such as the power of press when unfortunately manipulated. Others argue that journalists are the mirror of the society they are reporting from and divisiveness is the essence of democracy; it is the very question it considers. Moreover, their job is to report the facts and not uniting public opinion; if the facts are pluralistic, then so be it. But freedom of expression can be exercised only in a free and pluralistic media environment, including through independent media governance.[39]

In the modern world, information, for most of us, lies quite literally at our fingertips. Under these circumstances, it seemed natural enough to question what role the media plays in perceptions of identity and pluralism.[40] The media markets, in pursuit of efficiency through economies of scale and network effects, have a tendency to move away from the competitive form of organization to monopoly or oligopoly. This situation raises concern because the efficiency promoted in the form of large economies of scale also leads towards smaller number of competitors and might even lead to abuse of monopoly power. Monopoly in media market is different from monopoly in other markets because concentration in media markets, apart from the usual economic effects, can profoundly influence opinion and ideas.[41]

Case study: impact of BCCI's monopoly on cricket

Background

The Board for Control of Cricket in India (BCCI) is the main organizer of all the international cricket matches held in India. Furthermore, it has also established a monopoly over all the private T-20 leagues by stipulating that the Indian Premier League (IPL) shall be the only recognized private T-20 league in India. BCCI has now set up its own independent television production unit which produces the television content related to all the cricket matches in India, and the television channels can merely buy the right to telecast the content but cannot set up their own production.[42]

Reason for the monopoly: barriers to entry

BCCI has created a monopoly in the market for the private T-20 leagues and cricket telecasts by imposing barriers to entry by other organizations. BCCI is in such a position that it is not only a regulator of cricket but also an organizer of cricket. BCCI requires all international matches held in India to be approved by it and furthermore has bound itself not to give official recognition to any other private cricket league except the IPL, which BCCI itself organizes. Finally, BCCI also retains to itself the right to sell the telecast rights of the cricket matches. Thus, by misuse of its regulatory powers, the BCCI has put up great barriers to entry for other firms wishing to organize cricket and thus ensured that it has a monopoly.

Underproduction due to monopoly status

For a monopolist, the market demand curve and the monopoly firm's demand curve is the same since it is the only firm in that market. A monopoly firm can thus sell more of its goods or services only by lowering the price. Therefore, its average revenue curve (AR curve) is downward sloping. The marginal revenue curve (MR curve) lies below it and has twice the gradient of AR. Since the BCCI aims to maximize profits, it will keep increasing the output of cricket telecasts or cricket leagues till the point that the marginal revenue derived from the broadcast is equal to the marginal cost. Thus, the short-run equilibrium quantity shall be Q_{mon}, as shown in Figure 14.1, at the point where the MC curve cuts the MR curve from below. However, the price shall be P_x, since BCCI wishes to maximize its profit. This price P_m is greater than price P_c, while quantity Q_{mon} is lesser than quantity $Q_{comp.}$ The socially efficient equilibrium is at the point where the MC curve cuts the AR curve from below, that is at price P_c and quantity Q_{comp}. (Refer to Figure 14.1.)

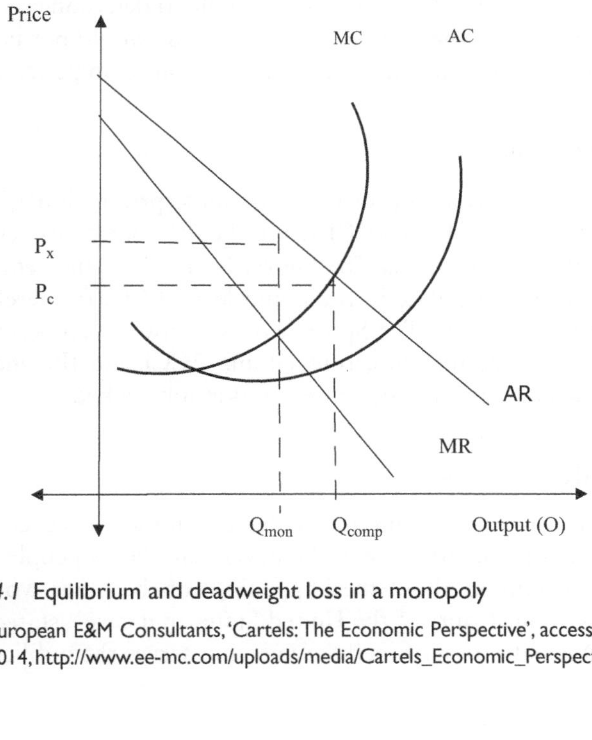

Figure 14.1 Equilibrium and deadweight loss in a monopoly

Source: European E&M Consultants, 'Cartels: The Economic Perspective', accessed 10 September 2014, http://www.ee-mc.com/uploads/media/Cartels_Economic_Perspective_03.pdf.

Thus, the BCCI is earning excessive profit, and there is underproduction of cricket telecasts and private T-20 cricket leagues due to BCCI's monopoly. This is clear from the fact that before BCCI assumed monopoly position by binding itself to not recognize any other private T-20 leagues apart from IPL, in India there had existed both the Indian Cricket League and the IPL. Today, after the monopoly came into being, the total number of matches played in IPL is still lesser than the sum of the matches that were held in the two leagues.

Imperfect information

Being a monopoly helps BCCI to control the information regarding its product, that is the cricket telecasts. Sunil Gavaskar and Ravi Shastri were employed by the BCCI in 2008 and then regardless of who owned the television rights, BCCI made it mandatory for the telecasters to have 'Sunny & Ravi' on commentary duty whenever India played at home. Furthermore, BCCI used this influence over commentary to ensure that the commentators on the home networks never brought up on air the topic of selection, administration and the Umpire Decision Review System. The impact of a biased commentary is that the general public would not be able to determine the quality of the cricket that they are watching and thus would not be able to determine its true value, leading to further market imperfections.

Possible solutions

One way of solving the problem of underproduction of cricket due to the monopoly of BCCI would be to separate its regulatory and organizing functions. The Sports Ministry of the central government should regulate in India and leave BCCI to merely be an organizer of matches. The Sports Ministry could also permit other firms to organize matches, thus ending BCCI and IPL monopoly and allowing a vibrant and larger market for cricket.

Diversity in news

Diversity in news is an important element in the media sector. This is because it is the diversity in the news that allows people to form their own opinion about the happenings of the outer world. The Federal Circuit Court of the United States in a case[43] stated as follows: 'Diversification of media ownership serves the public interest by promoting diversity of program and service viewpoints as well as by preventing undue concentration of economic power.'

At the global level, many international treaties and conventions such as the Universal Declaration of Human Rights, the International Covenant on Civil and Political Rights, the American Convention on Human Rights and the European Convention on Human Rights recognize the right of individuals to receive information and opinions from a diversity of sources. Thus, they speak about imposing an obligation on government to ensure media pluralism.

Therefore, in order to promote diversity and control the growing monopoly among media companies, countries like the United States, Australia, the United Kingdom, Germany, South Africa, Canada, South Korea and France have regulated cross-media ownership. In most of these countries, the restrictions imposed were stringent before the 1990s or the emergence of the Internet. After the digitalization and introduction of Internet media, the cross-media ownership rules have been relaxed. This is because many economists are of the view that emergence of the Internet as a medium for conveying news would not allow the growth of monopoly among media companies. This conclusion stems from the assumption that the new media technologies will bring about a significant increase in the number of media outlets and that the restrictions established for the old media will become unnecessary, ineffective and/or irrelevant.[44]

Herman and McChesney[45] have pointed out that the Internet has been profitable for only a few providers because while many people are keen to pay for web access, they are, to date, reluctant to pay for extra information and other Internet content. Thus, nobody generally generates profit from Internet media content. However, assuming Internet media content was to become profitable, the existing firm will have a strong advantage over potential Internet rivals. The reason for this is that it takes time and money to attract audiences to a website, and websites of already-existing firms enjoy a ready market. In their conclusion, the authors stated that 'the internet and digital revolution do not pose an immediate or even foreseeable threat to the market power of the media giants'.[46]

Efficiency

Cross-media business models are one way the sector could respond. This could provide consumer benefits (e.g. a cross-platform experience) and be an efficient and effective way of delivering news content.[47] Cross-media concentration is common, but it does have some effect on economic variables or motives. This is amply demonstrated in a model where a single producer operates in any one of the other media, such as television or radio or newspaper, which could involve methods of reducing cost (per unit consumption of output), leading to an increase in the general economic efficiency. For example, a combination of print and electronic publishing creates obvious synergies through opportunities for reuse of text and graphic content. However, less efficiency is created when collective resources will arise as a direct result of cross-media ownership among the radio, television and newspaper sectors.[48] The combinations of cross-media ownership that yield the most significant economic efficiencies are those that facilitate sharing of common specialized content or of a distribution infrastructure when a media firm's output is characterized by a particular theme or subject matter; then expanding operations into several different sectors will create important synergies. For example, specialization in providing one particular form of content enables it to exploit the economies of scale and scope across different products, and there is availability of different modes of delivery.[49]

Risk reduction can always provide incentive under diagonal expansion. It provides the producers an additional secured system as they are sure of the fact that if their newspaper is not the best-selling one, they reduce the risk by earning profits through broadcasting news on the channel which they own. They get an opportunity to diversify out of their own sector and try hands at faster-growth areas of commercial radio or television broadcasting. Managerial benefits that accrue due to the reduction in cost of production and increased efficiency rates are gratification and better-quality products. However, one of the disadvantages of cross-media ownership is that the profit which is earned by the media personnel is not put for increased efficient use of available limited resources but for favouring the private interests of the shareholders, which allows them to get hold of the market more. Thus, initially we see an upward sloping curve for efficiency, and then it becomes stagnant for some time and then it drops down. The preceding situation leads to monopoly, and it becomes very easier to influence such media news and activities.

Conclusion

Media ownership is a subject of intense debate and government review in both developed and developing countries around the world.

Unfortunately, there is scanty research, with no agreed parameters or techniques for the measurement of media concentration and diversity, and there is little agreement about how to define, measure and regulate it. This notion is best summed up by Ben Bagdikian, author of *The Media Monopoly* and Pulitzer Prize–winning journalist and professor: 'Modern democracies need a choice of politics and ideas, and that choice requires access to truly diverse and competing sources of news, literature, entertainment and popular culture.'

India has taken a positive step, and the Ministry of Information and Broadcasting has asked the ASCI to conduct a survey and publish a report on the cross-media scenario in India. Cross-media ownership has been a debatable topic attracting both appreciators and haters for the concept. Some are of the view that if businessmen and other influential members are not allowed to control media houses' properties, then there are other methods devisable that will allow them to own it. ASCI[50] performed a survey-cum-study to find out about cross-media ownership. In the Indian scenario, through the survey it has been proved that cross-media ownership has found its base and is expanding day by day. However, the concern is whether it will be possible to keep the ownership in control, or if it would amount to any kind of concentration. When the report was submitted, certain comments were given by the Ministry of Information and Broadcasting in March and July 2009.[51]

The ASCI's study on cross-media ownership in India in July recommended that India needs legislation regulating cross-media ownership as there is evidence of market dominance in certain relevant markets. They said that the rules on ownership must include broadcasting, print and the new media, thus covering Internet media segment as well. Further, the report emphasized that a periodic study on the media industry needs to be conducted and the rules on ownership should be changed accordingly. The Indian government has not, as of yet, prescribed any rules to control cross-media ownership rules. However, the government had made a reference to TRAI with respect to the same and the latter gave some recommendations, but India is yet to see a legislation that restricts cross-media ownership.

Draft report submitted by ASCI

ASCI affirms the fact that media has been growing over the past few years and a lot of money goes into this sector and its development. The media ownership has not been only restricted to electronic media but has also been spread to frequency modulation (FM) radio and other broadcasting routes. Media has been a part of any individual from time immemorial, and now the new age of technology has arrived where people are switching from cable TV to dish TV, and there is a tussle between newspapers and the newsroom.

The report, after an exhaustive survey, brings out in percentage the popularity of any well-known media house and also voices its concern that in the era of pluralism, regulations should not be imposed upon cross-media ownership. It argues that new media sources will guarantee that a diverse range of information and options will be freely exchanged in accessible and commonly used forums.[52] It has been noticed that unlike other sectors, traditional media has not lost its importance and new media sources are joining it. But pertaining to the same fact, that traditional media houses own the new one, concentration increases. The report gives a picture of who is the head honcho of the media sector and who is leading than the others.[53] The report also lays down certain regulations that need to be implemented, including the fact that the distributors and broadcasters should not have common ownership controlling rights as the consultation paper draws a direct link between 'uncontrolled ownership' and 'paid news, corporate and political lobbying by television channels, propagation of biased analysis and forecast . . . and irresponsible reporting to create sensationalism'. Regulating media ownership is 'essential in the public interest as a guarantee of plurality and diversity of opinion'.[54]

A seminar was also held in New Delhi on 4 August which discussed the heated topic of cross-media ownership and what steps should be taken to protect and foster its growth in the near-future. The main reason given by media stalwarts for cross-media ownership was that audiences are fragmented in today's world and thus it was necessary to engage the audiences at every point; thus, diversion through various domains becomes pertinent.[55] It is believed that every medium has its own advantage, and thus, it was necessary to make every medium operational so as to gauge the attention of the audiences. All the media houses want to enter into verticals, that is magazines, radio, television; however, it is not very easy to sell combinations. However, a looming danger hangs on the media houses that are entering into the realms of cross-media ownership, as media houses resort to malpractices when in search of news and materials. India still lacks a policy or law governing cross-media holding patterns.[56]

'Cross media holdings will not only give people the formula of selling their business successfully, it will, at the same time, dilute their risks by being in multiple verticals. However, in India, cross media holding will take some time before it can command that power', as has been held by Rahul Thappa of *Mail Today*. Thus, India is still to experience cross-media ownership in its full form and is still considered to be at inception stage. TRAI had in its consultation paper made a point that cross-media ownership does not want to entertain central government keeping a check on them; on the contrary, states like Tamil Nadu and West Bengal have applied for state ownership of either television channels or signal distribution.[57] While bodies like the Delhi Union of Journalists have suggested dismantling of existing monopolies and cross-media empires, Times Television Network wants a ban on entry of lobbyists having association with public relations or political parties, religious bodies, urban and local administrative bodies, central government ministries and departments and central government–owned companies undertakings.[58] However, the Indian Newspaper Society is of the view that TRAI should not regulate the media sector as it would mean placing restrictions on the print media and TRAI does not have the ability or authorization to deal with any dispute that would arise from the print media sector. Certain advancements have been made in the cross-media sector where new rules have been brought forth, which propose to extend the direct-to-home licences around the industry for another 20 years and the licence fee tax has been reduced from 10% to 8%.[59]

In the face of poor economic situation of the country, the cross-media ownership restrictions seem to threaten the economies of scale they might otherwise promote. Thus, the rules for cross-media ownership should essentially aim at striking a balance between the following twin objects:

1 To ensure media pluralism
2 To provide freedom to companies to expand, innovate and invest

The first objective is vital for democracy, and the second one benefits citizens and consumers by providing a basis for delivering higher-quality programmes, greater creativity and more risk taking. In India, there is proliferation of publications, radio stations, television channels and Internet websites. It ensures one thing – plurality, diversity and consumer choice. Over 82,000 publications were registered with the Registrar of Newspapers as on 31 March 2011. There are over 250 FM radio stations in the country (and the number is likely to cross 1,200 in five years).[60] The Ministry of Information and Broadcasting has allowed nearly 800 television channels to uplink or downlink from the country, including over 300 that claim to be television channels broadcasting 'news and current affairs'. There is an unspecified number of websites aimed at Indians. But the number of registration and domination is not the same. The media scenario is dominated by fewer than 100 large groups or conglomerates, which exercise considerable influence on what is read, heard and watched, says Guha Thakurta. One example will illustrate this contention. Delhi is the only urban area in the world with 16 English daily newspapers; the top three publications, the *Times of India*, the *Hindustan Times*, and the *Economic Times*, would account for over three-fourths of the total market for all English dailies.[61]

Therefore, there is evidence of cross-media ownership in India, as indicated by TRAI and ASCI in their respective reports. This calls for formulation of rules for the same. There have been different views with respect to presence of cross-ownership rules. While some experts favour it, there are some who do not think that such rules are necessary. Many publishers and media owners will suffer from loss of ad revenue in case the regulations controlling cross-media ownership are brought forth. It also needs to be pointed out that media ownership should be confined to one jurisdiction only. If an individual owns a newspaper in one jurisdiction, he or she should not be allowed to own a television channel or a radio station in the same jurisdiction. However, the individual can own a channel in another jurisdiction.[62]

Many analysts and observers equate media pluralism with a diversity of ownership and that concentration of ownership will skew information and public discussion by not exploring all viewpoints and interests. In their view, this can lead to abuse of media power in political and policy decision-making. But there are others who express the view that cross-media ownership rules are outdated and think that media should not be controlled on an assumption that owners or stakeholders try to promote their agenda through the platforms. Some of the editors opined that news-savvy audiences are intelligent and well read. They can easily differentiate what is black, grey and white, and therefore the correctness of the news should be best left to the people and the masses.

The media ownership rules are designed to strike a balance between ensuring a degree of plurality on the one hand and providing freedom to companies to expand, innovate and invest on the other hand. The first is vital for democracy since plurality of ownership helps to ensure that citizens have access to a variety of sources of news, information and opinion.[63] Cross-media ownership allows the media houses to expand, and this ensures the cost of production to be low at the later stages. The cost of production is higher at the initial levels, and later in the whole process, it gets curbed down. Thus, it ensures efficiency and allows for economies of scope and scale. However, economies of scale are diminishing in today's world as the consumers get all the products at cost of transmission rather than cost of production. Cross-media conglomeration reduces competition and denies entry to newcomers. Fewer sources fill more outlets more of the time with ever more standardized fare. Alternative perspectives vanish from the mainstream.

Cross-media ownership, though prevalent in the foreign countries, has not found its place in the Indian territories. It has just penetrated due to foreign influence but has not received its dues. However, it has already made its advent and has been adopted by the media houses. They are traversing in both horizontal and vertical integration of media sector. But there has been a lot of governmental interference, and thus the media sectors want to do away with it. Various studies and surveys have been conducted and recommendations have been brought out by TRAI based on such research; however, nothing has been implemented in its entirety. One thing is very clear in conclusion. Cross-media ownership has a lot of scope for development in India, and if the working of the media houses can be in consonance with the media laws of the country, then it does have a brighter future.

Notes

1 Mehjabeen Jagmag, 'The Invisible Fourth Pillar', *Accountability Initiative, India*, accessed 26 July 2014, http://www.accountabilityindia.in/accountabilityblog/2557-invisible-fourth-pillar.

2 Telecom Regulatory Authority of India, 'Recommendations on Media Ownership', 2009, accessed 30 September 2013, http://www.trai.gov.in/WriteReadData/Recommendation/ Documents/recom25feb09.pdf.

3 *Merriam Webster*, 'Cross Ownership', accessed 11 September 2013, http://www.merriam-webster.com/dictionary/cross-ownership.

4 Vivekananda International Foundation, 'Cross Media Ownership: A Threat to Vibrant Democracy', accessed 2 February 2014, http://

www.vifindia.org/article/2013/august/22/cross-media-ownership-can-india-checkmake-it.

5 Hakan Bilir, 'Media Ownership Control – To What Extent Is Competition Law and Policy Sufficient to Provide for Diversity and Plurality in Media?', *Middle East Technical University*, accessed 10 September 2014, http://stps.metu.edu.tr/sites/stps.metu.edu.tr/files/0508.pdf.

6 Ibid.

7 Tim Dickinson, 'Why Economies of Scale Don't Matter in the Media Anymore', *TechFruit*, accessed 15 March 2014, http://techfruit.com/2012/02/21/why-economies-of-scale-dont-matter-in-the-media-anymore.

8 'Gains of Markets or Loss of Audiences Media Essay', *UK Essays*, accessed 10 September 2014, http://www.ukessays.com/essays/media/gain-of-markets-or-loss-of-audiences-media-essay.php.

9 Marc Bourreau, Michel Gensollen and Jerome Perani, 'Economies of Scale in the Media Industry', accessed 10 September 2014, http://www.gensollen.net/scale.pdf.

10 Anita Elberse, 'Should You Invest in the Long Tail?', 2008, accessed 10 September 2014, http://www.geminis.ufscar.br/wp-content/uploads/2009/05/shouldyouinvestinthelongtail.pdf.

11 Ibid.

12 Dickinson, 'Why Economies of Scale Don't Matter in the Media Anymore'.

13 Bilir, 'Media Ownership Control – To What Extent Is Competition Law and Policy Sufficient to Provide for Diversity and Plurality in Media?'.

14 Jagmag, 'The Invisible Fourth Pillar'.

15 Sanjay Gupta, 'Music World to Shut All Stores Due to Falling Margins', *The Economic Times* (13 June 2013), accessed 10 September 2014, http://articles.economictimes.indiatimes.com/2013-06-13/news/39952181_1_music-world-music-retailing-business-business-model.

16 Jagmag, 'The Invisible Fourth Pillar'.

17 Gillian Doyle, *Understanding Media Economics* (London: Sage, 2013): 17–18.

18 W. James Potter, *Arguing for a General Framework for Mass Media Scholarship* (Los Angeles: Sage, 2009): 65.

19 Ibid.

20 Dickinson, 'Why Economies of Scale Don't Matter in the Media Anymore'.

21 Bilir, 'Media Ownership Control – To What Extent Is Competition Law and Policy Sufficient to Provide for Diversity and Plurality in Media?'.

22 Poulami Chatterjee, 'Horizontal Merger Guidelines', accessed 10 September 2014, http://www.competitioncommission.gov.in/advocacy/HorrizontalMergerGuidelinesPoulami%20chatterjee09022007.pdf.

23 Frederick R. Warren-Boulton, 'The Contribution of the Merger Guidelines to the Analysis of Non-Horizontal Mergers', *United States Department of Justice Public Documents*, accessed 10 September 2014, http://www.justice.gov/atr/hmerger/11709.htm.

24 Ibid.

25 Robert Cooter and Thomas Ulen, *Law and Economics*, 6th ed. (New Delhi: Pearson Education, 2012): 114.
26 Anthony J. Pennings, 'Media Content as a Public Good', accessed 23 February 2014, http://apennings.com/technologies-of-meaning/the-move-to-smart-tv/.
27 Bilir, 'Media Ownership Control – To What Extent Is Competition Law and Policy Sufficient to Provide for Diversity and Plurality in Media?'.
28 Ibid.
29 Telecom Regulatory Authority of India, 'Recommendations on Media Ownership'.
30 Potter, *Arguing for a General Framework for Mass Media Scholarship*.
31 Ibid.
32 Enrico Adriano Raffaelli, 'Oligopolies and Anti-Trust Law', *Fordham International Law Journal*, The Berkeley Electronic Press, accessed 14 July 2014 at http://ir.lawnet.fordham.edu/cgi/viewcontent.cgi?article=1474&context=ilj.
33 Ibid.
34 Gillian Doyle, *Media Ownership: The Economics and Politics of Convergence and Concentration* (London: Sage Publications Ltd, 2002): 75–77.
35 Anne Kartin Arnold, 'Indirect Media Effects', *The World Bank Blog, People, Spaces, Deliberation*, accessed 2 February 2014, http://blogs.worldbank.org/publicsphere/indirect-media-effects-unknown-quantity-policy-making.
36 Jagmag, 'The Invisible Fourth Pillar'.
37 Ibid.
38 Jessica Weiss, 'Media Pluralism Divisive or Democratic', accessed 5 February 2014, https://ijnet.org/community/groups/10189/media-pluralism-divisive-or-democratic.
39 European Commission, Digital Agenda for Europe: A Europe 2020 Initiative, 'Media Freedom and Pluralism', accessed 8 February 2014, http://ec.europa.eu/digital-agenda/en/media-freedom-and-pluralism.
40 Serene Kasim, 'Media and Religious Identity in Contemporary India', accessed 20 September 2014, http://www.hivos.net/Hivos-Knowledge-Programme/Themes/Pluralism/Countries/India/Publications/Media-and-Religious-Identity-in-Contemporary-India.
41 Telecom Regulatory Authority of India, 'Recommendations on Media Ownership'.
42 Sharda Ugra, 'Big Brother BCCI's Watching!', *Economic and Political Weekly*, XLVIII, 2013, accessed 17 March 2014, http://www.epw.in/journal/2013/38/postscript/big-brother-bccis-watching.html.
43 *Prometheus Radio Project v. FCC*, 373 F.3d 372, 383 (3rd Cir. 2004).
44 Allan Brown, 'The Economics of Media Ownership', 1999, accessed 9 July 2014, http://www.pc.gov.au/inquiries/completed/broadcasting/submissions/sub152/sub152.pdf.
45 Herman, Edward S. and Robert W. McChesney, *The Global Media: The New Missionaries of Corporate Capitalism* (London: Cassell, 1997): 123.
46 *Prometheus Radio Project v. FCC*.

47 Ofcom, 'Media Ownership Rules Review', accessed 2 February 2014, http://stakeholders.ofcom.org.uk/binaries/consultations/morr/summary/morrcondoc.pdf.
48 Anne Kartin Arnold, 'Indirect Media Effects', *The World Bank Blog, People, Spaces, Deliberation*, accessed 2 February 2014, http://blogs.worldbank.org/publicsphere/indirect-media-effects-unknown-quantity-policy-making.
49 *Prometheus Radio Project v. FCC.*
50 ParamitaDasgupta, UshaRamachandra andAshitaAllamraju, 'Study on Cross Media Ownership in India (Draft Report)', 2009, accessed 20 July 2014, http://www.cablequest.org/pdfs/i_b/ASCI%20Cross%20Media%20ownership%20in%20India%202009.pdf.
51 'ASCI's Response to Comments Made by STAR India on the ASCI Report in STAR India's Submissions on the TRAI Consultation Paper on Issues Relating to Media Ownership', 2013, accessed 20 July 2014, http://www.trai.gov.in/WriteReadData/ConsultationPaper/Document/201305080305142594586Comments%20on%20Star%20Report.pdfhttp://www.trai.gov.in/WriteReadData/ConsultationPaper/Document/201305080305142594586Comments%20on%20Star%20Report.pdf.
52 Telecom Regulatory Authority of India, 'Recommendations on Media Ownership'.
53 Sashi Kumar, 'Cross Media Currents', accessed 1 August 2014, http://www.frontline.in/columns/Sashi_Kumar/cross-media-currents/article4478587.ece#.
54 Prashant Jha, 'Media Cross Holding in Cross Hairs', *The Hindu* (24 May 2013), accessed 10 September 2014, http://www.thehindu.com/todays-paper/tp-opinion/media-crossholding-in-cross-hairs/article4744594.ece.
55 Afaqs! News Bureau, 'How Will Cross Media Ownership Change the Rules of the Game', accessed 1 August 2014, http://www.afaqs.com/news/story/31324_The-Future-of-News-2011:-How-will-cross-media-ownership-change-the-rules-of-the-game.
56 Ibid.
57 Rahul Khullar, 'TRAI Recommendation on Media and Ownership Including Cross-Media Issues Expected Next Month', accessed 23 July 2014, http://www.indiantelevision.com/regulators/trai/trai-recommendation-on-media-and-ownership-including-cross-media-issues-expected-next-month-140723.
58 Khullar, 'TRAI Recommendation on Media and Ownership Including Cross-Media Issues Expected Next Month'.
59 Asia-Pacific Broadcasting Union, 'India Proposes New Cross Media Ownership Rules', accessed 2 August 2014, http://www.abu.org.my/Latest_News-@-India_proposes_new_cross-media_ownership_rules.aspx.
60 Khullar, 'TRAI Recommendation on Media and Ownership Including Cross-Media Issues Expected Next Month'.
61 Shivaji Sarkar, 'Cross Media Ownership: A Threat to Vibrant Democracy', accessed 2 February 2014, http://www.vifindia.org/article/2013/august/22/cross-media-ownership-can-india-checkmake-it.

62 Abhinav Trivedi, 'Cross Media Ownership – Monopoly or Market Demand?', accessed 3 February 2014, http://www.exchange4media.com/51597_cross-media-ownership-%E2%80%93-monopoly-or-market-demand-debate-continues.html.

63 Rahul Khullar, 'TRAI Recommendation on Media Control and Ownership by August', accessed 2 February 2014, http://www.firstpost.com/india/trai-recommendation-media-control-ownership-august-1631111.html.

Chapter 15

Comparative advertising

Case analysis of *Colgate Palmolive v. Hindustan Unilever Ltd*

Shivansh Agarwal and Ifrah Shaikh

Background note

Advertising, undoubtedly, has emerged as one of the main aspects of marketing today. In a market where the consumer is spoilt for choices, all firms try to play on consumer psychology in order to attract more and more customers. One way by which they manage to tap the market is through an aggressive advertisement campaign which figures most prominently on their marketing agenda. The people who argue in favour of advertising say that it is a necessary evil, helping firms publicize their products and helping buyers make informed choices. Considering the diverse market for products today, especially fast-moving consumer goods (FMCGs), this proposition indeed tends to hold credence. However, more often than not, these ad campaigns turn into major advertisement wars between monopolistic and oligopolistic firms. In this chapter, the authors have focused on comparative advertising as an efficient tool of marketing and have analysed the efficiency of the same in the light of the highly publicized case, *Colgate Palmolive v. Hindustan Unilever*. The chapter analyses comparative advertising on the basis of sound principles of law and economics and concludes by answering the question as to whether the judgement in the aforementioned case is proficient from a law and economics standpoint.

The Pepsodent–Colgate advertisement war started on 9 August 2013 with the release of Pepsodent's latest advertisement, which claimed, in its ad, that Pepsodent provided 130% better protection than Colgate. This led Colgate to file a case in Delhi High Court on 13 August 2013. The court did not uphold the claim of Pepsodent having denigrated Colgate and said that the ad was in no way a deliberate attempt by Hindustan Unilever to portray Colgate in a negative light. Further, the Delhi High Court by its judgement dated 21 August 2013 dismissed the injunction petition filed by Colgate against Pepsodent. The facts of the case and the judgement that the court arrived at are as follows.

Facts of the case

Colgate Palmolive (India) Ltd ('Colgate') filed a suit against Hindustan Unilever Ltd ('HUL') on 13 August 2013 for an interim injunction. HUL had launched its PepsodentGermicheck's germ attack power with Colgate Strong Teeth, claiming that PepsodentGermicheck has '130% superior' germ attack power over Colgate Strong Teeth after four hours of brushing. Colgate claimed an interim injunction on the following grounds:

1 The claim made by HUL that PepsodentGermicheck had 130% attack power was a false statement and in violation of several provisions of the Code of Advertising Standards Council of India, 1985 (ASCI), as well as the Drugs and Cosmetics Act, 1940, as it amounted to 'misbranding'.
2 The television commercial commenced on 9 August 2013, and the print advertisement appeared on the front page of the Delhi edition of *Hindustan Times* dated 11 August 2013, portraying the bad image of Colgate's product and falsely conveying that the use of Colgate could cause cavities. The advertisements were viewed in the court several times during the course of arguments, and the observation made was that the television commercial portrays that Triclosan, an ingredient in Pepsodent, stays in the mouth for four hours after brushing and qualifies a 'preventive cavity test'. But Colgate contended that no such test exists in the world. Then again, the Colgate Boy was shown brushing his teeth in an improper manner, whose teeth had cavities and he seemed to be unhappy, which implies that Colgate's toothpaste could cause cavities.
3 Colgate contended that HUL's past record showed that HUL has made a habit of introducing false and misleading advertisements and increasing its market share dishonestly. It had a history of making false claims in respect of its products.
4 It was argued that the words 'Pepsodent now better than Colgate Strong Teeth' in the print advertisement were meant to convey that Colgate Strong Teeth was no longer a good product.

Also, the word 'Attaaaack' used in the ad was an attack on Colgate and not on the cavity-causing germs.

5 Colgate apprehended a loss of market share if HUL was not restrained from circulating these ads.

The submissions made by HUL in reply to the case filed were as follows:

1 In this regard, the decision in *Dabur India Limited v. Colortek Meghalaya Pvt. Ltd*[1] was cited to show that the courts have allowed comparative advertising.
2 HUL requested the court not to treat the advertisement as some sort of breach of agreement as its intention was not to misbrand Colgate.
3 Furthermore, HUL submitted that using the name of Colgate in the advertisement was to portray it as a premium product and compare Pepsodent to it accordingly. Moreover, HUL's main aim was to compete with Colgate in the price segment.

Judgement

On the basis of the judgements given in the earlier cases such as *Dabur India Ltd v. Colortek Meghalaya Pvt. Ltd* and *Reckitt and Colman of India Ltd v. M.P. Ramchandran and Anr.*,[2] the Hon'ble Court dismissed the case by saying that HUL is not denigrating the product of Colgate. It said that it is unable to identify any unfairness in this practice that may attract the clauses of the ASCI Code. Comparative advertising is permissible as long as the competitor's product is not denigrated or defamed. In the case *Dabur India Ltd v. Colortek Meghalaya Pvt. Ltd*, it was held that certain factors have to be kept in mind while describing a question of disparagement. These factors are:

- Intent of the commercial
- Manner of the commercial
- Storyline of the commercial and the message sought to be conveyed

Further, in the case *Reckitt and Colman of India Ltd v. M.P. Ramachandran and Anr.*, it was held that

1 a seller is entitled to declare his goods to be best in the world, even though his statement is not true;
2 he can say that his goods are better than his competitor's goods, even though his statement is not true;
3 he can compare the advantages of his goods over the goods of others;
4 however, he cannot say that his competitor's goods are bad.

According to the court 'too much could not be read into the expressions of each individual character in the advertisements'. The expressions and effects used in the advertisement only showed that Pepsodent was a better product but did not disparage Colgate's product. Also, the court said that as there is a comparison of products and an attempt to show that one is better than the other, obviously 'both boys cannot have happy faces'. Also, the court held that the word 'attack' in the print was related to Pepsodent's germ-fighting capability and was not an attack on Colgate.

Before proceeding onto the economic analysis of the case, it is important to state what the Advertising Standards Council of India says on comparative advertising. The ASCI has adopted a code in 1985 for self-regulation in advertising. It is a commitment to honest advertising and to fair competition in the market place. ASCI Code deals with the various provisions pertaining to advertisements. Colgate claimed that HUL has violated the provisions of Chapter IV of the ASCI Code. Chapter IV of the code is regarding the fairness in competition. The broad aspects covered by it are as follows:

1 Advertisements containing comparisons with other manufacturers or suppliers or with other products including those where a competitor is named are permissible in the interests of vigorous competition and public enlightenment, provided:
   a It is clear what aspects of the advertiser's product are being compared with what aspects of the competitor's product.
   b The subject matter of comparison is not chosen in such a way so as to confer an artificial advantage upon the advertiser or so as to suggest that a better bargain is offered than is truly the case.
   c The comparisons are factual, accurate and capable of substantiation.

- d There is no likelihood of the consumer being misled as a result of the comparison, whether about the product advertised or that with which it is compared.
- e The advertisement does not unfairly denigrate, attack or discredit other products, advertisers or advertisements, directly or by implication.

2 Advertisements shall not make unjustifiable use of the name or initials of any other firm, company or institution, nor take unfair advantage of the goodwill attached to the trademark or symbol of another firm or its product or the goodwill acquired by its advertising campaign.

3 Advertisements shall not be similar to any other advertiser's earlier-run advertisements in general layout, copy, slogans, visual presentations, music or sound effects, so as to suggest plagiarism.

4 As regards matters covered by sections 2 and 3, complaints of plagiarism of advertisements released earlier abroad will lie outside the scope of this Code except in the under-mentioned circumstances:

- a The complaint is lodged within 12 months of the first general circulation of the advertisements/campaign complained against.
- b The complainant provides substantiation regarding the claim of prior invention/usage abroad.

The court kept in mind all these principles before arriving at the judgement of the case. The court held that there is no denigration of Colgate as a brand. The advertisement just holds Pepsodent to be a superior product. It is not saying explicitly that Colgate is an inferior product. Hence, the court says that it cannot be concluded that Hindustan Unilever is trying to disgrace Colgate as a brand. However, in the earlier judgement of *Tata Press Ltd v. MTNL*,[3] the Supreme Court opined that it is not good to declare one's own goods to be the best and/or better than his competitors', but if a party does so, then the advertiser must have some reasonable factual basis for the assertion made. The Federal Trade Commission of the United States has defined comparative advertising as 'advertisement that compares alternative brands on objectively measurable attributes or price, and identifies the alternative brand by name, illustration or other distinctive information'.[4]

Economic analysis

Efficiency of judiciary

In this chapter, it has been assumed that the judiciary of a country functions reasonably efficiently. In litigations concerning comparative advertising, various claims are made at various stages of the proceedings, and it is up to the court to determine what claim to allow and what claim to reject. These involve considerable use of time and other resources, as it may be very difficult to determine the exactness of the claim made, and whether it is technically and monetarily feasible.

The model presented in this chapter shows that with efficient courts that are able to obtain precise information about the entrant's product quality and are willing to impose damages, comparative advertising should be a widely used marketing instrument. In spite of some researchers in marketing being cautious about the general effectiveness of comparative advertising, the marketing literature agrees that if a brand has a small market share, or is unfamiliar to

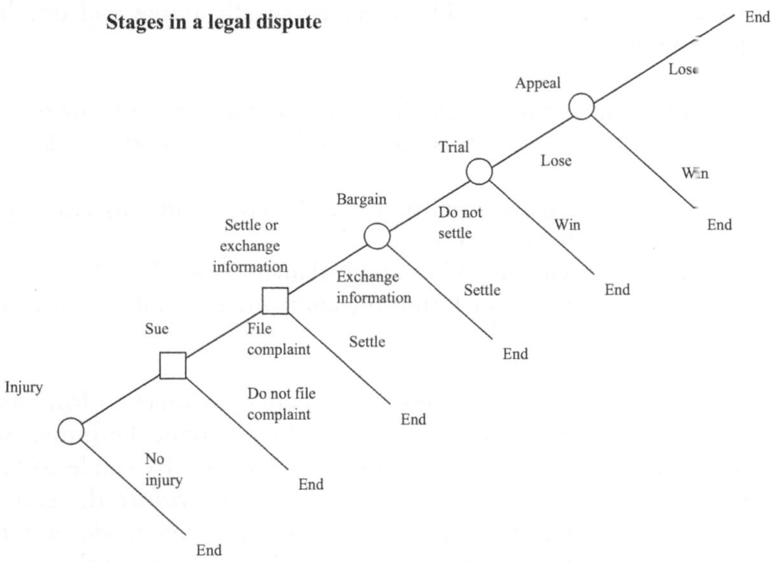

Figure 15.1 Stages in a legal dispute

Source: Robert Cooter and Thomas Ulen, *Law and Economics*, 6th ed. (Boston, MA: Pearson Education, 2012): 383.

buyers, it can enhance the relevance of an ad by naming a leading brand, which is regularly purchased or is familiar to consumers.[5] For example, according to Mitsubishi's marketing manager, the company used comparative advertising when entering the European market, 'to guide the consumer by making associations with top brand names'.

First and foremost, the parties involved in the dispute should decide what exactly their expectations from the litigation are. The first, most important, task of a company facing a dispute (in conjunction with the attorneys handling that dispute) is to determine reasonable goals and expectations for the outcome of the dispute. This is not always an easy process. Indeed, in many instances attorneys are faced with clients who have unreasonable expectations and unreachable goals in addressing comparative advertising conflicts. However, these issues can be far more easily overcome if they are identified and addressed early.[6] Specifically, advertisers (or those companies challenging a competitor's comparative advertising) should identify the range of acceptable outcomes of the dispute. The following questions would further streamline the process of dispute settlement and reduce avoidable deadweight unallocated losses, if the parties are able to unequivocally frame and decide upon the following questions:

- If the company is challenging the comparative advertising of its competitors, does that company seek only to modify or clarify the advertising?
- Does the company seek to force the competitor to cease its advertising in its entirety?
- Has there been real and provable damage caused by the advertising in question, such that the company is seeking monetary damages?

The answers to these questions would help companies to form an effective roadmap (as shown in Figure 15.1), about the future of the litigation which would significantly reduce the avoidable costs. During the litigation, important questions arise before the court pertaining to whether the claims and counterclaims made by the parties are substantially correct in nature. For instance, in the present case *Colgate Palmolive India (Ltd) v. Hindustan Unilever Limited*, the defendants claimed that their toothpaste has the chemical substance called Triclosan, which stays in the mouth for four hours, even after brushing the teeth, and hence provides better protection against germs and cavities. Colgate made a counterclaim saying that no such test exists in the world to determine such claim.

Now it is up to the court to determine whether this claim substantially affects the proceedings; if yes, then it must appoint an independent body, which is technologically and scientifically proficient, and verify this claim. This is a laborious process, and it may take some time for the court to appoint such a body and for this body to come up with its detailed report after a thorough investigation. In this time, the litigant may incur a lot of monetary loss because of any potential loss of sales, as an alleged direct result of the impugned advertisement. An option before the court may be to grant a temporary injunction against the circulation of this advertisement. Again, the injunction order, if passed, would impose additional costs on the advertising agency, as it would not be able to recover the advertisement costs through sales. Also, it would be unjust if the advertisement is found not to contain any derogatory substance; this cost of injunction would go unallocated, and this may act as a deterrent in the future for companies to go for comparative advertising, in its true sense, for achieving perfect information in the market for ensuring a more competitive environment. Due to this, the authors respectfully submit that Indian courts should, in the ordinary course, refrain from granting such injunctions The main aim should be to hasten judicial proceedings and reduce all the extra costs, which can be easily mitigated.

The basic underlying point behind the judgement should be to increase overall information and competitiveness, as was done in this judgement. This would simultaneously ensure that some ongoing harm, if any, would be stopped as early as possible. This would essentially ensure a Pareto efficient outcome, with parties gaining through sales, the market gaining due to perfect information and the consumers gaining through cheaper prices caused by the resultant competition and technology. The so-called victim of the comparative advertisement would have to improve its own product and incorporate better technology, to come up with a better product, which would enhance its sales and would be beneficial for consumers as well. So essentially, if the parties in the litigation are clear on what exactly they want out of the litigation, the litigation itself would become more efficient. They should not brazenly go to court to compel the competitor to stop its impugned advertisement and pay damages. They should do so only when they are convinced that their product is superior to the competitor's, and the claim made in the impugned advertisement is patently wrong and must be rectified as soon as possible. Damages, if any, should be left to the wisdom of the court to decide. The court, in turn, should dispose of these matters in a very fast and decisive manner, keeping in mind the principles of perfect competition and perfect information.

With the clear verdict in the case which was delivered at a reasonably quick pace, the courts have cleared the stage for more comparative advertising, in which the companies should be careful not to denigrate or defame the other product, which would lead to more competitive markets, and since the number of such instances is bound to increase. This landmark decision can be seen as a set precedent, which would lead to a lessened number of future lawsuits, hence increasing the efficiency of both the judiciary and the markets.

Game-theoretical perspective

Game theory revolves around strategic decision-making involving two or more players. The decisions made by a particular player will affect the potential interests of other players as well. Game theory focuses on conflict and cooperation.[7] It is an offshoot of the negotiation theory whose crux lies in how negotiation is an all-pervasive concept inherent in any interaction between persons, whether natural or artificial. In the case of firms, depending on the type of market they operate in, the actions taken by rival firms are more or less interdependent. In the case of an oligopoly, intense interfirm competition exists, which frequently results in heavy price cutting and aggressive ad wars. The oligopolists generally face an indeterminate demand curve as each and every action taken by one firm produces an equal and opposite reaction by the other firm. Considering the market for FMCGs like toothpaste in this case, the market is characterized by oligopolistic features. Looking at interfirm interaction from a game-theoretical perspective thus becomes very important. In a game theory model, every player undertakes a particular strategy, which is one of the given possible actions of the player.[8] Each strategy results in a particular pay-off to the player, which is the utility derived out of choosing a particular strategy.

This chapter deals with comparative advertising wherein we attempt to provide an efficiency analysis of the same by using the case of *Colgate Palmolive* v. *Hindustan Unilever* as an example. In a market where a few firms have market power, a strong interfirm rivalry in terms of cost-cutting and marketing strategies is bound to exist. Advertising becomes integral in such a situation. Firms opt either for generic advertising, which involves advertising one's own product only, or for comparative advertising, which again forks into comparative price advertising and comparative non-price advertising. In a market characterized by heavy interfirm interaction, a particular firm may or may not disclose all details about its product. Taking comparative advertising into account, the firm discloses attributes of its products and at the same time differentiates between the horizontal attributes of its own product and that of the rival. In the case of comparative price advertising, price becomes the distinguished feature, whereas in the case of comparative non-price advertising, the focus lies more on informing the consumers about the quality of the product. Comparative advertising, especially comparative non-price advertising, increases product differentiation as a result of which the firm whose product is being used as a comparison has to reduce its price so as to prevent consumers from deflecting towards the rival brand. Price reduction in the case of comparative non-price advertising is more than what it is in the case of comparative price advertising. Given here is the game-theoretical model that supports the contention of why firms will opt for comparative advertising in a given competitive environment.

In our game-theoretical model, we take the case of two well-established firms operating in an oligopolistic market, namely Firm 1 and Firm 2. For the sake of simplicity, we shall consider the case of just two firms in the market, which technically makes it a duopoly, but the decisions taken by each will be the same as that of an oligopolistic firm as duopoly is an offshoot of oligopoly. Let us say that Firm 1 manufactures a product of a certain quality q1. Firm 2 manufactures a homogeneous product of a particular quality q2. It is to be noted that these two products are close substitutes and not perfect substitutes of each other. Consumer expectations for Firm 1's product quality are denoted by qc and expectations for Firm 2's product quality are denoted by qc1. But before enumerating the strategies of both the firms and declaring their pay-offs, certain necessary assumptions need to be highlighted:

1 Both the firms, that is Firm 1 and Firm 2, do not know of each other's product quality or the type of technology used by the

rival firm. However, both firms do have perfect information about consumer expectations regarding quality of both products. That is Firm 1 is ignorant of q2 and Firm 2 is ignorant of q1. However, Firm 1 not only has knowledge of qc (consumer expectations regarding its own product quality) but also possesses information about qc1. Similarly, Firm 2 has information about both qc and qc1.
2. Consumers in the given market do not have rigid tastes and preferences. They are rational and will choose only that product which gives them the maximum utility.
3. Advertising has a considerable influence over consumer psychology.
4. Comparative advertising for the purpose of this model means only comparative non-price advertising.
5. The firms are not risk averse and make decisions on the basis of probabilistic events.
6. The product quality of both firms is high even though consumer expectations regarding the said quality might be different.
7. Firms advertise about their product truthfully.

Assumption 2 highlights the fundamental principle of *rational choice theory*. Given the aforementioned assumptions, both the firms have a couple of strategies available. Strategy 1 is comparative advertising. Strategy 2 is non-comparative advertising. Now let us discuss the various outcomes when both firms choose either Strategy 1 or 2.

If Firm 1 chooses comparative advertising as its marketing strategy and so does Firm 2, then overall product differentiation in the market will increase, and since both the firms have compared each other's product, both will be induced to reduce prices in order to retain consumers. This reduction in prices will enable new consumers, who previously could not afford to buy the product at the prevailing price, to enter the market, which will lead to an increase in market share of both the firms. This will result in a win–win scenario for both firms and will also increase overall welfare in the economy as consumers are able to avail the products at lower prices, thereby increasing their utility. Thus, both firms face a pay-off of [2, 2].

If Firm 1 chooses comparative advertising as its strategy and Firm 2 decides to opt for non-comparative advertising, then Firm 1 will manage to increase its market share by luring more consumers towards its brand but will also face litigation costs if Firm 2 decides to litigate. If we assume profits made out of comparative advertising to be higher than advertising costs and cost of litigation, Firm 1 stands in a favourable position although it would have preferred not facing any litigation costs at all. Hence, the pay-off to Firm 1 is [1]. Firm 2 on the other hand stands to risk the chance of losing consumers due to comparative advertising, and in order to avoid that, it is compelled to reduce its product price, thereby lowering profits. If it opts for litigation, it will face litigation costs and will recover its losses only if the courts decide to grant it compensation. Hence, overall, Firm 2 is put in an unfavourable position due to which it faces a pay-off of [–1]. If Firm 2 opts for comparative advertising whereas Firm 1 goes for non-comparative advertising, then Firm 1 will have a pay-off of [–1] and Firm 2 will have a pay-off of [1] for the reasons elucidated earlier.

If both the firms decide to choose non-comparative advertising, then their actions, although still independent by virtue of being in an oligopolistic market, are neutral with regard to each other. Hence, they face a pay-off of [0, 0]. Figure 15.2 is a pay-off matrix for both the firms.

Earlier, we analysed the various outcomes and the resultant pay-offs for both the firms when they choose either strategy. Using the *incentive analysis* approach, let us derive the dominant strategy for both the firms. In a general context, a firm is hurt by information disclosure of its product.[9] If a firm knows that the quality of its rival brand is low, it is encouraged to provide that information

	Firm 1	
Firm 2	Comparative advertising	Non-comparative advertising
Comparative advertising	2; 2	–1; 1
Non-comparative advertising	1; –1	0; 0

Figure 15.2 Pay-off matrix for two firms' advertising strategy in an oligopolistic market

Source: Author's own compilation.

to the consumers through comparative advertising.[10] However, in the aforementioned model, we have assumed that a firm is unaware of the quality of its rival's product but does have knowledge about the consumer expectations regarding its rival's product quality. For example, if Firm 1 knows that consumer expectations regarding Firm 2's product quality are high, then Firm 1 would choose comparative advertising as a marketing strategy to show that its product is better than even that of Firm 2's product which is perceived to be of high quality by the consumers. On the other hand, if Firm 1 knows that the consumer expectations regarding Firm 2's product quality are low, then Firm 1 would want to uphold that public psychology by opting for comparative advertising and declaring that its product is way better than that of Firm 2. Thus, in both cases, Firm 1 would opt for comparative advertising. This is irrespective of Firm 1's knowledge about consumer expectations regarding its own product quality. Firm 2 will also apply the same reasoning and hence choose comparative advertising as its dominant strategy. Further, both firms also know that each will apply the same reasoning and choose comparative advertising as a strategy that gives each firm the maximum pay-off, and thus, no firm has an incentive to deviate from the dominant strategy.

Thus, ultimately, both the firms will choose comparative advertising, which will give them a pay-off of [2, 2] rendering them in a *Nash equilibrium* as they do not have any reason or incentive to choose another strategy. This equilibrium is also *Pareto efficient* as it results in maximum pay-offs for both the firms. The same result is supported by a graph based on the application of an indifference curve. Let us consider a firm whose utility function is defined by two goods, namely price and market share. An indifference curve shows all possible combinations of two goods that give maximum utility to a consumer. In this case, the indifference curve depicts all possible combinations of price and market share that give the same satisfaction to the firm. The downward sloping shape of the indifference curve represents a trade-off between the two goods and also shows that the firm is willing to let go of price for market share and vice versa. Given in Figure 15.3 is a graph depicting the same.

As seen in Figure 15.3, price is represented on the x-axis and market share on the y-axis. The original indifference curve is $IC_{1,}$ with point A being a point on the indifference curve showing the combination of both the goods that give the same utility to the firm. The original price charged by the firm, say, Firm 1 for its

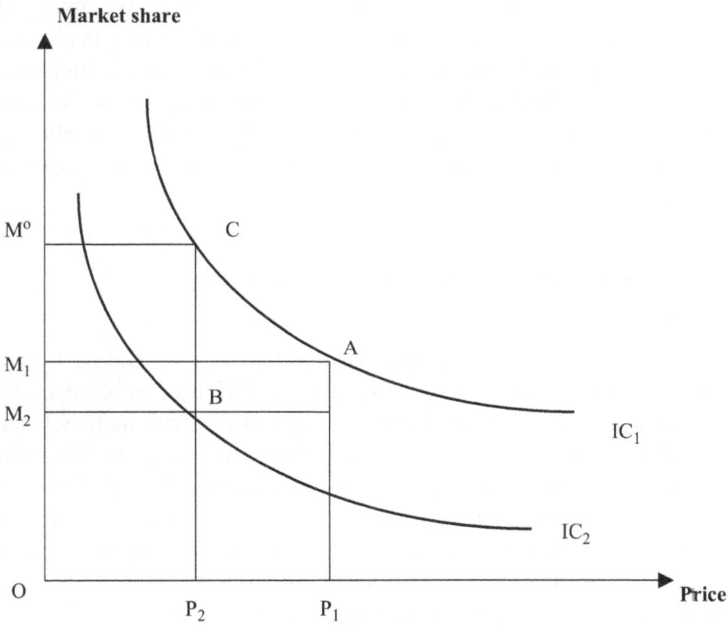

Figure 15.3 Indifference curve trade-off between market share and price

Source: Author's own compilation.

product is OP_1 and the original market share is OM_1. Now suppose another rival firm in the market, say, Firm 2, opts for comparative advertising wherein it shows its product in a more favourable light as compared to Firm 1, then Firm 1 will have to reduce its price as a result of increased product differentiation. It will reduce its price so as to retain its consumers. Thus, the price now becomes OP_2. However, there will be consumers who prefer quality over price and hence will deflect towards Firm 2, causing a loss in market share to Firm 1. The new market share is now OM_2. OP_2 and OM_2 correspond to point Q on the indifference curve IC_2. Assuming that the price level cannot be increased by Firm 1 as it will lead to reduction in demand, the only option that Firm 1 has in order to restore its original utility on IC_1 is to increase its market share. Considering that Firm 1 is a well-established firm operating in an oligopolistic market, it is already into advertising its product. Thus, in order to increase its market share now, it has to devise a different marketing strategy, which will be comparative advertising. By opting for comparative advertising, it can publicize its product in a favourable light as compared to the rival firm's products, thereby increasing market share to OM°. Thus, in the face of one firm opting for comparative advertising, it will be economically efficient for the firm whose product is being compared to opt for comparative advertising as well.

Alternate dispute resolution in comparative advertising

An effective way of reducing the costs to be borne by the parties can be found in alternative dispute resolution (ADR) mechanisms like mediation and arbitration. Important questions arise as to whether these alternative solutions actually reduce the costs, whether they should be legal in the country's judicial framework and if they are allowed, what impact would these have on the minds of the consumers about these products. These questions would be discussed in the context of efficient outcomes by the application of Coase Theorem and competitiveness in the market.

Coase Theorem is defined as follows: 'When transaction costs are zero, an efficient use of resources results from private bargaining, regardless of the legal assignment of property rights'.[11] For a more detailed understanding, when one activity interferes with another, the law must decide whether one party has the right to interfere or whether the other party has the right to be free from interference. Efficiency requires allocating the right to the party that values it the most. When the parties follow the law non-cooperatively, the legal allocation of rights does not matter to efficiency. When the parties bargain successfully, the legal allocation of rights does not matter to efficiency. Given successful bargaining, the use of resources is efficient, regardless of the legal rule.[12]

All this is true only when the transaction costs are theoretically equivalent to zero, and it can be assumed that for practical real-world application, efforts must be made so that these transaction costs must be as close to zero as possible. It would be worthwhile for the parties to make this effort, as the final outcome, if efficient, would save much more money and resources, compared to the amount of resources spent in this effort to save transaction costs.

In the present case of comparative advertising, the transaction costs, which would act as barriers to the two rival parties coming together to negotiate, would include selective perception in making evaluations, wrong baselines, gaps in information, anger and embarrassment, preoccupation with winning: ego and market perception.[13]

Mediation

In a mediation procedure, a neutral intermediary, the mediator, helps the parties to reach a mutually satisfactory settlement of their dispute. Any settlement is recorded in an enforceable contract. Experience shows that intellectual property litigation often ends in settlement. Mediation is an efficient and cost-effective way of achieving that result while preserving, and at times even enhancing, the relationship of the parties.[14] The principal characteristics of mediation are as follows:

- Mediation is a non-binding procedure controlled by the parties. A party to a mediation cannot be forced to accept an outcome that it does not like.
- Mediation is a confidential procedure. In a mediation, the parties cannot be compelled to disclose information that they prefer to keep confidential. Mediation's confidentiality allows the parties to negotiate more freely and productively, without fear of publicity.
- Mediation is an interest-based procedure. In court litigation or arbitration, the outcome of a case is determined by the facts of the dispute and the applicable law. In a mediation, the parties can also be guided by their business interests. Therefore, the parties are free to choose an outcome that is oriented as much to the future of their business relationship as to their past conduct.

When the parties refer to their interests and engage in dialogue, mediation often results in a settlement that creates more value than would have been created if the underlying dispute had not occurred. Because mediation is non-binding and confidential, it involves minimal risk for the parties and generates significant benefits. Indeed, one could say that even when a settlement is not achieved, mediation never fails, as it causes the parties to define the facts and issues of the dispute, thus in any event preparing the ground for subsequent arbitration or court proceedings. Mediation is often used in conjunction with litigation. After a lawsuit has been filed, the judge, recognizing that settlement may be preferable to spending an enormous amount of money on discovery and the rest of the litigation process, can push the parties into mediation. It can often be helpful to get a clear-eyed third-party view of the case early on in the proceedings – a view that often enables the litigants to reevaluate where they stand.[15]

Arbitration

Another method of ADR parties can engage in is arbitration. Arbitration combines many of the attributes of litigation with many of the attributes of mediation. Arbitration generally is binding – the decision of the arbitrator or the panel of arbitrators can generally be enforced in a court of law. The parties, however, agree upon the process by which the determination will be made. The parties can agree to limit discovery and generally have some discretion over the choice of the arbitrators to decide the dispute in question.[16] In theory, the advantage of arbitration is that it can be less expensive than full-scale litigation. Because the parties have the discretion to limit the proceedings and limit the discovery, it can be a less expensive way of proceeding to a final decision.

In many instances, however, the goal of reducing costs is not met. Unless the parties are meticulous in crafting the specifics of the procedure to be used, the arbitrator has enormous discretion in determining what amount of discovery and/or hearing preparation is necessary. In addition, appealing an arbitrator's decision can often be more difficult than appealing a decision of a court. Courts generally uphold the decisions of arbitrators – even when those decisions may be unsupported – based on the theory that the parties have agreed that the arbitrator's decision shall be final, until and unless the award is contrary to the Public Policy of India, against the interest of India, against justice or morality, or is patently illegal.[17] By contrast, while trial judges have a significant amount of discretion, their decisions are nonetheless subject to review in the appellate courts. As a result, if parties decide to submit themselves to arbitration, they would be wise to outline in significant detail the procedures and procedural limitations to be employed in the dispute resolution process.

The difference between mediation and arbitration is that mediation is a voluntary dispute resolution process; all parties must consent to participate in good faith and work toward a mutually agreeable resolution. Mediating parties are not bound to resolve their dispute (although mediated settlements, once reached, can be made binding if the parties decide to draft a contract called a settlement agreement). Mediations are not 'decided' in favour of one party or another; rather, the mediator simply facilitates the negotiation process. In evaluative mediation, the mediator will counsel parties on the strengths and weaknesses of their case and gauge each party's likelihood of success if the dispute proceeds to arbitration or litigation. Arbitration, on the other hand, is a dispute resolution process in which a neutral party (the arbitrator) hears a dispute between one or more parties and, after considering all relevant information, renders a final decision in favour of one of the parties. Arbitration decisions may be either binding or non-binding, depending on the terms of the arbitration agreement. Binding arbitration decisions may be confirmed by a court and carry the same significance as a court judgement.[18]

Impact of ADR on sales and on consumers

An important aspect to consider in respect of these internal settlements, which are legal when the issue involved is of a civil nature, is their impact on the consumers. Of course, the assumption is that at first, there was a disputed advertisement, and later there was some form of dispute settlement that took place. Since in this case there are only two dominant firms in the market, Colgate and HUL, any sort of internal dispute resolution between them may be perceived as an indication of collusion between these two firms. The aim of the advertisement by one firm was meant to highlight the differences between the products of their firm compared to the other firm, and to emphasize upon the superiority of one's product over the other (of course without disparaging the other's product).

Product sales = category sales × market share,[19] which implies that sales can be improved by increasing category sales, that is the primary consumer demand itself, or by increasing the market share. Primary consumer demand can be increased by way of generic advertising. The goal of generic advertising is to increase the primary demand (i.e. the size of the pie) of a product without influencing the market share of any one producer. Generic advertising is

Table 15.1 Impact of ADR on the sales of the competitors

	Firm's product	*Competitor's product*
Sales before advertisement	X	Y
Sales after advertisement	X + S	Y – R
Sales after ADR	X + (S – R)	Y

Source: Author's own compilation.

designed to enhance category beliefs, increase across category differentiation and reduce the advertised category's price elasticity.[20] Operationally, generic advertising generates new sales by targeting beliefs about the product category while downplaying or oftentimes not mentioning the sponsoring brand. In contrast, brand advertising provided consumers with information about the brand's value proposition that differentiates it from its competitors, thereby encouraging consumers to choose the advertised brand over competing brands.[21] Comparative advertising on the other hand is, in the authors' view, essentially a form of brand advertising with traces of generic advertising, where the firm aims to increase its market share (i.e. the size of its slice), by directly comparing its product with the competitor's, and as the product information is increased in the market because of this exercise, the market consumer demand itself rises (i.e. the size of the pie), but this is not very significant, as the main aim of the firm is not this.

The respective sales have been explained in Table 15.1.

Assumptions

1 There is a dispute regarding the advertisement; if there is no dispute, there is no need for any sort of dispute resolution.
2 It is implicit that the firm not opting for comparative advertising undergoes a loss in sales or else there would arise no dispute. We denote this loss in sales as R.
3 Also, a dispute between the two firms will arise only in case of a pecuniary loss suffered by the firm not opting for comparative advertising. Any loss in reputation of the brand image or the product is not quantifiable and hence not considered.
4 There are some consumers in the market who possess strong brand loyalty. There are others whose tastes and preferences are

prone to be influenced by advertisements. The loss R is a result of the consumers' diverting from Firm Y towards Firm X.

Now the firm not opting for comparative advertising and suffering a loss equivalent to R should be made good the loss by the amount R. This is in consonance with the Kaldor–Hicks efficiency criterion, which states that anyone made better off due to a particular outcome should compensate those who were made worse off by the operation of that same outcome. However, there also might be a situation where R is much greater than S, in which case only litigation would make sense, as the loss R would not be covered by S, causing more loss to the firm opting for comparative advertising, in addition to its advertising costs. The difference between S and R should be large enough for a suitable ADR mechanism. If R is only nominally less than S, the firm opting for comparative advertising will choose to litigate rather than go for ADR, as after compensating the other firm for its loss (i.e. R), its benefit will be less than the advertisement costs, thus acting as a disincentive for it to go for ADR. As we can see from the table, sales of both the firms are comparatively better off than the other, than they both were before the advertisement, as a result of the ADR mechanism. Though the sales of Y come back to the original level as they were, this outcome achieved through ADR mechanisms is essentially better than litigation mechanisms, as the exorbitant litigation costs are avoided altogether, and also, the continued damage to the brand in case of awaiting the verdict of the court is avoided.

Decreasing information asymmetry and increasing competition

The authors assert that competitive advertising, when not denigrating the product of the other company, is in the interest of the market and the consumers. These advertisements lead to a better-off situation where the consumers are better aware of the products they use and how these are better compared to the competitor's product. If there are any litigations and disputes involved, it is highly unlikely that the consumer would come to know about the proceedings, and the nitty-gritties of the investigations, or matter discussed in closed-door ADR meetings. The consumer would come to know only about the final outcome of the deliberations. If it is a verdict of a court, then the message would be clear-cut, and the consumers would come to know about the correctness of the claims and defences of each company. In case of out-of-court settlements, the settlement would be done by the companies and the exact terms and conditions will not be publicized, and thus, the consumer's choice is likely to be not affected, as he or she would not know about the compromises made by the companies. This does not mean that the claims and counterclaims made were totally false; it is just that compromises made during the negotiations were in the interest of all interested parties, thus reducing social costs and increasing social welfare.

Conclusion

Much conjecture remains on the use of comparative advertising by firms as a device to increase their sales. Out of the various options available, firms can choose either comparative or non-comparative advertising. These two branches further fork into comparative price and non-price advertising and non-comparative price and non-price advertising. In our chapter, except for the game-theoretical perspective, we have considered comparative advertising in both its forms. The crux of the chapter lies in determining whether comparative advertising is efficient from a law and economics standpoint and whether the judgement passed in *Colgate Palmolive* v. *Hindustan Unilever*, which has been used as a case analysis study, is efficient.

Using the game-theoretical perspective and the indifference curve approach, we have proved that firms should opt for comparative advertising and that no stringent rules should be passed against it as long as it provides useful, precise, accurate and reliable information to the consumers, thereby encouraging them to make more informed choices. The end aim of comparative advertising as a marketing tool should be increase in total welfare rather than individual gains. Of course, the presumption justifying this premises is that firms provide truthful information in their advertisements, and although they might engage in puffery, the claims made by them are not false. However, if the firms do use comparative advertising to make false claims and denigrate rival products, the courts should intervene and set up compliance mechanisms. Efficiency of judiciary plays an integral role in this. The firms also have an option of choosing ADR mechanisms, which have their own advantages and disadvantages. Firms should choose between ADR and litigation on the basis of economic efficiency. In this particular case, the judgement of the court is sound from a law and economics perspective. The court by not allowing an ad interim injunction to HUL not only prevented a major waste of resources but also encouraged comparative advertising as long as it adheres to certain standards. Hence, it was a proficient judgement as a result of an efficient judiciary.

Notes

1 *Dabur India Ltd v. Colortek Meghalaya Pvt. Ltd* (2009) 42 PTC 88.
2 *Reckitt and Colman of India Ltd v. M.P. Ramchandran and Anr.* 1999) PTC 19 741.
3 *Tata Press Ltd v. MTNL* (1995) AIR 2438, 1995 SCC (5) 139.
4 John E. Villafranco, 'The Law of Comparative Advertising in the United States', *Litigator* 16 (1) (2010): 97–104.
5 Francesca Barigozzi, Paolo G. Garella and Martin Peitz, 'With a Little Help from My Enemy: Comparative Advertising as a Signal', *Journal of Economics & Management Strategy* 18 (4) (2009): 1071–1094.
6 David Hosp, 'Weighing the Risks: A Practical Guide to Comparative Advertising', In *Advertising and Marketing Litigation Best Practices: Leading Lawyers on Preventing Conflicts, Mitigating Risks, and Deciding When to Settle vs. Litigate*, 1st ed. (Boston, MA: Aspatore Books, 2007): 45–63.
7 Theodore L. Turocy and Bernhard Von Stengel, 'Game Theory', 8 October 2001, accessed 27 September 2014, http://www.cdam.lse ac.uk/Reports/Files/cdam-2001-09.pdf.
8 Ibid.
9 Maarten Janssen and Mariya Teteryanikova, 'Competition and Disclosure of Comparative or Non-Comparative Horizontal Product Information', *European Economic Association & Econometric Society* (2005), accessed 25 July 2014, http://homepage.univie.ac.at/maarten.janssen/working papers/disclosure_revision4.pdf.
10 Ibid.
11 Robert Cooter and Thomas Ulen, *Law and Economics*, 4th ed. Singapore: Pearson Education, 2004): 88–89.
12 Ibid.
13 Robert H. Moonkin, 'Why Negotiations Fail: An Exploration of Barriers to the Resolution of Conflict', *Ohio State Journal on Dispute Resolution* 8 (2) (1993): 235.
14 World Intellectual Property Organization, 'What Is Mediation?', accessed 28 August 2014, http://www.wipo.int/amc/en/mediation/what-mediation.html.
15 Hosp, 'Weighing the Risks'.
16 Ibid.
17 R.S. Bachawat and Ruma Pal, *Justice Bachawat's Law of Arbitration and Conciliation: Including International Commercial Arbitration and ADR* (Gurgaon: LexisNexis Butterworths Wadhwa, 2005): 1477.
18 ONLINE TOOLS, 'National Arbitration Forum: FAQ', accessed 30 August 2014, http://www.adrforum.com/faq.aspx?faq=876.

19 Frank M. Bass, Anand Krishnamoorthy, Ashutosh Prasad and Suresh P. Sethi. 'Generic and Brand Advertising Strategies in a Dynamic Duopoly', *Marketing Science* 24 (4) (2005): 556–568.
20 Amitav Chakravarti and Chris Janiszewski, 'The Influence of Generic Advertising on Brand Preferences', *Journal of Consumer Research* 30 (2) (2004): 487–502.
21 S. Krishnamurthy, 'Enlarging the Pie vs. Increasing One's Slice: An Analysis of the Relationship between Generic and Brand Advertising', *Marketing Letters* 11 (1) (2000): 37–48.